# KNOWLEDGE
# MANAGEMENT

# KNOWLEDGE MANAGEMENT

## Challenges, Solutions, and Technologies

**Irma Becerra-Fernandez**
*Florida International University*

**Avelino Gonzalez**
*University of Central Florida*

**Rajiv Sabherwal**
*University of Missouri at St. Louis*

Upper Saddle River, New Jersey, 07458

**Library of Congress Cataloging-in-Publication Data**

Becerra-Fernandez, Irma
  Knowledge management: challenges, solutions, and technologies / Irma Becerra-Fernandez, Avelino Gonzalez, Rajiv Sabherwal.
    p. cm.
  Includes bibliographical references and index.
  ISBN 0-13-101606-7 (case)
    1. Knowledge management. I. Gonzalez, Avelino J. II. Sabherwal, Rajiv. III. Title.

HD30.2.B437 2004
658.4′038—dc22                                                      2003058249

**Executive Editor:** Bob Horan
**Project Manager:** Kyle Hannon
**Editorial Assistant:** Robyn Goldenberg
**Publisher:** Natalie E. Anderson
**Media Project Manager:** Joan Waxman
**Senior Marketing Manager:** Sharon M. Koch
**Marketing Assistant:** Danielle Torio
**Managing Editor (Production):** John Roberts
**Production Editor:** Maureen Wilson
**Permissions Supervisor:** Suzanne Grappi
**Manufacturing Buyer:** Michelle Klein
**Cover Design:** Bruce Kenselaar
**Cover Illustration/Photo:** Digital Vision Ltd.
**Composition/Full-Service Project Management:** Progressive Publishing Alternatives

Credits and acknowledgments borrowed from other sources and reproduced, with permission, in this textbook appear on appropriate page within text.

Pearson Education LTD.
Pearson Education Singapore, Pte. Ltd
Pearson Education, Canada, Ltd
Pearson Education-Japan

Pearson Education Australia PTY, Limited
Pearson Education North Asia Ltd
Pearson Educación de Mexico, S.A. de C.V.
Pearson Education Malaysia, Pte. Ltd

10 9 8 7 6 5 4
ISBN 0-13-101606-7

We would like to dedicate this book to our families, for their guidance, encouragement, love, and support

—Irma Becerra-Fernandez and Rajiv Sabherwal

I would like to dedicate this book to my mother Consuelo. The immense strength of character she continually demonstrated during the hard times in our family has been a source of great inspiration to her children. Besides, I know how she likes to brag about her kids' accomplishments, even if her kids are no longer kids.

—Avelino Gonzalez

# Brief Contents

# Contents

ix

# Preface

*Knowledge Management: Challenges, Solutions, and Technologies* is targeted toward students and managers who seek detailed insights into contemporary knowledge management (KM). It explains the concepts, theories, and technologies that provide the foundation for KM, the systems and structures that constitute KM solutions, and the processes for developing and deploying these KM solutions. We hope this book will help our readers acquire the relevant suite of managerial, technical, and theoretical skills for managing knowledge in the modern business environment.

The purpose of this book is to provide a thorough and informative perspective on the emergent practices in knowledge management. Information technology has been, and will continue to be, an important catalyst of this innovative field. Artificial intelligence, expert systems, and Web-based technologies continue to support and transform the field of knowledge management. However, these technologies would not be effective without the day-to-day social aspects of organizations, such as "water-cooler conversations," brainstorming retreats, and communities of practice. To further complicate matters, the current business environment renders new skills obsolete in years or even months. In essence, we are witnessing a new era, where advanced industrial economies are being revolutionized with the advent of the knowledge age, and highly skilled knowledge-based workers are replacing industrial workers as the dominant labor group.

Knowledge management is defined in this book as *doing what is needed to get the most out of knowledge resources*. KM is an increasingly important discipline that promotes the discovery, capture, sharing, and application of the firm's knowledge. Although the benefits of KM may be obvious, it may not necessarily be so obvious how to effectively manage this valuable resource. In this book, the discussion of knowledge management reflects the intimacy the authors have with this topic, from a theoretical as well as practical standpoint, through their substantial and diverse experiences.

The book is divided into three parts:

*Part I: Principles of Knowledge Management:* This part provides a more detailed discussion of the concepts of knowledge and knowledge management, and describes the key constituents of KM solutions, including infrastructure, processes, systems, tools, and technologies. The impacts of KM, the factors that influence KM, and the essential steps for performing a KM assessment are also described.

*Part II: Technologies for Knowledge Management:* This part describes the underlying technologies that support KM systems. These include data mining techniques that enable the creation of new knowledge, knowledge elicitation techniques, and techniques based on artificial intelligence, specifically, rule-based expert systems and case-based reasoning systems.

*Part III: Knowledge Management Systems:* This part describes the different types of KM systems: knowledge discovery systems, knowledge capture systems, knowledge sharing systems, and knowledge application systems. The mechanisms and technologies to support these KM systems are discussed, and case studies related to their implementation are presented.

This book may be adapted in several different ways, depending on the course and the students. The book is primarily designed for a two-semester course on knowledge management for graduate MIS students. In such a context, the first semester would cover Parts I and II to provide the student a solid grounding on the fundamentals of KM and its associated technologies. The second semester would cover Part III with its emphasis on KM systems and the prototypes included in the book package CD. Alternatively, this book can be used as a one semester traditional course on KM for graduate MIS students by covering selected topics from Parts I and III. An instructor wishing to concentrate on KM technologies and systems in one semester could do so by covering Chapter 1, and Parts II and III. MBA students would mostly benefit from Part I, and selected topics from Part III. Finally, a KM course for engineering or computer science students should concentrate on Parts II and III, and selected topics from Parts I.

## Student and Instructor Resources

To complement the text and enhance the learning and pedagogical experience, we provide the following support materials:

- *Student's Resource CD-ROM.* The CD-ROM features video clips of the KM systems presented in Chapters 13–16. These video clips are used to enhance the students' ability to visualize the functionality and impact of these systems. These clips highlight real-world KM systems that have been developed to support the needs of organizations, and illustrate key concepts discussed in the textbook.
- *Web site.* The textbook is supported by a Web site at http://www.prenhall.com/ becerra-fernandez. PowerPoint slides which describe the key concepts explained in the text are available for both students and instructors. Additional support materials may be downloaded from the secure faculty section of the Web site. In addition, faculty adopting the book are encouraged to share with the authors relevant material that could be included on the Web site to reinforce and enhance the students' experience.

# Acknowledgments

We have so many people to acknowledge! First, we want to recognize our families—especially our spouses, children, siblings, and parents—who were so understanding during the time we spent with our heads buried in word processors.

We further thank those organizations that provided us with the fertile ground to develop many of our ideas about KM: NASA Kennedy Space Center, NASA Goddard Space Flight Center, NASA Ames Research Center, National Semiconductor, NAVY Center for Advanced Research in Artificial Intelligence, and the Institute for Human and Machine Cognition. We especially thank the individuals at these organizations, who made it possible for us to formalize some of the concepts and techniques presented in this book: David Aha, Gregg Buckingham, Alberto Cañas, Chris Carlson, Steve Chance, John Coffey, Martha Del Alto, Ken Ford, Mike Glynn, Milt Halem, Susan Hoban, James L. Jennings, Art Hamilton, Chris Knight, Nancy Laubenthal, Orlando Melendez, Mike Meltzer, Amir Razavi, Shannon Roberts, Joel Shealy, Pat Simpkins, and Helen Stewart.

We also thank our administrators, who were very understanding when our other academic commitments couldn't be completed on time. These include Joyce Elam and Christos Koulamas at Florida International University, and Doug Durand, Tom Eysell, and Marius Janson at the University of Missouri–St. Louis. Our sincere thanks are also directed towards Doug Dankel at the University of Florida, who directly and selflessly contributed to the material on expert systems contained in this book.

We also gratefully acknowledge the contributions of the students who have worked at the FIU Knowledge Management Lab, and who collaborated in the development of the KM systems described here. We also thank the students of FIU's Masters in MIS Cohorts 6 and 7 for reviewing the book prior to publication. Special thanks go to Rajesh Chatrani, Bertha Correa, and Maria Rivera from Florida International University for their help in the creation of the demos presented in the CD-ROM, and to Charles Chowa, Anosh Wadia, Chris Kang, and Vandita Prabhu from University of Missouri–St. Louis for their research assistance and help in developing the end-of-chapter questions and their solutions for some of the chapters.

Our heartfelt thanks are directed toward the various anonymous reviewers for Prentice Hall. We appreciate their valuable suggestions and contributions to the final product.

Finally, we are deeply indebted to many individuals at Prentice Hall who enabled us to publish this book. Among those with whom we directly worked are our editor Bob Horan, and the Prentice Hall staff including Joan Waxman, Kyle Hannon, and Lori Cerreto.

# Introducing Knowledge Management

## ◇ ◇ ◇ Introduction

The scientific endeavor that culminated on July 20th, 1969, with the first American walking on the Moon is considered one of the most significant accomplishments in the history of humankind. Especially noteworthy about this undertaking is that when President John F. Kennedy issued the promise in 1961 that the United States would land a man on the Moon and return him safely to Earth before the end of that decade, most of the scientific and technological knowledge required to take this "one small step for man, one giant leap for mankind" did not exist. The necessary science and technology essentially had to be discovered and developed to accomplish this extraordinary task. However, many of those technological advances now have a permanent presence in the landscape of our lives, from cordless tools to cellular phones. These first missions to space carried less computer power onboard than what some of us typically lug around through airports in our laptop computers and PDAs. The computers on board *Apollo 11,* considered state-of-the-art in the 1960s, had 4 KB of random access memory (RAM), no disk drive, and a total of 74 KB of auxiliary memory. From the knowledge management (KM) perspective, how did they manage the extraordinary quantities of knowledge that had to be developed in order to accomplish the task? The required knowledge about space travel, rocketry, aerodynamics, control systems, communications, biology, and many other disciplines had to be developed and validated prior to use in the space mission. From the knowledge creation perspective, this was an extraordinarily successful endeavor. On the other hand, a closer look reveals that attempts to elicit and capture the knowledge resulting from these efforts may have been largely unsuccessful, and some studies even suggest that the National Aeronautics and Space Administration (NASA) may have actually lost that knowledge. In fact, in the words of Sylvia Fries, NASA's chief historian between 1983 and 1990, who interviewed 51 NASA engineers who had worked on the Apollo program:

> The 20th anniversary of the landing of an American on the surface of the Moon occasioned many bittersweet reflections. Sweet was the celebration of the historic event itself. . . . Bitter, for those same enthusiasts, was the knowledge that

during the twenty intervening years much of the national consensus that launched this country on its first lunar adventure had evaporated . . . a generation of men and women who had defined their lives to a large extent in terms of this nation's epochal departure from Earth's surface was taking its leave of the program they had built [Fries, 1992].

In this text, we hope to impart to the readers what we know about the important field of KM—what it is and how to implement it successfully, with the tools provided by the technological advances of our times. The book presents a balanced discussion between theory and application of KM to organizations. In this book the reader can find an overview of KM theory and implementation, with a special emphasis on the technologies that underpin KM and how to successfully integrate those technologies. The book includes implementation details about both KM mechanisms and technologies.

In this chapter, we first describe what KM is and what the forces are that drive KM. We also discuss organizational issues related to KM. Specifically, we introduce knowledge management systems and their role in the organization. Finally, we explain how the rest of the book is organized.

## ◇ ◇ ◇ What Is Knowledge Management?

**Knowledge management (KM)** may simply be defined as *doing what is needed to get the most out of knowledge resources.* Although KM can be applied to individuals, it has recently attracted the attention of organizations. KM is viewed as an increasingly important discipline that promotes the creation, sharing, and leveraging of the organization's knowledge. Peter Drucker [1994], whom many consider as the father of KM, best defines the need for KM:

> Knowledge has become the key resource, for a nation's military strength as well as for its economic strength . . . is fundamentally different from the traditional key resources of the economist—land, labor, and even capital . . . we need systematic work on the quality of knowledge and the productivity of knowledge . . . the performance capacity, if not the survival, of any organization in the knowledge society will come increasingly to depend on those two factors (pp. 66–69).

Thus, it can be argued that the most vital resource of today's enterprise is the collective knowledge residing in the minds of an organization's employees, customers, and vendors. Learning how to manage organizational knowledge has many benefits, some of which are readily apparent; others are not. These benefits may include leveraging core business competencies, accelerating innovation and time to market, improving cycle times and decision making, strengthening organizational commitment, and building sustainable competitive advantage [Davenport and Prusak, 1998]. In short, they make the organization better suited to compete successfully in a much more demanding environment. Organizations are increasingly valued for their intellectual capital. An example of this fact is the widening gap between corporate balance sheets and investors' estimation of corporate worth. It is said that knowledge-intensive companies around the world are valued at three to eight times their financial capital. Consider, for example, Microsoft, the highest valued company in the world, with a market capitalization that was estimated at around $284 billion as of July 2003. Clearly, this figure represents more than Microsoft's net worth in buildings, computers, and other physical assets. Microsoft's valuation also represents an estimation of its intellectual assets. This includes structural capital in the form of copyrights, customer databases, and business process software. It also includes human capital in the form of the knowledge that resides in the minds of all of Microsoft's software developers, researchers, academic collaborators, and business managers.

In general, KM focuses on organizing and making available important knowledge, wherever and whenever it is needed. The traditional emphasis in KM has been on knowledge that is recognized and already articulated in some form. This includes knowledge about processes, procedures, intellectual property, documented best practices, forecasts, lessons learned, and solutions to recurring problems. Increasingly, KM has also focused on managing important knowledge that may reside solely in the minds of an organization's experts.

Consider, for example, the knowledge of the Shuttle Processing Director at NASA—Kennedy Space Center (KSC). By 1999, the Shuttle Processing Director at NASA had been supervising Shuttle launches for 20 years and had supervised each of the Shuttle launches until its liftoff. During the countdown, he was responsible to make the final call if an anomaly justified calling off the mission. As Shuttle Processing Director, he depended on his experience to weigh the severity of the problem and decide on the spot whether indeed it required stopping the mission. A decision to stop the launch could cost the organization millions of dollars, but on the other hand it could save lives, a priceless alternative. When facing its director's retirement, how can an organization like NASA KSC elicit and catalog his knowledge so that new generations may benefit?

KM is also related to the concept of intellectual capital. Composed of both human and structural capital, **intellectual capital** is considered by many as the most valuable enterprise resource. Human capital refers to the body of knowledge the company possesses. Human capital may reside not only in the minds of the company's employees, but also in its vendors and customers. **Structural capital,** on the other hand, is everything that remains when the employees go home: databases, customer files, software, manuals, trademarks, and organizational structures: in other words, organizational capability. Intellectual capital is ubiquitous, yet there are no standard tools to manage it as an asset.

## ❖ ❖ ❖  Forces Driving Knowledge Management

Today, organizations rely on their decision makers to make "mission-critical" decisions based on inputs from multiple domains. Ideal decision makers possess a profound understanding of specific domains that influence the decision-making process, coupled with the experience that allows them to act quickly and decisively on the information. This profile of the ideal decision maker usually corresponds to someone who has lengthy experience and insights gained from years of observation. Although this profile does not mark a significant departure from the past, the following four underlying trends increase the stakes in the decision-making scenario:

1. ***Increasing domain complexity.*** The complexity of the underlying knowledge domains is increasing. As a direct consequence, the complexity of the knowledge that is required to complete a specific business process task has increased as well. Intricacy of internal and external processes, increased competition, and rapid advancement of technology all contribute to increasing domain complexity. For example, new product development no longer requires only brainstorming sessions by the freethinking product designers of the organization, but instead it requires the partnership of interorganizational teams representing various functional subunits—from finance to marketing to engineering. Thus, we see an increased emphasis from professional recruiters around the world seeking new job applicants who not only possess excellent educational and professional qualifications, but also have outstanding communication and team collaboration skills. These skills can enable them to share their knowledge for the benefit of the organization.

2. ***Accelerating market volatility.*** The pace of change, or volatility, within each market domain has increased rapidly in the past decade. For example, market and environmental influences can result in overnight changes in an organization. Corporate announcements of a missed financial quarterly target could send a company's capitalization, and perhaps that of a whole industry, in a downward spiral. Stock prices on Wall Street have become increasingly volatile in the past few years, resulting in the phenomenon of day trading where many nonfinancial professionals make a living from taking advantage of the steep market fluctuations.

3. ***Intensified speed of responsiveness.*** The time required to take action based on subtle changes within and across domains is decreasing. The rapid advance in technology continually changes the decision-making landscape, making it imperative that decisions be made and implemented quickly, lest the window of opportunity closes. For example, in the past, the sales process incorporated ample processing time, thus allowing the stakeholders a "comfort zone" in the decision-making process. Typically in response to a customer request, individual sales representatives would return to the office, discuss the opportunity with their manager, draft a proposal, and mail the proposal to the client, who would then accept or reject the offer. The time required by the process would essentially provide the stakeholders sufficient time to ponder the most adequate solution at each of the decision points. Contrast the sale process of yesterday with that of today, for example, the process required by many online bidding marketplaces thriving on the Web. Consider the dilemma faced by a hotel manager that participates in an Internet auctioning market of hotel rooms: "Should I book a $200 room for the bid offer of $80 and fill the room, or risk not accepting the bid hoping to get a walk-in customer that will pay the $200?" Confronted with a decision to fill a room at a lower rate than what the hotel typically advertises poses an important decision that the hotel manager must make within minutes of a bid offer.

4. ***Diminishing individual experience.*** High employee turnover rates have resulted in individuals with decision-making authority having less tenure within their organizations than ever before. Consider, for example, the average age of a chief executive officer (CEO) in the new millennium. The number of CEOs below the age of 50 in Fortune 300 companies in the year 2000 was about 15%, an increase from about 5% in 1980. Furthermore, the median tenure of CEOs in office in 1980 was 7 years, down to about

5 years in 2000 [Neff and Ogden, 2000]. Because trends change so rapidly, even when a decision maker has been with a company for several years, that individual's experience may not be relevant to the decision that needs to be made. This creates a great disadvantage when making mission-critical decisions. One principal effect of these trends is immature intuition, where decision makers are less likely to understand the nuances of domain inputs due to the complexity in specific domains and their own tenure within an organization. Another such effect is the responsiveness of the decision maker. When facing external pressures, the need to respond is more urgent due to competitive pressures such as shortening product development cycles. Finally, the decision must be made clearly and correctly. This is because the need for swiftness in implementing an action after a decision has been made allows little market tolerance for wrong or unclear decision responses.

So, what does this mean? Faced with increased complexity, market volatility, and accelerated responsiveness, today's younger manager feels less adequate to make the difficult decisions faced each day. In the decision-making scenario described above, it is evident that knowledge can greatly assist the decision maker. In the past, this knowledge resided mostly in the decision maker. These previously discussed complications indicate that in modern organizations, the knowledge necessary to make good decisions cannot possibly all reside with the individual decision makers, hence the need to provide them with the requisite knowledge for making correct, timely decisions.

Perhaps nothing has made more evident the need for KM than the corporate downsizing trend at public and private organizations that marked the reengineering era of the 1990s, a well-known feature of the economic landscape of the late 20th century. The dominant driver of downsizing in most organizations is well understood: rapidly reduce costs to survive against competitors. Clearly, a negative side effect of downsizing is the dissipation of the knowledge resources of the organization, resulting in devitalized organizations. Some of the symptoms of such organizations are decreased morale, reduced commitment, inferior quality, lack of teamwork, lower productivity, and lost of innovative ability [Eisenberg, 1997]. The fact is many of the individuals who were laid off as a result of downsizing had performed significant tasks and had acquired considerable and valuable skills over the years. Many companies are typically not prepared for downsizing, and few take any steps to prevent the escape of knowledge that usually follows. To minimize the impact of downsizing, organizations should first identify what skills and information resources are needed to meet mission-critical objectives. Therefore, effective methodologies, including tools and techniques to capture vital knowledge, are essential for an organization to maintain its competitive edge.

In short, KM is important for organizations that continually face downsizing or a high turnover percentage due to the nature of the industry. KM is important for all organizations because today's decision makers face the pressure to make better and faster decisions in an environment characterized by a high domain complexity and market volatility, even though they may in fact lack the experience typically expected from the decision maker, and even though the outcome of those decisions could have such a considerable impact on the organization. In short, KM is for everybody. Vignette 1-1 illustrates this fact.

---

 VIGNETTE 1-1

### Is Knowledge Management for Everybody?

John Smith owns an independent auto repair shop in Stillwater, Oklahoma, which he established in 1975. Prior to opening his own shop, he had been repairing foreign cars as a mechanic for the local Toyota dealership. In these days of increasing complexity in automobiles, he had to learn about such new technologies as fuel injection, computer-controlled ignition, and multivalve and turbo-charged engines. This was not easy, but he managed to do it. At the same time, he created a successful business, one with an outstanding reputation. As his business grew, he had to hire mechanics to help him with the workload. At first, training them was easy, because cars were simpler. That has radically changed in the last 10 years. He now finds himself spending more time training and correcting the work of his mechan-ics, instead of working on cars himself, which is what he truly enjoys. To further complicate matters, his mechanics are so well trained that the local Toyota dealership is hiring them away from him for significant salary increases. As a small business, he cannot afford to compete with Toyota, so he finds himself doing more and more training and correcting all the time. The turnover has now begun to affect the quality of the work he turns over to his customers, increasing complaints and damaging his hard-earned reputation. Basically, he has a knowledge problem. He has the knowledge, and needs to capture it in a way that it is easy to disseminate to his mechanics. He must find a way to manage this knowledge to survive. How successful he is can dictate his future survival in this business.

---

##  Knowledge Management Systems

Rapid changes in the field of KM have to a great extent resulted from the dramatic progress we have witnessed in the field of information technology (IT). IT facilitates sharing as well as accelerated growth of knowledge. IT allows the movement of information at increasing speeds and efficiencies. For example, computers capture data from measurements of natural phenomena, and then quickly manipulate the data to better understand the phenomena they represent. Increased computer power at lower prices enables the measurement of increasingly complex processes, which we possibly could only imagine before. According to Bradley [1996]:

> Today, knowledge is accumulating at an ever increasing rate. It is estimated that knowledge is currently doubling every 18 months and, of course, the pace is increasing . . . Technology facilitates the speed at which knowledge and ideas proliferate.

Thus, IT has provided the major impetus for enabling the implementation of KM applications. Moreover, as learning has accrued over time in the area of social and structural mechanisms, such as mentoring and retreats that enable effective knowledge sharing, it has made it possible to develop KM applications that best leverage these improved mechanisms by deploying sophisticated technologies.

In this book we therefore place significant focus on the applications that result from the use of the latest technologies used to support KM mechanisms. Knowledge Management mechanisms are organizational or structural means used to promote KM. The use of leading-edge information technologies (e.g., Web-based conferencing) to support KM mechanisms in ways not earlier possible (e.g., interactive conversations along with instantaneous exchange of voluminous documents among individuals located at remote locations) enables dramatic improvement in KM. We call the applications resulting from such synergy between the latest technologies and social/structural mechanisms as **knowledge management systems,** as described in Part III of this book. KM systems utilize a variety of KM mechanisms and technologies to support the KM processes. Based on observations on the KM systems implementations under way at many organizations, a framework emerges for classification of KM systems as:

1. *Knowledge discovery systems*  (discussed in Chapter 13).
2. *Knowledge capture systems*  (discussed in Chapter 14).
3. *Knowledge sharing systems*  (discussed in Chapter 15).
4. *Knowledge application systems*  (discussed in Chapter 16).

Artificial intelligence (AI) and machine learning technologies play an important role in the processes of knowledge discovery, capture, sharing, and application, enabling the development of KM systems. Chapters 7 through 12 will provide an introduction to these technologies. Because KM systems provide access to explicit company knowledge, it is easy to learn from previous experiences. **Experience management** is another recent term also related to KM. Basically, experience develops over time, to coalesce into more general experience, which then combines into general knowledge. Experiences captured over time can be managed by the use of technology. We discuss how intelligent technologies are used to manage experiences, as well as create new knowledge.

## ◇ ◇ ◇  Issues in Knowledge Management

In practice, given the uncertainty in today's business environments, and the imminent reality of continuing layoffs, what could make employees feel compelled to participate in KM initiatives? Although many attempts have been made to launch KM initiatives, including the design and implementation of KM systems, not all KM implementations have been successful. In fact, many KM systems implementations, for example, of lessons learned systems (discussed in Chapter 15), have fallen short of their promise. Many KM systems implemented at organizations have failed to enable knowledge workers to share their knowledge for the benefit of the organization. The case in point is that effective KM is not about making a choice between "software vs. wetware, classroom vs. hands-on, formal vs. informal, technical vs. social" [Stewart, 2002]. Effective KM uses all the options available to motivated employees to put knowledge to work. Effective KM depends on recognizing that all these options basically need each other.

One of the primary differences between traditional information systems and KM systems is the active role that users of KM systems play in building the content of such systems. Users of traditional information systems are typically not required to actively contribute to building the content of such systems, an effort typically delegated to the management information systems (MIS) department or to information systems (IS) consultants. Therefore, traditional IS research has concentrated much of its efforts in understanding what factors are leading users to accepting, and thereby using IT.[1] As we see later in Chapter 15, users of lessons learned systems not only utilize the system to find a lesson applicable to a problem at hand, but also typically contribute lessons to the system database. As a result, the successful implementation of KM systems requires that its users not only effectively "use" such systems as in traditional IS but also contribute to the knowledge base of such systems. Therefore, seeking to understand the factors that lead to the successful implementation of KM systems is an important area of research that is still in its infancy.

Whereas technology has provided the impetus for managing knowledge, we now know that effective KM initiatives are not solely limited to a technological solution. An old adage states that effective KM is 80% related to organizational culture and human factors, and is 20% related to technology. This means that there is an important human component in KM. This finding addresses the fact that knowledge is first created in people's minds. First, KM practices must identify ways to encourage and stimulate the ability of employees to develop new knowledge. Second, KM methodologies and technologies must enable effective ways to elicit, represent, organize, reuse, and renew this knowledge. Third, KM should not distance itself from the knowledge owners, but instead celebrate and recognize their position as experts in the organization. This, in effect, is the essence of knowledge management. More about such issues related to KM are presented in future chapters, specifically in Chapters 3 and 5, and the epilogue.

## ◇ ◇ ◇  Text Overview

This book is composed of 16 chapters, divided into 3 parts, and an epilogue:

### PART I: PRINCIPLES OF KNOWLEDGE MANAGEMENT

This section of the book includes the overview of knowledge management presented in Chapter 1, as well as the role that IT plays in KM. Chapter 2 discusses the concept of knowledge in greater detail and distinguishes it from data and information, summarizes the perspectives commonly used to view knowledge, describes the ways of classifying knowledge, and identifies some key characteristics of knowledge. Chapter 3 explains in greater detail the concept of KM; specifically it describes in detail a variety of KM solutions, including KM infrastructure, KM systems, KM tools and technologies, and KM processes. Chapter 4 presents a discussion of the impacts of KM, examining the impact on several important aspects of business organizations. Chapter 5 presents the factors that influence KM, including the type of knowledge, the organization's strategy, and the environment. This chapter also describes a methodology to prioritize implementation of KM solutions based on knowledge, organization, and industry characteristics. Chapter 6 discusses the steps necessary for

---

[1]Much of the IS research has concentrated on the development of the technology acceptance model (TAM) [Davis, 1989] which identifies two factors associated with user acceptance of information technology to be *perceived usefulness* and *perceived ease of use.*

an organization to perform a KM assessment, including the reasons why the assessment is needed, alternative approaches to evaluating various related aspects, and overall approaches.

## PART II: TECHNOLOGIES FOR KNOWLEDGE MANAGEMENT

This section of the book is devoted to a discussion on the underlying technologies that enable the creation of knowledge management systems. Chapter 7 will introduce the reader to AI, an important field of computer science for its impact on KM. This chapter discusses the historical perspective of AI, its relationship with knowledge, and why it's an important aspect of KM. Chapter 7 also serves as a transition to the next three chapters, which introduce in greater detail some of the AI techniques that serve a significant role in KM systems. Chapter 8 discusses how to represent human expertise through rule-based expert systems, the most traditional and the most basic of the AI techniques used in KM. This chapter introduces the basics of knowledge representation in rules and frames, reasoning mechanisms, and the types of problems for which this technique is used. It also provides an analysis of the strengths and weaknesses of these types of systems. Chapter 9 discusses how explicit past history can be used as knowledge through case-based reasoning systems. This chapter includes a discussion of the weaknesses of rule-based systems that case-based reasoning systems try to address. Chapter 10 presents the topic of knowledge elicitation, including the various ways to query experts automatically to obtain and represent their knowledge, using techniques such as repertory grids. Chapter 11 explains the Internet and the World Wide Web, and how they are used to facilitate communications and the organization of knowledge to a level unparalleled in history. Knowledge communities and forums are discussed as a means to create, share, and capture knowledge; and search techniques used in Web-based searches and related technologies for the purpose of sharing knowledge are also discussed. Finally, Chapter 12 describes how technology can enable the creation of new knowledge through the use of data mining (DM) techniques. Several techniques are used to perform DM, of which inductive learning, neural networks, and statistical methods are the most common. How to select the appropriate DM technique to meet the project requirements is also presented. This discussion is essential for the understanding of knowledge discovery systems in later chapters.

## PART III: KNOWLEDGE MANAGEMENT SYSTEMS

This section of the book is dedicated to a discussion on the different types of KM systems and is composed of four chapters. Chapter 13 introduces knowledge discovery systems. The chapter presents a description of knowledge discovery in databases and DM, including both mechanisms and technologies to support the discovery of knowledge. The material covers design considerations and the CRISP-DM process. Two very relevant topics, DM and its relationship to discovering knowledge on the Web and to customer relationship management (CRM), are also presented including the importance of knowing about your customer. Barriers to the use of knowledge discovery are discussed. Specific attention is placed on two knowledge discovery systems, and case studies related to their implementation are presented. Also included in this chapter is a discussion on mechanisms for knowledge discovery and the use of socialization to catalyze innovation in organizations. Chapter 14 discusses knowledge capture systems. These refer to systems that elicit and preserve the knowledge of experts, so that it can be shared with others. Issues related to how to design the knowledge capture system, including the use of intelligent technologies, are discussed. Specific attention is placed on two knowledge capture systems and case studies related to their implementation are presented: Cmap Tools and CITKA. Also included in the chapter is a discussion on mechanisms for knowledge capture and the use of storytelling in organizations. The chapter concludes with a short discussion about research trends on knowledge capture systems. In Chapter 15, we describe knowledge sharing systems, which refer to systems that organize and distribute knowledge and comprise the majority of the KM systems currently in place. Design considerations and special types of knowledge sharing systems are discussed: lessons learned systems and expertise locator systems. Two case studies are given based on the experience gained from their development: SAGE Expert Finder, an expertise locator system to locate experts in Florida; and Expert Seeker, an expertise locator system used to identify experts at NASA. The chapter concludes with a discussion on mechanisms to exchange tacit knowledge and communities of practice. Chapter 16 covers knowledge application systems and the specific types of intelligent technologies that enable such systems. The chapter discusses different types of knowledge application systems: expert systems, help desk systems, and fault diagnosis systems. Three case studies that describe the implementation of knowledge application systems are presented, each based on different intelligent technologies and designed to accomplish different goals: provide advice, fault detection, and creative reasoning. Finally, limitations of knowledge application systems are discussed.

Finally, the book concludes with an epilogue, a view into the future of knowledge management. Issues related to protecting intellectual property, ethics, privacy, and trust are also discussed in the context of KM.

## Summary ❖ ❖ ❖

In this chapter, you have learned about several KM issues as they relate to the learning objectives. KM ranging from the system perspective to the organizational perspective is described. The relevance of KM in today's dynamic environments augmented with increasing technological complexity is discussed. Benefits and considerations about KM are presented, including an overview of the nature of the KM projects currently in progress at public and private organizations around the world. Finally, IT plays an important role in KM. The enabling role of IT is discussed, but the old adage, "KM is 80% about organization, and 20% about IT" still holds today.

## Key Terms ❖ ❖ ❖

- experience management—p. 7
- intellectual capital—p. 3
- knowledge management (KM)—p. 2
- knowledge management systems—p. 7
- structural capital—p. 3

## REVIEW QUESTIONS ◇ ◇ ◇

1. Describe what knowledge management (KM) is.
2. Discuss the forces driving KM.
3. What are knowledge management systems? Enumerate the four types of KM systems.
4. Describe some of the issues facing KM.

## APPLICATION EXERCISES ◇ ◇ ◇

1. Identify an example of a KM initiative that has been undertaken in your organization. Has the initiative been successful? What are some of the issues, both technical and nontechnical, that were faced during its implementation?
2. Design a knowledge management initiative to support your business needs.
3. Describe the nontechnical issues that you will face during its implementation.
4. Consider the four forces driving KM described in this chapter. Think of another example that illustrates each of these forces.

## REFERENCES ◇ ◇ ◇

Bradley, K. 1996. Excerpts from his lecture at the Royal Society of Arts: "Intellectual Capital and the New Wealth of Nations," Stockholm, Sweden.

Davenport, T.H., and Prusak, L. 1998. *Working Knowledge: How Organizations Manage What They Know.* Boston: Harvard Business School Press.

Davis, F. 1989. Perceived usefulness, perceived ease of use, and user acceptance of information technology. *MIS Quarterly,* 13(3), 319–340.

Drucker, P. 1994. The age of social transformation. *The Atlantic Monthly,* 274(5), 53–70.

Eisenberg, H. 1997. Healing the wounds from reengineering and downsizing. *Quality Progress,* May.

Fries, S. 1992. *NASA Engineers and the Age of Apollo.* Washington, DC. (NASA SP-4104).

Neff, T., and Ogden, D. 2002. Anatomy of a CEO. Published at www.chiefexecutive.net/depts/routetop/anatomyofaceo.html.

Stewart, T. 2002. The case against knowledge management. *Business 2.0,* February.

# CHAPTER 2

# The Nature of Knowledge

## ◇◇◇ Introduction

In the previous chapter, we provided an introduction to the basic concepts of knowledge management (KM). In this chapter, we take the next step by explaining in detail what we mean by knowledge. We distinguish knowledge from data and information and illustrate these three concepts using some examples. In this chapter, we also summarize some of the perspectives commonly used to view knowledge, including both subjective and objective viewpoints. Moreover, we describe some of the ways to classify knowledge, and identify some attributes that may be used to characterize different types of knowledge. Finally, we also explain the various reservoirs, or locations, in which knowledge might reside.

## ◇◇◇ What Is Knowledge?

**Knowledge** is quite distinct from **data** and **information,** although the three terms are sometimes used interchangeably. However, they are quite distinct in nature. In this section, we define and illustrate these concepts and differentiate among them. This discussion also leads to our definition of *knowledge in an area as justified beliefs about relationships among concepts relevant to that particular area.*

*Data* comprises facts, observations, or perceptions (which may or may not be correct). Alone, data represents raw numbers or assertions, and may therefore be devoid of context, meaning, or intent. Let us consider three examples of what is considered to be data. We then build on these examples to examine the meaning of information and knowledge.

*Example 1.* A restaurant sales order including two large burgers and two medium-sized vanilla milkshakes is an example of data.
*Example 2.* The observation that a tossed coin lands on heads also illustrates data.
*Example 3.* The wind component ($u$ and $v$) coordinates for a particular hurricane's trajectory, at specific instances of time, are likewise considered data.

Although data is devoid of context, meaning, or intent, it can be easily captured, stored, and communicated using electronic or other media.

*Information* is a subset of data, only including those data that possess context, relevance, and purpose. Information typically involves the manipulation of raw data to obtain a more meaningful indication of trends or patterns in the data. Let us continue with the three previously mentioned examples:

> **Example 1.**   For the manager of the restaurant, the numbers indicating the daily sales (in dollars, quantity, or percentage of daily sales) of burgers, vanilla milkshakes, and other products are considered information. The manager can use such information to make decisions concerning pricing and raw material purchases.
>
> **Example 2.**   Let us assume that the context of the coin toss is a betting situation where John is offering to pay anyone $10 if the coin lands heads but to take $8 if the coin lands tails. Susan, considering whether to take up John's bet, benefits from knowing that the last 100 times the coin was tossed it landed on heads 40 times and on tails 60 occasions. The result of each individual toss (head or tail) is data, but is not directly useful. It is therefore data but not information. By contrast, the 40 heads and 60 tails resulting from the last 100 tosses are also data, but they can be directly used to compute probabilities of heads and tails, and hence to make the decision. These data are useful, and therefore they are also considered information for Susan.
>
> **Example 3.**   Based on the *u* and *v* components, hurricane software models may be used to create a forecast of the hurricane trajectory. The hurricane forecast is information.

As can be seen from these examples, whether certain facts are considered information or only data depends on the individual who is using those facts. The facts about the daily sales of burgers represent information for the store manager but only data for a customer. If the restaurant is one out of a chain of 250 restaurants, these facts about daily sales are also data for the chief executive officer (CEO) of the chain. Similarly, the facts about the coin toss are simply data for an individual who is not interested in betting.

*Knowledge* has been distinguished from data and information in two different ways. A more simplistic view considers knowledge to be at the highest level in a hierarchy with information at the middle level, and data to be at the lowest level. According to this view, knowledge refers to information that enables action and decisions, or information with direction. Hence, knowledge is intrinsically similar to information and data, although it is the richest and deepest of the three, and is consequently also the most valuable. Based on this view, data refers to bare facts void of context, for example, a telephone number. Information is considered as data in context, for example, a phone book. Knowledge is information that facilitates action, for example, individuals who are the domain experts within an organization. An example of knowledge includes recognizing that a phone number belongs to a good client, who needs to be called once per week to get orders.

Although this simplistic view of knowledge may not be completely inaccurate, we believe it does not fully explain the characteristics of knowledge. Instead, we use a more complete perspective, according to which knowledge is intrinsically different from information. Instead of considering knowledge as richer or more detailed set of facts, *we define knowledge in an area as justified beliefs about relationships among concepts relevant to that particular area.* This definition has support in the literature [Nonaka, 1994]. Let us now consider how this definition works for the preceding examples.

> ***Example 1.***    The daily sales of burgers can be used, along with other information (e.g., information on the quantity of bread in the inventory), to compute the amount of bread to buy. The relationship between the quantity of bread that should be ordered, the quantity of bread currently in the inventory, and the daily sales of burgers (and other products that use bread) is an example of knowledge. Understanding this relationship (which could conceivably be stated as a mathematical formula) helps to use the information (on quantity of bread in the inventory, daily sales of burgers, etc.) to compute the quantity of bread to be purchased. However, the quantity of bread to be ordered should be considered information and not knowledge. It is simply more valuable information.
>
> ***Example 2.***    The information about 40 heads and 60 tails (out of 100 tosses) can be used to compute the probability of heads (0.40) and tails (0.60). The probabilities can then be used, along with information about the returns associated with heads ($10 from Susan's perspective) and tails (−$8, again from Susan's perspective) to compute the expected value to Susan from participating in the bet. Both probabilities and expected values are information, although more valuable information than the facts that 40 tosses produced heads and 60 produced tails. Moreover, expected value is more useful information than the probabilities; the former can directly be used to make the decision, whereas the latter requires computation of expected value.
>
> The relationship between the probability of heads, the number of times the coin lands heads, and the total number of tosses [i.e., that probability of heads, or $p_H = n_H/(n_H + n_T)$, assuming that the coin can only land heads or tails] is an example of knowledge. This relationship helps compute the probability from the data on outcomes of tosses. The similar formula for probability of tails is knowledge as well. In addition, the relationship between expected value (EV) and the probabilities $(p_H, p_T)$ and returns $(R_H, R_T)$ for heads and tails (i.e., $EV = p_H \times R_H + p_T \times R_T$) is also knowledge. Using these components of knowledge, probability of heads and tails can be computed as 0.40 and 0.60, respectively. Then the expected value for Susan can be computed as $0.40 \times (+\$10) + 0.60 \times (-\$8) = -\$0.80$.
>
> ***Example 3.***    The knowledge of a hurricane researcher is used to analyze the *u* and *v* wind components, as well as the hurricane forecast produced by the different software models, to determine the probability that the hurricane will follow a specific trajectory.

Thus, knowledge helps produce information from data or more valuable information from less valuable information. In that sense, this information facilitates action, such as the decision of whether to bet. Based on the new generated information of the expected value of the outcome, as well as the relationship with other concepts, such as Susan's anticipation that the coin may be fair or not, knowledge enables Susan to decide whether she can expect to win at the game. This aspect of the relationship between data and information is depicted in Figure 2-1, which shows the relationship between data (which have zero or low value in making the decision), and information (which has greater value than data, although different types of information might have differing values).

The preceding relationships between data, information, and knowledge are illustrated using Example 2 in Figure 2-2. As may be seen from Figure 2-2, knowledge of how

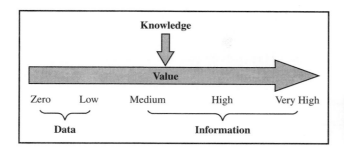

**FIGURE 2-1 Data, Information, and Knowledge**

to count helps convert data on coin tosses (each toss producing a head or a tail, with the set of 100 tosses producing 100 such observations, shown as H and T, respectively) into information (number of heads and number of tosses). This information is more useful than the raw data, but it does not directly help the decision maker (Susan) to decide on whether to participate in the bet. Using knowledge of how to compute probabilities, this information can be converted into more useful information (i.e., the probabilities of heads and tails). Moreover, combining the information about probabilities with information about returns associated with heads and tails, it is possible to produce even more information (i.e., the expected value associated with participation in the bet). In making this transition, knowledge of the formula for computing expected value from probabilities and returns is utilized. Figure 2-2 illustrates how knowledge helps produce information from data (e.g., probabilities based on outcomes of tosses of 60 heads and 40 tails) or more valuable information (expected value) from less valuable information (e.g., probabilities and payoffs associated with heads and tails).

The preceding distinction between data, information, and knowledge is consistent with Nonaka and Takeuchi's [1995] definition of knowledge as "a justified true belief." It is also consistent with Wiig's [1999, p. 3-2] view of knowledge as fundamentally different from data and information:

> Knowledge consists of truths and beliefs, perspectives and concepts, judgments and expectations, methodologies and know-how and is possessed by humans, agents, or other active entities and is used to receive information and to recognize and identify; analyze, interpret, and evaluate; synthesize and decide;

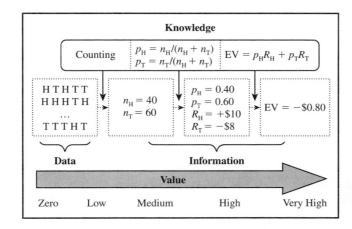

**FIGURE 2-2 An Illustration of Data, Information, and Knowledge**

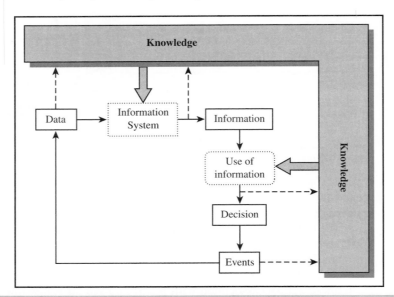

◇ ◇ ◇ **FIGURE 2-3** Relating Data, Information, and Knowledge to Events

plan, implement, monitor, and adapt—i.e. to act more or less intelligently. In other words, knowledge is used to determine what a specific situation means and how to handle it.

Figure 2-3 depicts how knowledge, data, and information relate to information systems, decisions, and events. As discussed above, knowledge helps to convert data into information. The knowledge could be stored in a manual or computer-based information system, which receives data as input and produces information as output. Moreover, the use of information to make the decision requires knowledge as well (e.g., in the context of the preceding Example 2, the knowledge that expected value above zero generally suggests that the decision is a good one). The decisions, as well as certain unrelated factors, lead to events, which cause generation of further data. The events, the use of information, and the information system might cause modifications in the knowledge itself. For example, in the context of Example 1 on ordering raw materials based on sales, information about changes in suppliers (e.g., a merger of two suppliers) might cause changes in the perceived relationship (i.e., knowledge) between the quantity on hand, the daily sales, and the quantity to be ordered. Similarly, in Example 2 on betting on the outcome of a coin toss, the individual's risk aversion, individual wealth, and so on might cause changes in beliefs related to whether expected value above zero justifies the decision to participate in the bet.

## ◇ ◇ ◇ Alternative Views of Knowledge

Knowledge can be viewed from a subjective or an objective stance. The subjective view represents knowledge using two possible perspectives: as a state of mind, or as a practice. On the other hand, the objective view represents knowledge in three possible perspectives: as an object, as an access to information, or as a capability. The perspectives on knowledge are shown in Figure 2-4.

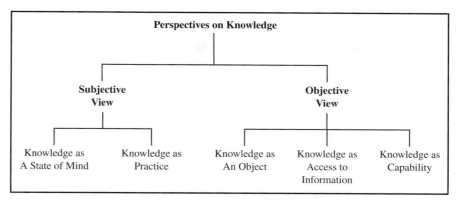

❖❖❖  **FIGURE 2-4** Various Perspectives on Knowledge

## SUBJECTIVE VIEW OF KNOWLEDGE

According to the subjective view, reality is socially constructed through interactions with individuals [Schultze, 1999]. Knowledge is viewed as an ongoing accomplishment, which continuously affects and is influenced by social practices [Boland and Tenkasi, 1995]. Consequently, knowledge cannot be placed at a single location, because it has no existence independent of social practices and human experiences. According to the subjective view, knowledge could be considered from two perspectives, either as state of mind or as practice.

### Knowledge as State of Mind

This perspective considers knowledge as a state of an individual's mind. Organizational knowledge is viewed as the beliefs of the individuals within the organization. Moreover, to the extent the various individuals have differing experiences and backgrounds, their beliefs, and hence knowledge, could differ from one another. Consequently, the focus is on enabling individuals to enhance their personal areas of knowledge so that they can apply them to best pursue organizational goals [Alavi and Leidner, 2001].

### Knowledge as Practice

According to this perspective, knowledge also is considered to be subjective but is viewed to be held by a group and not decomposable into elements possessed by individuals. Thus, from this perspective, knowledge is "neither possessed by any one agent, nor contained in any one repository" [Schultze, 1999, p. 10]. Moreover, knowledge resides not in anyone's head but in practice. Knowledge is composed of beliefs, consistent with our definition earlier, but the beliefs are collective instead of individual, and therefore are better reflected in organizational activities than in the minds of the organization's individuals. Viewed from this perspective, knowledge is "inherently indeterminate and continually emerging" [Tsoukas, 1996, p. 22].

## OBJECTIVE VIEW OF KNOWLEDGE

The objective view is the diametrical opposite of the subjective stance. According to the objective view, reality is independent of human perceptions and can be structured in terms of *a priori* categories and concepts [Schultze, 1999]. Consequently, knowledge can be located in the form of an object or a capability that can be discovered or improved by human agents. In the objective view knowledge is considered from three possible perspectives.

### Knowledge as Objects

From this perspective knowledge is something that can be stored, transferred, and manipulated. Consistent with the definition of knowledge as a set of justified beliefs, these knowledge objects (i.e., beliefs) can exist in a variety of locations. Moreover, they can be of several different types, as discussed in the next section.

### Knowledge as Access to Information

From this perspective knowledge is the condition of access to information [Alavi and Leidner, 2001]. Thus, knowledge is viewed as enabling access and utilization of information. This perspective extends the preceding view of knowledge as objects, emphasizing the accessibility of these objects.

### Knowledge as Capability

This perspective is consistent with the last two perspectives of knowledge as objects or as access to information. However, this perspective differs in that the focus is on the way in which knowledge can be applied to influence action. This perspective places emphasis on knowledge as a strategic capability that can potentially be applied to seek a competitive advantage.

Thus, the five perspectives discussed above differ in their focus in viewing knowledge, but they are all consistent in viewing knowledge as a set of beliefs about relationships. The first perspective, knowledge as a state of mind, focuses on beliefs within human minds; whereas the second perspective, knowledge as a practice, focuses on beliefs implicit to actions or practice. In either case, the beliefs, and the knowledge they comprise, are considered subjective. In contrast, the last three perspectives (knowledge as objects, knowledge as access to information, and knowledge as capability) view knowledge as objective, focusing on beliefs as objects to be stored and managed; as the condition of access to information; and as a capability that affects action. We recognize all five perspectives as important, and consider them as simply providing different ways of examining knowledge. However, in the remainder of the book, we adopt a position that is more objective than subjective.

We next examine the different forms of knowledge, which are clearly consistent with the objective perspective of knowledge. However, an argument could also be made that at least some types of knowledge discussed below (e.g., tacit) are not inconsistent with a subjective view either.

## ❖❖ ❖❖ ❖❖ Different Types of Knowledge

Knowledge has been classified and characterized in several different ways. For example, knowledge has been categorized as individual, social, causal, conditional, relational, and pragmatic [Alavi and Leidner, 2001], and also as embodied, encoded, and procedural [Venzin et al., 1998]. In this section, we examine some of the more important classifications of knowledge. It is important to understand the nature of these various types of knowledge because different types of knowledge should be managed differently, as discussed in detail in some of the later chapters.

## PROCEDURAL OR DECLARATIVE KNOWLEDGE

The first distinction we examine is that between **declarative knowledge** (facts) and **procedural knowledge** (how to ride a bicycle) [Singley and Anderson, 1989; Kogut and Zander 1992]. Declarative knowledge (or substantive knowledge, as it is also called) focuses on beliefs about relationships among variables. For example, all other things being equal, greater price charged for a product would cause some reduction in its number of sales. Declarative knowledge can be stated in the form of propositions, expected correlations, or formulas relating concepts represented as variables.

Procedural knowledge, in contrast, focuses on beliefs relating sequences of steps or actions to desired (or undesired) outcomes. An example of such procedural knowledge is the set of justified beliefs about the procedure that should be followed in a government organization in deciding on whom to award the contract for a particular area (e.g., information system development).

Declarative knowledge may be characterized as "know what," whereas procedural knowledge may be viewed as "know how." To further understand the difference between these two types of knowledge, let us consider the example of a hypothetical automobile-manufacturing firm. An instance of declarative knowledge in this context is the set of justified beliefs about the effect that the quality of each component would have on the final product. This could include the effect of quality on such features as reliability, fuel consumption, deterioration over time, and quality of the ride of a particular model. Such declarative knowledge, combined with information about the set of components needed for each model and the prices of various alternatives for each component, would help determine the specific components that should be used in each model. An example of procedural knowledge in the same context would be the set of beliefs about the process used to assemble a particular model of the car. This could include the steps in the engine assembly process, which tasks can be performed in parallel, the amount of time that each step should take, the amount of waiting time between successive steps, and so on.

## TACIT OR EXPLICIT KNOWLEDGE

Another important classification of knowledge views it as tacit or explicit [Nonaka, 1994; Polanyi, 1966]. **Explicit knowledge** typically refers to knowledge that has been expressed into words and numbers. Such knowledge can be shared formally and systematically in the form of data, specifications, manuals, drawings, audio and video tapes, computer programs, patents, and the like. For example, the basic principles for stock market analysis contained in a book or manual are considered explicit knowledge. This knowledge can be used by investors to make decisions about buying or selling stocks. It should also be noted that although explicit knowledge might resemble data or information in form, the distinction mentioned earlier in this chapter is preserved; although explicated, the principles of stock market analysis are justified beliefs about relationships instead of simple facts or observations.

In contrast, **tacit knowledge** includes insights, intuitions, and hunches. This knowledge is difficult to express and formalize, and therefore difficult to share. Tacit knowledge is more likely to be personal and based on individual experiences and activities. For example, through years of observing a particular industry, stock market analysts might gain knowledge that helps them make recommendations to investors in the stock market concerning the likely short-term and long-term market trends for the stocks of firms within that industry. Such knowledge would be considered tacit, unless the analyst can verbalize it in the form of a document that others can use and learn from.

As discussed earlier, explicit and tacit forms of knowledge are quite distinct. However, it is possible to convert explicit knowledge into tacit, as occurs, for example, when an individual reads a book and learns from it, thereby converting the explicit knowledge contained in the book into tacit knowledge in the individual's mind. Similarly, tacit knowledge can sometimes be converted into explicit knowledge, as happens when an individual with considerable tacit knowledge about a topic writes a book or manual formalizing that knowledge. These possibilities are discussed in greater detail in the next chapter on KM solutions.

## GENERAL OR SPECIFIC KNOWLEDGE

The third classification of knowledge focuses on whether the knowledge is possessed widely or narrowly. **General knowledge** is possessed by a large number of individuals and can be transferred easily across individuals. For example, knowledge about the rules of baseball can be considered general, especially among the spectators at a baseball stadium. One example of general knowledge in this context is knowing that when a baseball player takes the fourth "ball," he gets a walk; when he takes the third "strike," he is out. It is general because everyone with a basic understanding of baseball would possess this knowledge.

Unlike general knowledge, **specific knowledge,** or "idiosyncratic knowledge," is possessed by a very limited number of individuals, and is expensive to transfer [Hayek, 1945; Jensen and Meckling, 1996]. Consider the distinction between a professional coach and a typical fan watching a baseball game. The coach has the knowledge needed to filter, from the chaos of the game, the information required to evaluate and help players by advising such as when to try to hit the ball or when to steal a base. For example, if Barry Bonds is at bat, with a slow man on first, his team has two outs and is behind by one run against a left-handed pitcher, Bonds should be allowed to swing away. Few fans may have this knowledge, and so it is considered specific.

Specific knowledge can be of two types: technically specific knowledge and contextually specific knowledge. **Technically specific knowledge** is deep knowledge about a specific area. It includes knowledge about the tools and techniques that may be used to address problems in that area. This kind of knowledge is often acquired as a part of some formal training and is then augmented through experience in the field. Examples include the scientific knowledge possessed by a physicist and the knowledge about computer hardware possessed by a computer engineer.

On the other hand, **contextually specific knowledge** refers to the knowledge of particular circumstances of time and place in which work is to be performed [Hayek, 1945; O'Reilly and Pondy, 1979]. Contextually specific knowledge pertains to the organization and the organizational subunit within which tasks are performed. For example, the detailed knowledge design engineers possess about the idiosyncrasies of the particular design group in which they are working is contextually specific. Another example is a baseball catcher's knowledge of the team's pitching staff. Contextually specific knowledge cannot be acquired through formal training, but instead must be obtained from within the specific context (such as membership in the same design group or baseball team).

## COMBINING THE CLASSIFICATIONS OF KNOWLEDGE

The preceding classifications of knowledge are independent. In other words, procedural knowledge could be either tacit or explicit, and either general or specific. Similarly, declarative knowledge could be either tacit or explicit, and either general or specific. Combining the previous three classifications, and considering technically specific and contextually specific knowledge as distinct, 12 ($2 \times 2 \times 3$) types of knowledge can be identified as indicated and illustrated in Table 2-1.

## KNOWLEDGE AND EXPERTISE

We define **expertise** to be knowledge of higher quality. It addresses the degree of knowledge. That is, one who possesses expertise is able to perform a task much better that those who do not. This is specific knowledge at its best. The word *expert* can be used to describe people possessing many different levels of skills or knowledge. A person can be an expert at a particular task irrespective of how sophisticated that area of expertise is. For example, there are expert bus drivers just as there are expert brain surgeons. These experts excel in the performance of tasks in their respective fields.

Thus, the concept of expertise must be further classified for different types of domains. The skill levels of experts from different domains should not be compared. All experts require roughly the same cognitive skills. The difference lies in the depth of their expertise when compared with that of others from their own domains. For example, a highly skilled bus driver has greater abilities than a novice driver, just as an expert brain surgeon has greater skills than a surgical intern.

The expertise of interest can be classified into three distinct categories. Expert systems have had varying degrees of success when representing expertise from each of these categories. These categories, discussed in the following subsections, are (1) associational (black box), (2) motor skills, and (3) theoretical (deep) expertise.

### Associational Expertise

In most fields, it is usually desirable that experts have a detailed understanding of the underlying theory within that field. However, is this absolutely necessary? What about the television repair technician considered an expert repairman, but who does not understand all of the complex internal workings of a transistor or a picture tube? This technician can *associate* the observations of the performance of the device to specific causes purely based on experience. This individual may have expert-level associational understandings of these devices and may be able to fix almost any problem encountered. However, when encountering a new, previously unseen problem, the technician may not know how to proceed because of not understanding the inner workings of the device.

**TABLE 2-1  Illustrations of the Different Types of Knowledge**

|  | *General* | *Contextually Specific* | *Technically Specific* |
|---|---|---|---|
| *Declarative* | | | |
| *Explicit* | A book describing factors to consider when deciding whether to buy a company's stock. This may include price to earnings ratio, dividends | A company document identifying the circumstances under which a consultant team's manager should consider replacing a team member who is having problems with the project. | A manual describing the factors to consider in configuring a computer so as to achieve performance specifications |
| *Tacit* | Knowledge of the major factors to consider when deciding whether to buy a company's stock. | A human relations manager's knowledge of factors to consider in motivating an employee in a particular company. | A technician's knowledge of symptoms to look for in trying to repair a faulty television set. |
| *Procedural* | | | |
| *Explicit* | A book describing steps to take in deciding whether to buy a company's stock. | A company document identifying the sequence of actions a consultant team's manager should take when requesting senior management to replace a team member having problems with the project. | A manual describing how to change the operating system setting on a computer so as to achieve desired performance changes |
| *Tacit* | Basic knowledge of the steps to take in deciding whether to buy a company's stock. | A human relations manager's knowledge of steps to take in motivating an employee in a particular company. | A technician's knowledge of the sequence of steps to perform in repairing a television set. |

❖❖❖❖

### Motor Skills Expertise

Motor skill knowledge is predominantly physical instead of cognitive; therefore, knowledge-based systems cannot easily emulate this type of expertise. Humans learn these skills by repeatedly performing them. Although some people have greater abilities for these types of skills than others, real learning and expertise result from persistent practice. For example, consider the tasks of riding a bicycle; hitting a baseball; and snow skiing downhill. When you observe experts performing these activities, you notice that their reactions seem spontaneous and automatic. These reactions result from the experts' continual and persistent practice. For example, when skilled baseball players bat, they instinctively react to curve balls, adjusting their swing to connect with the ball. This appropriate reaction results from encountering thousands of curve balls over many years. A novice batter might recognize a thrown curve ball, but due to a lack of practice reacts slower and, consequently, may strike out.

These processes do not involve conscious thinking per se. The batter merely reacts instinctively and almost instantaneously to the inputs. In fact, many coaches maintain that thinking in such situations degrades performance. Of course, some cognitive activity is necessary—the batter must follow the track of the ball, recognize its motion (curve, changeup, etc.), and make a decision on what to do (swing, let it go, etc.). The issue, however, is that the result of the decision making is manifested in very quick physical actions and not in carefully pondered statements.

### Theoretical (Deep) Expertise

Finding a solution to a technical problem often requires going beyond a superficial understanding of the domain. We must apply creative ingenuity—ingenuity based on our theoretical knowledge of the domain. This type of knowledge allows experts to solve problems that have not been seen before and, therefore, cannot be solved via associational expertise.

Such deeper, more theoretical knowledge is acquired through formal training and hands-on problem solving. Typically, engineers and scientists who have many years of formal training possess this type of knowledge. Because of its theoretical and technical nature, this expertise is very easily forgotten unless continually used.

## ◇ ◇ ◇ Some Concluding Remarks on the Types of Knowledge

In addition to the preceding types of knowledge, some other classifications also deserve mention. One of these classifications views knowledge as either simple or complex. Whereas *simple knowledge* focuses on one basic area, *complex knowledge* draws upon multiple distinct areas of expertise. Another classification focuses on the role of knowledge within organizations. It divides knowledge into *support knowledge,* which relates to organizational infrastructure and facilitates day-to-day operations; *tactical knowledge,* which pertains to the short-term positioning of the organization relative to its markets, competitors, and suppliers; and *strategic knowledge,* which pertains to the long-term positioning of the organization in terms of its corporate vision and strategies for achieving that vision.

Based in part on the above types of knowledge, a number of characteristics of knowledge can be identified. One such characteristic is *explicitness* of knowledge, which reflects the extent to which knowledge exists in an explicit form so that it can be stored and transferred to others. As a characteristic of knowledge, explicitness indicates that instead of simply classifying knowledge as either explicit or tacit, it may be more appropriate to view explicitness as a continuous scale. Explicit and tacit kinds of knowledge are at the two ends of the continuum, with explicit knowledge high in explicitness and tacit knowledge low in this regard. Any specific knowledge would then be somewhere along this continuum of explicitness.

Zander and Kogut [1995] argue that instead of considering explicit and tacit knowledge, we should consider two characteristics of knowledge—codifiability and teachability. **Codifiability** reflects the extent to which knowledge can be articulated or codified, even if the resulting codified knowledge might be difficult to impart to another individual. In contrast, **teachability** reflects the extent to which the knowledge can be taught to other individuals, through training, apprenticeship, and so on. Of course, some knowledge could be high in both teachability and codifiability, whereas some knowledge could be low in both teachability and codifiability. The former would clearly be considered explicit, whereas the latter would clearly be considered tacit. However, teachability and codifiability do not need to be correlated. In other words, some knowledge could be high in teachability but low in codifiability (e.g., knowledge of how to play basketball). Alternatively, some knowledge could be high in codifiability but low in teachability (e.g., knowledge of how to fix problems in a personal computer).

Specific knowledge is directly related to the concept of knowledge specificity [Choudhury and Sampler, 1997]. A high level of *knowledge specificity* implies that the knowledge can be acquired or effectively used only by individuals possessing certain specific knowledge [Jensen and Meckling, 1996]. Knowledge specificity implies that the knowledge is possessed by a very limited number of individuals, and is expensive to transfer [Choudhury and Sampler, 1997]. Taking this a step further, technically specific and contextually specific knowledge lead us to break down knowledge specificity into *contextual knowledge specificity* and *technical knowledge specificity.* Of course, contextually specific knowledge and technically specific knowledge are high in contextual knowledge specificity and technical knowledge specificity, respectively.

In addition, the distinction between simple and complex knowledge may be represented using *complexity* as a knowledge attribute. Similarly, the *organizational role* of knowledge reflects the distinction between support, tactical, and strategic knowledge.

## ◇ ◇ ◇  Locations of Knowledge

Knowledge resides in several different locations or reservoirs, which are summarized in Figure 2-5. They encompass people, including individuals and groups; artifacts, including practices, technologies, and repositories; and organizational entities,

◇ ◇ ◇   **FIGURE 2-5** The Reservoirs of Knowledge

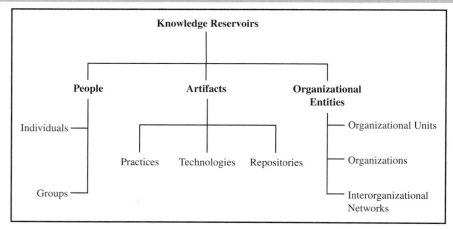

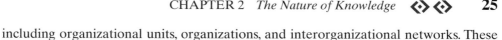

including organizational units, organizations, and interorganizational networks. These locations of knowledge are discussed in the rest of this section.

## KNOWLEDGE IN PEOPLE

A considerable component of knowledge is stored in people. Some of this knowledge is stored in *individuals* within organizations. For instance, in professional service firms, such as consulting or law firms, considerable knowledge resides within the minds of individual members of the firm [Argote and Ingram, 2000]. The knowledge stored in individuals is the reason several companies continually seek ways to retain knowledge that might be lost because of individuals retiring or otherwise leaving the organization.

In addition, considerable knowledge resides within *groups* because of the relationships among the members of the group. When three individuals have worked together for a long time, they instinctively know each other's strengths and weaknesses, understand the other's approach, and recognize aspects that need to be communicated and those that could be taken for granted [Skyrme, 2000]. Consequently, groups form beliefs about what works well and what does not, and this knowledge is over and above the knowledge residing in each individual member. In other words, the collective knowledge is synergistic—greater than the sum of each individual's knowledge. Communities of practice, which develop as individuals interact frequently with each other (physically or virtually) to discuss topics of mutual interest, illustrate such embedding of knowledge within groups.

## KNOWLEDGE IN ARTIFACTS

Over time, a significant amount of knowledge is stored in organizational artifacts as well. Some knowledge is stored in *practices,* organizational routines, or sequential patterns of interaction. In this case knowledge is embedded in procedures, rules, and norms that are developed through experience over time and guide future behavior [Levitt and March, 1988]. For example, fast-food franchises often store knowledge about how to produce high-quality products in routines [Argote and Ingram, 2000].

Considerable knowledge is also often stored in *technologies* and systems. As discussed earlier in this chapter, in addition to storing data, information technologies and computer-based information systems can store knowledge about relationships. For example, a computerized materials requirement planning system contains considerable knowledge about relationships between demand patterns, lead times for orders, and reorder quantities.

*Knowledge repositories* represent a third way of storing knowledge in artifacts. Knowledge repositories could be either paper based, such as books, papers, and other documents, or electronic based. An example of a paper-based repository is a consultant's own set of notes about the kind of things the client might focus more on, when examining the proposals submitted by the consultant firm's and its competitors. On the other hand, a Web site containing answers to frequently asked questions (FAQs) about a product represents an electronic knowledge repository.

## KNOWLEDGE IN ORGANIZATIONAL ENTITIES

Knowledge is also stored within organizational entities. These entities can be considered at three levels: as organizational units (parts of the organization), as an entire organization, and as interorganizational relationships (such as the relationship between an organization and its customers).

Within an organizational unit, such as a department or an office, knowledge is stored partly in the relationships among the members of the units. In other words, the organizational unit represents a formal grouping of individuals, who come together not because of common interests, but instead because of organizational structuring. Over time, as individuals occupying certain roles in an organizational unit depart and are replaced by others, the incumbents inherit some, but not all, of the knowledge developed by their predecessors. This knowledge may have been acquired through the systems, practices, and relationships within that unit. Moreover, contextually specific knowledge is more likely to be related to the specific organizational unit.

An organization, such as a business unit or a corporation, also stores certain knowledge, especially contextually specific knowledge. The norms, values, practices, and culture within the organization, and across its organizational units, contain knowledge that is not stored within the mind of any one individual. The way in which the organization responds to environmental events is dependent, therefore, not only on the knowledge stored in individuals and organizational units but also in the overall organizational knowledge that has been developed through positive and negative experiences over time.

Finally, knowledge is also stored in interorganizational relationships. As organizations establish and consolidate relationships with customers and suppliers, they draw on knowledge embedded in those relationships. Customers who use the focal organization's products, and suppliers who provide the basic components from which the products are made, often have considerable knowledge about the strengths and weaknesses of those products. Consequently, organizations often learn from their customers' experience with products about how these can be improved. They can also learn about new products that might be appealing to customers.

## SUMMARY ◆ ◆ ◆

In this chapter we have explained the nature of knowledge in considerable detail. We have distinguished knowledge from data and information, highlighting that knowledge should best be considered as fundamentally different from data and information instead of considering data, information, and knowledge as part of a hierararchy. We defined knowledge in an area as justified beliefs about relationships among concepts relevant to that particular area. Furthermore, we examined subjective and objective perspectives for viewing knowledge including perspectives that consider knowledge as a state of mind, as a practice, as an object, as an access to information, and as a capability. We then distinguished between procedural and declarative knowledge, between tacit and explicit knowledge, and between general and specific knowledge. Some other ways of classifying knowledge were also described. Based on the various classifications of knowledge, we introduced knowledge characteristics, such as tacitness and specificity. In this chapter we also described the possible locations of knowledge, including people, artifacts, and organizational entities. In the next chapter, we build on this chapter by describing various knowledge management solutions.

## KEY TERMS <>  <>  <>

- associational expertise—p. 21
- codifiability—p. 23
- contextually specific knowledge—p. 20
- data—p. 12
- declarative knowledge—p. 19
- deep expertise—p. 23

- expertise—p. 21
- explicit knowledge—p. 19
- general knowledge—p. 20
- information—p. 12
- knowledge—p. 12
- motor skills expertise—p. 22
- procedural knowledge—p. 19

- specific knowledge—p. 20
- tacit knowledge—p. 20
- teachability—p. 24
- technically specific knowledge—p. 20

## REVIEW QUESTIONS <>  <>  <>

1. How do the terms *data* and *knowledge* differ? Describe each term with the help of a similar example, elucidating the difference between the two.
2. *Information* contains *data* but not all data is information. Justify this statement.
3. Explain why the same set of data can be considered as useful information by some and useless data by others. Further, could this useful information be termed as *knowledge?* Explain why.
4. Describe the ways in which *knowledge* differs from *data* and *information.* Justify your answer with a relevant diagram.
5. Explain the importance of knowledge in creation and utilization of information.
6. How does the subjective view of knowledge differ from the objective view? Explain how knowledge can be viewed as a state of mind, as a practice, as an object, as an access to information and as a capability.
7. What is the difference between knowledge characterized as "know what" and "know how"? In these situations, how would you classify the knowledge a computer programmer has?
8. Does a player in a card game use tacit or explicit knowledge? Explain why. Define and explain the difference between the two.
9. What is general knowledge? How does it differ from specific knowledge? Describe the types of specific knowledge with suitable examples.
10. What is *expertise?* Distinguish between the three types of expertise.
11. Contrast the differences between knowledge in people and knowledge in artifacts. Describe the various repositories of knowledge within organizational entities.
12. List three primary knowledge reservoirs discussed in the chapter and compare those with respect to accessibility to knowledge.

## APPLICATION EXERCISES <>  <>  <>

1. Consider five decisions you have made today. (They could be simple, such as taking a turn while driving or even choosing a soda at a convenience store.) In each case determine the data, information, or knowledge that were involved in the decision.
2. Now consider how those decisions would have been influenced by the lack of preexisting data, information, or knowledge.
3. You have recently invented a new product. Collect demographic data from a sample population, determine how you would use this data, and convert it into information and possibly knowledge for marketing the product.
4. Interview a manager in a manufacturing organization, and one in a services-based organization. Determine the contrasting views of knowledge between the two due to the nature of their businesses.
5. Determine the various locations of knowledge within your organization (or that of a friend or family member). Classify them appropriately.

6. Now speculate on the negative effects of not having one or more of those knowledge repositories and accordingly determine which repository is the most critical to the organization. Which is the least?

7. Determine the various types of knowledge you used to read this chapter. You should be able to state at least one of each type.

8. Interview organizations in your area to determine the explicit and tacit knowledge within the organization. Rank the explicit knowledge on the basis of its codifiability and teachability. Further, suggest ways in which the tacit knowledge could be made explicit.

9. You are considering buying a new 2003 Ford Taurus. Gather tacit knowledge and explicit knowledge on buying cars from various resources (e.g., the Ford Web site (www.ford.com). List your findings and explain what source of knowledge is important for your choice.

10. Go to the Microsoft Web site (www.microsoft.com). Find the *Support* tab at the upper right corner of the Web page. Click the tab and you can find *Knowledge Base* at the pull-down menu. Try to find the *Knowledge Base* structure and usage. What types of knowledge can be applied at the Microsoft *Knowledge Base?* You should use at least four types of knowledge discussed in this chapter.

11. Suppose you desperately need technical advice on a Microsoft product. You have two options: (1) call computer experts or (2) use Microsoft FAQs. *Ceteris paribus,* define preferred option and briefly explain your choice with the concepts of accessibility to knowledge reservoir.

12. Wal-Mart (www.walmart.com) is said to be one of the leading employers of older workers and considers seniors vital to its unique corporate culture. Store managers are encouraged to recruit from senior citizen groups, local American Association of Retired Persons (AARP) chapters, and churches. Analyze this Wal-Mart strategy in terms of knowledge management.

## References ❖ ❖ ❖

Alavi, M., and Leidner, D. 2001. Knowledge management and knowledge management systems: Conceptual foundations and research issues. *MIS Quarterly,* 25(1), 107.

Argote, L., and Ingram, P. 2000. Knowledge transfer: basis for competitive advantage in firms. *Organizational Behavior and Human Decision Processes,* 82(1), May, 150–169.

Boland, R.J., and Tenkasi, R.V. 1995. Perspective making and perspective taking in communities of knowing. *Organization Science,* 6(4), 350–372.

Choudhury, V., and Sampler, J. 1997. Information specificity and environmental scanning: An economic perspective. *MIS Quarterly,* 21(1), 25–53.

Hayek, F.A. 1945. The use of knowledge in society. *American Economic Review* (XXXV:4), September, 519–530.

Jensen, M.C., and Meckling, W.H. 1996. Specific and general knowledge, and organizational structure, In Myers, P.S. (Ed.), *Knowledge Management and Organizational Design.* Butterworth-Heinemann, Newton, MA, pp. 17–38.

Kogut, B., and Zander, U. 1992. Knowledge of the firm, combinative capabilities and the replication of technology. *Organization Science,* 3(3), 383–397.

Levitt, B., and March, J.G. 1988. Organizational learning. *Annual Review of Sociology,* 14, 319–340.

Nonaka, I. 1994. A dynamic theory of organizational knowledge creation. *Organization Science,* 5(1), 14–37.

Nonaka, I., and Takeuchi, H. 1995. *The Knowledge Creating Company: How Japanese Companies Create the Dynamics of Innovation.* Oxford University Press, New York.

O'Reilly, C.A., and Pondy, L. 1979. Organizational communication. In Kerr, S. (Ed.), *Organizational Behavior.* Grid, Columbus, OH, 119–150.

Polanyi, M. 1966. *The Tacit Dimension.* Routledge and Keoan, London.

Schultze, U. 1999. Investigating the contradictions in knowledge management. In Larsen, T.J., Levine, L., and De Gross, J.I. (Eds.), *Information Systems:*

*Current Issues and Future Changes.* IFIP, Laxenberg, Austria, 155–174.

Singley, M., and Anderson, J. 1989. *The Transfer of Cognitive Skill.* Harvard Press, Cambridge, MA.

Skyrme, D.J. 2000. Developing a knowledge strategy: From management to leadership. In Morey, D., Maybury, M., and Thuraisingham, B. (Eds.), *Knowledge Management: Classic and Contemporary Works.* MIT Press, Cambridge, MA, pp. 61–84.

Tsoukas, H. 1996. The firm as a distributed knowledge system: A constructionist approach. *Strategic Management Journal,* 17 (Winter), 11–25.

Venzin, M., von Krogh, G., and Roos, J. 1998. Future research into knowledge management. In von Krogh, G., Roos, J., and Kleine, D. (Eds.), *Knowing in Firms: Understanding, Managing and Measuring Knowledge.* Sage Publications, Thousand Oaks, CA, 1998.

Wiig, K. 1999. Introducing knowledge management into the enterprise. In *Knowledge Management Handbook.* CRC Press, Boca Raton, FL, 3-1-41.

Zander, U., and Kogut, B. 1995. Knowledge and the speed of the transfer and imitation of organizational capabilities: An empirical test. *Organization Science,* 6, 76–92.

# CHAPTER 3

# Knowledge Management Solutions

### ❖ ❖ ❖ Introduction

In Chapter 2, we examine the nature of knowledge as well as its various forms and locations. In this chapter, we first discuss in some detail what we mean by **knowledge management (KM).** This is followed by an overview of KM solutions, and subsequently, a detailed discussion of the variety of KM solutions, including KM infrastructure, KM mechanisms and technologies, and KM processes.

### ❖ ❖ ❖ Knowledge Management and Knowledge Management Solutions

Managing any resource may be defined as doing what is necessary to get the most out of that resource. Therefore, at a very simple level, KM may be defined as *doing what is needed to get the most out of knowledge resources*. Let us now consider this simple definition in some detail by providing a few elaborations.

First, it is important to stress that this definition can be applied at the individual as well as organizational levels. Depending on the level, *knowledge resources* might be the knowledge resources that are relevant to the decisions, goals, and strategies of an individual or an organization. The *organization* may be a corporation, a firm, a field office of a firm, a department within a corporation or firm, etc. Moreover, the term *knowledge resources* refers not only to the knowledge currently possessed by the individual or the organization but also to the knowledge that can potentially be obtained (at some cost if necessary) from other individuals or organizations.

Second, *get the most* reflects the impacts of KM on the goal achievement of the individual or the organization. Considering the impact knowledge can have on individuals and organizations (as summarized in Chapter 1 and to be discussed in greater detail in Chapter 4), the objective of KM is to enhance the extent to which knowledge facilitates the achievement of individual or organizational goals. Furthermore, a cost–benefit assumption is implicit. In other words, the objective is to enhance the impact of knowledge in a cost-effective fashion, such that the benefits of KM exceed the costs of doing so.

Finally, *what is needed* refers to a variety of possible activities involved in KM. These activities are broadly intended to (1) discover new knowledge, (2) capture existing knowledge, (3) share knowledge with others, or (4) apply knowledge.

Based on the above elaborations, a more detailed definition of KM can now be offered.

> Knowledge management can be defined as performing the activities involved in discovering, capturing, sharing, and applying knowledge so as to enhance, in a cost-effective fashion, the impact of knowledge on the unit's goal achievement.

**Knowledge management solutions** refer to the variety of ways in which KM can be facilitated. KM solutions may be divided into four broad levels, as shown in Figure 3-1: (1) KM processes, (2) KM systems, (3) KM mechanisms and technologies, and (4) KM infrastructure.

KM processes are the broad processes that help in discovering, capturing, sharing, and applying knowledge. These four KM processes are supported by KM systems and seven important types of KM subprocesses (e.g., exchange), which we describe later in this chapter.

**Knowledge management systems** are the integration of technologies and mechanisms that are developed to support the above four KM processes. KM systems are examined further in a later section of this chapter, and are discussed in considerable detail in Part III of the book.

**FIGURE 3-1** Overview of Knowledge Management Solutions

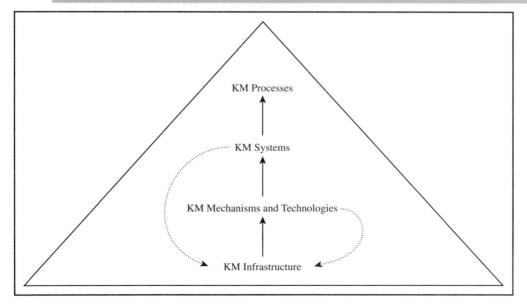

*KM mechanisms and technologies* are used in KM systems, with each KM system utilizing a combination of multiple mechanisms and multiple technologies. Moreover, the same KM mechanism or technology could, under differing circumstances, support multiple KM systems. We further discuss KM mechanisms and technologies in a later section of this chapter. Moreover, we discuss the various KM technologies in considerable detail in Part II of this book.

KM mechanisms and technologies, in turn, rely on the **KM infrastructure,** which reflects the long-term foundation for KM. In an organizational context, KM infrastructure includes five major components (e.g., organization culture and the organization's information technology infrastructure). These are also discussed in a later section of this chapter.

Thus, KM infrastructure supports KM mechanisms and technologies, and KM mechanisms and technologies are used in KM systems that enable KM processes. However, over time, KM infrastructure benefits from KM mechanisms and technologies as well as KM processes, as shown by the curved arrows in Figure 3-1.

In the next section we describe the processes used to support the discovery, capture, sharing, and application of knowledge. In discussing these KM processes, we also examine the seven subprocesses that facilitate them. We then provide a brief overview of KM mechanisms and technologies and KM systems. Finally, the KM infrastructure is described.

## ◇◆ ◇◆ ◇◆  Knowledge Management Processes

We earlier define KM as "performing the activities involved in discovering, capturing, sharing, and applying knowledge so as to enhance, in a cost-effective fashion, the impact of knowledge on the unit's goal achievement." Thus, KM relies on four main kinds of **KM processes.** As shown in Figure 3-2, these include the processes through which knowledge is discovered or captured. Figure 3-2 also includes the processes through which this knowledge is shared and applied. These four KM processes are supported by a set of seven KM subprocesses, as shown in Figure 3-2, with one subprocess—socialization—supporting two KM processes (discovery and sharing). Of

◇◆ ◇◆ ◇◆  **FIGURE 3-2** Knowledge Management Processes

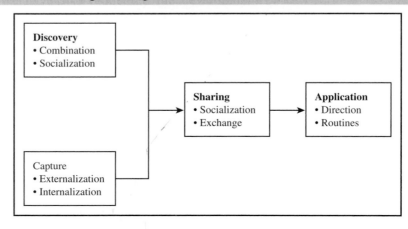

the seven KM subprocesses, four are based on Nonaka [1994]; focusing on the ways in which knowledge is converted through the interaction between tacit and explicit knowledge, Nonaka identified four ways of managing knowledge: socialization, externalization, internalization, and combination. The other three KM subprocesses—exchange, direction, and routines—are largely based on Grant [1996a, 1996b] and Nahapiet and Ghoshal [1998].

## KNOWLEDGE DISCOVERY

**Knowledge discovery** may be defined as *the development of new tacit or explicit knowledge from data and information or from the synthesis of prior knowledge.* The discovery of new explicit knowledge relies most directly on combination, whereas the discovery of new tacit knowledge relies most directly on socialization. Combination and socialization are discussed next.

New explicit knowledge is discovered through **combination,** wherein the multiple bodies of explicit knowledge (also data or information) are synthesized to create new, more complex sets of explicit knowledge [Nonaka, 1994]. Through communication, integration, and systemization of multiple streams of explicit knowledge, new explicit knowledge is created—either incrementally or radically [Nahapiet and Ghoshal, 1998]. Existing explicit knowledge, data, and information are reconfigured, recategorized, and recontextualized to produce new explicit knowledge. For example, when creating a new proposal to a client, explicit data, information, and knowledge embedded in prior proposals may be combined into the new proposal. Also, data mining techniques may be used to uncover new relationships among explicit data that may lead to predictive or categorization models that create new knowledge.

In the case of tacit knowledge, the integration of multiple streams for the creation of new knowledge occurs through the mechanism of socialization [Nonaka, 1994]. **Socialization** is the synthesis of tacit knowledge across individuals, usually through joint activities instead of written or verbal instructions. For example, by transferring ideas and images, apprenticeships help newcomers to see how others think. Davenport and Prusak [1998] describe how conversations at the watercooler helped knowledge sharing among groups at IBM.

## KNOWLEDGE CAPTURE

As we discuss in Chapter 2, knowledge can exist within people (individuals or groups); artifacts (practices, technologies, or repositories); and organizational entities (organizational units, organizations, or interorganizational networks). Moreover, knowledge can be either explicit or tacit. It may sometimes reside within an individual's mind, without that individual having the ability to recognize it and share it with others. Similarly, knowledge may reside in an explicit form in a manual but few people may be aware of it. It is important to obtain the tacit knowledge from the individual's minds as well as the explicit knowledge from the manual, such that the knowledge can then be shared with others. This is the focus of **knowledge capture,** which may be defined as *the process of retrieving either explicit or tacit knowledge that resides within people, artifacts, or organizational entities.* Also, the knowledge captured might reside outside the organizational boundaries, including consultants, competitors, customers, suppliers, and prior employers of the organization's new employees.

The knowledge capture process benefits most directly from two KM subprocesses—externalization and internalization. Based on work by Nonaka [1994], externalization and internalization help capture the tacit knowledge and explicit knowledge, respectively.

**Externalization** involves converting tacit knowledge into explicit forms such as words, concepts, visuals, or figurative language (e.g., metaphors, analogies, and narratives) [Nonaka and Takeuchi, 1995]. Externalization also helps translate individuals' tacit knowledge into explicit forms that can be more easily understood by the rest of their group. This is a difficult process because tacit knowledge is often difficult to articulate. Nonaka [1994] suggested that externalization may be accomplished through the use of metaphor (i.e., understanding and experiencing one kind of thing in terms of another). An example of externalization is a consultant team writing a document that describes the lessons the team has learned about the client organization, client executives, and approaches that work in such an assignment. This captures the tacit knowledge acquired by the team members.

**Internalization** is the conversion of explicit knowledge into tacit knowledge. It represents the traditional notion of "learning." The explicit knowledge may be embodied in action and practice, so that the individual acquiring the knowledge can reexperience what others have gone through. Alternatively, individuals could acquire tacit knowledge in virtual situations, either vicariously by reading manuals or others' stories, or experientially through simulations or experiments [Nonaka and Takeuchi, 1995]. An example of internalization is having new software consultants read a book on innovative software development, and learn from it. This learning helps the consultants and their organization capture the knowledge contained in the book.

### Knowledge Sharing

**Knowledge sharing** is the process through which explicit or tacit knowledge is communicated to other individuals. Three important clarifications are in order. First, knowledge sharing means *effective transfer*, so that the recipient of knowledge can understand it well enough to act on it [Jensen and Meckling, 1996]. Second, what is shared is knowledge instead of recommendations based on the knowledge; the former involves the recipient acquiring the shared knowledge as well as having the ability to take action based on it, whereas the latter (which is direction, as we discuss in the next section) simply involves utilization of knowledge without the recipient internalizing the shared knowledge. Third, knowledge sharing may take place across individuals as well as across groups, departments, or organizations [Alavi and Leidner, 2001].

If knowledge exists at a location that is different from where it is needed, either knowledge sharing or knowledge utilization without sharing (discussed in the next subsection) is necessary. Sharing knowledge is clearly an important process in enhancing organizational innovativeness and performance. This is reflected in the fact it was one of the three business processes for which General Electric chief executive officer (CEO) Jack Welch took personal responsibility (the others were allocation of resources and development of people) [Stewart, 2000].

Depending on whether explicit or tacit knowledge is shared, exchange or socialization processes are used. Socialization, which we discuss above, facilitates the sharing of tacit knowledge in cases in which new tacit knowledge is created (see previous subsection) as well as when new tacit knowledge is not created.

**Exchange,** in contrast, focuses on the sharing of explicit knowledge. It is used to communicate or transfer explicit knowledge between individuals, groups, and organizations [Grant, 1996b]. In its basic nature, the process of exchange of explicit knowledge does not differ from the process through which information is communicated. An example of exchange is a product design manual transferred by one employee to another, who can then use the explicit knowledge contained in the manual.

## KNOWLEDGE APPLICATION

Knowledge contributes most directly to organizational performance when it is used to make decisions and perform tasks. Of course, the process of **knowledge application** depends on the available knowledge, and the latter depends on the processes of knowledge discovery, capture, and storage, as shown in Figure 3-2. The better the processes of knowledge discovery, capture, and storage, the greater is the likelihood that the knowledge needed for effective decision making is available.

In applying knowledge, the party that makes use of it does not necessarily need to comprehend it. All that is needed is that somehow the knowledge is used to guide decisions and actions. Therefore, knowledge utilization benefits from two processes that do not involve the actual transfer or exchange of knowledge between the concerned individuals—routines and direction [Grant, 1996a].

**Direction** refers to the process through which individuals possessing the knowledge direct the action of another individual without transferring to that person the knowledge underlying the direction. This preserves the advantages of specialization and avoids the difficulties inherent in the transfer of tacit knowledge. Direction is the process used when a production worker calls experts to ask them how to solve a particular problem with a machine, and then proceeds to solve the problem based on the instructions given by the experts. This production worker does so without acquiring the experts' knowledge, so that if a similar problem reoccurs in the future, he would be unable to identify it as such and would therefore be unable to solve it without calling an expert. Note the difference between direction and socialization or exchange, in which the knowledge is actually internalized by the other person.

**Routines** involve the utilization of knowledge embedded in procedures, rules, and norms that guide future behavior. Routines economize on communication more than directions because they are embedded in procedures or technologies. However, they take time to develop, relying on constant repetition [Grant, 1996a]. An inventory management system utilizes considerable knowledge about the relationship between demand and supply, but neither the knowledge nor the directions are communicated through individuals.

## KNOWLEDGE MANAGEMENT MECHANISMS

**KM mechanisms** are organizational or structural means used to promote KM. They enable KM systems and by themselves are supported by the KM infrastructure.

KM mechanisms may (or may not) utilize technology, but they do involve some kind of organizational arrangement or social or structural means of facilitating KM.

Examples of KM mechanisms include learning by doing, on-the-job training, learning by observation, and face-to-face meetings. More long-term KM mechanisms include the hiring of a chief knowledge officer, cooperative projects across departments, traditional hierarchical relationships, organizational policies, standards, initiation process for new employees, and employee rotation across departments. To illustrate KM mechanisms, in Vignette 3-1 we briefly examine the approach one company, Viant, takes to manage knowledge.

## KNOWLEDGE MANAGEMENT TECHNOLOGIES

**KM technologies** also support KM systems and benefit from the KM infrastructure, especially the information technology infrastructure. KM technologies constitute a key component of KM systems. Technologies that support KM include artificial intelligence (AI) technologies encompassing those used for knowledge acquisition and case-based reasoning systems, electronic discussion groups, computer-based simulations, databases, decision support systems, enterprise resource planning systems, expert systems, management information systems, expertise locator systems, videoconferencing, and information repositories encompassing best practices databases and lessons learned systems.

---

   VIGNETTE 3-1

### Knowledge Management Mechanisms at Viant

Viant[1] is a Boston-based consulting company specializing in helping clients build e-commerce businesses. It considers KM as a key objective of the processes through which new employees are initiated into the organization and existing employees are rotated across functions and locations as mechanisms for KM. Viant makes excellent use of the orientation process to provide newcomers with knowledge of key clients, some company-specific skills, and the beginnings of an informal network. New employees begin their Viant career with 3 weeks in Boston. On arrival, employees receive their laptop, loaded with off-the-shelf and proprietary software. Later that week they learn team skills and take a course in the company's consulting strategy and tools. For the next 2 weeks they switch back and forth between classroom work and teams, doing a mock consulting assignment. They bond, meet all the officers, listen to corporate folklore, and party with the CEO.

Employee rotation also plays an important role in KM at Viant. In fact, conventional reporting relationships do not work at this company. Because people rotate in and out of assignments, consultants have no fixed relationship to a boss; instead, senior managers act as "advocates" for a number of "advocados." Performance reviews emphasize the growth in the employee's own skill level, and stock options recognize the knowledge they share [Stewart, 2000].

---

[1]See www.viant.com

Examples of the use of KM technologies include the World Bank's use of a combination of video interviews and hyperlinks to documents and reports to systematically record the knowledge of employees that are close to retirement [Lesser and Prusak, 2001]. Similarly, at British Petroleum (BP), desktop videoconferencing has improved communication and enabled many problems at off-shore oil fields to be solved without extensive traveling [Skyrme, 2000].

In the next subsection, we identify the roles of several specific KM technologies in enabling KM systems. Furthermore, we describe KM technologies in considerable detail in Part II of this book, discussing AI technologies (Chapter 7), rule-based expert systems (Chapter 8), case-based reasoning systems (Chapter 9), knowledge elicitation technologies (Chapter 10), computer communications technologies (Chapter 11), and data mining technologies (Chapter 12). Therefore, KM technologies are not discussed further in this subsection.

# ◆▷ ◁▷ ◆▷  Knowledge Management Systems

KM systems utilize a variety of KM mechanisms and technologies to support the KM processes discussed in an earlier section. Depending on the KM process most directly supported, KM systems can be classified into four kinds that we discuss in detail in Part III: knowledge discovery systems (Chapter 13), knowledge capture systems (Chapter 14), knowledge sharing systems (Chapter 15), and knowledge application systems (Chapter 16). In this section, we provide a brief overview of these four kinds of systems and examine how they benefit from KM mechanisms and technologies.

### KNOWLEDGE DISCOVERY SYSTEMS

As discussed in an earlier section, knowledge discovery systems support the process of developing new tacit or explicit knowledge from data and information or from the synthesis of prior knowledge. These systems support two KM sub-processes associated with knowledge discovery: combination, enabling the discovery of new explicit knowledge; and socialization, enabling the discovery of new tacit knowledge.

Thus, mechanisms and technologies can support knowledge discovery systems by facilitating combination or socialization. *Mechanisms* that facilitate combination include collaborative problem solving, joint decision making, and collaborative creation of documents. For example, at the senior management level, new explicit knowledge is created by sharing documents and information related to midrange concepts (e.g., product concepts) augmented with grand concepts (e.g., corporate vision) to produce new knowledge about both areas. This newly created knowledge could be, for example, a better understanding of products and a corporate vision [Nonaka and Takeuchi, 1995]. Mechanisms that facilitate socialization include apprenticeships, employee rotation across areas, conferences, brainstorming retreats, cooperative projects across departments, and initiation process for new employees. For example, Honda "sets up brainstorming camps (*tama dashi kai*) — informal meetings for detailed discussions to solve difficult problems in development projects" [Nonaka and Takeuchi, 1995, p. 63].

*Technologies* facilitating *combination* include knowledge discovery systems (see Chapters 13 and 16), databases, and Web-based access to data. According to Nonaka and Takeuchi [1995, p. 67], "reconfiguration of existing information through sorting, adding, combining, and categorizing of explicit knowledge (as conducted in computer databases) can lead to new knowledge." Repositories of information, best practices and lessons learned (see Chapter 15) also facilitate combination. Technologies can also facilitate socialization, albeit to less extent than they can facilitate combination. Some of the technologies for facilitating socialization include video-conferencing, and electronic support for **communities of practice** (see Chapter 11).

## KNOWLEDGE CAPTURE SYSTEMS

Knowledge capture systems support the process of retrieving either explicit or tacit knowledge that resides within people, artifacts, or organizational entities. These systems can help capture knowledge that resides within or outside organizational boundaries, including within consultants, competitors, customers, suppliers, and prior employers of the organization's new employees. Knowledge capture systems rely on mechanisms and technologies that support externalization and internalization.

KM mechanisms can enable knowledge capture by facilitating externalization (i.e., the conversion of tacit knowledge into explicit form), or internalization (i.e., the conversion of explicit knowledge into tacit form). The development of models or prototypes, and the articulation of best practices or lessons learned are some examples of mechanisms that enable externalization. Vignette 3-2 illustrates the use of externalization to capture knowledge about projects in one organization.

Learning by doing, on-the-job training, learning by observation, and face-to-face meetings are some of the mechanisms that facilitate internalization. For example, at one firm, "the product divisions also frequently send their new-product development

---

 VIGNETTE 3-2

### Knowledge Capture at Viant

Viant, the Boston-based company we discuss in Vignette 3-1, uses a variety of means to capture knowledge. The firm uses a number of simple but unavoidable forms. Before every project, consultants are required to complete a "quicksheet" describing the knowledge they need, what aspects of knowledge can be leveraged from prior projects, and what they need to create, along with the lessons they hope to learn that they can share with others later. A longer report, a sunset review, is produced at a team meet-ing to document what worked and what did not work well. Forgetting these reports is hard due to several reasons: "First, almost every document ends up on Viant's internal Website, hot-linked every which way. Second, sunset reviews are done with a facilitator who wasn't on the team, which helps keep them honest. Third, every six weeks Newell's knowledge-management group prepares, posts, and pushes a summary of what's been learned" [Stewart, 2000].

people to the Answer Center to chat with the telephone operators or the 12 specialists, thereby "'reexperiencing' their experiences" [Nonaka and Takeuchi, 1995, p. 69].

*Technologies* can also support knowledge capture systems by facilitating externalization and internalization. Externalization through knowledge elicitation (described in detail in Chapter 10) is necessary for the implementation of intelligent technologies such as expert systems (see Chapter 8), and case-based reasoning systems (see Chapter 9). Technologies that facilitate internalization include computer-based training and communication technologies (see Chapter 11). Using such communication facilities, an individual can internalize knowledge from a message or attachment thereof, sent by another expert, an AI-based knowledge capture system (see Chapter 14), or computer-based simulations.

## KNOWLEDGE SHARING SYSTEMS

Knowledge sharing systems support the process through which explicit or implicit knowledge is communicated to other individuals. They do so by supporting exchange (i.e., sharing of explicit knowledge) and socialization (which promotes sharing of tacit knowledge).

Mechanisms and technologies that were discussed in a previous subsection as supporting socialization also play an important role in knowledge sharing systems. *Discussion groups* or *chat groups* facilitate knowledge sharing by enabling individuals to explain their knowledge to the rest of the group. In addition, knowledge-sharing systems also utilize mechanisms and technologies that facilitate exchange. Some of the mechanisms that facilitate exchange are memos, manuals, progress reports, letters, and presentations. Technologies facilitating exchange include groupware and other team collaboration mechanisms (see Chapter 11); Web-based access to data, and databases (see Chapter 11); and repositories of information, including best practice databases, lessons learned systems, and expertise locator systems (see Chapter 15). Vignette 3-3 provides one illustration of the importance of knowledge sharing.

## KNOWLEDGE APPLICATION SYSTEMS

Knowledge application systems support the process through which some individuals utilize knowledge possessed by other individuals without actually acquiring, or learning, that knowledge. Mechanisms and technologies support knowledge application systems by facilitating routines and direction.

*Mechanisms* facilitating *direction* include traditional hierarchical relationships in organizations, help desks, and support centers. On the other hand, mechanisms supporting *routines* include organizational policies, work practices, and standards. In the case of both direction and routines, these mechanisms may be either within an organization (e.g., organizational hierarchies) or across organizations (e.g., software support help desks).

*Technologies* supporting direction include experts' knowledge embedded in expert systems (see Chapter 8) and decision support systems, as well as troubleshooting systems based on the use of technologies like case-based reasoning (see Chapter 9). On the other hand, some of the technologies that facilitate routines are expert systems (see Chapters 8 and 16), enterprise resource planning systems, and traditional management information systems. As mentioned for KM mechanisms, these technologies can also facilitate directions and routines within or across organizations. These are discussed in detail in Chapter 16.

 VIGNETTE 3-3

### Knowledge Sharing at VHA

Until 1997, the Veteran's Health Administration (VHA) did not have any systematic mechanism to enable its 219,000 employees to share their informal knowledge, innovations, and best practices. To address this need and also to serve as a place where any VHA employee can access knowledge capital of colleagues, the VHA Lessons Learned Project and its Web site, the Virtual Learning Center (VLC), were initiated in 1997. The VHA indicates that a major reason for initiating this project was a recognized need to transform the organization into a learning organization. In 1999, the VLC became available on the Internet.[2] The site now has international participation from Korea, Canada, Spain, Pakistan, and elsewhere. By reducing red tape, cutting across organizational silos, partnering and benchmarking with others, and establishing best processing, the VHA is "saving countless hours of staff time by not having to reinvent the wheel at its 173 medical centers, more than 600 clinics, 31 nursing home care units, 206 counseling centers, and other federal and private healthcare institutions, Veterans Benefits and National Cemetery offices."[3]

[2]See www.va.gov/vlc
[3]See www.infotoday.com/kmw01/kmawards.htm

Table 3-1 summarizes the above discussion of KM processes and KM systems, and also indicates some of the mechanisms and technologies that might facilitate them. As may be seen from Table 3-1, the same tool or technology can be used to support more than one KM process.

## ◆◇◆ Knowledge Management Infrastructure

**KM insfrastructure** is the foundation on which KM resides. It includes five main components: organization culture, organization structure, communities of practice, information technology infrastructure, and common knowledge. These components are discussed in the next five subsections.

### ORGANIZATIONAL CULTURE

Organizational culture reflects the norms and beliefs that guide the behavior of the organization's members. It is an important enabler of KM in organizations. Indeed, a survey of KM practices in U.S. companies [Dyer and McDonough, 2001] indicated that the four most important challenges in KM are nontechnical in nature, and include, in order of importance: (1) the organization's employees have no time for KM; (2) the current organization culture does not encourage knowledge sharing; (3) inadequate understanding of KM and its benefits to the company; and (4) inability to measure the financial benefits from KM. Although the second of these challenges specifically mentions organization culture, the first and third challenges are also directly dependent on organization culture—a supporting organization culture helps motivate employees to

**TABLE 3-1  KM Processes, Mechanisms, and Technologies**

| KM Processes | KM Systems | KM Sub-Processes | Illustrative KM Mechanisms | Illustrative KM Technologies |
|---|---|---|---|---|
| *Knowledge discovery* | Knowledge discovery systems | Combination | Meetings, telephone conversations, and documents, collaborative creation of documents | Databases, Web-based access to data, data mining, repositories of information, Web portals, best practices and lessons learned |
| | | Socialization | Employee rotation across departments, conferences, brainstorming retreats, cooperative projects, initiation | Video-conferencing, electronic discussion groups, e-mail |
| *Knowledge capture* | Knowledge capture systems | Externalization | Models, prototypes, best practices, lessons learned | Expert systems, chat groups, best practices, and lessons learned databases. |
| | | Internalization | Learning by doing, on-the-job training, learning by observation, and face-to-face meetings | Computer-based communication, AI-based knowledge acquisition, computer-based simulations |
| *Knowledge sharing* | Knowledge sharing systems | Socialization | See above | See above |
| | | Exchange | Memos, manuals, letters, presentations | Team collaboration tools, Web-based access to data, databases, and repositories of information, best practices databases, lessons learned systems, and expertise locator systems |
| *Knowledge application* | Knowledge Application Systems | Direction | Traditional hierarchical relationships in organizations, help desks, and support centers | Capture and transfer of experts' knowledge, troubleshooting systems, and case-based reasoning systems; decision support systems |
| | | Routines | Organizational policies, work practices, and standards | Expert systems, enterprise resource planning systems, management information systems |

understand the benefits from KM and also to find time for KM. Indeed, getting people to participate in knowledge sharing is considered the hardest part of KM. Carla O'Dell, president of the American Productivity & Quality Center, believes that of the companies trying to implement KM, less than 10% have succeeded in making it part of their culture [Koudsi, 2000].

Attributes of an enabling organizational culture include understanding of the value of KM practices, management support for KM at all levels, incentives that reward knowledge sharing, and encouragement of interaction for the creation and sharing of knowledge [Armbrecht et al., 2001]. In contrast, cultures that stress individual performance and hoarding of information within units encourage limited employee interaction, and lack of an involved top management creates inhibited knowledge sharing and retention. Moreover, people are often afraid of asking others if they know the answer to a certain question, and especially posting a question for the entire company to see, might reveal their ignorance [Koudsi, 2000].

A case study of a baby food manufacturer revealed that built-in competition within the corporate structure inhibited knowledge sharing practices that could have significantly increased revenues. The performance of frontline salespeople was evaluated based on that of other salespeople. Because of this, a group of sales people found a market niche in selling baby food to aging adults who could no longer eat hard food, but they kept knowledge of their customer base to themselves and let only their successful sales indicate their find. Because the company's culture bred competition between employees and offered incentives based on a curve, it missed out not only on increased revenues from additional sales in that market but also on potential product development to better fill this niche [DeTienne and Jackson, 2001].

In another case study, the male CEO of a Web-consulting company instituted several measures to enhance the use of the company's KM system [Koudsi, 2000]. He started publicly recognizing people who stood out as strong knowledge contributors. He also made use of the KM system a part of everyone's job description. He even started paying employees to use this system. Each task on the KM system was assigned points. If consultants placed their resume in the system, they would receive one point. If consultants created a project record, they would receive five points. The company's knowledge manager acted as judge, deciding whether entries deserved points. The totals were tallied every 3 months, and the resulting score accounted for 10% of a consultant's quarterly bonus. Before these metrics were introduced in January 1999, only a third of the company's employees were rated as good or better in the use of the KM system, but 2 months later, that use had almost doubled [Koudsi, 2000].

## ORGANIZATION STRUCTURE

KM also depends to a considerable extent on the organization structure. Several aspects of organization structure are relevant. First, the *hierarchical structure* of the organization affects the people with whom individuals frequently interact, and to or from whom they are consequently likely to transfer knowledge. Traditional reporting relationships influence the flow of data and information, and the nature of groups who make decisions together, consequently affecting the sharing and creation of knowledge. By decentralizing or flattening their organizational structures, companies often seek to eliminate organizational layers, thereby placing more responsibility with each individual and increasing the size of groups reporting to each individual. Consequently, knowledge sharing is likely to occur with a larger group of individuals in more decentralized organizations. In addition, matrix structures and an emphasis on leadership instead of management also facilitate greater knowledge sharing primarily by cutting across traditional departmental boundaries.

Second, organizational structures can facilitate KM through **communities of practice.** A community of practice is an organic and self-organized group of individuals who are dispersed geographically or organizationally but communicate regularly to discuss issues of mutual interest [Lave and Wenger, 1991]. For example, a tech club at DaimlerChrysler includes a group of engineers who do not work in the same unit but meet regularly, on their own initiative, to discuss problems related to their area of expertise. Similarly, at Xerox, a strategic community of information technology (IT) professionals, involving frequent informal interactions among them, promotes knowledge sharing [Storck and Hill, 2000].

Communities of practice provide access to a larger group of individuals than is possible within traditional departmental boundaries. Consequently, there are more numerous potential helpers, and this increases the probability that at least one of them can provide useful knowledge. Communities of practice also provide access to external knowledge sources. An organization's external stakeholders (e.g., customers, suppliers, and partners) provide a far greater knowledge reservoir than just that of the organization [Choo, 1998]. For instance, relationships with university researchers can help new biotechnology firms to maintain their innovativeness.

Although communities of practice are usually not part of a company's formal organization structure, company executives can facilitate them in several ways. For example, the executives can legitimize these practices through support for participation in them. Moreover, the executives can enhance the perceived value of participation in communities of practice by seeking advice from them. The executives can also help communities of practice by providing them with resources, such as money or connections to external experts.

Third, organization structures can facilitate KM through *specialized structures* and *roles* that specifically support KM. Three possibilities deserve special mention. First, some organizations appoint an individual to the position of chief knowledge officer and make this individual responsible for the organization's KM efforts. Second, some organizations establish a separate department for KM, which is often headed by the chief knowledge officer. Finally, two traditional KM units—the research and development (R&D) department and the corporate library—also facilitate KM, although they differ in focus. Whereas the R&D department supports management of knowledge about the latest or future developments, the corporate library supports business units by serving as a repository of historical information about the organization and its industry and competitive environment.

## INFORMATION TECHNOLOGY INFRASTRUCTURE

KM is also facilitated by the organization's information technology infrastructure. Although certain information technologies and systems are directly developed to pursue KM, the organization's overall information technology infrastructure, developed to support the organization's information systems (IS) needs, also facilitates KM. The IT infrastructure includes data processing, storage, and communication technologies and systems. This infrastructure comprises the entire spectrum of organization's information systems, including transaction processing and management information. The IT infrastructure consists of databases and data warehouses, as well as enterprise resource planning systems. One possible way of systematically viewing the IT infrastructure is to consider the capabilities it provides in four important aspects: *reach, depth, richness,* and *aggregation* [Daft and Lengel, 1986; Evans and Wurster, 1999].

Reach pertains to access and connection, and the efficiency of such access. Within the context of a network, reach reflects the number and geographic locations of the nodes that can be efficiently accessed. Keen [1991] also uses the term *reach* to refer to the locations an IT platform is capable of linking, with the ideal able to connect to "anyone, anywhere." Much of the power of the Internet is attributed to its reach and the fact that most people can access it quite inexpensively. Reach is enhanced not only by advances in hardware but also by progress in software. For instance, standardization of cross-firm communication standards, and languages such as XML, make it easier for firms to communicate with a wider array of trading partners, including those with whom they do not have long-term relationships.

*Depth*, in contrast, focuses on the detail and amount of information that can be effectively communicated over a medium. This dimension closely corresponds to the aspects of bandwidth and customization included by Evans and Wurster [1999] in their definition of richness. Communicating deep and detailed information requires high bandwidth. At the same time, it is the availability of deep and detailed information about customers that enables customization. Recent technological progress, for instance, in channel bandwidth, has enabled considerable improvement in depth.

Communication channels can be arranged along a continuum representing their "relative richness" [Carlson and Zmud, 1999]. The richness of a medium is based on its ability to: (1) provide multiple cues (e.g., body language, facial expression, tone of voice) simultaneously; (2) provide quick feedback; (3) personalize messages; and (4) use natural language to convey subtleties [Daft and Lengel, 1984]. IT has traditionally been viewed as a lean communication medium. However, given the progress in IT we are witnessing a significant increase in its ability to support rich communication.

Finally, rapid advances in IT have significantly enhanced the ability to store and quickly process information. This enables the *aggregation* of large volumes of information drawn from multiple sources. For instance, data mining and data warehousing together enable the synthesis of diverse information from multiple sources, potentially to produce new insights. Enterprise resource planning (ERP) systems also present a natural platform for aggregating knowledge across different parts of an organization. A senior IS executive at Price Waterhouse Coopers, for example, remarks, "We're moving quite quickly on to an intranet platform, and that's giving us a greater chance to integrate everything instead of saying to people, 'use this database and that database and another database.' Now it all looks—and is—much more coordinated" [Thomson, 2000, p. 24].

To summarize, the above four IT capabilities enable KM by enhancing common knowledge or by facilitating the four KM processes. For example, an expertise locator system (also called knowledge yellow pages, or a people-finder system) is a special type of knowledge repository that pinpoints individuals having specific knowledge within the organization. These systems rely on the reach and depth capabilities of IT by enabling individuals to contact remotely located experts and seek detailed solutions to complicated problems. Another IS solution attempts to capture as much of the knowledge in an individual's head as possible and archive it in a searchable database. This is primarily the aim of projects in artificial intelligence (AI), which capture the expert's knowledge in systems based on various technologies, including rule-based and case-based reasoning, among others [Wong and Radcliffe, 2000]. However, the most sophisticated systems for eliciting and cataloging experts' knowledge in models that can easily be understood and applied by others in the organization (see, e.g., Ford et al. [1996]) require strong knowledge engineering processes to develop. Such sophisticated KM systems have typically not been advocated for use in mainstream business environments, primarily because of the high cost involved in the knowledge engineering effort.

## COMMON KNOWLEDGE

**Common knowledge** [Grant, 1996b] represents another important component of the infrastructure that enables KM. Common knowledge also refers to the organization's cumulative experiences in comprehending a category of knowledge and activities, and the organizing principles that support communication and coordination [Zander and Kogut, 1995]. In addition, common knowledge provides unity to the organization, including a common language and vocabulary, recognition of individual knowledge domains, common cognitive schema, shared norms, and elements of specialized knowledge that are common across individuals sharing knowledge [Nahapiet and Ghoshal, 1998; Grant, 1996b].

Common knowledge helps enhance the value of an individual expert's knowledge by integrating it with the knowledge of others. However, because the common knowledge, based on the above definition, is common only to an organization, this increase in value is also specific to that particular organization and does not transfer to its competitors. Thus, common knowledge supports knowledge transfer within the organization but impedes the transfer (or leakage) of knowledge outside the organization [Argote and Ingram, 2000].

## PHYSICAL ENVIRONMENT

The physical environment within the organization is often taken for granted, but it is another important foundation on which KM rests. Key aspects of the physical environment include the design of buildings and the separation between them; the location, size, and type of offices; the type, number, and nature of meeting rooms; and so on. Physical environment can foster KM by providing opportunities for employees to meet and share ideas. Even though knowledge sharing is often not by design, coffee rooms, cafeterias, watercoolers, and hallways do provide venues where employees learn from, and share insights with, each other. A 1998 study found that most employees thought they gained most of their knowledge related to work from informal conversations around watercoolers or over meals instead of formal training or manuals [Wensley, 1998].

A number of organizations are creating spaces specifically designed to facilitate this informal knowledge sharing. For example, the London Business School created an attractive space between two major departments, which were earlier isolated, to enhance knowledge sharing between them. Reuters News Service installed kitchens on each floor to foster discussions. Moreover, a medium-sized firm in the United States focused on careful management of office locations to facilitate knowledge sharing [Stewart, 2000]. This company developed open-plan offices with subtle arrangements to encourage what one senior executive calls *knowledge accidents*. Locations are arranged in this company so as to maximize the chances of face-to-face interactions among people who might be able to help each other. For example, a female employee might walk down the hall so that she might meet someone who knows the answer to her question, and she might meet such an individual not due to chance but because a snack area is positioned where four project teams' work areas intersect.

Table 3-2 summarizes the above five dimensions of KM infrastructure, indicating the key attributes related to each dimension.

**TABLE 3-2    A Summary of Knowledge Management Infrastructure**

| Dimensions of KM Infrastructure | Related Attributes |
|---|---|
| *Organization culture* | ■ Understanding of the value of KM practices<br>■ Management support for KM at all levels<br>■ Incentives that reward knowledge sharing<br>■ Encouragement of interaction for the creation and sharing of knowledge |
| *Organization structure* | ■ Hierarchical structure of the organization (decentralization, matrix structures, emphasis on "leadership" rather than "management")<br>■ Communities of practice<br>■ Specialized structures and roles (Chief Knowledge Officer, KM department, traditional KM units) |
| *Information technology infrastructure* | ■ Reach<br>■ Depth<br>■ Richness<br>■ Aggregation |
| *Common knowledge* | ■ Common language and vocabulary<br>■ Recognition of individual knowledge domains<br>■ Common cognitive schema<br>■ Shared norms<br>■ Elements of specialized knowledge that are common across individuals |
| *Physical environment* | ■ Design of buildings (offices, meeting rooms, hallways)<br>■ Spaces specifically designed to facilitate informal knowledge sharing (coffee rooms, cafeterias, water coolers) |

◆◇ ◇◆ ◆◇ ◇◆

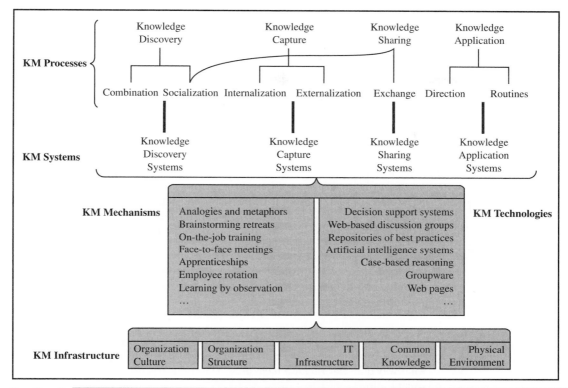

❖ ❖ ❖ **FIGURE 3-3** Detailed View of Knowledge Management Solutions

## SUMMARY ❖ ❖ ❖

Building on the discussion of knowledge in Chapter 2, we describe the key aspects of KM in this chapter. We provide a working definition of KM, and examine KM solutions at four levels: KM processes, KM systems, KM mechanisms and technologies, and KM infrastructure. Figure 3-3 provides a summary of the key aspects of this chapter, indicating the various aspects of KM processes (including the four overall processes as well as the seven specific processes that support them), KM systems, KM mechanisms and technologies, and KM infrastructure (including its five dimensions). The next chapter examines the value of knowledge and KM solutions, highlighting their importance for organizational performance.

## KEY TERMS ❖ ❖ ❖

- combination—p. 33
- common knowledge—p. 45
- communities of practice—p. 38
- direction—p. 35
- exchange—p. 35
- externalization—p. 34

- information technology infrastructure—p. 43
- internalization—p. 34
- knowledge application—p. 35
- knowledge capture—p. 33
- knowledge discovery—p. 33
- knowledge management—p. 30

- knowledge management infrastructure—p. 32
- knowledge management mechanisms—p. 36
- knowledge management processes—p. 32

- knowledge management solutions—p. 31
- knowledge management systems—p. 31
- knowledge management technologies—p. 36
- knowledge sharing—p. 34
- routines—p. 35
- socialization—p. 33

## REVIEW QUESTIONS ◆◇ ◆◇ ◆◇

1. What is knowledge management (KM)? What are its objectives?
2. Describe the ways to facilitate KM, along with suitable examples.
3. Define knowledge discovery and describe two important ways of managing knowledge discovery.
4. Briefly describe the processes involved in KM within a unit. How would these processes relate to each other?
5. Compare and contrast internalization and externalization processes for managing knowledge.
6. What is *knowledge sharing* as opposed to *knowledge application*?
7. Briefly describe why General Electric's CEO Jack Welch may have suggested knowledge sharing as important.
8. How does direction differ from routines in regard to knowledge application?
9. Explain the importance of KM mechanisms and KM technologies to KM systems. Give examples of each.
10. Briefly explain the four kinds of classifications for KM systems based on the process supported.
11. State the roles of (a) organizational culture and (b) organizational structure for the development of a good KM infrastructure.
12. In what way does information technology (IT) infrastructure contribute to KM within an organization?

## APPLICATION EXERCISES ◆◇ ◆◇ ◆◇

1. How would you, as a CEO of a manufacturing firm, facilitate the growth of practices within your organization?
2. Interview a manager of an organization where knowledge management (KM) practices have recently been implemented. Identify the processes involved.
3. Did you observe knowledge discovery, knowledge capture, knowledge sharing, and knowledge application in the organization? Accordingly identify what in your opinion was the most critical stage for the organization, and which was the least important.
4. Choose a company that has well-established groupware without a KM system yet. Based on this company, briefly explain how the communications between employees were made and compare the difference between KM system and the company's legacy system in terms of knowledge sharing.
5. How would you develop a KM system. What are the possible mechanisms and technologies you could utilize?
6. How would you utilize knowledge discovery systems and knowledge capture systems in an organization that is spread across the globe? Does geographic distance hamper the utilization of these systems?
7. Cisco (www.cisco.com) developed a new KM system. Because Cisco is an Internet-centered company, a Web-based resource is essential. However, instead of building the resource, the company looked to a partner to speed the KM development process. Describe strengths and weaknesses of employing an outsourcing company for developing KM system.

8. Suggest reasons why a knowledge sharing system could be established between rival organizations (e.g., Mastercard and Visa) for the mutual benefit of both organizations.

9. Dell Computer Corporation (www.dell.com) has developed a host of Microsoft Exchange Server–based KM solutions that have helped the company increase productivity and cut costs while improving customer service. Find information on types of KM technology and solutions used these days and compare with those of Dell.

10. Determine ways in which a law firm would implement and utilize knowledge application systems. Conduct interviews if necessary.

11. Interview at least three managers from local organizations that have recently implemented KM. Contrast the differences in organization culture, structure, IT infrastructure, common knowledge, and physical knowledge within the organizations.

12. Critique the following statement: "We have implemented several IT solutions: expert systems, chat group, and best practices and lessons learned databases. These powerful solutions can surely induce our employees to internalize knowledge."

13. Many small to midsize firms were only investing in ERP system packages—no KM system at all. Comment on what you think may be particularly important parts of the decision process when an organization expands its IT infrastructure to a KM system.

## REFERENCES ❖ ❖ ❖

Alavi, M., and Leidner, D. 2001. Knowledge management and knowledge management systems: Conceptual foundations and research issues. *MIS Quarterly*, 25(1), 107–136.

Argote, L., and Ingram, P. 2000. Knowledge transfer: Basis for competitive advantage in firms. *Organizational Behavior and Human Decision Processes*. May, 82(1), 150–169.

Armbrecht, F.M.R., Chapas, R.B., Chappelow, C.C., Farris, G.F., Friga, P.N., Hartz, C.A., McIlvaine, M.E., Postle S.R., and Whitwell, G.E. 2001. Knowledge management in research and development. *Research Technology Management*, 44(4), 28–48.

Carlson, J.R., and Zmud, R.W. 1999. Channel expansion theory and the experiential nature of media richness perceptions. *Academy of Management Journal*, 42(2), 153–170.

Choo, C.W. 1998. *The Knowing Organization: How Organizations Use Information to Construct Meaning, Create Knowledge, and Make Decisions.* Oxford University Press, New York.

Daft, R.L., and Lengel, R.H. 1986. Organization information requirements, media richness, and structural design. *Management Science*, 32(5), 554–571.

Davenport, T., and Prusak, L. 1998. *Working Knowledge.* Harvard Business School Press, Boston, MA.

DeTienne, K.B., and Jackson, L.A. 2001. Knowledge management: Understanding theory and developing strategy. *Competitiveness Review*, 11(1), 1–11.

Dyer, G., and McDonough, B. 2001. The state of KM. *Knowledge Management*, May, 31–36.

Evans, P., and Wurster, T.S. 1999. Getting real about virtual commerce. *Harvard Business Review*, November/December, 85–94.

Grant, R.M. 1996a. Prospering in dynamically-competitive environments: Organizational capability as knowledge integration. *Organization Science*, 7(4), 375–387.

Grant, R.M. 1996b. Toward a knowledge-based theory of the firm. *Strategic Management Journal*, 17, 109–122.

Jensen, M.C., and Meckling, W.H. 1996. Specific and General Knowledge, and Organizational Structure. In Myers, P.S. (Ed.), *Knowledge Management and Organizational Design.* Butterworth-Heinemann, Newton, MA, pp. 17–38.

Keen, P. 1991. *Shaping the Future: Business Design Through Information Technology.* Harvard Business School Press, Boston, MA.

Koudsi, S. 2000. Actually, it is like brain surgery. *Fortune*, March 20, 233–234.

Lave, J., and Wenger, E. 1991. *Situated Learning: Legitimate Peripheral Participation.* Cambridge University Press, Cambridge, MA.

Lesser, E., and Prusak, L. 2001. Preserving knowledge in an uncertain world. *Sloan Management Review*, Fall, 101–102.

Nahapiet, J., and Ghoshal, S. 1998. Social capital, intellectual capital, and the organizational advantage. *Academy of Management Review,* 23(2), 242–266.

Nonaka, I. 1994. A dynamic theory of organizational knowledge creation. *Organization Science,* 5(1), February, 14–37.

Nonaka, I., and Takeuchi, H. 1995. *The Knowledge Creating Company: How Japanese Companies Create the Dynamics of Innovation.* Oxford University Press, New York.

Skyrme, D.J. 2000. Developing a knowledge strategy: From management to leadership. In Morey, D., Maybury, M., and Thuraisingham, B. (Eds.), *Knowledge Management: Classic and Contemporary Works.* MIT Press, Cambridge, MA, pp. 61–84.

Stewart, T.A. 2000. The house that knowledge built, *Fortune,* October 2, 278–280.

Storck, J., and Hill, P. 2000. Knowledge diffusion through "strategic communities." *Sloan Management Review,* 41(2), 63–74.

Thomson, S. 2000. Focus: Keeping pace with knowledge. *Information World Review,* Issue 155, February, 23–24.

Wensley, A. 1998. The value of story telling. *Knowledge and Process Management,* 5(1–2), 1–2.

Wong, W., and Radcliffe, D. 2000. The tacit nature of design knowledge. *Technology Analysis and Strategic Management,* 12(4), 493–512.

Zander, U., and Kogut, B. 1995. Knowledge and the speed of the transfer and imitation of organizational capabilities: An empirical test. *Organization Science,* 6, 76–92.

CHAPTER 4

# Organizational Impacts of Knowledge Management

*The wise see knowledge and action as one.*
—FROM THE BHAGWAD GITA

## ◇◇◇ Introduction

In the previous chapter we examined what we mean by knowledge management (KM), and discuss the variety of KM solutions, including KM infrastructure, KM mechanisms and technologies, and KM processes. In this chapter, we examine the impacts of KM. Consistent with our emphasis on the use of KM in organizations, we focus our discussion on the impact of KM on companies and other private or public organizations.

The importance of knowledge (and KM processes) is well recognized. KM can impact organizations and organizational performance at several levels: people, processes, products, and the overall organizational performance. It is important to note that KM processes can impact organizations at these four levels in two main ways. First, KM can help create knowledge, which can then contribute to improved performance of organizations along these four dimensions. Second, KM can directly cause improvements along these four dimensions. These two ways in which KM can impact organizations are summarized in Figure 4-1.

Figure 4-2 depicts the impacts of KM on the four dimensions mentioned above, and shows how the effect on one dimension can have an impact on another. The impact at three of these dimensions—individuals, products, and the organization—was clearly indicated in a joint survey by IDC[1] and *Knowledge Management Magazine* in May 2001 [Dyer and McDonnough, 2001]. This survey examined the status of KM practices in U.S. companies, and found three top reasons why U.S. firms adopt

---

[1]IDC is one of the world's leading providers of technology intelligence, industry analysis, market data, and strategic and tactical guidance to builders, providers, and users of information technology. More information on it can be obtained from www.idc.com.

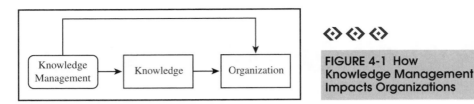

❖ ❖ ❖

**FIGURE 4-1 How Knowledge Management Impacts Organizations**

KM: (1) retaining expertise of employees, (2) enhancing customers' satisfaction with the company's products, and (3) increasing profits or revenues. We look at these issues closely in the next four sections.

## ❖❖❖ Impact on People

KM can affect the organization's employees in several ways. First, KM can facilitate their learning (from each other as well as from external sources). This learning allows the organization to be constantly growing and changing in response to the market and the technology. Second, KM also causes employees to become more flexible, and enhances their job satisfaction. This is largely because of their enhanced ability to learn about solutions to business problems that worked in the past, as well as those solutions that did not work. We discuss these effects in the next subsections.

### IMPACT ON EMPLOYEE LEARNING

KM can help enhance employees' learning and exposure to the latest knowledge in their fields. This can be accomplished in a variety of ways, including externalization and internalization, socialization, and communities of practice, which are all discussed in Chapter 3.

We earlier described **externalization** as the process of converting tacit knowledge into explicit forms, and **internalization** as the conversion of explicit knowledge into tacit knowledge [Nonaka and Takeuchi, 1995]. Externalization and internalization work together in helping individuals learn. One possible example of externalization is preparing a report on lessons learned from a project. In preparing the report, the team members document, or externalize, the tacit knowledge they have acquired during

❖❖ ❖ **FIGURE 4-2 Dimensions of Organizational Impacts of Knowledge Management**

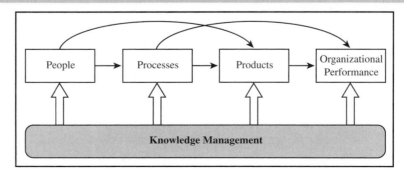

the project. Individuals embarking on later projects can then use this report to acquire the knowledge gained by the earlier team. These individuals acquire tacit knowledge through internalization (i.e., by reading the explicit report and thereby reexperiencing what others have gone through). Thus, experts writing a book are externalizing their knowledge in that area, and students reading the book are acquiring tacit knowledge from the knowledge explicated in the book.

**Socialization** also helps individuals acquire knowledge, but usually through joint activities, such as meetings and informal conversations. One specific, but important, way in which learning through socialization can be facilitated involves the use of a **community of practice,** which we define in Chapter 3 as an organic and self-organized group of individuals who are dispersed geographically or organizationally but communicate regularly to discuss issues of mutual interest. In Vignette 4-1, we give an example.

The experience of Xerox illustrates the way in which KM can enable the organization's employees to learn from each other as well as from prior experiences of former employees. This experience is also indicative of how such processes for individual learning can lead to continued organizational success.

 VIGNETTE 4-1

### Strategic Communities of Practice at Xerox

Xerox Corporation accomplished such individual learning through a strategic community of practice. Consistent with our definition of a community of practice, the group at Xerox included geographically distributed individuals, from the headquarters as well as business units. However, this group was somewhat different from a traditional community of practice because it was not voluntarily formed by the individuals, but was instead deliberately established by the top management at Xerox with the goal of providing strategic benefits through knowledge sharing. This is the reason Storck and Hill [2000] characterized it as a "strategic" community. In this strategic community, which had been formed to help in the management of technology infrastructure, a large group of information technology (IT) professionals provided leading-edge solutions, addressed unstructured problems, and stayed in touch with the latest developments in hardware and software.

According to the group members surveyed by Storck and Hill, about two-thirds of the group's value resulted from face-to-face networking at the group's meetings. This attention to KM by focusing on informal groups of employees has helped Xerox in its recent push in global services. Jim Joyce, a senior executive at Xerox remarked, "It is about understanding where knowledge is and how it is found. By working with human elements of this, there are real things you can do to help people embrace the technology and incorporate it into the workflow" [Moore, 2001]. Similarly, Tom Dolan, president of Xerox Global Services, recognized, "At the core of Xerox's heritage of innovation is a deep understanding of how people, processes and technology interact with each other in the creation of great work. As a result, our practical, results-oriented, knowledge management solutions can help businesses streamline work processes, enable better customer service and grow revenue" [Business Wire, 2002].

## IMPACT ON EMPLOYEE ADAPTABILITY

When the KM process at an organization encourages its employees to continually learn from each other, the employees are likely to possess the information and knowledge needed to adapt whenever organizational circumstances so require. Moreover, when employees are aware of ongoing and potential future changes, they are less likely to be caught by surprise. Awareness of new ideas and involvement in free-flowing discussions not only prepare employees to respond to changes but also make them more likely to accept change. Thus, KM is likely to engender greater adaptability among employees.

When Buckman Laboratories, a privately owned U.S. specialty chemicals firm with about 1,300 employees, was named "the 2000 Most Admired Knowledge Enterprise," chairman Bob Buckman remarked that the company's KM efforts were intended to continually expose its employees to new ideas and enable them to learn from these ideas [Business Wire, 2000]. He also emphasized that the employees were prepared for change as a result of being in touch with the latest ideas and developments, and they consequently embraced change instead of fearing it. The increased employee adaptability due to KM enabled the company to become a very fast changing organization around the needs of its customers.

## IMPACT ON EMPLOYEE JOB SATISFACTION

Two benefits of KM that accrue directly to individual employees have been discussed above; (1) they are able to learn better than employees in firms that are lacking in KM; and (2) they are better prepared for change. These impacts cause the employees to feel better because of the knowledge acquisition and skill enhancement, and also enhance their market value relative to other organizations' employees. A recent study found that in organizations having more employees sharing knowledge with one another, turnover rates were reduced, thereby positively affecting revenue and profit [Bontis, 2003]. Indeed, exit interview data in this study indicated that one of the major reasons many of the brightest knowledge workers changed jobs was because "they felt their talent was not fully leveraged." Of course, it is possible to argue for the reverse causal direction; that is, more satisfied employees are likely to be more willing to share knowledge. The causal direction of the relationship between employee job satisfaction and knowledge sharing needs to be examined further in empirical research.

In addition, KM also provides employees with solutions to problems they face in case those same problems have been encountered earlier, and effectively addressed. This provision of tried-and-tested solutions (e.g., through the direction mechanism discussed in Chapter 3) amplifies employees' effectiveness in performing their jobs. This helps keep those employees motivated, because successful employees would be highly motivated whereas employees facing problems in performing their jobs would likely be demotivated.

Thus, as a result of their increased knowledge, improved market value, and greater on-the-job performance, KM facilitates employees' job satisfaction. In addition, some approaches for KM, such as mentoring and training, are also directly useful in motivating employees, and therefore increasing employee job satisfaction. Similarly, communities of practice provide the involved employees intimate and socially validated control over their own work practices [Brown and Duguid, 1991].

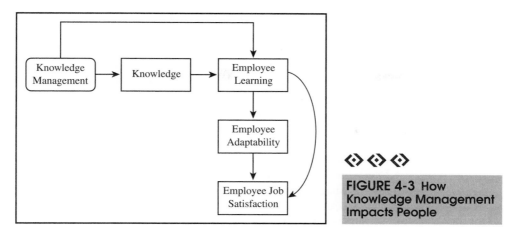

❖ ❖ ❖

**FIGURE 4-3** How Knowledge Management Impacts People

Figure 4-3 summarizes the above impacts KM and knowledge can have on employees of organizations.

## ❖ ❖ ❖ Impact on Processes

KM also enables improvements in organizational processes such as marketing, manufacturing, accounting, engineering, and public relations. These impacts can be seen along three major dimensions: effectiveness, efficiency, and degree of innovation of the processes. These three dimensions can be characterized as follows:

- *Effectiveness.*   Performing the most suitable processes and making the best possible decisions.
- *Efficiency.*   Performing the processes quickly and in a low-cost fashion.
- *Innovation.*   Performing the processes in a creative and novel fashion, that improves effectiveness and efficiency—or at least marketability.

KM can improve the above interrelated aspects of organizational processes through several means, including better knowledge imparted to individuals (through exchange, socialization, etc.), and the provision of workable solutions (through directions and routines) for employees to solve the problems faced in their tasks. The effects of KM on effectiveness, efficiency, and innovation are discussed in more detail in the following three subsections, respectively.

### IMPACT ON PROCESS EFFECTIVENESS

KM can enable organizations to become more effective by helping them to select and perform the most appropriate processes. Effective KM enables the organization's members to collect information needed to monitor external events. This results in fewer surprises for the leaders of the organization, and consequently reduces the need to modify plans and settle for less effective approaches. In contrast, poor KM can result in mistakes by organizations because they risk repeating past mistakes or not foreseeing otherwise obvious problems. For example, Ford and Firestone incurred numerous problems that may have been reduced through greater knowledge sharing, either by exchanging explicit knowledge and information or by using meetings (and other means of socialization) to share tacit knowledge. These firms did possess the necessary information to warn them about the mismatch of Ford Explorers and Firestone tires. However, the information was not integrated across the two companies, which might have inhibited either company from having the "full picture." It is interesting to note that although Ford had a good KM process (the Best Practices Replication Process, discussed later in this chapter), it was not used to manage the information and knowledge relating to the Ford Explorer and the Firestone tires [Stewart, 2000]. The result was significant loss in lives for their customers, and unprecedented legal liability.

KM enables organizations to quickly adapt their processes according to the current circumstances, thereby maintaining process effectiveness in changing times. On the other hand, organizations lacking in KM find it difficult to maintain process effectiveness when faced with turnover of experienced and new employees. An illustrative example is from a large firm that reorganized its engineering department in 1996. This reorganization achieved a 75% reduction of the department's workforce. An external vendor subsequently absorbed many of the displaced engineers. However, like many organizations undergoing significant downsizing, this company failed to institutionalize any mechanisms to capture the knowledge of the employees that were leaving the department. A 2-month review of the results following the reorganization effort showed that several key quality indicators were not met. This was a direct result of the loss of human knowledge with the displacement of the workforce. One important reason for the lack of attention to retaining knowledge is that the alternative approaches for capturing individual knowledge (which is introduced in Chapter 3) are not well understood. We discuss some of these methods and technologies to capture knowledge in Chapter 14.

In Vignette 4-2 we cite an example of how KM helps organizations to adapt to current circumstances.

## IMPACT ON PROCESS EFFICIENCY

Managing knowledge effectively can also enable organizations to be more productive and efficient. While exploring the "black box" of knowledge sharing within Toyota's network, Dyer and Nobeoka [2000] found that Toyota's ability to effectively create and manage network-level knowledge sharing processes, at least partially, explains the relative productivity advantages enjoyed by Toyota and its suppliers. Knowledge diffusion was found to occur more quickly within Toyota's production network than in competing automaker networks. This was because Toyota's network had solved three fundamental dilemmas with regard to knowledge sharing by devising methods to: (1) motivate members to participate and openly share valuable knowledge (while preventing undesirable spillovers to competitors); (2) prevent free riders (i.e., individuals who learn from others without helping others learn); and (3) reduce the costs associated with finding and accessing different types of valuable knowledge.

Another example of improved efficiency through KM comes from British Petroleum (BP) [Echikson, 2001]. A BP exploration geologist located off the coast of

◆◇ ◆◇ ◆◇ ◆◇   VIGNETTE 4-2   ◆◇ ◆◇ ◆◇ ◆◇

### Knowledge Management at Tearfund[2]

Tearfund, a large relief and development agency based in the United Kingdom, regularly responds to natural and humanitarian disasters, such as floods, hurricanes, typhoons, famine, and displacement. The KM efforts of this agency have been founded on the recognition that learning from successes and failures during responses to disasters, both natural and man-made, should improve responses to later ones. Tearfund has proved this by identifying, consolidating, and then utilizing lessons learned in response to floods in Bangladesh, the Orissa Cyclone in India, the Balkan crisis, and other disasters. This agency's KM efforts are composed of two main components. The first component is utilizing the learning opportunities that arise during and after any major activity, by involving key participants in the activity to perform after-action reviews that describe lessons learned from the activity. In each project, the key project members participate in a structured, facilitated process to identify the key lessons learned, and retrieve them again when they are next required. Second, Tearfund creates communities of practice to connect people with similar roles, issues, challenges, and knowledge needs. This enables Tearfund's employees to share their knowledge with its 350 U.K. and overseas partner organizations. Both these steps rely on cultural change and use of technology.

Through these KM efforts, Tearfund has been consciously learning different disaster responses, in each case identifying specific and actionable recommendations for future application. The explicit and conscious sharing of these recommendations provides Tearfund with the confidence and shared understanding needed to implement some of the lessons its many individuals had learned. The outcome has been a more proactive and integrated response to disasters that provides help to the beneficiaries more effectively. For example, Tearfund has modified its processes so that someone would be in the field no later than 48 hours after a disaster. It has also identified 300 specific and actionable recommendations. In this context, success depends on not simply identifying the lessons, but actually implementing them on the next occasion. It should to be a part of someone's job to ensure that learning occurs and lessons are embedded in the processes we follow in subsequent disaster responses [Wilson, 2002].

---

[2]Visit www.tearfund.org for more information on this organization.

◇ ◇ ◇ ◇

Norway discovered a more efficient way of locating oil on the Atlantic seabed in 1999. This improved method involved a change in the position of the drill heads to better aim the equipment and thereby decrease the number of misses. The employee posted a description of the new process on BP's intranet for everyone's benefit in the company. Within 24 hours, another engineer working on a BP well near Trinidad found the posting and e-mailed the Norwegian employee, requesting necessary additional details. After a quick exchange of e-mail messages, the Caribbean team successfully saved 5 days of drilling, and $600,000.[3] This case study points to a real instance where knowledge sharing and taking advantage of information technology to quickly disseminate it, resulted in a major cost savings to a company. Overall, the use of KM and Internet technologies enabled BP to save $300 million during the year 2001, while also enhancing innovation at every step of its value chain.

### IMPACT ON PROCESS INNOVATION

Organizations can increasingly rely on knowledge shared across individuals to produce innovative solutions to problems as well as to develop more innovative organizational processes. KM has been found to enable riskier brainstorming [Storck and Hill, 2000], and thereby enhance process innovation.[4] J.P. Morgan Chase recognizes the impact knowledge can have on process innovation when the following statement appeared in bold in their debut annual report [Stewart, 2001]: "The power of intellectual capital is the ability to breed ideas that ignite value."

Buckman Laboratories, discussed earlier in this section, linked its R&D personnel and technical specialists to its field-based marketing, sales, and technical support staffs to ensure that new products were developed with the customers' needs in mind and that customers' needs were quickly and accurately communicated to the product development group [Zack, 1999]. As a result, new knowledge and insights were effectively exploited in the marketplace, leading to better products. In addition, the regular interactions with customers generated knowledge to guide future developments.

Another example of the impact of KM on process innovation (and efficiency) may be seen in the case of the Office of Special Projects, Veteran's Health Administration (VHA), which we discuss in Chapter 3. VHA significantly enhanced innovation by reducing bureaucracy, breaking down organizational barriers, benchmarking and partnering with others, and institutionalizing best processes.

Figure 4-4 summarizes the above impacts of KM and knowledge on organizational processes.

##  Impact on Products

KM also impacts the organization's products. These impacts can be seen in two respects: **value-added products** and **knowledge-based products.** Whereas the impacts on these dimensions come either through knowledge or directly from KM, the impacts that follow arise primarily from knowledge created through KM. This is depicted in Figure 4-5.

### IMPACT ON VALUE-ADDED PRODUCTS

KM processes can help organizations offer new products or improved products that provide a significant additional value as compared with earlier products. One such

---

[3]Of course, in utilizing this knowledge, the employees of the Caribbean unit needed to either trust their Norwegian colleagues, or be able to somehow assess the reliability of that knowledge. Issues of trust, knowledge ownership, and knowledge hoarding, are important, and need to be examined in future empirical research.

[4]In this context, Nonaka's [1998] concept of "ba"—which is equivalent to "place" in English, and refers to a shared space (physical, virtual, or mental) for emerging relationships—is relevant. Unlike information, knowledge cannot be separated from the context. In other words, knowledge is embedded in ba, and therefore a foundation in ba is required to support the process of knowledge creation.

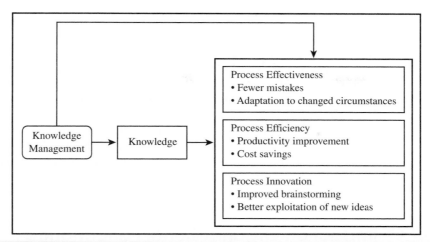

**◆◆ ◆◆ ◆◆  FIGURE 4-4** How Knowledge Management Impacts Organizational Processes

example is Ford's best practices replication process in manufacturing. Every year Ford headquarters provides a task to managers, requiring them to come up with a 5%, 6%, or 7% improvement in key measures, for example, improvements in throughput or energy use. On receiving their task, the managers turn to the best practices database to seek knowledge about prior successful efforts. Ford claims that its best practice replication system, whose use Ford tracks in meticulous detail, saved the company $245 million from 1996 to 1997 [Anthes, 1998]. Over a 4-1/2 year period from 1996 to 2000, more than 2,800 proven superior practices were shared across Ford's manufacturing operations. The documented value of the shared knowledge in 2000 was $850 million, with another $400 million of value anticipated from work in progress, for a total of $1.25 billion [Stewart, 2000].

Value-added products also benefit from KM due to the effect the latter has on organizational process innovation. For example, innovative processes resulting from KM at Buckman Laboratories enables sales and support staff to feed customer problems into their computer network, to access relevant expertise throughout the company, and to develop innovative solutions for the customers. Similarly, Steelcase uses information obtained through video ethnography from its customers, the end users of office furniture, to understand how its products are used, and then to redesign the products to make them more attractive to customers [Skyrme, 2000].

## IMPACT ON KNOWLEDGE-BASED PRODUCTS

KM can also have a major impact on products that are inherently knowledge based (e.g., in consulting and software development industries). For example, consultants at

**◆◆ ◆◆ ◆◆  FIGURE 4-5** How Knowledge Management Impacts Products

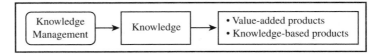

ICL[5] can quickly access and combine the best available knowledge and bid on proposals that would otherwise be too costly or too time-consuming to put together. Indeed, in such industries, knowledge management is *necessary* for mere survival.

Knowledge-based products can also sometimes play an important role in traditional manufacturing firms. A classic example is Matsushita's development of an automatic bread-making machine. To design the machine, Matsushita sought a master baker, observed the master baker's techniques, and then incorporated them into the machine's functionality [Nonaka and Takeuchi, 1995]. Similarly, companies such as Sun have enhanced the level of customer service by placing solutions to customer problems in a shareable knowledge base. Moreover, customers can download software patches from the Internet based on their answers to an automated system that prompts customers with a series of questions aimed at diagnosing the customer needs.

## ❖ ❖ ❖ Impact on Organizational Performance

In addition to potentially impacting people, products, and processes, KM may also affect the overall performance of the organization. The Deutsche Bank put it all in a nutshell when it took out a big advertisement in the *Wall Street Journal* [Stewart, 2001] that said, "Ideas are capital. The rest is just money." This advertisement reflects the belief that investments in KM should be viewed as capital investments. This investment may be capable of producing long-term benefits to the entire organization, instead of assets providing value only at the present time.

KM can impact overall organizational performance either directly or indirectly, as discussed next.

### DIRECT IMPACTS ON ORGANIZATIONAL PERFORMANCE

Direct impact of KM on organizational performance occurs when knowledge is used to create innovative products that generate revenue and profit, or when the KM strategy is aligned with business strategy (this aspect is discussed in greater detail in Chapter 5). Such a direct impact concerns revenues or costs, and can be explicitly linked to the organization's vision or strategy. Consequently, measuring direct impact is relatively straightforward. It can be observed in terms of improvements in *return on investment (ROI)*. For example, one male account director at British Telecom indicated that his sales team generated about U.S.$1.5 million in new business based on briefings from a new KM system [Compton, 2001]. Similarly, speaking to the Knowledge Management World Summit in San Francisco, California, on January 11, 1999, Kenneth T. Derr, the chairman and CEO of Chevron Corporation stated:

> Of all the initiatives we've undertaken at Chevron during the 1990s, few
> have been as important or as rewarding as our efforts to build a learning

---

[5]ICL, which was formed in 1968 and once projected as Britain's answer to IBM, was bought by STC in 1984. Fujitsu bought an 80% stake in ICL-UK from STC in 1990. In 2002, ICL-UK was split into two companies: its consulting arm was merged with U.S.-based DMR Consulting to become Fujitsu Consulting, and its service division became Fujitsu Services.

organization by sharing and managing knowledge throughout our company. In fact, I believe this priority was one of the keys to reducing our operating costs by more than $2 billion per year—from about $9.4 billion to $7.4 billion—over the last seven years.

The experience of another large company—Shell—in computing the ROI for its expenditure in KM communities of practice is described in Vignette 4-3 below.

## INDIRECT IMPACTS ON ORGANIZATIONAL PERFORMANCE

Indirect impact of KM on organizational performance results from activities that are not directly linked to the organization's vision, strategy, revenues, or costs. Such effects occur, for example, through the use of KM to demonstrate intellectual leadership within the industry, which, in turn, might enhance customer loyalty. Alternatively, it could occur through the use of knowledge to gain an advantageous negotiating position with respect to competitors or partner organizations. Unlike direct impact, however, indirect impact cannot be associated with transactions and, therefore, cannot be easily measured.

 VIGNETTE 4-3

### Evaluating Returns on Knowledge Management at Shell

Oil exploration often involves extrapolating from sketchy data and comparing exploration sites to known ones. This allows geoscientists to decide whether enough reserves exist on a site to make developing it worthwhile. For example, one site contained layers of oil-bearing sand that were less than an inch thick. A Shell exploration team needed to decide whether thin sand beds could extend over a large enough area for the oil in them to be efficiently pumped out. This would normally require drilling and testing a number of exploratory wells. The team asked one of Shell's communities of practice, including geoscientists from several disciplines, for help. By comparing this site to others, the community helped in the team's analysis of where to drill more accurately, resulting in fewer exploratory wells.

Community members estimated that the discussions of such comparisons enabled them to drill and test three fewer wells a year, saving U.S.$20 million in drilling and an additional U.S.$20 million in testing costs for each well (i.e., an annual saving of U.S.$120 million). It is possible that they might have reached the same conclusions on where to drill, but the leader estimated that the community could claim 25% of the savings and was 80% sure of this estimate. Thus, it may be argued that the community saved 25% of 80% of U.S.$120 million (i.e., U.S.$24 million annually). Because it cost between U.S.$300,000 and $400,000 annually to run the community, this represented an annual return of 40 times the investment. This was not the only benefit, but it was sufficient to address the senior executives' need to know whether the community was worth the investment. For further details on this case study, please refer to Wilson (2002).

One example of indirect benefits is the use of KM to achieve economies of scale and scope. Before examining these effects, we briefly examine what we mean by economies of scale and scope.

A company's output is said to exhibit **economy of scale** if the average cost of production per unit decreases with increase in output. Due to economy of scale, a smaller firm has higher costs than those of larger firms, which makes it difficult to compete with the larger firms in terms of price. Some of the reasons that result in economies of scale include large setup cost makes low-scale production uneconomic, possibilities for specialization increase as production increases, and greater discounts from suppliers are likely when production is large scale.

A company's output is said to exhibit **economy of scope** when the total cost of that same company producing two or more different products is less than the sum of the costs that would be incurred if each product had been produced separately by a different company. Due to economy of scope, a firm producing multiple products has lower costs than those of its competitors focusing on fewer products. Some of the reasons that result in economies of scope include joint use of production facilities and joint marketing or administration. Economy of scope can also arise if the production of one good provides the other as a byproduct.

KM can contribute to economies of scale and scope by improving the organization's ability to create and leverage knowledge related to products, customers, and managerial resources across businesses. Product designs, components, manufacturing processes, and expertise can be shared across businesses, thereby reducing development and manufacturing costs, accelerating new product development, and supporting quick response to new market opportunities. Similarly, shared knowledge of customer preferences, needs, and buying behaviors can enable cross-selling of existing products or development of new products. Finally, economies of scope also result from the deployment of general marketing skills and sales forces across businesses. Although economies of scale and scope could, and usually do, lead to improvements in ROIs, the effect of KM on scale and scope economies and their subsequent effect on return on investments cannot be directly linked to specific transactions; this is, therefore, considered as an indirect impact.

Another indirect impact of KM is to provide a **sustainable competitive advantage.** Knowledge can enable the organization to develop and exploit other tangible and intangible resources better than the competitors can, even though the resources might not be unique. Knowledge, especially context-specific tacit knowledge, tends to be unique and therefore difficult to imitate. Moreover, unlike most traditional resources, this knowledge cannot easily be purchased in a ready-to-use form. To obtain similar knowledge, the company's competitors have to engage in similar experiences, but obtaining knowledge through experience takes time. Therefore, competitors are limited in the extent to which they can accelerate their learning through greater investment.

LeaseCo, an industrial garment and small equipment leasing company described by Zack [1999], illustrates the use of KM to gain a sustainable competitive advantage. LeaseCo's strategy involved occasionally bidding aggressively on complex, novel, or unpredictable lease opportunities. These bidding, and subsequent negotiation, experiences provided the company with unique and leverageable knowledge, while reducing the opportunity for competitors to gain that same knowledge. LeaseCo realized two significant benefits over its competitors, first by investing in its strategic knowledge platform and second by learning enough about the particular client to competitively and profitably

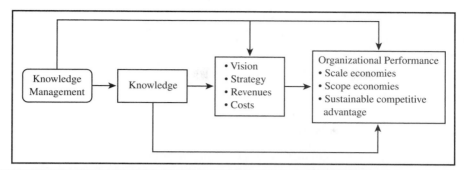

❖ ❖ ❖ **FIGURE 4-6** How Knowledge Management Impacts Organizational Performance

price leases for future opportunities with the same client. Often, sufficient mutual learning occurred between LeaseCo and the client that the client contracted the company for future leases without even going out for competitive bids. In essence, LeaseCo created a sustainable (or renewable) knowledge-based barrier to competition.

Thus, sustainable competitive advantage may be generated through KM by allowing the organization to know more than its competitors about certain things; competitors, on the other hand, would need considerable time to acquire that same knowledge.

Figure 4-6 summarizes the direct and indirect impacts KM and knowledge can potentially have on organizational performance.

## SUMMARY ❖ ❖ ❖

Table 4-1 summarizes the various impacts of KM we examine in this chapter. It needs to be reiterated that the impact KM has on one level might lead to synergistic impacts on another level as well. For example, employee learning facilitates impacts on processes and on products. Thus, KM has the potential to produce several interrelated impacts on people, products, processes, and organizations, as we describe in this chapter.

**TABLE 4-1** A Summary of Organizational Impacts of Knowledge Management

| Levels of Impact | Impacted Aspects |
|---|---|
| People | Employee learning |
| | Employee adaptability |
| | Employee job satisfaction |
| Processes | Process effectiveness |
| | Process efficiency |
| | Process innovativeness |
| Products | Value-added products |
| | Knowledge-based products |
| Organizational performance | *Direct Impacts* |
| | Return on investment |
| | |
| | *Indirect Impacts* |
| | Economies of scale and scope |
| | Sustainable competitive advantage |

❖ ❖ ❖ ❖

## KEY TERMS ❖ ❖ ❖

- community of practice—p. 53
- economy of scale—p. 62
- economy of scope—p. 62
- effectiveness—p. 55
- efficiency—p. 55

- externalization—p. 52
- innovation—p.55
- internalization—p. 52
- knowledge-based products—p. 58

- socialization—p. 53
- sustainable competitive advantage—p. 62
- value-added products—p. 58

## REVIEW QUESTIONS ❖ ❖ ❖

1. Briefly enumerate the ways in which knowledge management (KM) can impact an organization.
2. Describe the impact of internalization, externalization, socialization, and communities of practice on employee learning.
3. State the importance of KM with specific reference to its impact on employee adaptability and job satisfaction.
4. Explain why poor KM reduces the effectiveness of organizational processes.
5. What three dimensions are relevant for examining the impact of KM on business processes?
6. State reasons how KM helps improve process effectiveness, efficiency, and innovation.
7. Describe how KM can contribute to an organization's products.
8. How can we assess the direct impact of KM on organizational performance?
9. Describe the ways in which the indirect impacts of KM in an organization may be observed.
10. KM is an invaluable tool to the oil Industry. Justify this statement with suitable examples.

## APPLICATION EXERCISES ❖ ❖ ❖

1. Identify the possible ways in which knowledge management (KM) (or the lack of) in your organization (it could be your academic institution or your workplace) affects your learning and job satisfaction.
2. Identify two organizations within the same industry that have well-established KM systems. Based on these companies, compare and contrast the impact of KM in terms of impact on employees.
3. Identify the biggest positive impact on your organization (it could be your academic institution or your workplace) due to the implementation of KM. Speculate on the possibilities if there were no KM practices in place.
4. Now identify the biggest negative impact on your organization (it could be your academic institution or your workplace) due to improper or insufficient KM practices and suggest ways of improvement.
5. Interview a friend or a family member who works at a different organization than you and examine the overall effects of KM on that organization.
6. BP-Amoco (www.bpamoco.com) introduced *Connect* as its KM system. Over 12,000 staffs use *Connect* for sharing and disseminating their knowledge and expertise. Find information on *Connect* at BP-Amoco and compare the KM of BP-Amoco with that of Shell, which is discussed in the previous chapter of this book.
7. Dow Chemical (www.dow.com) introduced the Intellectual Asset Management Model (IAM) for managing its intellectual assets. It involves six phases: strategy; competitive assessment; classification; valuation; investment; and portfolio of its managing intellectual assets. Compared with Ford's best practice replication process system, what are the similarity and difference of IAM in terms of impact on employee, business process, and organizational performance?

8. SUN (www.sun.com) offered SunTAN as a KM system that consolidated sales training information, sales support resources, product updates and materials, competitive intelligence, and an array of other content on the Sun intranet. Gather information on SunTAN and describe its strength and potential weaknesses in terms of sustainable competitive strategy.

9. You are a CEO who considers implementing a KM system to your company. You have to decide on one option out of two: (a) our KM system can be accessed by customers, (b) our KM system cannot be accessed by customers. Describe your decision and provide the reason in terms of organizational performance.

10. Critique the following analysis: Our investment on KM seems to be unsuccessful. The return on investment (ROI) decreased from 10% to 5% at the year of system implementation. Because direct measure of organizational performance decreased, we need to uninstall the KM system right away.

## REFERENCES ◆ ◆ ◆

Anthes, G. 1998. Defending knowledge. *Computerworld,* 32(7), February 16, 41–42.

Bontis, N. 2003. HR's role in knowledge management. *Canadian HR Reporter,* March 10, 16(5), G8.

Brown, J.S., and Duguid, P. 1991. Organizational learning and communities-of-practice: Toward a unified view of working, learning, and innovation. *Organization Science,* 2(1), 40–57.

Business Wire. 2002. Xerox ranked as one of North America's most admired knowledge enterprises: Winning practices available to customers through Xerox Global Services. *Business Wire,* May 6, http://home.businesswire.com/portal/site/home/index.jsp.

Business Wire. 2000. 2000 Most admired knowledge enterprises announced. *Business Wire,* June 5, http://home.businesswire.com/portal/site/home/index.jsp.

Compton, J. 2001. Dial K for knowledge. *CIO,* June 15, 136–138.

Dyer, G., and McDonough, B. 2001. The state of KM. *Knowledge Management,* May, 21–36.

Dyer, J.H., and Nobeoka, K. 2000. Creating and managing a high-performance knowledge-sharing network: The Toyota case. *Strategic Management Journal,* 23(3), 345–367.

Echikson, W. 2001. When oil gets connected. *Business Week,* December 3, EB28–EB30.

Moore, C. 2001. Xerox makes global services push. *InfoWorld Daily News,* November 19, InfoWorld.com.

Nonaka, I. 1998. The concept of "ba": Building a foundation for knowledge creation. *California Management Review,* Spring, 40(3), 40–54.

Nonaka, I., and Takeuchi, H. 1995. *The Knowledge Creating Company: How Japanese Companies Create the Dynamics of Innovation.* Oxford University Press, New York.

Skyrme, D.J. 2000. Developing a knowledge strategy: From management to leadership. In Morey, D., Maybury, M., and Thuraisingham, B. (Eds.), *Knowledge Management: Classic and Contemporary Works.* MIT Press, Cambridge, MA, pp. 61–84.

Stewart, T.A. 2000. Knowledge worth $1.25 billion. *Fortune,* November 27, 302–303.

Stewart, T.A. 2001. Intellectual capital: Ten years later, how far we've come. *Fortune,* May 28, 192–193.

Storck, J., and Hill, P. 2000. Knowledge diffusion through "strategic communities." *Sloan Management Review,* 41(2), 63–74.

Wilson, J. (Ed.). 2002. *Knowledge Management Review: The Practitioner's Guide to Knowledge Management.* Melcrum Publishing, Chicago, IL.

Zack, M.H. 1999. Developing a knowledge strategy. *California Management Review,* Spring, 41(3), 125–145.

# CHAPTER 5

# Factors Influencing Knowledge Management

## ❖ ❖ ❖ Introduction

In the previous chapter we examine the impacts of knowledge management (KM) on companies and other private or public organizations. These impacts result either directly from KM solutions, or indirectly through knowledge created by these KM solutions. These solutions, as we discuss in Chapter 3, include KM infrastructure, mechanisms, technologies, and processes. In this chapter, we argue that various KM solutions may have different impacts on performance, depending on the circumstances, and examine the key factors affecting the suitability of KM solutions. This perspective, which is called *contingency perspective,* we discuss next, and then outline the overall approach. In the subsequent sections we examine the effects of several important factors.

## ❖ ❖ ❖ Contingency View of Knowledge Management

A **universalistic view of KM** would imply that there is a single best approach of managing knowledge, which should be adopted by all organizations in all circumstances. This seems to be implicit in the literature on KM; for example, knowledge sharing is recommended as useful to all organizations, although we believe that direction may sometimes represent an equally effective but more efficient alternative. In contrast to this universalistic view, a **contingency view,** which has previously been used, for example, in the literature on organization design, suggests that no one approach is best under all circumstances. Whereas a universalistic view focuses on identifying a single path to successful performance, a contingency perspective considers the path to success to include multiple alternative paths, with success achieved only when the appropriate path is selected. For instance, an organization design with few rules or procedures is considered appropriate for small organizations whereas one with extensive rules and procedures is recommended for large organizations.

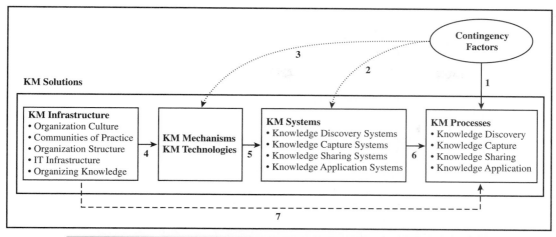

◈ ◈ ◈  **FIGURE 5-1** Contingency Factors and KM Solutions

A similar contingency view of KM is presented in this chapter. When asked what kind of a KM solution should an organization use, we often find ourselves responding, "It depends," instead of unequivocally recommending a specific solution. We need to understand the circumstances within and surrounding the organization to identify the most suitable KM solution. This indicates that a certain KM solution is contingent on the presence of certain circumstances, hence the name.

A contingency perspective for KM is supported by prior empirical research [Becerra-Fernandez and Sabherwal, 2001]. For example, based on a detailed study of Nortel networks, Massey et al. [2002, p. 284] conclude, "Thus, a key finding of our study is that successful KM initiatives like Nortel's cannot be disentangled from broader organizational factors and changes."

Figure 5-1 summarizes the way in which we examine the relationship between the contingency factors and KM solutions in this chapter. As we discuss in Chapter 3, KM solutions include KM infrastructure, KM mechanisms and technologies, KM systems, and KM processes. In much of this chapter, we focus on KM processes, with the choice of appropriate KM process depending on contingency factors, as shown by arrow 1 in Figure 5-1. Once the appropriate KM processes are recognized, the KM systems, mechanisms, and technologies needed to support them can be identified as well. Thus, the contingency factors indirectly affect KM systems, mechanisms, and technologies, as shown using arrows 2 and 3. Moreover, the KM infrastructure supports KM mechanisms and technologies (arrow 4), which in turn affect KM systems (arrow 5), and KM systems support KM processes (arrow 6). Thus, the KM infrastructure indirectly affects KM processes (arrow 7).

Several contingency factors influence the choice of KM processes. They include characteristics of the tasks performed, the knowledge managed, the organization, and the organization's environment. Figure 5-2 summarizes these categories of contingency factors affecting KM processes. In the next two sections we examine the effects of task characteristics and knowledge characteristics, respectively; and then describe the effects of organizational and environmental characteristics.

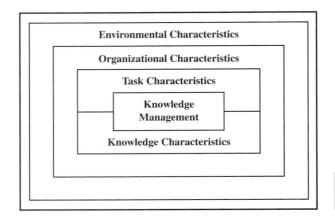

**FIGURE 5-2** Categories of Contingency Factors

In general, the contingency factors and KM infrastructure affect the suitability of KM processes in two ways: (1) by increasing or reducing the *need* to manage knowledge in a particular way; and (2) by increasing or reducing the organization's *ability* to manage knowledge in a particular way. For example, larger organizations have greater need to invest in knowledge sharing processes, whereas an organization culture characterized by trust increases the organization's ability to use knowledge sharing processes.

## ◈ ◈ ◈ Effects of Task Characteristics

The underlying argument in this section is that the KM processes that are appropriate for an organizational subunit (e.g., a department, a geographic location) depend on the nature of its tasks. This involves viewing each subunit at the aggregate level based on the predominant nature of its tasks. This approach has considerable support in prior literature. For example, Van de Ven and Delbecq [1974] offered a contingency view of the relationship between subunit tasks and organization structure. They suggest that the structure appropriate for a subunit depends on task difficulty, or on the problems in analyzing the work and stating performance procedures; and task variability, or on the variety of problems encountered in the tasks. Lawrence and Lorsch [1967] also focused on a task characteristic—task uncertainty—at the subunit level, and found subunits that perform certain, predictable tasks to be more effective when they were formally structured. Thus, a number of task characteristics have been studied at the level of organizational subunits. Here, two task characteristics—task uncertainty and task interdependence—are considered as influencing the appropriate KM processes [Spender, 1996].

Consistent with Lawrence and Lorsch [1967], greater **task uncertainty** is argued to reduce the organization's ability to develop **routines,** and hence knowledge application would depend on direction. Moreover, when task uncertainty is high, **externalization** and **internalization** would be more costly due to changing problems and tasks. Under such circumstances, knowledge is more likely to remain tacit, inhibiting the ability to use **combination** or **exchange.** Therefore, under high task uncertainty, **direction** or **socialization** would be recommended. For example, individuals responsible for product design when customer tastes are expected to change frequently would benefit most from socializing with, and receiving directions from, each other.

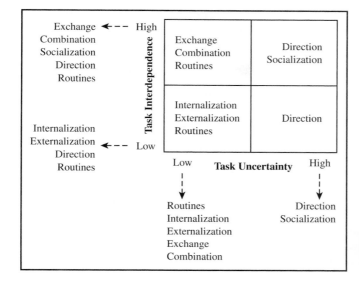

**FIGURE 5-3** Effects of Task Characteristics on KM Processes

On the other hand, when the tasks are low in uncertainty, routines can be developed for the knowledge supporting them. Moreover, the benefits from externalizing or internalizing knowledge related to any specific task would accumulate through the greater occurrence of that task. Finally, exchange and combination would be useful due to the externalization of potentially tacit knowledge. Therefore, under low task uncertainty, routines, exchange, combination, internalization, or externalization would be recommended. These conclusions are summarized in the bottom part of Figure 5-3. For example, for individuals performing tasks related to credit and accounts receivables, considerable benefits would be obtained from the use of routines (e.g., those for credit-checking procedures); exchange (e.g., sharing of standards and policies); combination (e.g., integration of explicit knowledge different credit analysts have generated from their experiences); and from externalization and internalization (e.g., to facilitate training and learning of existing policies by new credit analysts).

The second important task characteristic is **task interdependence,** which indicates the extent to which the subunit's achievement of its goals depends on the efforts of other subunits [Jarvenpaa and Staples, 2001]. Performing tasks that are independent of others primarily requires the knowledge directly available to the individuals within the subunit. These tasks rely mainly on distinctive units of knowledge, such as "functional knowledge embodied in a specific group of engineers, elemental technologies, information processing devices, databases, and patents" [Kusonaki et al., 1998]. They often require deep knowledge in a particular area. With internalization (such as when individuals acquire knowledge by observing or by talking to others), as well as with externalization (such as when they try to model their knowledge into analogies, metaphors, or problem-solving systems), the learning processes are personal and individualized. Through externalization, the individual makes the knowledge more agreeable and understandable to others in the group, whereas through internalization the individual absorbs knowledge held by others in the group [Maturana and Varela, 1987]. Internalization and externalization are thus fundamental to KM in an independent task domain. Performance of interdependent tasks relies mainly on dynamic interaction in which individual units of knowledge are combined and transformed through communication and coordination across different functional groups. This creates greater causal ambiguity, because knowledge is integrated across multiple groups that may not have a high level of shared understanding. Socialization and combination processes, both of which help integrate prior knowledge to create new knowledge, are therefore appropriate for interdependent tasks [Grant, 1996].

The left portion of Figure 5-3 shows that internalization and externalization should be preferred for independent tasks, whereas exchange, combination, and socialization should be preferred for interdependent tasks. Moreover, directions and routines can be used for independent as well as interdependent tasks; their suitability depends more on task uncertainty, as discussed earlier.

Combining the above arguments concerning the effects of task uncertainty and task interdependence, we obtain the four-cell matrix in Figure 5-3. As shown in the matrix, direction is recommended for uncertain independent tasks; direction and socialization are recommended for uncertain interdependent tasks; exchange, combination, and routines are recommended for certain interdependent tasks; and internalization, externalization, and routines are recommended for certain independent tasks.

## ◆◇ ◆◇ ◆◇ Effects of Knowledge Characteristics

Three knowledge characteristics—explicit vs. tacit, procedural vs. declarative, and general vs. specific—are examined in Chapter 2. The first two of these knowledge characteristics directly affect the suitability of KM processes. The underlying contingency argument is that certain KM processes may have greater impact on the value that one type of knowledge contributes to the organization, whereas some other KM processes might affect the value of another type of knowledge [Spender, 1996].

Figure 5-4 shows the KM processes that were presented earlier in Figure 3-2, and also depicts the effects of the two knowledge classifications. The difference between

◆◇ ◆◇ ◆◇ **FIGURE 5-4** Effects of Knowledge Characteristics on KM Processes

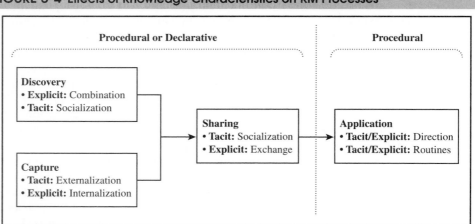

KM processes appropriate for **explicit and tacit knowledge** is based directly on the main difference between these knowledge types. For **knowledge discovery,** combination would be appropriate for integrating multiple streams of explicit knowledge for example, with knowledge discovery systems that are presented in Chapter 13, where socialization would be suitable for integrating multiple streams of tacit knowledge. For **knowledge capture,** externalization would be appropriate for tacit knowledge because it helps convert tacit knowledge into explicit, for example, in the knowledge capture systems that are presented in Chapter 14, whereas internalization would be appropriate for explicit knowledge because it helps convert tacit into explicit knowledge, for example, in learning. For **knowledge sharing,** exchange helps transfer explicit knowledge whereas socialization is needed for tacit knowledge. These intuitively obvious recommendations are also based on the logic that a KM process would contribute much to the value of knowledge if it is both effective and efficient for managing that knowledge [Gupta and Govindarajan, 2000]. Some KM processes might not contribute to the value of a given type of knowledge either because they are not effective in managing it (e.g., combination and exchange would not be effective for managing tacit knowledge), or because they are too expensive or too slow (i.e., an alternative process would be able to integrate it more quickly) or at a lower cost (e.g., socialization would be too expensive and slow for sharing explicit knowledge, especially in comparison to exchange).

No difference between the suitability direction and routines is expected between tacit and explicit knowledge. In other words, either direction or routines could be used to apply either tacit or explicit knowledge. However, these processes should be used mainly for **procedural knowledge,** or "know how," which focuses on the processes or means that should be used to perform the required tasks, such as how to perform the processes needed to achieve the specific product design. This is shown in the right portion of Figure 5-4. Procedural knowledge differs from **declarative knowledge,** substantive knowledge, or "know what," which focuses on beliefs about relationships among variables, as we discuss in Chapter 2. As shown in the left part of Figure 5-4, all the KM processes supporting knowledge discovery, capture, and sharing can be used for either declarative or procedural knowledge.

Thus, either direction or routines could be used to apply procedural knowledge, whether tacit or explicit. KM processes used to discover, capture, or share knowledge are the same for both procedural and declarative kinds of knowledge. However, these processes differ between tacit and explicit knowledge, as discussed above and shown in Figure 5-4 within the boxes for knowledge discovery, capture, and sharing.

## ◇ ◇ ◇ Effects of Organizational and Environmental Characteristics

Two organizational characteristics—size and strategy—and one environmental characteristic—uncertainty—affect the suitability of various KM processes. Table 5-1 summarizes the effects of organizational and environmental characteristics.

*Organization size* affects KM processes by influencing the choice between the two processes supporting knowledge application (direction, routines) and the two processes supporting knowledge sharing (socialization, exchange). For knowledge application, large and more bureaucratic organizations would benefit more from

**TABLE 5-1  Effect of Environmental and Organizational Characteristics on KM Processes**

| Characteristic | Level/Type | Recommended KM Processes |
|---|---|---|
| *Organization size* | Small | Knowledge sharing (socialization) |
| | | Knowledge application (direction) |
| | | Knowledge discovery (combination, socialization) |
| | | Knowledge capture (externalization, internalization) |
| | Large | Knowledge sharing (exchange) |
| | | Knowledge application (routines) |
| | | Knowledge discovery (combination) |
| | | Knowledge capture (externalization, internalization) |
| *Business strategy* | Low cost | Knowledge application (direction, routines) |
| | | Knowledge capture (externalization, internalization) |
| | | Knowledge sharing (socialization, exchange) |
| | Differentiation | Knowledge discovery (combination, socialization) |
| | | Knowledge capture (externalization, internalization) |
| | | Knowledge sharing (socialization, exchange) |
| *Environmental uncertainty* | Low | Knowledge sharing (socialization, exchange) |
| | | Knowledge capture (externalization, internalization) |
| | High | Knowledge discovery (combination, socialization) |
| | | Knowledge application (direction, routines) |

routines because of their greater use of standards. Small organizations, on the other hand, are usually not very bureaucratic. They would, therefore, benefit more from direction, which does not rely on standardization and rules. The circumstances needed for direction (e.g., the knowledge user's trust in the individual providing direction [Connor and Prahalad, 1996]) are also more likely to exist in smaller organizations. Knowledge sharing across greater distances would be needed in large organizations, whereas knowledge is more likely to be shared across shorter distances in smaller organizations. Therefore, knowledge sharing through exchange is recommended for large organizations whereas socialization is recommended for small organizations. Socialization for knowledge discovery is also recommended for small organizations, although combination could be used in either small or large organizations. Finally, small and large organizations do not differ in terms of the suitability of the alternative knowledge capture processes (externalization, internalization). For example, a small financial consulting firm with 25 employees would have only a few experts in any area (e.g., customer relations' practices). Consequently, others in the organization are likely to trust these experts and depend on their direction. Moreover, the small number of employees would have frequent opportunities to interact with each other, thereby enabling greater use of socialization for knowledge discovery as well as sharing. On the other hand, a large consulting firm, with over 5,000 employees would find it infeasible or overly expensive to rely on socialization, especially across large geographic distances. Instead, in such an organization, knowledge sharing would rely more on exchange of knowledge explicated in reports, lessons learned documents, and so on. Furthermore, this firm would find it beneficial to develop and use routines for applying knowledge. Routines would be more economical due to their greater frequency of use in such larger firms and also more needed by individuals seeking help.

The effect of *business strategy* may be examined using Porter's [1980, 1985] popular typology of low-cost and differentiation strategies. Organizations pursuing a low-cost strategy should focus on applying existing knowledge instead of creating new knowledge, whereas organizations following a differentiation strategy are more likely to innovate [Langerak et al., 1999], seek new opportunities [Miles and Snow, 1978], and frequently develop new products [Hambrick, 1983]. They would, therefore, benefit more from knowledge discovery and capture processes (combination and socialization). Organizations pursuing either low-cost or differentiation strategy would benefit from knowledge capture and sharing processes, because these processes can be used to capture or share knowledge on ways of reducing costs as well as innovating with products or services. For example, a supermarket chain competing through a low-cost strategy would seek to reuse prior knowledge about ordering, inventory management, supplier relations, and pricing. This company would, therefore, use organizational routines (if the company is large) or direction (if the company is small) to support the application of prior knowledge. In contrast, an exclusive fashion boutique, trying to differentiate itself from its competitors would seek new knowledge about attracting competitors' customers, and retaining its own customers, developing innovative products, and so on. This boutique would significantly benefit from socialization and combination processes for creating new knowledge about these aspects, using prior tacit and explicit knowledge, respectively.

The *environmental uncertainty* encountered by the organization also affects the suitability of various KM processes. When the organization faces low levels of uncertainty, knowledge sharing and knowledge capture processes would be recommended because the captured and shared knowledge would be relevant for longer periods of time. On the other hand, under higher uncertainty, **knowledge application and discovery** would be recommended. Knowledge application contributes in uncertain environment by enabling individuals to address problems based on solutions indicated by those possessing the knowledge, instead of the more time-consuming processes of sharing knowledge [Connor and Prahalad, 1996; Alavi and Leidner, 2001].

Knowledge discovery processes contribute by enhancing the organization's ability to develop innovative solutions to emergent problems [Davenport and Prusak, 1998]. For example, the environment would be rather certain and predictable for an automobile manufacturing firm that has a relatively stable product line and competes with a small number of competitors, especially when each firm has its own, clear market niche. For such an organization, knowledge about product design, manufacturing, marketing, sales, etc. would be generally stable, benefiting from the sharing of prior knowledge through socialization or exchange, and the capture of knowledge through internalization and externalization. Knowledge sharing, as well as internalization and externalization, would have long-term benefits because the knowledge remains inherently stable. On the other hand, an international mobile phone manufacturer having a dynamic product line and evolving customer base would face a highly uncertain environment. This organization would seek to create new knowledge and quickly apply existing knowledge by investing in combination and socialization for knowledge discovery, and routines and direction for knowledge application.

# ◇ ◇ ◇ Identification of Appropriate Knowledge Management Solutions

Based on the above discussion, we recommend a methodology for identifying appropriate KM solutions. The methodology includes the following seven steps:

1. Assess the contingency factors.
2. Identify the KM processes based on each contingency factor.
3. Prioritize the needed KM processes.
4. Identify the existing KM processes.
5. Identify the additional needed KM processes.
6. Assess the KM infrastructure.
7. Develop additional needed KM systems, mechanisms, and technologies.

These seven steps are discussed below.

Step 1: **Assess the contingency factors.** This step requires assessing the organization's environment in terms of the contingency factors—characterizing the tasks, the knowledge, the environment, and the organization—and how they contribute to uncertainty. The variety of tasks for which KM is needed should be characterized in terms of task interdependence and task uncertainty. Furthermore, the kind of knowledge those tasks require, should be classified as general or specific, declarative or procedural, and tacit or explicit. Environmental uncertainty may arise from changes in competition, government regulations and policies, economic conditions, and so on. Additionally, the organization's business strategy—low cost or differentiation—should be identified. Finally, the organization should be classified as small or large relative to its competitors. In some instances, it may be labeled as midsized, in which case the KM processes would be based on considerations of both small and large organizations.

Step 2: **Identify the KM processes based on each contingency factor.** Next, the appropriate KM processes based on each contingency factor should be identified. In doing this, Table 5-2, which summarizes the effects of various contingency factors, should be useful. Table 5-2 shows the seven contingency factors, and the effects they have on the KM processes. It is important to note, however, that Table 5-2 only provides some of the most important factors that need to be considered in making this choice. There are several other factors, such as the information intensity of the organization's industry, that would also affect the appropriateness of KM processes, but they have been excluded to simplify the presentation.

Step 3: **Prioritize the needed KM processes.** Once the KM processes appropriate for each contingency factor have been identified, they need to be considered together to identify the needed KM processes. In doing so, it is useful to assign a value of 1.0 to situations where a KM process is appropriate for a contingency variable, and 0.0 where it is not appropriate. Moreover, where a KM process is appropriate for all possible states of a contingency variable, a value of 0.5 could be assigned. As a result, a prioritization of the importance of various KM processes can be developed, and a cumulative priority score can be computed. For example, if KM process A has a composite score of 6.0 based on the seven contingency factors, whereas another one (B) has a

**TABLE 5-2  Appropriate Circumstances for Various KM Processes**

| KM Processes | Task Uncertainty | Task Interdependence | Contingency Factors | | | Organizational Size | Business Strategy* | Environmental Uncertainty |
|---|---|---|---|---|---|---|---|---|
| | | | Explicit (E) or Tacit (T) Knowledge | Procedural (P) or Declarative (D) Knowledge | | | | |
| Combination | Low | High | E | P/D | | Small/large | D | High |
| Socialization for knowledge discovery | High | High | T | P/D | | Small | D | High |
| Socialization for knowledge sharing | High | High | T | P/D | | Small | LC/D | Low |
| Exchange | Low | High | E | P/D | | Large | LC/D | Low |
| Externalization | Low | Low | T | P/D | | Small/large | LC/D | Low |
| Internalization | Low | Low | E | P/D | | Small/large | LC/D | Low |
| Direction | High | High/low | T/E | P | | Small | LC | High |
| Routines | Low | High/low | T/E | P | | Large | LC | High |

*Low cost—LC; differentiation—D

75

composite score of 3.0, greater attention is needed toward KM process A instead of B. This computation is shown in greater detail using an illustrative example in the next section.

**Step 4:** **Identify the existing KM processes.** Next, the KM processes that are currently in use should be identified. In doing so, a short survey of some of the employees, assessing the extent to which each KM process is used, may be helpful. Possible approaches for such assessments are discussed in detail in Chapter 6.

**Step 5:** **Identify the additional needed KM processes.** Based on the needed KM processes (identified in step 3) and the existing KM processes (identified in step 4), the additional needed KM processes can be identified. This comparison might also find some of the existing KM processes to not be very useful. In other words, if a KM process is identified as needed (step 3) but it is not currently in use (step 4), it should be added; whereas if a KM process is not identified as needed (step 3) but it is currently in use (step 4), it could potentially be dropped, at least based on KM considerations.

**Step 6:** **Assess the KM infrastructure and identify the sequential ordering of KM processes.** The KM infrastructure indirectly affects the KM processes as we discuss earlier. Specifically, organization culture, organization structure, and physical environment can facilitate or inhibit knowledge sharing and creation. Additionally, information technologies can support all KM processes, and organizing knowledge can help enhance the efficiency of knowledge sharing (e.g., through common language and vocabulary) and application processes (e.g., by enhancing recognition of individual knowledge domains). These aspects of the KM infrastructure should be considered with respect to the additional KM processes needed (as identified in step 5) to identify the KM processes for which supporting infrastructure currently exists. This step is especially important when deciding the sequence in which KM processes that are nearly equal in importance (as identified in step 3) should be developed.

**Step 7:** **Develop additional needed KM systems, mechanisms, and technologies.** Steps 1 through 6 have helped identify the KM processes, and the order in which they should be developed. Now the organization needs to undertake steps to initiate the creation of KM systems, mechanisms, and technologies that would support those KM processes. This might require creation of teams, acquisition of technologies, development of systems, and so on. In the long run, these systems, mechanisms, and technologies would also contribute to the KM infrastructure.

## ◇ ◇ ◇ Illustrative Example

As an illustration, which is kept somewhat simple to prevent this discussion from becoming overly complex, let us consider the fictional Doubtfire Computer Corporation, a manufacturer of low-end personal computers for home users. A small player in this industry, Doubtfire has recently undergone some difficult times due to new competition for its product line. Competitors make frequent changes in technology in an attempt to gain the upper hand in the marketplace with more state-of-the-art products. Having belatedly recognized this, Doubtfire recently hired a new president and a new sales manager to turn the situation around. The new president called a meeting of the staff to discuss possible strategies for the financial turnaround of the company. The main thrust of this presentation was that the staff needed to better manage knowledge so as to creatively identify areas where new technology can improve the company's products and operations. Based on inputs from the senior management, the president hired a KM consulting firm, KM-Consult Inc., to help improve its KM strategy.

A team of consultants from KM-Consult conducted an in-depth study of Doubtfire, using interviews with several employees and examination of company documents. Based on their investigation, the consultants concluded that Doubtfire is a small organization that has pursued a low-cost business strategy to operate in an uncertain environment. KM is needed for its tasks, which are highly interdependent and also highly uncertain due to changing environmental conditions. Doubtfire relies mainly on the tacit, procedural knowledge possessed by its employees instead of seeking the explication of that knowledge or management of declarative knowledge. Then, based on Table 5-2, the consulting team arrived at the following conclusions.

First, based on Doubtfire's *small organization size,* socialization (for knowledge sharing or knowledge discovery) and direction processes would be appropriate. In addition, combination, internalization, and externalization could be used regardless of organization size. However, exchange and routines would be inappropriate because Doubtfire is a small organization.

Moreover, considering Doubtfire's *low-cost business strategy,* direction and routines would be appropriate. In addition, socialization (for knowledge sharing), exchange, internalization, and externalization could be used regardless of strategy. However, combination and socialization (for knowledge discovery) would be inappropriate because they are unsuitable for a low-cost strategy.

The consulting team also concluded that, based on the *uncertain environment* in which Doubtfire operates, direction, combination, and socialization (for knowledge discovery) would be appropriate. However, the remaining processes would be inappropriate because they are more suitable for certain, predictable environments.

The *high task interdependence* in Doubtfire suggests that socialization (for knowledge sharing or knowledge discovery), combination, and exchange would be appropriate. In addition, direction and routines could be used regardless of task interdependence. However, externalization and internalization would not be as useful. The *high task uncertainty* suggests that socialization (for knowledge sharing or knowledge discovery) and direction would be appropriate. However, the remaining processes would be less suitable.

The *procedural* nature of knowledge indicates that direction and routines would be useful for managing this knowledge. The *tacit* nature of knowledge suggests that socialization (for knowledge sharing or knowledge discovery) and externalization would be appropriate. In addition, direction and routines could be used regardless of tacit or explicit nature of knowledge.

Table 5-3 shows the results of this analysis by KM-Consult. The cells in the columns for each contingency factor show the suitability of the KM process in that row for that contingency variable. More specifically, "yes" indicates that KM process in that row is appropriate for the contingency variable in that column, which converts to a score of 1.0; "no" indicates that KM process in that row is inappropriate for the contingency variable in that column, which converts to a score of 0.0; and "OK" indicates that KM process in that row can be used for all possible values of the contingency variable in that column, which converts to a score of 0.5.

**TABLE 5-3** Prioritizing KM Processes for Doubtfire Computer Corporation

| Contingency Factors KM Processes | Task Uncertainty = High | Task Interdependence = High | Tacit Knowledge | Procedural Knowledge | Organizational Size = Small | Business Strategy = Low Cost | Environmental Uncertainty = High | Number of Yes | Number of OK | Number of No | Cumulative* Priority Score |
|---|---|---|---|---|---|---|---|---|---|---|---|
| Combination | No | Yes | No | OK | OK | No | Yes | 2 | 2 | 3 | 3.0 |
| Socialization for knowledge discovery | Yes | Yes | Yes | OK | Yes | No | Yes | 5 | 1 | 1 | 5.5 |
| Socialization for knowledge sharing | Yes | Yes | Yes | OK | Yes | OK | No | 4 | 2 | 1 | 5.0 |
| Exchange | No | Yes | No | OK | No | OK | No | 1 | 2 | 4 | 2.0 |
| Externalization | No | No | Yes | OK | OK | OK | No | 1 | 3 | 3 | 2.5 |
| Internalization | No | No | No | OK | OK | OK | No | 0 | 3 | 4 | 1.5 |
| Direction | Yes | OK | OK | Yes | Yes | Yes | Yes | 5 | 2 | 0 | 6.0 |
| Routines | No | OK | OK | Yes | No | Yes | Yes | 3 | 2 | 2 | 4.0 |

*Yes = 1; OK = 0.5; No = 0

The last four columns of Table 5-3 show the computation of the cumulative priority score for each KM process, based on the number of "yes," "OK," and "no" for the suitability of that KM process for the seven contingency variables. Based on this analysis, direction has the highest cumulative priority score (6.0), followed by socialization for knowledge discovery (5.5) and socialization for knowledge sharing (5.0). Routines are at an intermediate level of priority, with a cumulative priority score of 4.0, whereas combination, externalization, exchange, and internalization have low cumulative priority scores (3.0 or less).

Thus, the consideration of the contingency variables led KM-Consult to conclude that Doubtfire should focus its KM efforts primarily on direction and socialization (for both knowledge discovery and knowledge sharing), with attention to be given to combination and routines if the resources so allow (KM-Consult recognized the financial difficulties Doubtfire was facing). Moreover, KM-Consult had found that the current KM at Doubtfire was making little use of both socialization and direction. Therefore, KM-Consult recommended that Doubtfire should try to enhance the use of direction and socialization for KM. In the report KM-Consult also identified the specific technologies and systems for Doubtfire to pursue, recommending establishment and use of communities of practice to support socialization and an expertise locator system to support direction. It also recommended that Doubtfire should enhance socialization through more frequent meetings, rituals, brainstorming retreats, etc. The consultants argued that this socialization would also enhance mutual trust among Doubtfire's employees, thereby increasing their willingness to provide and accept direction. Moreover, KM-Consult found Doubtfire to be currently making considerable use of internalization, spending considerable resources on employee training programs. In the light of the low cumulative score for internalization, KM-Consult advised Doubtfire to consider reducing the budget allocated toward employee training.

## SUMMARY ◆ ◆ ◆

Following our discussion of KM impacts in Chapter 4, we describe how an organization can seek to enhance these impacts by targeting its KM solutions according to the circumstances in which KM is used. In doing so, we examine the variety of KM processes, systems, mechanisms, as well as technologies discussed in Chapter 3, while focusing mainly on the KM processes. Table 5-2 summarizes the conclusions concerning the suitability of the KM processes under various circumstances. We also describe a methodology for effectively targeting the KM solutions, and illustrated using a detailed example. In the next chapter we examine how we can evaluate the contributions of KM solutions.

## KEY TERMS ◆ ◆ ◆

- combination—p. 68
- contingency view of knowledge management—p. 66
- declarative knowledge—p. 71
- direction—p. 68
- exchange—p. 68
- explicit knowledge—p. 71
- externalization—p. 68
- internalization—p. 68
- knowledge application—p. 73
- knowledge capture—p. 71
- knowledge discovery—p. 71
- knowledge sharing—p. 71
- procedural knowledge—p. 71
- routines—p. 68
- socialization—p. 68
- tacit knowledge—p. 71
- task interdependence—p. 69
- task uncertainty—p. 68
- universalistic view of KM—p. 66

## REVIEW QUESTIONS ◈ ◈ ◈

1. What is the contingency view of knowledge management (KM)? How does it differ from the universalistic view of KM?
2. What do you understand by task uncertainty and task interdependence?
3. What are the knowledge characteristics that affect the appropriateness of KM processes? Explain why.
4. How does organizational size affect KM processes?
5. In what way do organizational strategy and environmental uncertainty affect KM processes?
6. What steps would one take in identifying appropriate KM solutions? Briefly describe them.
7. Explain how a large organization operating in a highly uncertain environment can pursue a low-cost business strategy using KM? State the assumptions made to arrive at your answer.
8. In the seven steps of identifying appropriate KM solutions, "cumulative priority score" was computed. Describe the function of the score and its application.

## APPLICATION EXERCISES ◈ ◈ ◈

1. Visit local area companies to study their knowledge management (KM) practices. Determine how they decided on the type of KM solution they use.
2. Consider reasons why an organization would chose the universalistic view to KM over the contingency view.
3. Visit an organization with a high level of task uncertainty in its business. Explore the extent to which KM is helping or could help them.
4. Similarly, visit an organization with high levels of task interdependence between the subunits. Explore the ways in which they have implemented KM to the benefit of the organization.
5. Visit any three organizations. Classify the characteristics of their organizational knowledge under the headings, explicit or tacit, procedural or declarative, and general or specific. Based on the data you collect, determine how appropriate their KM processes are.
6. Collect information from the Internet, *Business Week, Fortune,* etc., on either General Motors or Microsoft about the nature of the organization. Based on this information and the contingency approach presented in this chapter, identify how knowledge should be managed at this company.
7. You are a KM consultant for BP-Amoco (www.bpamoco.com). BP-Amoco is one of the world's largest petroleum and petrochemicals groups. Its main activities are exploration and production of crude oil and natural gas; refining, marketing, supply, and transportation; and manufacturing and marketing of petrochemicals. Because of the current political instability (e.g., war in Iraq) in the Middle East, environmental uncertainty is said to be relatively high these days.
    a. Gather information on BP-Amoco and decide whether its task uncertainty and task interdependence are high or low. Provide the reasons of your decision.
    b. What types of knowledge does BP-Amoco use most and suggest as an appropriate KM process for the certain type of knowledge?
    c. Assess (i) organization size of BP-Amoco (small or large), (ii) business strategy (low cost or differentiation), and (iii) environmental uncertainty (high or low).
    d. Now, compute the cumulate priority score of each KM process discussed in this chapter. Based on this analysis, what is your recommendation of appropriate KM solutions to BP-Amoco?

## REFERENCES

Alavi, M., and Leidner, D. 2001. Knowledge management and knowledge management systems: Conceptual foundations and research issues. *MIS Quarterly,* 25(1), 107–136.

Becerra-Fernandez, I., and Sabherwal, R. 2001. Organizational knowledge management processes: A contingency perspective. *Journal of MIS,* 18(1), Summer, 23–55.

Conner, K.R., and Prahalad, C.K. 1996. A resource-based theory of the firm: Knowledge versus opportunism. *Organization Science,* 7(5), 477–501.

Davenport, T.H., and Prusak, L. 1998. *Working Knowledge: How Organizations Manage What They Know.* Harvard Business School Press, Watertown, MA.

Grant, R.M. 1996. Toward a knowledge-based theory of the firm. *Strategic Management Journal,* 17, Winter, 109–22.

Gupta, A.K., and Govindarajan, V. 2000. Knowledge management's social dimension: Lessons from Nucor steel. *Sloan Management Review,* Fall, 71–80.

Hambrick, D.C. 1983. Some tests of the effectiveness and functional attributes of Miles and Snow's strategic types. *Academy of Management Journal,* 26(1), 5–26.

Jarvenpaa, S.L., and Staples, D.S. 2001. Exploring perceptions of organizational ownership of information and expertise. *Journal of MIS,* 18(1), Summer, 151–184.

Kusonaki, K., Nonaka, I., and Nagata, A. 1998. Organizational capabilities in product development of Japanese firms: A conceptual framework and empirical findings. *Organization Science,* 9(6), 699–718.

Langerak, F., Nijssen, E., Frambach, R., and Gupta, A. 1999. Exploratory results on the importance of R&D knowledge domains in businesses with different strategies. *R&D Management,* 29(3), 209–217.

Lawrence, P.R., and Lorsch, J.W. 1967. *Organization and Environment: Managing Differentiation and Integration.* Harvard University Press, Boston.

Massey, A.P., Montoya-Weiss, M.M., and O'Driscoll, T.M. 2002. Knowledge management in pursuit of performance: Insights from Nortel Networks., *MIS Quarterly,* 26(3), September, 269–289.

Maturana, H., and Varela, F. 1987. *The Tree of Knowledge.* New Science Library, Boston.

Miles, R.E., and Snow, C.C. 1978. *Organizational Strategy, Structure, and Process.* McGraw-Hill, New York.

Nahapiet, J., and Ghoshal, S. 1998. Social capital, intellectual capital, and the organizational advantage. *Academy of Management Review,* 23(2), 242–266.

Nonaka, I. 1994. A dynamic theory of organizational knowledge creation. *Organization Science,* 5(1), 14–37.

Pisano, G.P. 1994. Knowledge, integration, and the locus of learning: An empirical analysis of process development. *Strategic Management Journal,* Winter, 85–100.

Porter, M.E. 1980. *Competitive Strategy.* Free Press, New York.

Porter, M.E. 1985. *Competitive Advantage.* Free Press, New York.

Spender, J.C. 1996. Making knowledge the basis of a dynamic theory of the firm. *Strategic Management Journal,* 17, Winter, 45–63.

Van de Ven, A., and Delbecq, A. 1974. The effectiveness of nominal, delphi, and interacting group decision-making processes. *Academy of Management Journal,* 17, 314–318.

CHAPTER 6

# Knowledge Management Assessment of an Organization

## ❖❖❖ Introduction

In Chapter 4, we examined the impacts knowledge management (KM) can have on companies and other organizations. We indicated that these impacts result either from KM solutions, or through the knowledge created from using them. Then, in Chapter 5, we presented a contingency perspective of KM, and examine the effects of several important factors. In this chapter we build further on Chapters 4 and 5, by examining the way in which KM can be assessed in an organization. We begin the chapter by discussing the reasons why a KM assessment is needed, and then describe alternative approaches to assessing KM, first for evaluating various aspects related to KM and then for overall evaluating KM.

## ❖❖❖ Importance of Knowledge Management Assessment

In any aspect of organizational or individual task performance, it is imperative to track whether the efforts are enabling the organization or the individual to achieve underlying objectives. Without such assessment, it would be impossible to determine either the contribution of those efforts or whether, and where, improvements are needed. More specifically, a **KM assessment** is aimed at evaluating the need for KM solutions, the knowledge these solutions can help discover, capture, share, or apply, and the impact they can have on individual or organizational performance. A KM assessment can help establish the baseline for implementing those KM solutions, including the existing infrastructure and technologies that can help support those efforts.

Overall, assessment of KM is a critical aspect of a KM implementation; what is not measured cannot be managed well. A 1997 survey by Ernst & Young [1997] indicated that measuring the value and contribution of knowledge assets ranks as the second most important challenge faced by companies, with changing people's behavior the most important. However, only 4% of the firms surveyed by Ernst & Young claimed to be good or excellent at "measuring the value of knowledge assets and/or impact of knowledge management."

Several reasons attest to the need for conducting a KM assessment, as described below.

1. A KM assessment helps identify the contributions currently made by KM. It helps answer the question: Is KM improving the individual's or the organization's ability to perform various tasks, and thereby enhancing efficiency, effectiveness, or innovativeness?

2. A KM assessment enhances the understanding of the quality of efforts put into KM, as well as the intellectual capital produced through these efforts. It helps answer the questions: are the KM solutions employed adequate for the needs of the individual or the organization? Do these efforts produce the intellectual capital required to perform individual or organizational tasks?

3. A KM assessment helps us understand whether the costs of the KM efforts are justified by the benefits they produce. It helps answer the question: Do the direct and indirect benefits from KM together exceed or equal the various costs incurred? This is an important benefit for the overall KM solutions as well as the solutions pursued in a specific KM project. Thus, the overall KM solutions as well as specific KM projects can be cost justified through careful KM assessment.

4. A KM assessment helps recognize the gaps that need to be addressed in the KM efforts by individuals or the organization. It helps answer the question: What kind of potentially valuable KM solutions does the individual or organization currently lack? What potentially important knowledge is not adequately supported by the KM efforts?

5. Finally, a KM assessment can also help in making a business case to senior executives in an organization for additional investments in KM efforts. Based on the benefits currently provided by the organization's KM solutions (point 1 above) and the gaps in the organization's KM efforts (point 4 above), a business case can be built for the development of solutions that address these gaps.

Thus, KM assessments are important because of several reasons, as described above. We next examine the different types of KM assessments, and then discuss the alternative KM assessment approaches in some detail.

## ❖ ❖ ❖ Types of KM Assessment

KM assessments can be classified in a number of different ways. Three possible ways of considering alternative KM assessments are described next. They are related to the following aspects: (1) when is KM assessed, (2) how is KM assessed, and (3) what aspects of KM are assessed?

 VIGNETTE 6-1

## An Illustrative Tool for Assessing KM

Please indicate your level of agreement with each of the following statements by selecting a number from 1 (strongly disagree) to 5 (strongly agree).

1. I am satisfied with the availability of knowledge for my tasks.

2. It is easy for me to locate information I need to perform my job.

3. I always know where to look for information.

4. The available knowledge improves my effectiveness in performing my tasks.

5. My supervisor encourages knowledge sharing within my subunit.

6. The members of my group consistently share their knowledge.

7. I am satisfied with the management of knowledge in my subunit.

8. The available knowledge improves my subunit's effectiveness.

9. The organization directly rewards employees for sharing their knowledge.

10. The organization publicly recognizes employees who share their knowledge.

## TIMING OF KNOWLEDGE MANAGEMENT ASSESSMENT

A KM assessment can be performed on different occasions. Three possibilities are especially noteworthy. First, a KM assessment may be performed *periodically for an entire organization or a subunit.* The objective of such an assessment is to evaluate the overall quality of KM solutions, intellectual capital, and their impacts. This could help identify any areas that need improvement in KM. Such an assessment can be performed, for example, by surveying employees and inquiring about their degree of agreement with statements such as in Vignette 6-1 above.

Responses to the above statements may be averaged across a number of employees from various subunits of the organization. Averages for each subunit and the entire organization would then show where the individual subunits, as well as the overall organization, perform in terms of the overall quality of KM. Each assessment would be in terms of a number ranging from 1 (poor KM) to 5 (excellent KM).

KM assessments may also be conducted at *the start of a KM project* to build a business case for it. The purpose of such an assessment is to identify the gap in current KM at the organization, and delineate the potential benefits of the proposed KM project. For example, for a firm focusing on new products and increasing market share, so that research and development (R&D) represents a major cost center, the business plan might include the following statement describing the value of the proposed KM project:

> The target for the KM project will be to cut cycle time on specific new projects by 20 percent. In addition, . . . The project will identify cost savings and time savings for scientists in the unit of 25 percent [Wilson, 2002, p. 17].

The above example illustrates the outcome of a KM assessment conducted at the start of the project. It indicates there are currently problems in KM within the R&D

function, which is a critical component of the organization; and addressing these problems through the proposed project would be highly beneficial.

A KM assessment may also be done *following the conclusion of a KM project.* Such assessment aims to determine the impacts of the KM project, and may focus on the entire organization or a specific sub-unit. It may be necessary to establish historical KM performance to evaluate the effects produced by the KM project. Following are some of the aspects that can be evaluated during such a postproject assessment:

- Perceptions of improved KM in the area focused on by the project.
- Perceptions of greater availability of knowledge in the area focused on by the project.
- Some evidence of financial return (e.g., cost savings, increased returns, return on investment [ROI]), either for KM function or for the entire organization.
- Increased awareness of the importance of KM.
- Increased recognition of the different areas of knowledge, and their importance to the organization.
- Greater knowledge sharing throughout the organization.
- Greater comfort level throughout the organization with the concepts of KM and knowledge.

For example, a KM project at one large consulting firm caused a major transformation of the organization [Davenport and Prusak, 1998 p. 152]. This transformation was significant in both breadth and depth of impact across the organization. The KM project required line managers to reengineer their business processes to draw heavily from the organization's centralized knowledge, accessing earlier client presentations, work plans, system specifications, and other important documents. Consequently, the consulting firm's "win rate" in client proposals increased as well. In Vignette 6-2, we describe a KM assessment that relies on measuring the effectiveness of one specific KM tool—communities of practice.

 **VIGNETTE 6-2**

### Assessment of KM Through Communities of Practice

1. What was the overall value of this community to you and your team?

2. When your community discussed topic A, what specific knowledge, information, or data did you use?

3. What was the value of this knowledge, information, or data for you as an individual? Can you express the value in numerical terms, such as time saved?

4. Can you estimate the value of this knowledge, information, or data to your business unit in cost savings, reduced cycle time, improved quality of decision making, or lower risk?

5. What percentage of this value was obtained directly from the community? What is the likelihood you would have learned it without the community?

6. How confident are you of the above estimate?

7. Who else in your team used this knowledge, information, or data? [Wilson, 2002]

## NATURE OF KNOWLEDGE MANAGEMENT

KM assessments are also differentiated on the basis of the way in which KM assessment is done. There are two distinct and important methods to perform KM assessments: qualitative and quantitative.

**Qualitative KM assessments** aim to develop a basic understanding of whether the KM efforts are working. These assessments involve such simple tasks as walking around the halls and buildings of the organization and informally chatting with the employees about how things are going for them. They also include more formal interviews, based on semistructured or structured interview guides, individually conducted with a carefully selected set of employees. Regardless of the formality of these conversations, they are inherently qualitative, surfacing anecdotes about how well the KM efforts seem to be working, as well as examples of situations where the KM efforts did not produce the desired results. Such anecdotes of successes (or problems) may concern the quality of decisions, innovations, and technology transfer at the organizational level. In addition, they may point out issues related to career development, visibility, confidence, and staying up-to-date technologically, at the individual level. Furthermore, such qualitative assessments can be performed at certain periodic intervals, at the start of a project, or at the conclusion of a project, as discussed before. Consequently, they may focus on the organization's overall strategy for KM, or on more specific aspects, such as the development of a KM system, as a community of practice, or an expertise-locator system.

**Quantitative assessments of KM,** on the other hand, produce specific numerical scores indicating how well an organization, an organizational subunit, or an individual is performing with respect to KM. Such quantitative assessments may be based on a survey, such as the one described in Vignette 6-1. Alternatively, such quantitative KM assessments may be in financial terms, such as the *return on investment (ROI)* or the cost savings from a KM project. Finally, quantitative measures also include such ratios or percentages as employee retention rate (i.e., the percentage of employees most essential to the organization retained during the preceding year) or training expenditures as a proportion of payroll (i.e., total expenditures on training as a percentage of the organization's annual payroll).

Quantitative measures are more difficult to develop during an organization's early experiences with KM. During initial stages, qualitative assessments should be preferred, with greater use of quantitative measures as the organization gains experience with KM. This is depicted in Figure 6-1. However, it is important to note that even when an organization is very experienced with KM, it can obtain considerable benefits from using qualitative measurements, especially in uncertain environments.

## DIFFERENCES IN THE ASPECTS OF KNOWLEDGE MANAGEMENT ASSESSED

The third way of viewing KM assessment, which is used to structure the rest of this chapter, focuses on the aspect under assessment. As we discuss in Chapter 4, KM can directly or indirectly impact organizational performance at several levels: people processes, products, and overall organizational performance. These impacts either come about directly from the KM solutions or from the knowledge produced and shared through the KM solutions. Therefore, in the next three sections, the KM assessment can focus on: (1) the KM solutions, (2) the knowledge produced or shared

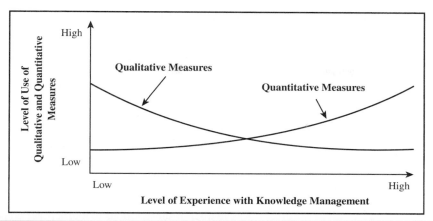

❖❖ ❖❖ ❖❖   **FIGURE 6-1** Qualitative and Quantitative Assessments of KM

through KM solutions, and (3) the impacts of KM solutions or knowledge on performance (including individuals or employees, processes, products, and the overall organizational performance), respectively.

## ❖❖ ❖❖ ❖❖ Assessment of Knowledge Management Solutions

Assessment of KM solutions involves evaluating the extent to which knowledge discovery, capture, sharing, and application processes that we discuss in Chapter 3 are utilized, and how well they are supported by KM technologies and systems. Table 6-1 provides some illustrative measures of the four aspects of KM solutions—discovery, capture, sharing, and application. Although most of the measures given in Table 6-1 are easy to quantify, some (e.g., extent of use of learning by doing) involve perceptions, at least to some extent. Moreover, further research is needed to establish these measures but some of them are based on prior empirical research.

Collison and Parcell [2001] describe another way of viewing KM solutions, especially for knowledge sharing in organizations that focuses on organizational subunits and the key activities they perform. Such organizational activities include increased morale and motivation; plan, schedule, and work execution; and management of spare parts and stores. Once these activities are identified for the organization, interviews with managers from each subunit are used to evaluate each subunit's target performance as well as actual performance for each activity. This process helps identify, for each combination of subunit and activity, the gap between actual and target performance. For each activity, actual as well as target performance for various subunits can then be placed along a matrix, as shown in Figure 6-2. Subunits that show a high level of actual performance and a high level of target performance, such as SU-1 in Figure 6-2, are the ones that both consider that activity as important and perform it well. These subunits should be emulated by subunits, such as SU-2, that consider that activity as important but perform it poorly, as shown by high level of target performance

| Dimension | Illustrative Measures |
|---|---|
| Knowledge discovery | Number of cooperative projects across subunits divided by the number of organizational subunits |
| | Extent of use of apprentices and mentors to transfer knowledge |
| | Employee rotation (i.e., number of employees who move to a different area each year) |
| | Annual number of brainstorming retreats or camps as a proportion of the total number of employees |
| | Number of patents published per employee |
| Capture | Average number of annual hits on each document in the document repository |
| | Number of subscriptions to journals per employee |
| | Attendance at group presentations as a proportion of invited attendees |
| | Number of annual presentations per employee |
| | Extent of use of learning by doing |
| Sharing | Proportion of information used that is available on Web pages (intranet and Internet) |
| | Proportion of organizational information that resides in databases |
| | Level of use of groupware and repositories of information, best practices, and lessons learned |
| | Size of discussion databases |
| | Annual number of shared documents published per employee |
| Application | Frequency of advice seeking per employee |
| | Corporate directory coverage (i.e., proportion of employees whose expertise areas are listed in the corporate directory) |
| | Annual number of improvement suggestions made per employee |
| | Level of use of decision support systems and expert systems |
| | Frequency of hits on KM Web sites |

**TABLE 6-1   Illustrative Measures of Key Aspects of KM Solutions**

◈ ◈ ◈ ◈

combined with a low level of actual performance. Therefore, the organization would benefit from knowledge sharing between these two kinds of subunits (SU-1 and SU-2), which both consider that activity as important (high level of target performance) but differ in actual performance. Subunits (such as SU-3) that consider the activity as less important (low level of target performance) may also benefit from knowledge sharing with subunits that consider that activity as important in case the focus of their operations changes.

Some specific tools for assessing KM solutions have also been proposed. One example is *Knowledge Advisors'* "Metrics that Matter"[1] [PR Newswire, 2001c], which provides a comprehensive solution to help training organizations to measure their learning investments. This approach has three components—learner based, manager

---

[1]More details about this approach may be found at www.knowledgeadvisors.com.

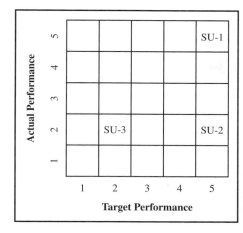

**FIGURE 6-2** Identifying
Knowledge Sharing
Opportunities

based, and analyst based. Each component helps measure learning across five levels of evaluation: (1) did they like it, (2) did they learn, (3) did they use it, (4) what were the results, and (5) what is the return on investment?

## ◇ ◇ ◇ Assessment of Knowledge

Assessment of knowledge requires: (1) the identification of the various areas of knowledge that are relevant to the organization or a specific subunit, followed by (2) an evaluation of the extent to which knowledge in each of these areas is available. The first of these steps—*identification of the relevant areas of knowledge*—may be performed using interviews with managers and other employees of that organization or subunit. In this step, it may be useful to first identify the "critical success factors" for the organization or the subunit. Critical success factors have been defined as "the limited number of areas in which results, if they are satisfactory, will ensure successful performance for the organization" [Rockart, 1979, p. 85]. Organizations should therefore give special attention to them, trying to perform exceedingly well in the few areas they represent instead of seeking to perform a larger number of tasks only reasonably well. By asking the senior executives to identify six to eight critical success factors, and then asking them to identify the knowledge needed to succeed with respect to each critical success factor, we can thus obtain the most important knowledge areas.

Once the relevant knowledge areas have been identified, *the extent and quality of available knowledge* in each area needs to be assessed. This is often a very tricky issue, for such knowledge can reside in individuals' minds, corporate databases and documents, organizational processes, and so on. To some extent, such measurement of available knowledge may be conducted through surveys or interviews of organizational employees, asking them to evaluate items such as the ones following, on a 5-point scale, ranging from 1 = strongly disagree to 5 = strongly agree. Statements 1 to 4 are coded such that a *high* score indicates excellent availability of this knowledge, whereas statements 5 and 6 are reverse coded, so that a *low* score on these items indicates excellent availability of this knowledge. Therefore, ratings on items 5 and 6 should be subtracted from 6 and the results can then be averaged with the ratings on items 1 to 4. The resulting average would range from 1 to 5, with 5 indicating excellent availability of this knowledge.

1. I can easily access knowledge in this area.
2. Everyone in the organization (or the subunit) recognizes the experts in this area of knowledge.
3. Available knowledge in this area is of a high quality.
4. Available knowledge in this area helps improve the organization's (or subunit's) performance.
5. I often have to perform my tasks without being able to access knowledge in this area.
6. The performance of this organization (or subunit) is often adversely affected due to the lack of knowledge in this area.

Another important aspect of KM assessment is the value each area of knowledge contributes to the organization. *Assessment of value of knowledge* is one way of attributing a **tangible measure** of benefits resulting from knowledge, which is often intangible [Sullivan, 2000]. In general, value has two monetary measures—cost and price. Price represents the amount a purchaser is willing to pay in exchange for the utility derived from that knowledge, whereas cost is the amount of money required to produce that knowledge. Both cost and price are direct, quantitative measures of value, but there are also other nonmonetary or indirect measures of value, such as the improvement in the quality of decisions enabled by this knowledge. Some of these benefits of knowledge are discussed in the next section. Moreover, **intangible measure** of value of knowledge is a key aspect of the **intangible assets** monitor approach, which focuses on the assessment of the value of intellectual capital and is discussed in a later section.

## ◇ ◇ ◇   Assessment of Impacts

As we discuss in Chapter 3, KM solutions and the knowledge they help to create, capture, share, and apply can impact individuals, products, processes, and overall performance of organizations. A KM assessment, therefore, involves not only the evaluation of KM solutions and knowledge (we discuss both in earlier sections) but also an evaluation of their impacts. In this section we describe how these impacts may be assessed.

### ASSESSMENT OF IMPACTS ON EMPLOYEES

KM can impact an organization's employees by facilitating their learning from each other, from prior experiences of former employees, and from external sources. KM can also enable employees to become more flexible, by enhancing their awareness of new ideas (which prepares them to respond to changes) and also by making them more likely to accept change. These impacts, in turn, can cause the employees to feel more satisfied with their jobs due to the knowledge acquisition and skill enhancement and their enhanced market value. Thus, KM can enhance learning, adaptability, and job satisfaction of employees. Some illustrative measures of impacts on each of these three dimensions are given in Table 6-2.

**TABLE 6-2    Illustrative Measures of Impacts on People**

| Dimension | Illustrative Measures |
|---|---|
| Employee learning | Average amount of time annually spent by an employee in training |
| | Average number of conferences or seminars annually attended by each employee |
| | Average amount of time annually spent by an employee in training others within the organization |
| | Average of employees' annual assessment of their learning during the year |
| Employee adaptability | Proportion of employees who have worked in another area (other than the area in which they currently work) for more than 1 year |
| | Average number of areas in which each employee has previously worked |
| | Number of countries in which each senior manager has worked as a proportion of the total number of countries in which the organization conducts business |
| Employee job satisfaction | Proportion of employees who express high level of satisfaction with the organization and their jobs |
| | Percentage of critical employees retained during the previous year |
| | Percentage of openings requiring advanced degrees or substantial experience filled in the previous year |

## ASSESSMENT OF IMPACTS ON PROCESSES

KM can improve organizational processes (e.g. marketing, manufacturing, accounting, engineering, and public relations). These improvements can occur along three major dimensions: effectiveness, efficiency, and degree of innovation of the processes, as we discuss in Chapter 4. For example, at Hewlett Packard, a KM system for computer resellers enhanced efficiency by considerably reducing the number of calls for human support and enabling the number of people needed to provide this support [Davenport and Prusak, 1998]. Table 6-3 lists some illustrative measures of the impacts KM and knowledge can have along each of these dimensions.

## ASSESSMENT OF IMPACT ON PRODUCTS

KM can also impact the organization's products, by helping to produce either value-added products or inherently *knowledge-based products*. Value-added products are new or improved products that provide a significant additional value as compared with earlier products. Inherently knowledge-based products refer, for example, to products from the consulting and software development industries. These impacts are discussed in Chapter 4. Table 6-4 provides some examples of possible measures of the impacts that KM can have on these two dimensions.

## ASSESSMENT OF IMPACTS ON ORGANIZATIONAL PERFORMANCE

KM can impact overall organizational performance either directly or indirectly. Direct impacts concern revenues or costs, and can be explicitly linked to the

| TABLE 6-3 Illustrative Measures of Impacts on Organizational Processes | |
|---|---|
| *Dimension* | *Illustrative Measures* |
| Efficiency | Reduced ratio of manufacturing costs to annual sales |
| | Shortening proposal times |
| | Quicker decisions |
| | Faster delivery to market |
| Effectiveness | Enhanced customer service |
| | Improved project management |
| | Fewer surprises due to external events |
| | Percentage of customers reporting complaints about products and services |
| Innovativeness | Percentage of all current products and services introduced in the previous year |
| | Greater number of patents per employee |
| | Organizational changes precede, instead of following competitors' moves |
| | Number of new ideas in KM databases |

◇ ◇ ◇ ◇

organization's vision or strategy. Consequently, direct impact can be observed in terms of increased sales, decreased costs, and higher profitability or ROI. For example, Texas Instruments generated revenues by licensing patents and intellectual property [Davenport and Prusak, 1998]. However, it is harder to attribute revenue increases to KM than cost savings [Davenport et al., 2001]. Indirect impacts on organizational performance come about through activities that are not linked to the organization's vision or strategy, and revenues; and cannot be associated with transactions. As we discuss in Chapter 4, indirect impacts include economies of scale and scope, and sustainable **competitive advantage.** Table 6-5 provides some examples of possible measures of these direct and indirect impacts KM can have on overall organizational performance.

The value of a KM investment should be evaluated based on how it affects discounted cash flow. Improved problem solving, enhanced creativity, better relationships with customers, and employees' more meaningful work, can eventually be

| TABLE 6-4 Illustrative Measures of Impacts on Organizational Products | |
|---|---|
| *Dimension* | *Illustrative Measures* |
| Value-added products | Increased rate of new product launch |
| | More frequent improvements in products |
| | Average of the ratio of profit margin to price across the range of products offered by the organizations |
| Knowledge-based products | Increased information content in products |
| | Greater product-related information provided to customers |
| | Proportion of customers accessing product-related knowledge that the organization places on the Internet |

◇ ◇ ◇ ◇

**TABLE 6-5    Illustrative Measures of Impacts on Organizational Performance**

| Types of Impacts | Illustrative Measures |
|---|---|
| Direct impacts | *Revenues.* Increase in total revenues per employee compared with those of the previous year |
| | *Costs.* Increase in total annual costs per employee compared with those of the previous year |
| | *ROI.* Increase in ROI compared with that of the previous year |
| Indirect impacts | *Economy of scale.* Average (across all products offered by the organization) change in total cost per unit sold as compared with that of the previous year |
| | *Economy of scope.* Average (across all products offered by the organization) change in the number of different products a salesperson can sell as compared with that of the previous year |
| | *Economy of scale.* Average (across all products offered by the organization) of the difference between the price of the organization's product and the mean price of competing products |
| | *Economy of scope.* Difference between the average number of different products produced in the organization's manufacturing plants and the average number of different products produced in the manufacturing plants of its main competitors |
| | *Competitive advantage.* Difference between return on investment for the organization and its key competitors |
| | *Competitive advantage.* Average number of years existing customers have been buying the organization's products and services |
| | *Competitive advantage.* Percentage of top customers ending sales contracts in the previous year |

◇ ◇ ◇ ◇

linked to real cash flows. Therefore, organizations can enhance their cash flow in the following ways:

- Reduce expenses by decreasing costs.
- Enhance margins by increasing efficiency to improve profit.
- Increase revenue through the sale of more products or services.
- Reduce taxes using smart strategies to minimize tax liabilities of the organization.
- Reduce capital requirements by lowering amount of capital needed by regulation.
- Reduce cost of capital by lowering the cost of loans, equity, and other financing. [Wilson, 2002]

It is important to keep the above drivers in mind during the implementation of KM projects. In other words, if KM initiatives are observed to help increase the company's cash flow, executives may listen and therefore find a viable way to fund them.

# ❖ ❖ ❖ Conclusions about Knowledge Management Assessment

We have examined, and provided illustrative measures for KM assessments. We also have discussed the direct and indirect impacts KM assessments can have on the overall organizational performance. In this section, we provide a broader discussion of KM assessment, including a discussion of who performs KM assessment, some overall approaches for KM assessment, the approach for the implementation of a KM assessment, and some caveats concerning KM assessments.

## WHO PERFORMS KNOWLEDGE MANAGEMENT ASSESSMENT?

To perform a KM assessment, it is helpful to form a team including internal and external members. The internal members provide the necessary context and help retain within the organization the knowledge acquired from the assessment, whereas the external members help identify KM-related assumptions and opportunities that may be missed by internal members. Overall, a KM assessment should incorporate: (1) peer review of internal performance; (2) external appraisal (by customers, suppliers, etc.) of the organization and its outputs; (3) business evaluation of effectiveness, efficiency, and innovativeness; and (4) evaluation of the knowledge assets created [Quinn et al., 1996].

The following example illustrates how these perspectives could be included and effectively integrated. Following each project, a major investment banking firm asks all team members, the team leader, and its customer group to rank all project participants in terms of their exhibited knowledge, specific contributions to the project, and support for the team. Customers also rate their overall satisfaction with the firm as well as with the specific project. Annual surveys, ranking the firm against competitors on 28 key dimensions, complement these evaluations. The firm also measures costs and profits for each project and allocates them among participating groups based on a simple, preestablished formula. Annually, for each division the firm computes the net differential between its market value (if sold) and its fixed asset base. This net intellectual value of the division is tracked over time as an aggregate measure of how well the division's management is building its intellectual assets.

## OVERALL APPROACHES FOR KNOWLEDGE MANAGEMENT ASSESSMENT

In the preceding sections we discuss a number of measures that can be used for KM assessment. Overall KM assessment approaches usually combine several of these measures, as illustrated above with the investment banking firm's example.

One such approach involves the use of **benchmarking,** or comparing KM at an organization or subunit with other organizations or subunits. Adopted as a systematic technique for evaluating a company's performance toward its strategic goals, benchmarking is based on the recognition that best practices are often the same within a company or even within an industry. Benchmark targets could therefore include other units within the same company, competing firms, the entire industry, or in some cases successful companies in other industries. For example, a leading manufacturer identifies outstanding operating units, formally studies them, and then replicates their practices throughout the rest of the company. This approach produced sales that exceed

 VIGNETTE 6-3

## The Most Admired Knowledge Enterprises Survey

The Annual Most Admired Knowledge Enterprises (MAKE) survey by Teleos, an independent KM research company, and the KNOW network (www.knowledgebusiness.com) is based on ranking of firms by a panel of chief knowledge officers and leading KM practitioners along eight specific criteria (PR Newswire, 2001a):

1. Success in establishing an enterprise knowledge culture.
2. Ability to develop and deliver knowledge-based products and services.

3. Top management support for KM.
4. Success in maximizing the value of the enterprise's intellectual capital.
5. Effectiveness in creating an environment of knowledge sharing.
6. Success in establishing a culture of continuous learning.
7. Effectiveness in managing customers' knowledge to increase their loyalty and the value to them.
8. Ability to manage knowledge to generate shareholder value.

goals by 5% [PR Newswire, 2001b]. Vignette 6-3 provides information on a cross-industry survey that may be used to benchmark in the arena of KM.

Another overall approach for KM assessment utilizes the **Balanced Scorecard Method,** which was originally developed by Kaplan and Norton [1996] to provide for a more "balanced view" of internal performance instead of KM assessment. The Balanced Scorecard provides a way of maintaining a balance between short-term and long-term objectives, financial and nonfinancial measures, lagging and leading indicators, and external and internal perspectives. It examines the goals, metrics, targets, and initiatives for the following four different perspectives [Tiwana, 2002]:

- *Customer perspective.*   How should our customers perceive us?
- *Financial perspective.*   What is the face that we want to present to our shareholders?
- *Internal business perspective.*   Are our internal operations efficient and effective, and performing at their best?
- *Learning and growth perspective.*   How can we sustain our competitive advantage over time?

In employing the Balanced Scorecard for KM assessment, the above four perspectives are used in a series of four steps, performed over time. The first step involves translating the KM vision (i.e., why we are managing knowledge, and what our vision is for KM). This vision then needs to be communicated within the organization, with rewards linked to knowledge use and contribution. The next step involves business planning, including the establishment of goals and the alignment of metrics and rewards to them. The fourth step—learning and feedback on whether KM is working and whether it can be improved—then feeds back to the first step to begin the cycle again. The above four complementary criteria from the Balanced Scorecard are used during each of these steps.

Like the Balanced Scorecard, the *Intangible Assets Monitor Framework* [Sveiby, 2000] also recognizes the importance of examining intangible knowledge assets instead of focusing only on financial or monetary assets. The Intangible Assets Monitor considers a firm's market value to depend on tangible net book value and intangible assets, which include external structure (relationships with customers and suppliers, brand names, trademarks, and image or reputation); *internal structure* (patents, concepts, models, and systems); and the competence of the organization's individual employees (skills, education, experience, values, and social skills). Based on these factors, WM-data, which is a large Swedish independent computer software and consulting company, has designed a set of nonmonetary indicators, which top management uses to follow up its operation on a weekly, monthly, and annual basis. The Intangible Assets Monitor Framework[2] evaluates growth, renewal, efficiency, and stability for tangible assets (financial value); external structure (customer value); internal structure (organizational value); and competence of people (competence value). For example, the following are some of the questions that may be used to evaluate growth: Is the existing customer base growing in value? Are the support staff and administrative management improving their competence? Are our tools and processes growing in value?

The *Skandia Method* is another approach to KM assessment that gives considerable attention to intangible assets. The Swedish insurance company Skandia developed this method, although it prefers using the term *intellectual capital* instead of knowledge. Skandia uses a number of ratios in which it looks at the past, present, and future. The following information is publicly provided by Skandia at its Web site.[3]

> At Skandia . . . we have . . . a number of methods and tools, among them the Skandia Navigator, to manage what we call our Intellectual Capital: the unique combination of our Customers, Employees and Processes that drive Skandia's future value creation. We understand how these separate pieces come together to form a coherent framework for the company's future, sustainable development.
>
> We have also pioneered the development of new forms of disclosing our intellectual capital to analysts and investors. This disclosure is driven by our firm belief that increased transparency leads to a greater understanding.

Another overall approach for KM assessment is the *real options approach,* which views KM initiatives as a *portfolio of investments* [Tiwana, 2002]. This approach focuses on the value-to-cost ratio (i.e., the ratio of the net value to the total cost) for each investment and the volatility faced by each investment. Using this approach, KM projects can be placed on an option space, as shown in Figure 6-3. A clockwise move from region 1 to 3 in the option space implies a shift from projects that are low risk

---

[2]See www.knowinc.com/demo/intangible-demo.htm.
[3]See www.skandia.com/en/sustainability/intellectualcapital.shtml.

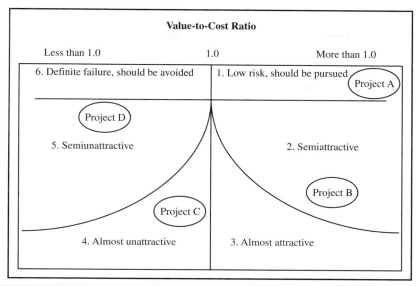

**FIGURE 6-3** KM Projects Mapped on the Option Space

and attractive to projects that are fairly attractive. Continuing further to region 6, the projects reduce further in attractiveness. Thus, projects A and B in Figure 6-3 are attractive, and projects C and D are not, with project A the most attractive and project D the least attractive. Such real option analysis combines strategic and financial approaches to evaluating investments. In positioning projects on the option space, it can benefit from the techniques discussed earlier in the chapter, especially for identifying the value-to-cost ratio. To conclude this section on overall KM assessment, Vignette 6-4 provides a summary of KM assessment at Siemens.[4]

## FURTHER RECOMMENDATIONS
## FOR KNOWLEDGE MANAGEMENT ASSESSMENT

So far in this chapter we have described a number of KM metrics and assessment approaches. In developing these measures and approaches, the following eight suggestions should be carefully considered (Tiwana, 2002; Wilson, 2002).

1. ***Remember why you are doing KM.***   When proposing a KM project, it is critical to define its measures of success based on things the organization cares about, such as reducing waste, lowering costs, and enhancing the customer experience.
2. ***Establish a baseline.***   It is important to identify and develop a baseline measure when you begin efforts, instead of scrambling after the effort to determine success. Establishing a baseline is essential to prove results down the line.
3. ***Consider qualitative methods.***   KM is a qualitative concept, and qualitative methods of measurement, such as analyzing the value of social networks, and telling success stories, should not be ignored.

[4]See www.siemens.com

 VIGNETTE 6-4

## KM Assessment at Siemens

To estimate ROI, Siemens computes the costs of a community of practice, including labor, meetings, and facilities and the effort spent by KM experts. Siemens then decides how much effort has been saved through the sharing of solutions in the community. Siemens also considers subcommunities and their generation of solutions in terms of community projects. If a group needs a solution and embarks on a knowledge-creation effort, it can determine the savings in time to market, *competitive positioning,* etc. To further determine the value of KM, Siemens has developed a master plan of KM metrics that contains measures for each of four dimensions of its holistic KM system:

- *Knowledge community.* The organization, community, and people dimensions.
- *Knowledge marketplace.* The IT involved.
- *Key KM processes.* Sharing and creation.
- *Knowledge environment.* All of the above.

Siemens has realized that it can assess the success of its communities and marketplaces with measures, such as how much knowledge comes in or out of the community, and the quality of feedback. Siemens believes communities are the heart of the KM system, and it has spent a great deal of time on communities-of-practice assessments—questionnaires for community members that provide ideas on how to improve the community.

Siemens has tried to check the health of KM processes to determine the performance of the sharing process. Ideally, the measures evaluate whether a person has managed the process correctly and set the right limits on it. This provides Siemens a good way to look at the marketplace and also to examine how much sharing and creation is taking place.

To monitor the entire KM system, Siemens performs a KM maturity assessment that defines whether KM is still *ad hoc* and *chaotic* or has progressed to an *optimized* state. To do this, Siemens measures its four dimensions and 16 enablers, each of which has a set of questions.

4. *Keep it simple.* An organization does not need hundreds of measures. A handful of relevant, robust, and easily measurable ones are better in demonstrating to yourself and your organization that KM is indeed adding value.
5. *Avoid KM metrics that are hard to control.* KM assessment should use metrics that are specific and within the control of the organization's employees. Broad and grand statements, such as "enable every individual in America to have a mobile phone by 2010" are visionary but impossible to control or measure.
6. *Measure at the appropriate level.* Measure at the project or application level in the beginning. Organizations that have implemented KM initiatives for a long time can then try to measure the total value of KM or their program.
7. *Link rewards to KM assessment results.* KM assessment should not be end–goal. Instead, the results of KM assessments should be used to provide rewards and incentives, thereby motivating improved KM results in the future.

**8. *Be conservative in your claims.*** When calculating a figure like ROI for KM projects, it is recommended to overestimate costs and underestimate value to make the results more believable to management.

## Summary

Following our discussion of KM impacts in Chapter 4 and factors affecting KM solutions in Chapter 5, in this chapter we describe KM assessments. We have examined assessment of KM systems and the impacts that assessments can have. We also summarize some overall KM assessment approaches and how a KM assessment can be implemented. The next few chapters examine KM technologies, beginning with artificial intelligence technologies in Chapter 7.

## Key Terms

- Balanced Scorecard Method—p. 95
- benchmarking—p. 94
- competitive advantage—p. 92
- intangible assets—p. 90
- knowledge management assessment—p. 82
- qualitative KM assessments—p. 86
- quantitative KM assessments—p. 86
- tangible measure—p. 90

## Review Questions

1. Why is it important to perform knowledge management (KM) assessment? Identify and discuss any three reasons.
2. Describe the different types of KM assessment, in terms of (a) the timing of KM assessment; and (b) the aspect assessed.
3. What are the differences between quantitative and qualitative assessments of KM assessment? How does their use depend on the organization's experience with KM?
4. Briefly describe some financial measures that can be used for KM assessment.
5. Briefly describe some nonfinancial measures that can be used for KM assessment.
6. Briefly discuss how the different impacts of KM on employees can be assessed.
7. How can the impacts of KM on efficiency, effectiveness, and innovation be evaluated?
8. How do the measures of the direct impacts of KM differ from the measures of its indirect impacts?

## Application Exercises

1. Visit a local area firm to study its KM assessment process. Determine how it decided on the type of KM solution it uses.
2. How would you conduct KM assessment at the firm you visited? Describe the suggested approach in some detail, making sure to connect this approach to the approaches described in this chapter.
3. Study how knowledge is managed at either your family physician's office or your dentist's office through 15-minute conversations with a few individuals that work at that office. Then recommend an approach for assessing KM at this office. Discuss the suggested approach with some senior employees (e.g., the family physician or the dentist) at this office, and seek their feedback concerning your suggestions.

4. Visit any three organizations of varying sizes and different industries. Examine how these organizations perform their KM assessments. For each organization, discuss how the KM assessment approach relates to the KM assessment approaches discussed in this chapter.
5. For each of the organizations you visited in question 4 above, examine how consistent the organization's KM assessment approach is with the recommendations in this chapter. Which organization seems most consistent with the recommended approach? Of the three organizations, is this organization the one that has the most experience with knowledge management?

## REFERENCES ◇ ◇ ◇

Collison, C., and Parcell, G. 2001. *Learning to Fly.* Capstone Publishing, Milford, CT.

Davenport, T.H., and Prusak, L. 1998. *Working Knowledge: How Organizations Manage What They Know.* Harvard Business School Press, Boston.

Davenport, T.H., Harris, J.G., De Long, D.W., and Jacobson, A.L. 2001. Data to knowledge to results: Building an analytic capability. *California Management Review,* Winter 43(2), 117–138.

Ernst & Young, LLP. 1997. *Executive Perspectives on Knowledge in the Organization.* Ernst & Young, Cambridge, MA.

Kaplan, R.S., and Norton, D.P. 1996. *The Balanced Scorecard.* Harvard Business School Press, Boston.

Lopez, K. 2001. How to measure the value of knowledge management. *KM Review,* March/April 4(2).

PR Newswire. 2001a. Siemens one of 10 most admired knowledge enterprises; named to MAKE hall of fame for world class knowledge management. *PR Newswire,* June 15, www.prnewswire.com.

PR Newswire. 2001b. Knowledge management: Best practice sharing overcomes barriers. *PR Newswire,* November 1, www.prnewswire.com.

PR Newswire. 2001c. Microsoft teams with knowledge advisors to measure training investments. *PR Newswire,* November 27, www.prnewswire.com.

Quinn, J.B., Anderson, P., and Finkelstein, S. 1996. Leveraging intellect. *Academy of Management Executive,* 10(3) 7–27.

Rockart, J.H. 1979. Chief executives define their own data needs. *Harvard Business Review,* 57(2), 81–92.

Sullivan, P.H. 2000. *Value-Driven Intellectual Capital.* John Wiley & Sons, New York.

Sveiby, K.-E. 2000. Measuring intangibles and intellectual capital. In Morey, D., Maybury, M., and Thuraisingham, B. (Eds.), *Knowledge Management: Classic and Contemporary Works.* MIT Press, Cambridge, MA, pp. 337–353.

Tiwana, A. 2002. *The Knowledge Management Toolkit: Orchestrating IT, Strategy, and Knowledge Platforms.* Prentice Hall PTR, Upper Saddle River, NJ.

Wilson, J. (Ed.). 2002. *Knowledge Management Review: The Practitioner's Guide to Knowledge Management.* Melcrum Publishing, Chicago, IL.

# Technologies to Manage Knowledge: Artificial Intelligence[1]

## ❖ ❖ ❖  Introduction

We now know what knowledge is and what knowledge management (KM) is all about. We have also stated that information technologies can and have facilitated the implementation of KM. In the next few chapters, we look at some of the technologies that have enabled KM. We begin with **artificial intelligence** (AI), the area of computer science that endeavors to build machines exhibiting human-like cognitive capabilities.

Progress in AI over the last two decades may well have been the spark that gave rise to the KM discipline. Like human intelligence, AI is inextricably associated with knowledge, making it a natural technology to deal with the management of intellectual assets. However, let us first examine AI and discuss its nature as a prelude to understanding its relationship with KM. In this chapter, you will learn what AI is, how it represents and manipulates knowledge, and the types of knowledge that can be represented and manipulated. We also present several examples and case studies to help explain the concepts described. We start with a definition of AI and a brief historical perspective.

## ❖ ❖ ❖  Artificial Intelligence: A Definition and Historical Perspective

A good definition of AI is elusive simply because human intelligence is not completely understood. Historically, computers have excelled at performing logical, repetitive tasks such as complex arithmetic calculations or database storage and retrieval. One aspect common across these repetitive tasks is that they are *algorithmic* in nature. That is, they involve a precise and logically designed set of instructions that yield a single correct output. Conventional computer programs are based on exactly such a way of

---

[1]Written in collaboration with Douglas D. Dankel.

expressing actions. Humans, on the other hand, excel at solving problems using symbols to which meaning can be attached, such as when planning a sequence of tasks or understanding a poem. The manipulation of these symbols is arguably the basis of AI. This process is called **symbol manipulation,** and it is and has been the subject of great controversy among some researchers in the community.

The many textbooks on AI provide several diverse definitions, each emphasizing the different perspectives of the field most important to its authors. Nevertheless, we like one general definition [Tanimoto, 1987] that provides a good, broad view of the field:

> Artificial intelligence is a field of study that encompasses computational techniques for performing tasks that apparently require intelligence when performed by humans. . . It is a technology of information processing concerned with processes of reasoning, learning, and perception.

However, we prefer to leave out the relationship to human intelligence, given its rather ill-defined nature. Therefore, our own definition of AI, in more specific terms, is:

> The science that provides computers with the ability to represent and manipulate symbols so they can be used to solve problems not easily solved through algorithmic models.

Most modern AI systems are founded on the realization that intelligence is tightly intertwined with knowledge. Knowledge is associated with the symbols we manipulate. We can informally describe human intelligence as our innate ability to learn and manipulate knowledge in order to communicate or to solve a problem. However, when we judge a student's performance in class or decide whom to hire, we generally focus on *how much* they know. People go to college to acquire knowledge, not intelligence. We are born with intelligence and thereafter acquire knowledge. Furthermore, without knowledge to exercise their intelligence, it becomes difficult to gauge a person's intelligence without subjecting them to formal psychological tests. Some AI systems (knowledge-based systems) attempt to emulate the problem-solving prowess of accomplished problem solvers in a particular subject matter (**domain knowledge**). They do this by using their knowledge to solve problems. Knowledge-based systems inherently present us with a way to manage knowledge, that is, to discover, capture, share, and apply it. Hopefully, our discussions in this part of the book will let the reader see this clearly.

The idea of intelligent machines has been with us since the beginning of the information age. Computing researchers in the 1950s boldly claimed that within a decade, they would build a machine that would be as intelligent as a human. Of course, this proclamation turned out to be rather naïve. They grossly underestimated the complexity of the human mind and overestimated the capability of the primitive computers of the time. Nevertheless, research in AI slowly began to make strides, as researchers became aware of its potential benefits as well as its inherent difficulties.

John McCarthy coined the term *artificial intelligence* in 1956 during a workshop he organized at Dartmouth College. This so-called Dartmouth Conference brought together four individuals who pioneered AI research: John McCarthy, Marvin Minsky, Allan Newell, and Herbert Simon. Although this event is generally considered the birth place of AI, related research had already been ongoing during the previous 10 years. In any case, research continued in earnest after this workshop, initially within academic centers throughout the world, and rapidly expanding to commercial and industrial laboratories.

The early emphasis in AI research was on game playing and machine translation of natural languages. In game playing, researchers developed a number of chess-playing programs over the years, including MacHack by Richard Greenblatt [1967], and Chess 4.5 by David Slate and Larry Atkin [1977], the last version of which had a tournament rating of 2552 [Hsu, 1990]. More recently, an AI program named Big Blue defeated Boris Kasparov, the reigning world champion in chess in a widely publicized match in 1997.

Other game-related AI programs have included a checkers-playing program developed by A. L. Samuel, which defeated R. W. Nealey, "one of the nation's foremost players" [Samuel, 1963]. Samuel's checkers program was also the first program able to learn from its experiences. Hans Berliner in 1979 developed a backgammon program that defeated the reigning world champion [Berliner, 1980]. A checkers-playing program called *Chinook* placed second in the U.S. National Open in 1991, winning the right to challenge for the world title [Peterson, 1991; Schaeffer, 1991].

However, efforts in machine translation of natural languages were not nearly as successful. Researchers originally believed that there was a one-to-one, context-free correspondence between words in one language and those in another. They thought that translation merely required finding the corresponding words and slightly changing the order of words. This was, of course, found not to be true.

One example of direct word-for-word translation that illustrates the obstacles faced by researchers is the case of Braniff International Airways, a now-defunct airline then based in Dallas–Ft. Worth. In the early 1980s, Braniff heavily marketed the comfort of its leather-upholstered seats. Although these commercials were presumably successful in convincing English-speaking travelers to fly with this airline, such was not the case when the firm translated the ads into Spanish for the large Hispanic market of the Southwestern United States. The motto, "fly in leather," when directly translated into Spanish unwittingly exhorted the Spanish-speaking travelers to "fly naked." Because of similar difficulties, the machine translation efforts were abandoned in the mid-1960s. Only recently have these efforts begun to yield fruit (e.g., babelfish.com and other online translation services).

Another major milestone in the early days of AI was the development of the General Problem Solver (GPS) by Simon and Newell [Newell, 1963]. GPS demonstrated the ability to solve some problems by searching for an answer in a solution space. This system was representative of the trends in AI of the time. We provide more about this approach later in this chapter

Although there were many other interesting advances in the early days of AI (1950 to 1980), it would be impractical to discuss all of them. However, one very interesting program was called *Eliza* [Weizenbaum, 1965]. Eliza used a natural language interface to act as an artificial psychoanalyst, carrying on a dialogue with a patient. It used a very simple approach, where keywords in the patient's response were used to trigger questions presented to the patient. It clearly had no understanding of the patient's response. However, at least for a while, a user felt as if it truly did. Eliza was created as a way to discredit AI by demonstrating that a program could sound intelligent without

**Artificial Intelligence**

**Knowledge-Based Systems**

- Rule-based systems
  - Classification
  - Diagnosis
  - Design
  - Decision support
  - Planning
  - Scheduling
- Case-based reasoning
  - Diagnostics
  - Design
  - Decision support
  - Classification
- Constraint-based reasoning
  - Planning
  - Scheduling
- Model-based reasoning
  - Monitoring
  - Diagnostics
  - Design

**Natural Language Processing**

- NL understanding
- NL synthesis
- Speech understanding
- Speech synthesis

**Computer Vision**

- Image processing
- Image understanding

**Machine Learning**

- Inductive learning
- Case-based learning
- Connectionist learning
- Learning from analogy
- Explanation-based learning
- Data mining
- Others

**Soft Programming Approaches**

- Neural networks
- Uncertainty management
  - Bayesian probability
  - Certainty factors
  - Bayesian belief nets
  - Fuzzy logic
- Evolutionary techniques
  - Genetic algorithms
  - Genetic programming

**Games**

- Chess
- Checkers
- Go
- Backgammon

**Robotics**

- Control
- Navigation and tactics

**Human Behavior Representation**

- Context-based reasoning
- Cognitively-inspired modeling
- Others

**Automated Know Acquisition**

- Repertory grids
- Conceptual maps

**FIGURE 7-1 Artificial Intelligence and Its Component Areas**

truly being so. Nevertheless, contrary to its author's intent, Eliza became a symbol of the successes of AI and many people wanted to consult with it. Eliza's main legacy, after all, was that it succeeded in showing people's acceptance of automated human-like behavior, and their willingness to interact with it.

One last project worthy of mention is Blocks World [Winograd, 1972]. This program assumed a robot arm and a set of blocks on the table. The blocks were of different size and shape, and their location could be defined as being on top of other blocks.

Blocks World consisted of giving commands to the robot arm to move specific blocks from one location in the table (possibly on top or below other blocks) to another location in the table, possibly already occupied. It had to plan a series of tasks removing any block on top of the desired block, placing it down elsewhere in the table, and clearing any obstacles in the destination before actually moving the target block. This project demonstrated the feasibility of automated task planning, an important feature in modern-day, human-like robotics.

One of the areas that have produced the greatest success and consequent popularity is that of knowledge-based systems. As the name indicates, these systems use knowledge to solve problems. This is the area that has the closest relationship to KM. We concentrate on this technology in this chapter as well as the next two.

Other areas of research within the AI umbrella, which are also knowledge-intensive in their own right, include natural language understanding, classification, diagnostics, design, machine learning, planning and scheduling, robotics, and computer vision (to a somewhat lesser degree). Figure 7-1 depicts the areas encompassing AI. Note that it is not an exhaustive listing of all areas of investigation under the AI umbrella.

You have now learned what we mean by AI and its historical background. Let us now look briefly at the evolution of AI techniques, all the way up to modern knowledge-based systems. We begin with *search-based methods*. We note their relevance to KM at every step.

## ◇▷ ◁◇ ◁◇ Early AI : Search-Based Systems

Automating the reasoning process is the basic objective of AI techniques. Interestingly enough, the strong link between intelligence and knowledge for problem solving was slow to be recognized. Early AI systems such as the GPS mentioned earlier, were rather primitive search engines. However, instead of searching for a piece of data in some preexisting data structure, these early systems searched for a solution to a problem presented to it. This brought about the concept of the **solution space**—a model of sorts of the problem domain. In a figurative manner, the solution space is where a solution to a problem can be found—we just have to search for it. The solution space contains the many actions, states, or beliefs that represent the status of the problem. One can imagine that a solution is a "path" (sequence of steps) through these actions, beliefs, or states, starting from the initial state (the current problem definition) to the goal state (the final desired state of the problem). Each successive state, action, or belief can be said to advance the partial solution toward the final one. A solution to the problem is, in effect, a path through the solution space between the initial state and the goal state. This path would compose all the actions to be done to solve the problem.

From the KM point of view, these early search techniques were not very good at managing knowledge. Although they certainly employed knowledge, it was very general knowledge and it was embedded in the solution space (the *operators,* as they were called). Explicit use of specific knowledge would not come about for a few years yet.

Let us now look at an example shown in **Vignette 7-1** to better understand the concept of solution space.

As we mention above, clearly there is knowledge in the solution space. However, the knowledge about the domain (car repair) is deeply embedded in the solution space. This knowledge is about how to check the battery, or how to replace the starter

  VIGNETTE 7-1

## Searching a Solution Space

Let us suppose that your automobile fails to start one cold, shivering morning— a problem that many of us have unfortunately encountered. The initial state is that your car does not start when you turn the ignition switch. Your desired goal state is that the car starts. Many things can cause your car to fail to start, with each of these problems possibly having several different solutions. All these problems and their solutions define the solution space, only a small portion of which is shown in Figure 7-2. In this figure, the lines (arcs) represent actions that can be taken and the nodes represent possible results that can occur from these actions. Note that not all possible results are represented (e.g., when

you turn the key, the engine might turn over but not start). Furthermore, we assume that only one problem exists.

Determining the source of the observed problem and taking appropriate corrective action is the essence of diagnosis and repair. In this example, the search engine explores the solution space, searching for complete paths between the initial state and the goal state. As it moves about the solution space, the search engine "visits" specific states. An operator at each state can indicate what possible new states can be reached from the current state. The search process, therefore, involves discovering the group of possible next states and determining which of these possible next

◆◇ ◆◇ ◆◇ FIGURE 7-2 **Representation of a Portion of a Solution Space for Automobile Diagnosis**

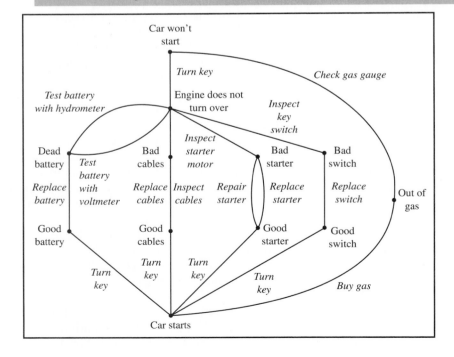

states to visit. The search ends either when the goal state is reached (the search engine knows what the goal state looks like) or all the possible states have been visited and paths navigated, yet none lead to the goal state. In this way, possibly after many false steps, an appropriate path from the initial state to the goal state is discovered. This path is the sequence of steps that solves the current problem. In our case, it is to repair the car so it starts. Searching the problem space to find this path can often be difficult, however.

Let us now put this concept into practice in our example. The first step in searching for a solution to your car's problem might be to see whether the engine turns over. The information obtained defines a new state in the solution space that you reach by turning the ignition key and seeing what results. For this example, let us say that the engine does not turn over. This new state, therefore, is described by the facts:

**The car does not start and its engine does not turn over.**

This is depicted in Figure 7-3a. Then scanning the solution space of Figure 7-2, we find several possible next steps in the solution. These include (1) determining the viability of the battery, (2) inspecting the starter motor, and (3) inspecting the cables. For example, should you find the battery to be defective, you can replace it and the problem is solved. Suppose that you choose to pursue this path. Two methods can be used to test the battery:

measuring the charge on the battery with a hydrometer or measuring its charge using a voltmeter as you turn the ignition switch. These two methods are shown in Figure 7-3b as dashed lines. You decide to use the hydrometer and discover that the battery is charged and functional (Figure 7-3c).

The new state is that the car does not start, the engine does not turn over, and the battery is charged. This state gets you nowhere, because replacing the battery does not solve the problem (the old battery is just fine). So, you have reached a dead end for this possible solution. You must now go back and consider other potential problems for why the engine fails to turn over.

Another possibility is that your car may have a bad starter motor (Figure 7-3d). When you inspect the starter motor, you discover that it has a broken wire. Taking one of two actions can correct this problem: replace the motor or repair the wire. You choose to replace the entire motor. On completion of the repair and reinstallation, you verify that you have reached the final state by turning the ignition key and finding that the car now starts, solving your problem (Figure 7-3e). The successor states—those that follow the current state—are determined by *operators* that contain knowledge about the domain, albeit at a most basic level. The concepts behind these operators may be a bit fuzzy for the reader—we cover them in detail later. Nevertheless, it is clear that a search was used to traverse this solution space. Furthermore, the path is a series of steps and new states that got us to our goal state, thus serving as the solution.

*Continued*

◆▷ ◁▷ ◆▷ **FIGURE 7-3** Searching a Portion of the Solution Space of Figure 7-2

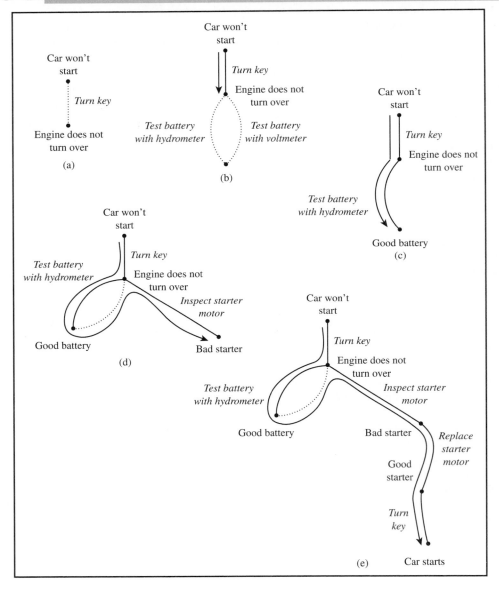

motor. Yet, there is no knowledge about how to find the appropriate path to get us to the desired state as soon and as effectively as possible. This search was rather unintelligent in that way.

## HOW SEARCHES USE KNOWLEDGE

The early researchers realized that the solution space searches were very inefficient. They addressed the problem partially by adding knowledge in the form of **heuristics** to assist the search process in determining which next state is more promising than the others. According to Webster's dictionary, a heuristic is ". . . helping to discover or invent." Heuristics represent rules of thumb and shortcuts that people develop after considerable experience to help them with a problem. Thus, **heuristic functions** were used to compute the desirability of moving on to each of the possible next states based on some general knowledge, and ranked these states in order of decreasing desirability.

This next example shown in Vignette 7-2 provides a glimpse into **heuristic search-based** AI systems. It also brings home the difference between these early systems and the traditional algorithmic approaches contained in traditional computer programs.

 VIGNETTE 7-2

Let us assume that we are visiting Paris for the first time and are trying to locate *la Tour d'Eiffel* (the Eiffel Tower). We know our initial state is at the Sorbonne University, on Boulevard St. Michel. We want to be at the tower (the goal state). We also know what the tower looks like from pictures in tour books— this can help us later. See the section of a simplified map of Paris shown in Figure 7-4. Yes, we know—we can take a taxi. However, to make things interesting, let us say we do not speak French and are flat broke, so a taxi is not an option. We have to walk. What we need is a path through the city from our current location to the tower (a solution).

Let us first try to find it through algorithmic methods. As we mentioned earlier, traditional computer programming involves a structured sequence of steps (instructions) to find a solution. Such procedures are known as **algorithms.** Additionally, we need a model or

data on which to execute our algorithms—a road network. To find our way to the Eiffel Tower algorithmically, we need the set of steps defined on this road network, to get us there. The directions can be easily obtained from the French Tourist Office. They might read something like:

1. Turn left at Boulevard St. Michel from the Sorbonne.
2. Continue on Boulevard St. Michel until you reach the intersection with Boulevard du Montparnasse.
3. Turn right at Boulevard du Montparnasse.
4. Continue on Boulevard du Montparnasse until you reach the roundabout intersecting with the Boulevard des Invalides.
5. Continue on Boulevard des Invalides until it becomes Avenue de Villars. Continue on Avenue De Villars until you reach the Hotel des Invalides and the intersection with Avenue de Tourville.

*Continued*

6. Turn left at Avenue. de Tourville.

7. Continue on Avenue de Tourville until you reach the Place de la Ecole Militaire and the Avenue de la Motte Picquet. You now are at the lower end of the Parc du Champs de Mars.

8. At the opposite end of the Parc du Champs de Mars is the Eiffel Tower.

Nevertheless, what if these directions are in French? (Remember, we do not speak French.) Clearly, no useful algorithm exists. Therefore, we must find an alternative solution method. We must then *search* for the Eiffel Tower!

Because of the conceivably infinite number of possible routes that could be taken (some of which could be by way of China), we need to constrain the area of our search. With our limited knowledge of Paris, we know that the Eiffel Tower is located in the southern half of Paris—within two physical barriers: the AutoRoute to the south and the Seine River on the north, east, and west sides,

roughly forming a semicircle. Reaching either of these can be considered a dead end, resulting in our having to go in some alternate direction.

Governing our search is a set of operators defining the legal paths we can follow. These operators reflect the road network in Paris. They state that on reaching any intersection, we have a choice of continuing on the same street to the next intersection or turning right or left onto other streets at this intersection. Because we are walking, we can safely assume that there are no one-way streets. We know when we get to the Eiffel Tower (the goal state) because we know what it looks like from pictures.

We can use various methods to search for our goal. For example, we could randomly turn at any street, hoping that eventually we will bump into the Eiffel Tower. Although in all probability this **random search** ultimately allows us to find the Eiffel Tower, it may take

◈ ◈ ◈ **FIGURE 7-4 Simplified Map of Paris**

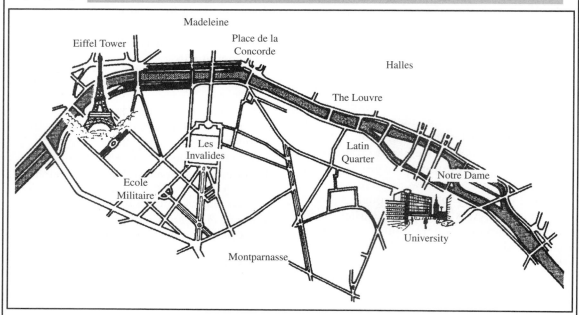

an awful long time. This is because the arbitrary manner with which we select a path to follow can result in paths taken multiple times. Furthermore, a random search cannot guarantee that it will explore all paths in the solution space and thereby cannot guarantee a solution (if one indeed exists). Therefore, we need an alternative, more systematic, method to explore the domain.

One such approach is to follow exhaustively every street to its end (i.e., the tower, the river, the AutoRoute, or a dead end). When we encounter an end (other than the tower, of course) we back up to the most recently visited intersection and from there find another road to walk on, regardless of whether we are moving closer to, or farther from, our goal. Eventually (if Paris followed a grid system, which it does not) this approach considers all locations in our solution space and guarantees that we ultimately find the tower. This type of systematic search is called a **systematic blind search** because it uses no knowledge of how close we are to a solution when picking the path to follow from our current location to a new location. A systematic blind search is a definite improvement over the uncontrolled process of the random search. For some applications, this approach can be quite effective.

Alternatively, we can use our knowledge of what the tower looks like to improve the efficiency of our search. Assuming the tip of the Eiffel Tower can be seen from everywhere in Paris (*not* actually true), we can look up and take whatever street appears to take us in its general direction. This is called a *heuristic* (or *directed) search,* because instead of blindly or randomly searching for our goal, we are directed by a heuristic function. Heuristic searches form the foundation of knowledge-based AI. The general knowledge, in the form of the heuristic function, was used to direct the search toward next states that are most promising. This is one way knowledge was added to the original blind searches to make them more intelligent. The knowledge was used to evaluate where the search mechanism should proceed for its next step. At every step of the way, it will have one or more options of where to go next. The knowledge is used to determine which of the potential next steps is the most promising one. In our example, we would always want to move to the intersection that gets us closer to the Eiffel tower, and not take us in the opposite direction. It is commonsense knowledge, and quite general, but it works in many cases.

## SEARCH-BASED METHODS: CONCLUSION

The solution spaces in both examples above do in fact contain basic domain knowledge. They capture and represent relevant knowledge and provide a way to re-use it. The car repair solution space represents the ways cars can fail and what can be done to fix them. This is indeed valuable knowledge. The Paris solution space is nothing more than a map, but this is still valuable information.

Yet, there is no knowledge about how to decide quickly and correctly what is the problem with the car based on the symptoms it displays. Knowing this, one can much more quickly navigate the solution space to the goal state. Good mechanics know right away that it is the starter motor based on the sound it makes. The mechanics may not have to test the battery. Likewise, knowledgeable guides in Paris know how to get there immediately, without having to search the city. Thus, these search-based systems, although far from useless, do not take full advantage of available knowledge. Search-based systems evolved somewhat to include general heuristic knowledge to guide the search. However, they were still knowledge-poor solutions.

The use of searches, even when they included general knowledge, was insufficient to solve the difficult problems. This was because this knowledge was too general to be useful for the really difficult problems. In many of these hard problems, such general knowledge simply does not exist, or if it does, it is not very helpful. This was one important reason why search-based systems did not effectively solve the hard problems faced by technical or business organizations. The rise of modern knowledge-based systems was sparked by the realization that general knowledge was not sufficient to solve the difficult problems, and that high-quality, domain-specific knowledge was the alternative. We dedicate Chapter 8 entirely to knowledge-based systems. However, it is appropriate to briefly introduce some concepts in this chapter to put them in context with the current discussion about AI.

## ❖ ❖ ❖ Knowledge-Based Systems: A Brief Introduction

In the early 1970s, some researchers in AI realized that what was required was specific knowledge about the particular (and rather narrow) application domains of interest, instead of the broad general knowledge used in the search-based systems. This recognition led to the development of knowledge-based (e.g., expert) systems.

The knowledge represented in knowledge-based systems is that possessed by people knowledgeable in the domain. Such knowledge may consist, in part, of simple cause-and-effect relationships. These relationships or rules of thumb originate from a person's past experiences and are the heuristics about which we learned earlier. More specifically, heuristics represent informal knowledge, rules of thumb, or shortcuts that allow knowledgeable persons to quickly reach a solution to a problem without having to perform a detailed analysis of the particular situation. This occurs because either an analysis of a similar problem was successfully performed previously, or the relationship may have been learned as a result of a past failed attempt to solve a similar problem. These persons may not remember, or even know, all the details of the original problem analysis. However, they may recognize that a particular approach worked once for a similar problem and that this same approach can probably work again for the current problem. Consider the example in Vignette 7-3 that illustrates this concept.

Nicole did not methodically analyze the operation of the engine to determine the malfunction. She may not even know how an internal combustion engine operates. Nicole also did not search for a solution using any of the search methods described earlier in this chapter. In fact, she did not even have a solution space in mind. Instead, she used heuristic knowledge based on her prior experience to determine that the problem was with the vacuum hose. The use of this type of heuristic knowledge is what makes knowledge-based systems such a powerful tool.

A heuristic, then, *often* provides a correct solution to some problem. However, because it does not represent an exhaustive in-depth analysis, it occasionally gives incorrect answers or even fails to give any answers at all. This failure to always be successful is based on its use of an acceptable choice instead of the *true* or *best* answer. This may be because: (1) the number of possibilities to be examined is too large; (2) the algorithmic evaluation function applied to each possible answer to determine correctness is too complex; or (3) the algorithmic evaluation function is unknown and must be approximated.

 **VIGNETTE 7-3**

### The Backfiring Car

While driving downtown one morning, Nicole suddenly notices a backfiring noise in her automobile while stopped at a light. Although she does not know what it is, she has been driving this particular automobile for a long time and remembers a similar situation that occurred several months earlier. At that time, she took the car to her mechanic for repair, and the mechanic told her the problem was simply a loose vacuum hose connection in the engine. This loose connection caused air to leak into the engine, resulting in the backfiring. The mechanic even showed her which hose caused the problem. Knowing this, Nicole stops the car, opens the hood, discovers that the same hose is loose, and proceeds to reconnect it. When the car is restarted, she finds that it no longer backfires.

As we shall see, the use of heuristics in knowledge-based systems is markedly different from the heuristic functions described in the previous section for use in directed searches. The heuristic functions described previously for directed searches represent general knowledge used to guide a search through the solution space. Heuristics in knowledge-based systems, on the other hand, refer to the heuristic knowledge used by a knowledgeable individual in the solution of a problem, which bypasses the solution space altogether.

Experts possess skills that allow them to draw on past experiences and quickly focus on the core of a given problem. Nonexperts may approach a problem in a systematic (algorithmic) manner, employing a specific procedurally oriented methodology (if one indeed exists). However, this approach may be too complicated and may consume an unacceptable amount of time and effort. This use of the methodology may result from limited understanding of the domain and its cause-and-effect relationships. Experts, on the other hand, have a much higher success rate in solving problems because they have acquired a set of powerful cause-and-effect relationships (heuristics) based on experience. Experts are able to utilize this knowledge to recognize quickly the salient features of the problem, categorize it according to these characteristics, and correctly devise a solution.

The differences between heuristic and algorithmic techniques can be further illustrated through another real-world example. Consider Vignette 7-4 on the following page.

Obviously, the advantage of Avelino's approach is that he is able to give Alex a timely quotation. The disadvantage is the possibility that a miscalculation (e.g., the price of lumber just went through the roof two days ago) may invalidate the estimate, and cost him a bundle. However, if he is a true expert, this is unlikely to occur.

The first approach is algorithmic: thorough, detailed, and highly accurate, but possibly inadequate because of its long development time and effort. The second method is heuristic: not as thorough or detailed, but probably just as accurate and developed within acceptable limitations on time and effort. Thus, although the results of an algorithmic process are always precise and accurate, it is often the case that a heuristic estimate of almost equal accuracy can be made with significantly less

 VIGNETTE 7-4

### The Building Contractor

Alex is a prospective homebuyer, who arrives for a meeting with Avelino, a residential building contractor. Alex is carrying a set of architectural plans describing the design of a house. He wants an estimate of the cost of the house before committing to employ Avelino to build him the house.

A contractor typically determines the price of the house by performing a detailed cost analysis. This involves carefully calculating the amount of material necessary to build the house; calling a building supply warehouse to obtain material prices; evaluating quotations from subcontractors on the cost of their labor; determining the appropriate contractors' fees; allowing a reasonable contingency figure; and so forth. This process has the advantage of nearly guaranteeing a correct result (assuming no computational errors are made) and entails relatively little risk for the contractor. The disadvantage, however, is that this process involves a significant amount of effort and time. However, Alex is leaving town that same evening and needs a quotation before he leaves.

Avelino is an experienced contractor (an expert), and as such, he has another option. He compares the size of this home to ones he recently completed. By finding a home that has approximately the same living area, he can obtain a rough estimate (based on his previous experience) for the price per square foot. He then looks for differences between the homes that might raise or lower the estimate. These differences might include additions like a swimming pool (raising his estimate by $15,000), modifications like pine kitchen cabinets instead of oak (decreasing his estimate by $1,500), or deletions such as two bathrooms instead of three (decreasing his estimate by $6,000). After evaluating these differences, Avelino is able to make an estimate in only 30 minutes.

effort. However, only experts are capable of doing the latter, and sometimes a greater risk exists of being wrong.

## KNOWLEDGE-BASED SYSTEMS AND KNOWLEDGE MANAGEMENT

What does this have to do with KM? It has quite a bit, actually, because knowledge is the essence of knowledge-based systems. Knowledge-based systems excel at capturing, sharing, and allowing users to apply knowledge. Although KM is much more than this, capturing, sharing, and applying knowledge are three of the main KM processes. Knowledge-based systems do this quite well.

Nevertheless, knowledge-based systems were designed to solve problems, not merely to passively represent knowledge. KM does not always need to use knowledge to solve problems, but it may also support knowledge capture for humans to learn in the future. We all know how powerful examples can be for teaching concepts. Knowledge-based systems can be used to demonstrate to the learner some of the subtle issues in a domain by executing example problems and indicating the heuristic knowledge it used to solve the problem. In this way, knowledge-based systems can also be used for knowledge dissemination.

At this point, you have seen what AI is and what it comprises. You have also seen and understood the early search-based systems that used general knowledge to solve problems. The next section sets the stage for a more detailed discussion of knowledge-based systems in Chapter 8 and how they address the problem of KM. You can learn the differences between knowledge-based systems and the traditional search-based methods in AI.

We now continue with this brief prelude to knowledge-based systems by defining them and providing a brief historical perspective.

## ◇ ◇ ◇ Knowledge-Based Systems: A Historical Perspective and Definition

In general terms, a knowledge-based system can be defined to be:

> A computerized system that uses domain knowledge to arrive at a solution to a problem within that domain. This solution is essentially the same as one concluded by a person knowledgeable about the domain, when confronted with the same problem.

If the above definition of knowledge-based systems is strictly followed, however, many conventional software systems could be incorrectly categorized as knowledge-based systems. For example, computer programs that calculate currents and voltages in an electric circuit, analyze the stress factors in bridge trusses, calculate loan default risk, or simulate traffic flow in a city could all be considered knowledge-based systems under the above definition. All perform the same analysis as an expert in the field (albeit much faster) and use the same knowledge (i.e., formulas). Programs such as these have been around for years and yet they are not considered knowledge-based systems. The reason is that knowledge-based systems involve more than simply duplicating the knowledge and expertise of a human expert from a specific domain. A better description of knowledge-based systems is now required to resolve this inconsistency.

Knowledge-based systems are different from general search systems and from conventional software because of three fundamental concepts:

1. The use of highly specific domain knowledge.
2. The heuristic nature of the knowledge employed instead of algorithmic.
3. The separation of the knowledge from how it is used.

The concept of using highly specific domain knowledge was initially exploited during the late 1960s and early 1970s in the development of DENDRAL and Meta-DENDRAL [Lindsay, 1980]. DENDRAL infers the molecular structure of unknown compounds from mass spectral and nuclear magnetic response data, whereas Meta-DENDRAL assists in the determination of the dependence of mass spectrometric fragmentation on substructural features. Both systems used highly specific domain knowledge to do their work. They were the first to do this.

The second concept of using heuristic knowledge arose from the ability of humans to solve difficult problems without the use of models or algorithms. We have discussed this previously.

The third idea addresses the point that there are clearly two kinds of knowledge involved in automatically making inferences—the knowledge of how to infer something (anything) and the knowledge about that something. There can be advantages gained by separating the two levels. If one knows how to diagnose a patient for blood disorders, can one also use that general diagnostic knowledge to diagnose respiratory problems if the specific knowledge for the human respiratory system is also known? If the answer is yes, then only the respiratory system knowledge needs to be created for a new diagnostic system. Knowledge-based systems make this assumption. Although not universally true, there is much truth to it. This has given rise to the rule-based development environments (**shells**) that possess the functionality to exercise whatever domain knowledge is expressed as rules, and arrive at solutions or answers to questions. One common knowledge-based system shell is the CLIPS system, developed originally by the National Aeronautics and Space Administration (NASA) in the early 1980s. It has become a popular tool, easily available on the Web.

It was not until the development of the **MYCIN** system at Stanford University in the early 1970s [Shortliffe, 1976; Buchanan, 1984] that these three concepts were merged, creating the modern field of knowledge-based systems. MYCIN is a knowledge-based system developed to diagnose and specify treatments for blood disorders through a question and answer (Q&A) session with a physician. It directs this conversation by asking questions about the signs and symptoms of the patient and by requesting the performance of certain laboratory tests. Once the list of possible infections afflicting the patient has been sufficiently narrowed, the system recommends a drug treatment to address the disorder.

Significant in MYCIN's development was the adherence of the researchers to the fundamental concepts shown above, which were actually not fully recognized at that time. Their adherence to these principles led them to realize that the basic structure used in manipulating knowledge within MYCIN (called the **inference mechanism**) could be used with knowledge from other domains to perform the same style of diagnostic analysis. Some of these domain included lung disease [Aikins, 1983], structural analysis [Bennett, 1978], geology [Bonnet, 1983], and software development [Underwood, 1981]. By removing the domain-specific knowledge (on diagnosis and treatment of blood disorders), they were left with the *essential* elements of MYCIN or the *empty* shell of MYCIN called *E*MYCIN. This development led to the evolution of knowledge-based system shells.

A number of knowledge-based systems developed during the 1970s demonstrated the wide applicability of the techniques developed in DENDRAL and MYCIN to other domains. These other domains were medicine (CASNET, INTERNIST, PUFF, TEIRESIAS), understanding natural language (HEARSAY), geology (**PROSPECTOR**), and manufacturing (**XCON**). In Vignette 7-5 that follows, we describe some pioneering knowledge-based systems. Their relevance to KM is noted.

# ◈ ◈ ◈ Knowledge and Expertise

There has been much confusion about the terms *expert systems* and *knowledge-based systems*. In this section, we hope to clarify this issue. Furthermore, we introduce another way to categorize knowledge, consistent with the definitions and classifications of knowledge given in Chapter 2. This categorization is the *level* of the knowledge. The level of knowledge is particularly relevant to knowledge-based systems, and how they differ from search-based systems.

 ◈ ◈ ◈ ◈  VIGNETTE 7-5  ◈ ◈ ◈ ◈

## Pioneering Knowledge-Based Systems

PROSPECTOR [Duda, 1978] assisted geologists in identifying geologic formations that might have contained mineral deposits. It was developed by SRI International between 1974 and 1983 and did not mature into a commercial system. It elicited, preserved, and applied geologic formation knowledge to assist in mineral exploration.

XCON [McDermott, 1982], one of the earliest commercially successful systems, was used to assist in the configuration of newly ordered VAX computer systems. Developed by Digital Equipment Corporation (DEC) in conjunction with Carnegie-Mellon University, XCON elicited, preserved, and applied the knowledge of human configurators of computer systems to automate and duplicate their functions.

MYCIN [Shortliffe, 1976; Buchanan, 1984] was the granddaddy of them all. MYCIN was a medical diagnostic system that determined the infectious agent in a patient's blood, and specified a treatment for this infection. MYCIN was probably the most significant and renowned research system, because it pioneered the separation of the knowledge from the way it is used. It only served its purpose as a research vehicle. Development ceased in the early to mid-1980s. It elicited, preserved, and applied medical diagnostic knowledge in a critical area of human safety.

**GUIDON** [Clancey, 1979] was an instructional program teaching students therapy for patients with bacterial infections. GUIDON was a descendant of MYCIN and was developed as a research tool at Stanford University. It is not commercially available. GUIDON's contribution was in training. Its contribution to KM was its ability to preserve and disseminate knowledge for other learners in an efficient manner.

**COOKER** [AInteractions, 1985] assists in the maintenance of soup-making equipment. Developed by Texas Instruments for the Campbell Soup Company, it uses a personal computer as the delivery platform. This is the classic case of developing a system to preserve the knowledge of a highly experienced individual who was contemplating retirement at the time.

**AUTHORIZER'S ASSISTANT** [Leonard-Barton, 1988] assists the credit authorization staff in determining the credit level for credit card customers. The system takes information from a number of databases and approves or disapproves a telephone request from a merchant to authorize a large purchase from a cardholder. Developed by Inference Corporation and American Express Company, it serves to elicit, preserve, and apply human knowledge in handling applications for AMEX credit cards.

**GenAID** [Gonzalez, 1986] remotely monitors and diagnoses the status of large electrical generators in real time. It issues a diagnosis with a confidence factor whenever the generator is operating outside its normal operating conditions. It was developed by Westinghouse Electric Corporation with assistance from Texas Utilities Generating Company and Carnegie-Mellon University. This program is presently in commercial operation at various sites throughout the United States. We discuss this one in more detail later in this chapter.

◈ ◈ ◈ ◈

Chapter 2 classifies knowledge into its many forms, from what kind of knowledge it is to where can it be found. In this chapter, we take three of those classifications of knowledge—*general* or *specific knowledge, simple* or *complex knowledge,* and the *three types of expertise*—and introduce the different levels of knowledge. We also put these definitions in the context of knowledge-based systems, what is complex knowledge to the overall population, may be simple knowledge to a subset of the overall population.

Thinking back to the examples and vignettes we discussed earlier in this chapter, there are clearly two levels of knowledge in the example about starting a car. One type of knowledge, which can be considered general knowledge, at least to all car mechanics—indicates the variety of inspections that could be done to the car based on the available information. For example, at the point where the engine does not turn over (see Figure 7-2), a mechanic can test the battery (in two different ways), inspect the cables, inspect the starter switch, or inspect the starter motor. This most definitely is knowledge of what can be done, but it is rather general support knowledge. Keep in mind that this knowledge is not known by the overall population, but only by a small group of people—car mechanics—but it is general to them. However, the knowledge of each individual inspection, and therefore knowledge of the set of inspections, is simple knowledge. Another level of knowledge, on the other hand, is more specific— possessed by more expert car mechanics—and more complex than the knowledge about the inspections. This other knowledge overlaps across the various inspections and may be used to decide on the order in which various inspections should be done. This higher level knowledge may be *tactical or strategic* in nature. To make the distinction more clear, we present another brief example that draws out the differences between these levels of knowledge. We use the game of chess to illustrate the differences in Vignette 7-6 on the facing page.

Therefore, we clearly see two levels of knowledge involved here.

1. ***The knowledge about the rules of the game.*** This is general (and possibly simple) support domain knowledge. It is embedded in the operators of the solution space. This knowledge tells the player which moves *can* be made.
2. ***The knowledge of how best to move the pieces to defeat the opponent.*** Let's call this *complex, specific,* **tactical knowledge,** and it may be based on experience. This knowledge tells the player which move *should* be made.

Preserving general knowledge about the rules of the game is certainly necessary. However, it is clearly not the same as specific knowledge. It is imperative that a successful player be able to manage (i.e., discover, capture, and apply) specific knowledge well. The early AI methods used and represented general knowledge very well in their solution spaces, but not specific knowledge.

General knowledge could be said to reside in all humans who participate in a game or work in a domain. The specific (and complex and tactical or strategic) knowledge, on the other hand, represents knowledge possessed only by people who perform the tasks or play the game in a proficient way. In other words, not all persons who participate in the game or work in the domain may possess this knowledge. If they do, they may not master it in a way to make them excel at it.

Knowledge-based systems employ both types of knowledge. However, specific knowledge does not always need to be that of a person truly excelling at the task or

 VIGNETTE 7-6

### The Game of Chess

To be able to play chess, one must know the rules of the game, that is, how each piece moves and what the goal of the game is. Novice chess players know this. They can move the pieces on the board, probably randomly at first. These rules of piece movement can be easily captured through operators in a solution space such as those in the previous examples. The states are the board states at any time, and the possible next states are determined by the legal moves available to the player whose turn it is to move. This type of knowledge, however, provides a player with no indication of *which* legal move would be the best one to make. We can categorize this knowledge as simple, support, and general. It merely permits the player to participate in the game, but not excel in it.

However, because the objective of playing chess is to win, deciding which move to make is a question of critical importance in terms of strategy and tactics. This knowledge can be considered specific as well as complex. Furthermore, the knowledge used by expert players on one single game can be categorized as tactical, whereas the knowledge that sets their strategy on a series of games can be considered *strategic*. The best chess players have developed such knowledge from experience, and they use it proficiently.

game when compared with that of the best in the world. There exist knowledgeable individuals who are not considered experts. Expert systems also contain the same two levels of knowledge. The difference is that the specific knowledge is at a level equivalent to an expert performer. Therefore, under our definition, expert systems are a subset of knowledge-based systems. All expert systems are knowledge-based, but not all knowledge-based systems are based on expert-level knowledge.

We have now introduced the categorization of knowledge according to the *degree* or the *quality* of the knowledge. This is particularly applicable to tactical and strategic, complex, specific knowledge. Therefore, for our purposes in this book, we refer to knowledge-based and expert systems generically as *knowledge-based systems*. There is little, if any, difference between expert and knowledge-based systems vis-à-vis their nature and construction. Their only difference is the degree or quality of the knowledge they reflect. Their only distinction is that although both employ general (and simple and support) knowledge as well as expert specific (and complex and tactical or strategic) knowledge, expert systems employ this knowledge at the level of a human expert. They are equivalent in every other way.

Let us now discuss how the three classifications of expertise found in Chapter 2 relate to expert systems.

First, knowledge-based systems excel at representing **associational knowledge.** This level of skill reflects heuristic ability or knowledge acquired mostly through the experience of a human, and elicited through the **knowledge engineering process** (see Chapter 10). The system's knowledge can then associate the observations (inputs) with specific causes (outputs). The knowledge used by this individual is typically in the form of if–then relationships that cover most, if not all, the possible situations. This is why *rules* are typically used to represent this knowledge. We discuss rule-based systems in great detail in Chapter 8.

Knowledge-based systems, on the other hand, are a poor fit for representing and solving problems requiring **motor skills expertise.** One reason is that knowledge about human physical performance, which motor skills typically represent, is very tacit. If a superstar tennis player is asked how he can hit the ball so hard, he would find it difficult to respond in a way that others could successfully copy. Second, much of this expert performance depends on his physical, and not cognitive, abilities. Present-day robots can use knowledge for making simple decisions well enough, but the actuators generally cannot react with the required speed and stability to perform physical tasks like human experts. Finally, robotic capabilities for processing of sensory data is not sufficiently developed at the present to permit them to navigate the physical world in a human-like fashion except when performing very limited tasks. Although robots have been able to tie knots in ropes for some time now [Inoue, 1985], they are still many years from becoming expert at playing tennis. Some progress has been made in this regard, however, as displayed by the RoboCup competition [Kitano, 1998].

The third type of knowledge is theoretical—understanding how things work internally. As you most likely have already guessed, theoretical expertise cannot be easily duplicated in knowledge-based systems at present. **Model-based reasoning (MBR) systems,** on the other hand, are a notable attempt to capture this deep knowledge and reason with it.

Finally, the terms *expert systems* and to a slightly lesser degree *knowledge-based systems* have been made synonymous with rule-based systems. This came about partly because heuristics are best represented as if–then rules. Additionally, early knowledge-based systems were invariably rule based. We do not agree with this generalization, and consider any system that uses knowledge to solve a problem to be knowledge-based. However, we admit that most traditional expert systems are rule based, and this characterization persists in the user community.

## ◇ ◇ ◇ Features of Knowledge-Based Systems

Knowledge-based systems have a number of distinct advantages as well as disadvantages when compared to other solutions, such as conventional software or human problem solvers.

### ADVANTAGES

A number of advantages encourage knowledge-based system development and use:

1. ***Wide distribution of scarce expertise.*** Knowledge-based systems reproduce the knowledge and skills possessed by experts—individuals who are considered to be experts because so few possess their specialized knowledge. This ability to reproduce an expert's knowledge allows for wide distribution of this expertise at a reasonable cost. For example, a company may have an expert on federal tax laws. If the company has various groups that need this expertise, it may profit by developing a knowledge-based system based on the knowledge and skills of its tax expert, thereby providing all these groups unlimited access to the expert's

knowledge. Although the development of this system may not be trivial, it may be less costly than hiring additional tax lawyers to handle the heavy demand.

2. ***Ease of modification.***   The fundamental concept of separating the knowledge from the reasoning mechanism eases the process of modifying the knowledge. This is an important feature in heuristic programming where changes may occur frequently. A tax expert system that could be easily modified year after year would illustrate this feature because tax legislation changes frequently. Ease of modification is a very desirable feature in these situations.

3. ***Consistency of answers.***   Different human experts often present dissimilar answers to the same problem. One human expert may even sometimes provide slightly different answers to the same problem on different occasions. In some cases, these variations are minor, with little or no consequence; in others, they are major flaws resulting from the poor health, emotional disposition, or stress of the expert. Knowledge-based systems, on the other hand, are always consistent in their problem-solving abilities, providing uniform answers at all times. There are no emotional or health considerations that can vary their performance.

4. ***Perpetual accessibility.***   Knowledge-based systems provide (almost) complete accessibility. They work 24 hours a day, weekends, and holidays. They take no sick leave or vacation.

5. ***Preservation of expertise.***   In situations where the turnover of experts is high, where an expert is in poor health, or about to retire, the experience and proficiency of an individual can be preserved for posterity in a knowledge-based system.

6. ***Solution of problems involving incomplete data.***   Knowledge-based systems, partially by virtue of their heuristic nature, are capable of solving problems with incomplete or inexact data. This is an important feature because complete and accurate information on a problem is rarely available in the real world.

7. ***Explanation of solution.***   Partly because of their heuristic nature, knowledge-based systems track the knowledge used to generate solutions. Thus, inquisitive or doubting users can query the system for explanations about how conclusions were derived. These explanations assist the user by clarifying and justifying the results and, additionally, provide a rudimentary form of tutoring, allowing the user to become more competent.

## DISADVANTAGES

Knowledge-based systems are not, however, the panacea some consider them to be. They have shortcomings of which a potential user needs to be aware:

1. ***Answers may not always be correct.***   Experts often make mistakes, so it is expected that knowledge-based systems may also make mistakes. These errors, however, can prove to be very costly, as might be the case with a tax expert system or a monitoring system that protects expensive equipment from serious malfunctions.

2. ***Limits not always recognized.***   Knowledge-based systems always endeavor to deduce a solution, regardless of whether the problem at hand is within the system's field of expertise. They do not know when they do not know. As a result, misleading or incorrect answers may be generated, which an unsuspecting user

may take as fact. Humans, in contrast, know the limits of their knowledge and, as a result, qualify their answers or do not attempt to solve problems outside the boundaries of their expertise.

3. ***Lack of common sense.*** Commonsense knowledge can be difficult to represent in knowledge-based systems. Some measure of common sense can be represented, but it must be done explicitly. For example, it is commonly known that under normal circumstances, if we drop a brick from the fifth-story window, it will fall to the ground, and possibly cause damage or injury. Unless explicitly told by its developer (through a rule), a knowledge-based system would not know this, because this fact is more common knowledge than specific domain knowledge. If a solution was to dispose of the brick by throwing it out a first story (open) window, a low probability of damage or injury would be expected. However, one would have to explicitly represent that throwing it from anything higher than that could, in fact, cause damage. Explicitly representing such knowledge can be impractical in most situations.

In summary, knowledge-based systems provide an excellent approach for solving a large class of problems, but each application must be chosen carefully so this technology is appropriately applied.

## ◆◇ ◆◇ ◆◇ Other Artificial Intelligence Technologies

Many other technologies either currently fall, or at one time fell, under the AI umbrella of technologies. We cover many of these in the following chapters because they directly impact KM systems. These include case-based reasoning, neural networks, and inductive learning. Others, such as conceptual maps, context-based reasoning, and repertory grids, indirectly affect KM systems, and we also discuss them in the next chapters. However, these are by no means the entire spectrum of "intelligent" technologies. In this section we briefly describe several others that also impact KM, albeit to a lesser degree.

### CONSTRAINT-BASED SYSTEMS

Many problems are defined by what *cannot* be done. While other systems use knowledge of what is typically done, constraint systems reflect what constraints restrict possible solutions. Limitations of this type are called *constraints.* For example, when we attempt to schedule a meeting, we first make sure that all individuals needing to attend the meeting are at the same location or can easily get to the same location. Then we must ensure that everyone is available at the same time. If we cannot ensure that everyone is in the same city, one of the constraints is violated. In some cases, constraints can be relaxed. For example, we could have a videoconference. *Constraint-based reasoning* is a problem-solving technique that, when given a set of variables and constraints on these variables, can find a set of values that satisfy all the constraints. Failing that, it relaxes these constraints until a solution can be found that meets all the other constraints that are not relaxed. Alternatively, a constraint can be viewed as a limitation on the set of values assigned to some set of variables. An equally common name for constraint-based reasoning is *constraint satisfaction,* and we often refer to problems of this type as *constraint satisfaction problems (CSPs).*

Reasoning thorough definition of constraints is certainly an attractive concept. Simply provide the computer program with the framework of the solution (the variables to be assigned a value and their legal potential values), what cannot be done (constraints between the values of the different variables), the criteria for a solution (all variables to be assigned with a legal value and no constraints to be violated), and sit back and wait for an answer. Many real-world problems can be easily defined in such terms, including scheduling, planning, and resource allocation. The problem is that inherently, CSP is nondeterministic polynomial (NP)-complete[1], an inherently difficult set of problems. Using heuristics and other nondeterministic procedures remedy the problem somewhat, but it is still a potentially infeasible situation for large problems.

## MODEL-BASED REASONING (MBR)

Models have been a part of scientific and engineering thinking for many years. As such, MBR can mean different things to different people. To philosophers of science, MBR implies the basis for scientific discovery. Kenneth Craik said in 1943 that people reason by performing ". . . thought experiments on internal models" [Magnani, 1999, p. 10]. MBR is an AI technique used to reason with, and about, models to explain the cause of abnormal behavior of engineered systems represented by these models. For example, consider fault detection, isolation, and recovery (FDIR) systems. The idea behind FDIR is that many system failures do not occur suddenly, but instead, begin as slight deviations from normal. These are called *incipient faults*. These faults progressively deteriorate at an arbitrary rate until the situation reaches the point of system failure. Examples of faults becoming disastrous failures are Three Mile Island, Chernobyl, TWA Flight 800, the Space Shuttles Challenger and Columbia accidents, and numerous other less publicized events. By detecting incipient faults at an early stage, diagnosing their causes, isolating them, and invoking a plan for recovery, disastrous consequences can be avoided. This can save lives, property, environmental damage, and ultimately, cost.

MBR, in our definition, is founded on the principle that knowledge about the internal workings of a *target system* can be used to recognize and diagnose its abnormal operation. MBR benefits from the knowledge about the internal workings of an engineered system, which is typically available from design specifications, drawings, books, and other such nonhuman sources. This knowledge is expressed as a system model. Therefore, model-based systems can be considered knowledge based, where the knowledge is the model of the system monitored. What we here consider to be model-based reasoning was developed in the late 1970s and early 1980s by several researchers, including Genesereth [1984], de Kleer [1976], and Davis [1984] among others. It has since drawn the interest of many researchers who have made significant contributions to the field. The underlying basis for MBR is the observation that engineers, scientists, and highly skilled technicians generally possess a much deeper understanding of the domain of interest. They use a model, mental or otherwise, to

---

[1]A problem is called *nondeterministic polynomial (NP)* if its solution (if one exists) can be guessed and verified in polynomial time; nondeterministic means that no particular rule is followed to make the guess. If a problem is NP and all other NP problems are polynomial-time reducible to it, the problem is NP-complete. When an NP-complete problem must be solved, one approach is to use a polynomial algorithm to approximate the solution; the answer thus obtained is not necessarily optimal but is reasonably close.

simulate its behavior. This enables them to successfully handle problems and situations they have never seen before. Model-based reasoning incorporates generic troubleshooting procedures common to diagnosing many types of systems. The general model-based diagnostic procedures can be roughly likened to experienced troubleshooters who use a measuring device and their knowledge of component behavior to test the system and identify the failed components. This technique is system independent, but requires the model of the target system to perform the troubleshooting. Thus, the same model-based reasoning technique can be used to diagnose other target systems by simply replacing the model. In any case, models are an integral part of model-based diagnostics.

Models have always played a large role in the diagnostic process. Detection of a fault starts when we note a change in the operation of the system. This change indicates that the system's behavior has deviated from normal, probably because of an abnormally operating component in the system. This implies that the normal operation of the system must be known and expressed to notice these changes. Traditionally, such normal behavior was modeled as a set of *threshold values* of several state variables measured in the target system. As long as these threshold values were not exceeded, the system was deemed to be operating normally. On the other hand, exceeding a threshold value was an indication that a deviation from normal had occurred in the system's behavior.

One of the advantages of MBR is that it can help diagnose faults not previously experienced. Thus, not every possible malfunction needs to be explicitly identified ahead of time. This is by virtue of modeling the normal behavior of the system, not its abnormal behavior. Furthermore, it can also use the model to effect some action to control, isolate, circumvent, or otherwise minimize the effect of the fault on the target system. By the nature of the model, it is assumed that every possible component described can be a cause of a failure, regardless of whether it ever has been before.

## DIAGRAMMATIC REASONING

Diagrammatic Reasoning refers to the understanding of concepts and ideas through the use of diagrams and imagery, as opposed to linguistic or algebraic representations [Glasgow et al., 1995]. Diagrammatic reasoning refers to utilizing diagrams and mental images in problem solving. The use of drawings for problem solving involves many of the same processes as using vision, which are scanning and perceiving. Drawings are used to represent information about some problem in a form that can be visually extracted easily, instead of attempting to reproduce the real world [Chandrasekaran et al., 1993]. The use of diagrammatic reasoning has been instrumental in developing systems such as Gelernter's Geometry Machine [Gelernter, 1963], which uses diagrams to prove geometric theorems, represented in a coordinate system. Other scientists extended this work, including the construction of systems that solve problems of qualitative structural analysis [Iwasaki et al., 1995]. For a detailed literature survey of early systems in diagrammatic reasoning refer to Jamnik [1996].

## FUZZY LOGIC

In the mid-1960s, Zadeh [1965] developed the concept of **fuzzy sets** to account for the numerous concepts used in human reasoning that are intrinsically vague and imprecise (e.g., tall, old). He later developed fuzzy logic to account for the imprecision of natural language quantifiers (e.g., many) and statements (e.g., not very likely). Because many experts express knowledge using a similar set of imprecise and subjective quantifiers, Zadeh's concepts appear to naturally apply to intelligent systems. Fuzzy logic, by its nature, addresses vagueness in natural language more than it does uncertainty.

In traditional set theory, membership in a set is binary—something either belongs to it or does not. Fuzzy sets theory addresses the inexactness in the world and in our common language by permitting partial membership in sets. In fuzzy logic, an agent or object's degree of membership in a set is determined by a **set membership function.** For example, a person of 6 ft 4 in. height is tall when compared with the general population. However, this person is likely to be considered short when compared to the population of professional basketball players. Thus, the person may have 0.82 membership in the fuzzy set of tall people, but might only enjoy a degree of membership of 0.32 in the fuzzy set of tall professional basketball players. Table 7-1 shows how a membership function might look.

Note that in Table 7-1 we have defined four fuzzy sets, *tall, short, statuesque,* and *NBA players.* The leftside column for each set depicts the height of a person, whereas the right-hand column depicts the corresponding degree of membership of a person with that height. This fuzzy representation can be used to express inexact quantities in business processes and facilitate the management of the knowledge.

## EVOLUTIONARY ALGORITHMS

Another technology making significant inroads in applications is that of evolutionary techniques. Encompassing *genetic algorithms* and *genetic programming,* these techniques mimic the natural selection process found in biological life forms. They adapt to their environment by making seemingly random changes to their offspring over the course of many centuries, and those that survive become living proof of the success of the changes made. They, in turn, can make further changes to adapt to current conditions even better. In this fashion, over millions of years, species become highly adapted to their environment, if only because only those lucky enough to have evolved with the right features managed to survive and pass these features on to their offspring.

Genetic algorithms work in generally the same way. A generation of *individuals* is created and each individual is compared to a *fitness function*—the equivalent of the

| TABLE 7-1  Fuzzy Sets Tall, Statuesque, Short, and NBA Players | | | | | | | |
|---|---|---|---|---|---|---|---|
| *Tall* | | *Statuesque* | | *Short* | | *NBA Players* | |
| 5′0″ | 0.00 | 5′0″ | 0.00 | 5′0″ | 1.00 | 5′0″ | 0.00 |
| 5′4″ | 0.08 | 5′4″ | 0.08 | 5′4″ | 0.92 | 5′4″ | 0.04 |
| 5′8″ | 0.32 | 5′8″ | 0.32 | 5′8″ | 0.68 | 5′8″ | 0.08 |
| 6′0″ | 0.50 | 6′0″ | 0.50 | 6′0″ | 0.50 | 6′0″ | 0.18 |
| 6′4″ | 0.82 | 6′4″ | 0.82 | 6′4″ | 0.18 | 6′4″ | 0.32 |
| 6′8″ | 0.98 | 6′8″ | 0.98 | 6′8″ | 0.02 | 6′8″ | 0.50 |
| 7′0″ | 1.00 | 7′0″ | 1.00 | 7′0″ | 0.00 | 7′0″ | 0.75 |

❖ ❖ ❖ ❖

environment. Those individuals that best perform to the fitness function survive and are adapted through two processes called *mutation* and *crossover.* These two processes make changes to the offspring of the surviving individuals of a generation to create slightly different features in such offspring, and thus possibly better equip them to satisfy the fitness function. The next generation then goes through the same process until no noticeable improvement vis-à-vis the fitness function is found in a group of individuals from one generation to the next. At that point, the individual that best fits the fitness function is said to be the optimal solution to the problem.

Genetic algorithms (GAs) are typically used for searching a problem space. They have also been shown to learn effectively if a good fitness function can be found. One disadvantage is the constraint in representing the data used as individuals so they can be easily mutated or crossed over. GAs can serve to optimize processes in organizations where many options exist and the best one is not readily clear.

## SUMMARY ◆ ◇ ◆

AI and its derivative area, knowledge-based systems, provide what are arguably the most important information technologies to fuel the growth of KM. The main reason is that human intelligence is very knowledge-intensive, and AI and knowledge-based systems deal intensively with knowledge. They employ knowledge of different types to address and solve problems. In fact, it can be said that the emergence of these technologies provided the spark that led to the KM systems discussed in this book.

The original AI approaches involved searches of a solution space, where domain knowledge was embedded in data structures or operators. The search-based AI methods navigated the solution space looking for a path between the initial state and the desired goal state. A path, therefore, represented a sequence of steps, decisions, or procedures that led to the goal state. Later versions of these methods added general knowledge, in the form of heuristic evaluation functions, to seek the most promising path to the goal. The use of such knowledge significantly facilitated finding an adequate path to the goal. However, they were still not sufficient to solve hard problems easily solved by humans.

Knowledge-based systems are an advance on the search-based methods. They replaced the general heuristic functions with more specific domain knowledge to solve more difficult problems. They employed experience-based heuristics in the form of cause-and-effect relationships to represent the domain. They replaced the solution spaces of the earlier systems that contained basic domain knowledge. These experience-based heuristics were typically in the form of if–then rules, thus the name *rule-based expert systems.*

AI and knowledge-based systems have several advantages as well as disadvantages. The advantages include wide distribution of scarce expertise, ease of modification, consistency of answers, perpetual accessibility, preservation of expertise, solution of problems involving incomplete data, and explanation of solution. The disadvantages include answers that may not always be correct.

Finally, this chapter briefly discusses other AI technologies that, although not employed heavily at the present in KM systems, have significant promise for application in future KM systems. These include model-based reasoning, constraint-based systems, diagrammatic reasoning, fuzzy logic, and evolutionary algorithms.

# KEY TERMS ◇ ◇ ◇

- artificial intelligence—p. 101
- algorithms—p. 109
- associational knowledge—p. 119
- AUTHORIZER'S ASSISTANT—p. 117
- COOKER—p. 117
- domain knowledge—p. 102
- fuzzy sets—p. 124
- GenAID—p. 117
- GUIDON—p. 117

- heuristics—p. 109
- heuristic functions—p. 109
- heuristic search—p. 109
- inference mechanism—p. 116
- knowledge engineering process—p. 119
- model-based reasoning systems—p. 120
- motor skills expertise—p. 120
- MYCIN—p. 116

- PROSPECTOR—p. 116
- random search—p. 110
- set membership function—p. 125
- shells—p. 116
- solution space—p. 105
- symbol manipulation—p. 102
- systematic blind search—p. 111
- tactical knowledge—p. 118
- XCON—p. 116

# REVIEW QUESTIONS ◇ ◇ ◇

1. What are the two types of knowledge typically found in intelligent systems? Describe each type and distinguish between them.
2. Why are knowledge-based (expert) systems more capable of solving real-world problems than search-based AI methods?
3. List the advantages of knowledge-based systems.
4. List the disadvantages of knowledge-based systems.
5. What is a heuristic?
6. What is a heuristic function?
7. What is a heuristic search?

# APPLICATION EXERCISES ◇ ◇ ◇

1. How would you draw the solution space for the game of tic-tac-toe? Do it for the first three moves.
2. Classify the following types of knowledge as *associational, motor skill,* or *theoretical.* Explain your classification.
   a. Repairing a broken vase
   b. Repairing a flat tire on a bicycle
   c. Tying a shoe lace
   d. Replacing a burned out light bulb
   e. Writing a computer program
   f. Debugging a computer program
   g. Assembling a model car from a set of instructions
   h. Baking a cake
   i. Diagnosing an automobile
3. Identify five commonly used heuristics to get into a house or apartment when you are locked out. Why is each of these a heuristic?
4. Consider a jigsaw puzzle. Identify a set of heuristics that can be used in assembling the puzzle.
5. Finding a path from one location to another within any city involves the use of heuristics because traffic patterns vary from hour to hour and day to day. Pick two places in your city (e.g., your apartment and campus) and identify a set of heuristics based on the time of day that you use daily when traveling from one to the other.

## REFERENCES ❖ ❖ ❖

Campbell's keeps kettles boiling with personal consultant. *Ainteractions,* 1(1) (August), 3–4.

Aikins, J.S., Kunz, J.C., and Shortliffe, E.H. 1983. PUFF: An expert system for interpretation of pulmonary function data. *Computers and Biomedical Research.* 16, 199–208.

Bennett, J., Creary, L., Engelmore, R., and Melosh, R. 1978. A Knowledge-Based Consultant for Structural Analysis, Report No. 78–23, Computer Science Department, Stanford University (September).

Berliner, H. 1980. Backgammon program beats world champ. *SIGART Newsletter,* 69 (January), 6–9.

Bonnet, A., and Dahan, C. 1983. Oil Well Data Interpretation Using Expert System and Pattern Recognition Techniques, Proc. 8th Int. Conf. Artificial Intelligence, Menlo Park, CA, pp. 185–189.

Buchanan, B.G., and Shortliffe, E.H. 1984. *Rule-Based Expert Systems.* Addison Wesley, Reading, MA.

Clancey, W.J. 1979. Tutoring rules for guiding a case-method dialogue. *International Journal of Man-Machine Studies,* 11(1) (January), 25–49.

Duda, R., Hart, P.E., Nilsson, N.J., Reboh, R., Slocum, J., and Sutherland, G. 1978. Development of the PROSPECTOR Consultation System for Mineral Exploration, SRI Report, Stanford Research Institute, Menlo Park, CA (October).

Gonzalez, A.J., Osborne, R.L., Kemper, C., and Lowenfeld, S. 1986. On-line diagnosis of turbine generators using artificial intelligence. *IEEE Transactions on Energy Conversion,* EC-1(2) (June), 68–74.

Greenblat, R.D., Eastlake, D.E., and Crocker, S.D. 1967. The Greenblat Chess Program, Proc. Int. Machine Learning Workshop, Ithaca, NY.

Hsu, F., Anantharaman, T., Campbell, M., and Nowatzyk, A. 1990. A grandmaster chess machine. *Scientific American,* 263(4) (October), 44–50.

Inoue, H. 1985. Building a Bridge Between AI and Robotics, Proc. 9th Int. Joint Conf. on Artificial Intelligence, pp. 1231–1237.

Kitano, H. (Guest Ed.). 1998. Special issue: RoboCup. *Applied Artificial Intelligence,* 12(2–3), www.robocup.org.

Leonard-Barton, D., and Sviokla, J.J. 1988. Putting expert systems to work. *Harvard Business Review,* (March/April), 91–98.

Lindsay, R.K., Buchanan, B.G., Feigenbaum, E.A., and Lederberg, J. 1980. *Applications of Artificial Intelligence for Organic Chemistry.* McGraw-Hill, New York.

McDermott, J. 1982. R1: A rule-based configurer of computer systems. *Artificial Intelligence,* 19(1) (September), 39–88.

Newell, A., and Simon, H.A. 1963. GPS, a program that simulates human thought. In Fiegenbaum, E.A., and Feldman, J. (Eds.), *Computers and Thought.* McGraw-Hill, New York, pp. 279–296.

Peterson, I. 1991. The checkers challenge. *Science News,* 140(3) (July), 40–41.

Samuel, A.L. 1963. Some studies in machine learning using the game of chess. In Feigenbaum, E.A., and Feldman, J. (Eds.), *Computers and Thought.* McGraw-Hill, New York, pp. 71–105.

Schaeffer, J., Culberson, J., Treloar, N., Knoght, B., Lu, P., and Szafron, D. 1991. Checkers program to challenge for world championship. *SIGART Bulletin,* 2(2), 3–5.

Shortliffe, E.H. 1976. *Computer-Based Medical Consultations: Mycin.* American Elsevier, New York.

Slate, D.J., and Atkin, L.R. 1977. CHESS 4.5: The Northwestern University chess program. In Frey, P.W. (Ed.), *Chess Skills in Man and Machine.* Springer-Verlag, Berlin, pp. 82–118.

Tanimoto, S.L. 1987. *The Elements of Artificial Intelligence.* Computer Science Press, New York.

Underwood, W.E., and Summerville, P.J. 1981. PROJ-CON: A Prototype Project Management Consultant, Proc. Int. Conf. Cybernetics and Society (October), pp. 149–155.

Webster's. 1960. *Webster's New World Dictionary of the American Language.* World Publishing, New York.

Weizenbaum, J. 1965. ELIZA: A computer program for the study of natural language communication between man and machine. *Communications of the ACM,* 9(1), 36–45.

Winograd, T. 1972. *Understanding Natural Language.* Academic Press, New York.

Zadeh, L.A. 1965. Fuzzy sets. *Information and Control,* 8(3), 338–353.

CHAPTER 8

# Preserving and Applying Human Expertise: Knowledge-Based Systems[1]

## ◇ ◇ ◇ Introduction

As we saw in the previous chapter, a computer's ability to "think" like a human is one of the technological keys to managing knowledge. It stands to reason—knowledge is only meaningful in the context of the human mind. If we are to preserve it, reuse it, and maintain it within an electronic machine, then that electronic machine must have some semblance of compatibility with the human brain. In this section, we expand on the important technology of **knowledge-based (KB) systems** that was introduced in the last chapter.

KB systems, as the name implies, deal with solving problems by exercising knowledge. KB systems are uniquely developed to work with knowledge in some way. Therefore, there is a natural association between them and KM systems.

KB systems were originally devised as problem-solving techniques, rather than frameworks for KM systems. As they matured, however, they were found to excel at representing human knowledge, especially as it relates to heuristics. As such, they became an almost ideal tool for preserving and reusing the human knowledge required for problem solving. If a problem could be solved through a representation of human knowledge, then preserving that knowledge becomes very important for repeatedly solving the same or similar problems in the future. Thus, KB systems are considered adept at *preserving* knowledge for later distribution and *application*. Furthermore, as we shall later see, the process of building a KB system naturally becomes the process of

---

[1]This chapter is written in collaboration with Douglas D. Dankel.

drawing out the knowledge from its sources and representing it in a form more natural for machines. The source of this knowledge, of course, is the human being—specifically, an expert in solving the kind of problems the system is designed to solve. This is the process of **knowledge engineering.** Although these tasks (preservation and application of knowledge) do not comprise the entire scope of KM (it also includes creation and sharing), KB systems do indeed provide extensive support for KM.

In the previous chapter, we introduce and define KB systems in a general way. In this chapter, we discuss in detail how KB systems work, and how they are built. We specifically focus on rule-based systems, because they are the most popular of all KB systems, but provide a brief discussion of frame-based systems as well. We start by examining KB systems from several different perspectives.

## ◈ ◈ ◈ Knowledge-Based Systems from Different Points of View

Describing KB systems reminds us of the story of the five blind men who encountered an elephant for the first time. After each touched the elephant, each described it from his uniquely different point of view—"it's a snake" (the trunk), "it's a spear" (a tusk), "it's a fan" (an ear), "it's a tree" (a leg), and "it's a wall" (the body). Similarly, a KB system can appear quite different depending on one's perspective.

Each blind man experienced some limited aspect about the elephant and formed his impression based on his own constrained information. When learning about KB systems, we must be careful to gain exposure to the whole, and not just to a few limited features. Without this perspective, we are like the blind men, having formed an incomplete and imprecise understanding of what a KB system really is. Consequently, we are unable to utilize its power effectively and efficiently.

We limit the discussion here to two perspectives, (1) the end user of the KB system, (2) and the developer of the KB system.

### Knowledge-Based Systems: End Users' Point of View

The first point of view is that of end users, the individuals for whom the KB system is developed. See Figure 8-1. From end users' perspective, a KB system consists of three components: the **intelligent program,** the **user interface**, and a **problem-specific database**.

The intelligent program is the core of the KB system from the end users' points of view. It is what solves the end users' problems. How exactly it works is not important to most end users—only that it works and works reliably. The end user sees the intelligent program as a black box. It is within this component that the knowledge is represented and stored. The intelligent program also "exercises" the knowledge to solve problems, answer questions, or otherwise accomplish the objectives of the KB system.

The user interface is the users' window to this program, albeit a narrow one. Through it, end users can control the system to solve their current problems. The user interface provides functions that permit end users to exercise the knowledge, but it does not typically provide them access to this knowledge. Such is rarely necessary and often dangerous from a system security standpoint.

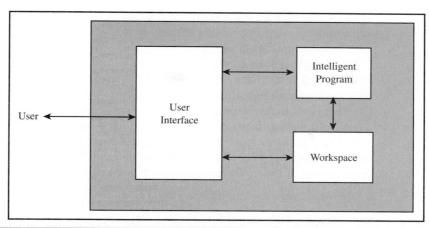

Some examples of what the user interface can do include:

1. Enabling the intelligent program to pose questions to the user about the problem at hand;
2. Providing explanations about why it (the intelligent program) is asking particular questions;
3. Allowing the user to query the intelligent program as to why or how a particular decision was made;
4. Displaying the results;
5. Providing graphic output for the results;
6. Allowing the user to save or print the results.

The problem-specific database contains the final component visible to the end user. The name *database* is a bit of a misnomer, as it is not really a database per se. It is merely the working space where the system reads any inputs and writes its outputs. It contains all the information provided (either automatically or by the user through the keyboard) about the current problem (the *inputs*), as well as all the conclusions that the intelligent program is able to derive. These conclusions include both the final ones representing the solution required by the user, as well as intermediate ones that act as stepping-stones in the intelligent program's path to the final conclusion. We refer to this database as the *workspace* in this textbook.

### Knowledge-Based Systems: Developers' Point of View

Developers of a KB system are commonly called *knowledge engineers* (KEs). Traditionally (for the last 20 years or so), a knowledge engineer would build a KB system by personally interacting with a domain expert or other knowledgeable person. Through a series of interviews with this individual or group of individuals, the KE elicits the knowledge possessed by the individual or group of individuals and incorporates it into the KB system using that system's representational paradigm (rules, frames, etc.). Nowadays, however, automated tools are used to assist the KE in this laborious task, although there is still a significant amount of face-to-face interviews.

From the KE's view, a KB system consists of two major components: the **intelligent program** and the **development environment** (Figure 8-2).

### Intelligent Program

The intelligent program is the same one we saw in the previous section. This program is identical to what the end user sees except that the KE can open the black box and see what is inside it. Instead of seeing the intelligent program as a big black box, the KE sees it as an open box made up of components critical to its essence. The components making up the intelligent program are the **knowledge base** and its associated **inference engine**. These components are the keys to understanding KB systems. Their importance comes from the third of the three fundamental characteristics of all KB systems we describe in Chapter 7—the clear and clean separation between the knowledge used by the system (knowledge base) and the program that utilizes it for problem solving (inference engine). The knowledge base contains the knowledge, whereas the inference engine contains the functionality for implementing the automated reasoning that exercises the knowledge and arrives at a solution. We focus on these two components in this chapter.

**Knowledge Base** The knowledge base is arguably the most important component of a KB system. It contains the entire relevant, domain-specific, problem-solving

◆ ◇ ◆ FIGURE 8-2 Knowledge Engineer's View of a Knowledge-Based System

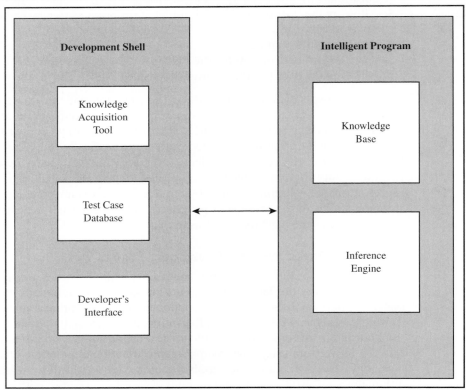

knowledge gathered by KEs from the various sources available to them. The knowledge base is the knowledge that is to be managed.

How to represent the knowledge depends basically on its nature—functional, heuristic, or structured. Functional knowledge is in the realm of traditional functions. Conventional programming techniques address this form of knowledge. On the other hand, most KB applications occur in domains where conventional computational problem-solving approaches either do not exist or do not work well. The knowledge, therefore, consists of the heuristics we discuss in the previous chapter—rules of thumb and shortcuts learned and developed by the expert over years of practical problem solving. The KE must elicit these to build the system. Heuristic knowledge is most naturally expressed as rules (*IF-THEN statements*). For example:

> *If the house plan includes a pool, then add $15,000 to the price.*

Alternatively, the knowledge may be more structured in nature. Such a structure could associate several components to an assembly. For instance, a traditional manufacturing corporation consists of several departments, including marketing, engineering, manufacturing, accounting, human resources, and information technology (IT), as well as the senior management staff. This knowledge is not naturally conditional, but structured, because it expresses an association of components to their whole. Representing this knowledge effectively requires a different paradigm, because rules do not naturally apply. A **frame** would be more conducive to representing this knowledge.

Several other knowledge representation schemes can be used to represent knowledge besides rules and frames: predicates, associative networks, and objects as well as others. Each of these schemes has different advantages and disadvantages, and a KE must be aware of them when developing a KB system. We only discuss rules and frames in this chapter, because they are by far the most popular. Please refer to Gonzalez and Dankel [1993] for a description of the others.

Regardless of its nature, knowledge enables the KB system to solve problems or answer questions in the domain of interest. This knowledge presents us with the challenge of managing it.

**Inference Engine**    The second important component of the intelligent program is the inference engine. The inference engine is the *interpreter* of the knowledge stored in the knowledge base. It examines the contents of the knowledge base and the input data accumulated about the current problem, and exercises the knowledge to derive the conclusions or answer the questions asked.

The knowledge base can be thought of as a very large graph (Figure 8-3). On the left side of the graph are a series of nodes representing all the signs, symptoms, characteristics, and features used as inputs when attempting to solve a relevant problem. Nodes representing all possible solutions to the problem are on the right side. All other nodes are the intermediate conclusions, which the system derives in the progression of deriving the final solution. The lines connecting the nodes in the graph depict the knowledge used by the expert during problem solving. This knowledge has been elicited from the expert and stored in the knowledge base. It specifies how new conclusions can be derived from existing facts or from earlier derived conclusions. The process of deriving a solution to a

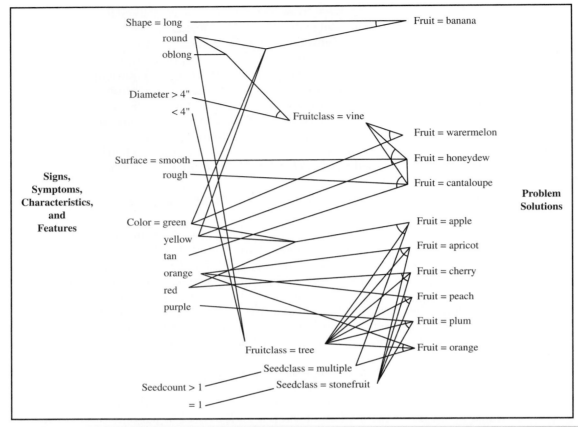

**FIGURE 8-3 Problem Description Graph**

problem can be viewed simplistically as one of finding a "knowledge path" (a *connection*) between the inputs and a conclusion that are capable of assigning a value to the conclusion. In this case, the knowledge associating the nodes is in the form of rules.

The system depicted in Figure 8-3 is a classification system for fruits. The answer sought is whether the fruit in question is a banana, a watermelon, a honeydew, a cantaloupe, an apple, an orange, a plum, a cherry, or an apricot. It can only be one of these. The inputs on the left-hand side are features of the fruit that can be observed and reported by a human user. These are, specifically, the color of the fruit and the texture of its skin (surface); and its diameter, shape, and seedcount. Finally, we see that there are some intermediate hypotheses, namely, *Fruitclass*, and *Seedclass*. These are abstractions of some knowledge to facilitate further derivations. The lines between the nodes are the rules that associate the inputs to intermediate or final conclusions. They are read by looking at the line's left- and right-side terminals. The nodes on the left side are the premises (*IF*s) of the rule. Those at the right side are its conclusions (*THEN*). For example, at the bottom of the figure, a line links *Seedcount* > 1 to *Seedclass* = *multiple*. This says that *IF* the seedcount is more than 1, *THEN* the seedclass is multiple, a rather obvious, but useful inference.

A short arc linking some lines together near the left-side terminals indicates that these associations are combined or "ANDed" together. For example, in the middle of the figure, where cantaloupe is located, it can be seen that *IF* the color is tan, *AND* If the surface is rough *AND* If the fruitclass is vine, *THEN* the fruit is a cantaloupe. In this way, the classification knowledge can be formalized and displayed in a form relatively easy for the human to see and understand. However, note that this is only an abstract representation for the benefit of humans because the system uses internal representations and the workspace to compute the solution. The rules are explicitly written in a later subsection.

The inference engine attempts to find these paths between the inputs and the solutions. These paths can be sought in several different ways. The inference engine might attempt to work from the inputs to the solutions (called **forward reasoning**), from the solutions back to the inputs **(backward reasoning),** or from both ends simultaneously **(bidirectional reasoning).** The particular method used depends on the characteristics of the problem domain and the reasoning of the expert. We discuss these in detail later in this chapter.

Although there are various means for representing knowledge in a knowledge base (e.g., rules, frames), it should be obvious that the inference engine must be able to support the representation scheme appropriate for the application. This problem is actually much more significant than it appears, because many inference engines may use the same knowledge representation paradigms but implement them using different methods or syntax. This problem is alleviated somewhat by the existence of development environments.

## Development Environment

The development environment is a set of tools that facilitates the creation of the knowledge within the intelligent program. The development environment assists the KE in structuring, debugging, modifying, and expanding the knowledge gathered from the expert. A development environment typically contains three components: a **knowledge acquisition tool,** a **test case database,** and the **developer's interface.** Depending on the type and size of the KB system, some of these components are not always necessary or always provided. Nevertheless, we describe them all below.

**Knowledge Acquisition Tool**   The knowledge acquisition tool assists the KE in the construction of the knowledge base. The KEs interact with experts and acquire knowledge from them. KEs must take this knowledge and incorporate it within the KB system.

In its simplest form, this tool merely serves as a knowledge base editor, providing a view of the knowledge and allowing the KE to edit it as desired. In its most complicated form, this tool can provide a wide range of features, for example, assisting the KE in locating "bugs" within the knowledge base. It can also compare existing knowledge to new knowledge in an attempt to second guess what the KEs really mean, should they not be as precise and exact as required. Additionally, it can provide bookkeeping functions to keep a record of all the modifications made, the person who made them, and when and why they were made. A tool that provides these features can greatly assist the KE and significantly shorten the KB system's development time.

**Test Case Database**   The KE often makes potentially significant changes to the knowledge base by deleting or modifying existing knowledge or adding new knowledge. Deleting existing knowledge might unwittingly eliminate important relationships. Likewise, modifying existing knowledge might incorrectly change important relationships. Finally, adding new knowledge might introduce contradictions with existing knowledge. Any of these could compromise the accuracy of the overall knowledge base. Therefore, checks must be made to ensure that these changes improve instead of degrade the problem-solving abilities of the KB system.

To aid the KE in verifying that these changes are appropriate, many KB systems include a test case database. The test case database consists of sample problems that have been successfully executed on the KB system. Whenever a change to the knowledge base is made, we can execute these test cases to verify that these benchmark test cases are still solved correctly.

**Developer's Runtime Interface**　The final component of the development shell is the developer's runtime interface. This is the same interface seen by the end user, as we discuss previously, except that it contains additional features to assist the KE in the development process.

Developers' runtime interface allows KEs to exercise the knowledge base, as it is modified and tested. This permits them to see exactly how the system can operate when delivered to the end user. Features within this interface include:

1. The ability to question the system about what portions of the knowledge are currently in use in the problem-solving process;
2. Explanations about why certain questions are asked;
3. Details on why and how particular results are derived;
4. A convenient interaction using menus, natural language, or graphic displays.

When combined with the features of the knowledge acquisition tool, this provides the KE with a powerful environment for developing a KB system.

## ◆ ◇ ◆ Representing Knowledge

We now know what KB systems are. Next we will see how they work. We first focus on how knowledge is represented in a KB system. In terms of the two major components of the intelligent program, representation is more closely associated with the knowledge base. This is important from the standpoint of KM, because to manage knowledge, we must first understand how it can be represented.

We suggest in an earlier section that there are two basic types of knowledge, heuristic and **structured knowledge.** Rules (also called *productions*) are the most popular (and natural) way to represent the former; frames are typically the most suitable way to represent the latter. We discuss both, but focus on rule-based systems.

### Rules

Rules are arguably the most important knowledge representation paradigm. This can be attributed to the excellent ability of rules to represent heuristic knowledge. Rule-based systems also tend to be highly intuitive to implement and to understand once implemented. Additionally, rules represent knowledge in a natural and very common form used by people to express knowledge in many types of domains.

If you question skilled problem solvers about how they solve problems or what causes them to draw certain conclusions, they typically respond with knowledge expressed in a rule format. For instance:

***Well, I noticed that A, B, and C were present in this problem, and these three facts imply that D is true.***

or

***If A, B, and C are present, then you can conclude D.***

People find it very natural to express knowledge using rules. This is especially true for domain knowledge they have accumulated over time, which has resulted in internal empirical associations (i.e., heuristics). Rules, therefore, represent knowledge using this *IF-THEN* format. The *IF* portion of a rule is a *condition* (also called a *premise* or an *antecedent*), which tests the truth-value of a set of facts. If these are found true, the *THEN* portion of the rule (also called the *action*, the *conclusion*, or the *consequent*) is inferred as a new set of facts.

Rules can be used to express a wide range of associations. They can express situations and actions that must be taken, for example:

- If dark clouds are rolling in from the west, the wind is increasing, and lightning strikes are occurring, then you should seek cover in a building.
- If you are driving a car and an emergency vehicle approaches, then you should slow down and pull to the side of the road to allow the emergency vehicle to pass.
- If baking a cake, test for completion by inserting a toothpick in the cake's center. If it emerges clean, the cake is ready to be taken out of the oven.

Rules can also express premises and conclusions that can be drawn from those premises:

- If your body temperature is above 100° F, then you are running a fever.
- If the outside temperature is below freezing, the gas gauge on your car does not register empty, and the engine turns over but will not start, then it is highly likely that you have a frozen gas line.
- If the loan applicant's salary is greater than $50,000, and the number of outstanding loans is less than two, then the applicant will pay the loan and is considered "good risk."

In addition, rules can express antecedents and their consequences:

- If you don't read the textbook or attend class, then you will flunk the exam.
- If the tub's drain is clogged and the water is left running, then the floor will become wet.
- If the electric bill is past due and your credit rating is bad, then your electricity will be cut off.

These rules can be categorized as situation–action, premise–conclusion, or antecedent–consequent.

With **pattern matching,** rule-based systems use automated reasoning methods to provide the logical progression from data to the desired conclusions. This progression causes new facts to be derived and leads to a solution of the problem. Thus, the process of problem solving in knowledge-based systems is to create a series of inferences that create a "path" between the problem definition and its solution. This series of inferences is progressive in nature and is called an **inference chain.**

To illustrate this idea, consider the following very simple example. Suppose we are building a KB system for forecasting the weather over the next 12 to 24 hours during the summer in Florida. Among many others, it would contain the following rule:

| | |
|---|---|
| *Rule 1* | |
| *IF* | The ambient temperature is above 90° F |
| *THEN* | The weather is hot |

Although rule 1 alone does not say much, the advantage of a rule-based system is that a group of rules can be created to form an inference chain capable of reaching a more meaningful conclusion. Adding the following two rules illustrates this idea:

| | |
|---|---|
| *Rule 2* | |
| *IF* | The relative humidity is greater than 65% |
| *THEN* | The atmosphere is humid |
| | |
| *Rule 3* | |
| *IF* | The weather is hot and the atmosphere is humid |
| *THEN* | Thunderstorms are likely to develop |

*Facts*, on the other hand, are statements considered true within the KB system. Practically speaking, facts represent the data used by the system. By definition, facts are assumed to be true and are typically found on the workspace. Let us suppose that the following facts exist:

***The ambient temperature is 92° F.***

and

***The relative humidity is 70%.***

Rules 1 and 2 would "see" these facts and have their conditions (IF's) "satisfied" by them. They can now deduce the following new facts:

***The atmosphere is humid.***

and

***The weather is hot.***

These newly derived facts, in turn, *satisfy* the premises of rule 3, causing it to derive the new fact:

**Thunderstorms are likely to develop.**

Of course, in this simple example, a single rule could have been written to reach the same conclusion directly:

| | |
|---|---|
| *Rule 1-A* | |
| *IF* | The ambient temperature is above 90° F and the atmospheric relative humidity >65% |
| *THEN* | Thunderstorms are likely to develop |

Nevertheless, the example shows how a chain of rules would work. Additionally, there may be other rules that use the facts "the weather is hot" and "the atmosphere is humid" for other purposes, making a good case for keeping the three rules separate.

The reasoning shown above always conveys complete certainty in its inferences. Unfortunately, in the real world, cause and effect relationships are not always completely understood and, thus, cannot always be said to be certain. In the thunderstorm example, the inference progresses from the cause to the effect. Yet, because our understanding of the meteorological phenomenon is incomplete, we hedge our bets and assign a measure of uncertainty to the conclusion derived (i.e., thunderstorms are *likely*). Uncertainty management is an important part of human reasoning. Therefore, it is very important in artificial intelligence, and specifically, in KB systems. A discussion of uncertainty management and the techniques available are beyond the scope of this book. Refer to Gonzalez and Dankel [1993] for more information.

## Frames

Recognizing that rules do not provide the ability to group facts into associated clusters or to associate relevant procedural knowledge with some fact or group of facts, Marvin Minsky developed the representation scheme called *frames* [Minsky, 1975]. Frames attempt to account for our ability to deal with new situations (either objects or actions) encountered each day by using our existing knowledge of previous events, concepts, and situations. Frames formed the basis of objects and object-oriented programming (OOP). In fact, OOP was once considered to be a branch of AI in the 1980s. Nowadays, however, OOP has severed all but its historical ties to AI, and is a separate field.

Frames are to structured knowledge what rules are to heuristic knowledge—an excellent way to represent these respective types of knowledge. Frames offer the ability to represent structured knowledge about physical or conceptual objects more easily than rules. They have become increasingly popular within KB systems as the limitations of rules for representing structured knowledge become obvious. Frames are also quite intuitive but in a different way than rules. The average person does not find frames to be as natural a way to express knowledge as rules. However, technically educated individuals (scientists, engineers, and technicians) find them very natural indeed as a way to express the attributes of things or concepts. We describe frames in two ways—a simple one and a more complex one. The simple one serves the needs of those readers only interested in a basic understanding of frames. The more complex one satisfies the more technically oriented readers.

### Simple Frames

Consider the concept of an automobile. On hearing the word or seeing a picture of one, we immediately associate many attributes to automobiles. We think of a means of transportation; we think of its physical attributes (e.g., four wheels, engine, number of doors, steering wheel, accelerator and brake pedals, air-conditioning and heating system, and sound system). The more mechanically inclined tend to think of its engine type, the turbocharger, the ignition control computer, etc. We may also think about abstract features such as its performance (0 to 60 mph time), its looks (red convertible), its safety implications (air bags, antilock brakes), its social implications (Rolls Royce vs. Yugo). We also associate functions to it (e.g., starting the car, driving a stick shift, or steering the car). The point is that we associate attributes with the word *automobile*. These attributes help in making decisions or answering questions about automobiles.

A frame provides the structure or framework for representing structured knowledge. Using a structure consisting of a frame name and a set of attribute-value pairs, a frame represents a stereotypical situation (i.e., an object, a concept, or a process) from the real world. In this way, frames are very similar to database records. For example, Avelino buys a brand new red Mustang convertible for his company car. A KB system that somehow needs to use this information (maybe asset inventory or maintenance management) builds a frame describing this automobile. Table 8-1 depicts this.

---

**TABLE 8-1  Basic Frame for Avelino's New Mustang**

*Frame:* Mustang
Manufacture: Ford
Country of manufacture: USA
Model: Mustang GT
Number of wheels: 4
Number of doors: 2
Year: 2002
Engine size: 4.6L-V8
Transmission: Standard
Reliability: Medium
Body style: Convertible
Color: Red
Miles per gallon: 19.7
Serial number: 12345A67890B
Owner: Avelino

The frame described in Table 8-1, although certainly not complete, provides a reasonable description of a Ford Mustang. It is clear that there is no heuristic knowledge involved here. Frames can be used to so describe things, ideas, concepts, organizations, policies, and relationships. However, to truly take advantage of the power of frames, we must delve into them a bit more deeply. We do so in the next section.

## Details about Frames

If we wish to describe an entire rental car fleet using frames, it would be silly to include the number of wheels in each and every frame. Everyone knows that all cars have four wheels. Less widely known is that all Mustangs have two doors, but it is likewise silly to include that information on each Mustang frame. The solution is to take all the attributes that do not change — the general ones — and move them up to a higher level frame. Then we allow the more specific frames to *inherit* that information. In this way, it is not necessary to repeat it.

Additionally, functional attributes (attributes whose values are executable functions) can add significant representational power to frames. If we wish to know the reliability of 2002 Mustangs based on the fleet's maintenance record, this number could conceivably change regularly. A function attached to this attribute that could access the up-to-date information on the fleets' experience with 2002 Mustangs and provide its value to the seeker would be significantly better than simply responding with *Medium*. Frames permit functional attachments such as these.

Finally, the value for each attribute could have secondary characteristics, which could become useful knowledge in determining a value. For example, if the function to determine the reliability history for some reason is not able to access the data, a default value could be provided that gives a best estimate of the value sought. We next look at frames in a deeper fashion, describing how these features are incorporated into the simple concept of frames presented in the previous subsection.

The attributes of the attribute-value pairs are often called **slots** whereas the values are called *fillers*. The fillers can additionally be subdivided into **facets,** each having its own associated value. The *VALUE:* facet is the most important of all facets. It contains the actual value assigned to that slot. It is analogous to holding the value of a variable. The following example illustrates this structure.

Continuing with our example of Table 8-1, Table 8-2 shows a small frame describing general information about an automobile. This frame indicates that automobiles have attributes (slots) for their manufacturer, country of manufacture, color, model, reliability, miles per gallon, year, and owner. Note that the frame is now significantly more complex, containing much more knowledge than the one of Table 8-1.

Several other facets besides the *VALUE:* facet can be associated with each slot. These include, but are not limited to:

- *Range.* The range of possible values for this slot;
- *Legal-values.* The set of discrete possible values the slot can take;
- *Default.* The value to assume if none is explicitly stated;
- *If–needed.* Procedure(s) for determining the actual value;
- *If–added.* Procedures to execute when a value is specified for the slot;
- *If–changed.* Procedures to execute if the value of the slot is changed.

**TABLE 8-2  Generic Frame for an Automobile**

Generic **Automobile** Frame
  *Specialization–of:* vehicle
  *Generalization–of:* (station-wagon coupe sedan convertible)
Manufacturer
  Value:
  Legal-values: (Ford Mazda BMW Saab GM Chrysler)
  Default: Ford
Country-of-manufacture
  Value:
  Legal-values: (USA Japan Germany Sweden)
  If–needed: (get-origin)
  Default: USA
Model
  Value:
  Legal-values: (Taurus Focus Mustang Crown-Victoria)
Color
  Value:
  Legal-values: (Black White Red Persian-Aqua)
  If–needed: (Examine-Title or Consult-Dealer or Look-at-automobile)
Reliability
  Value:
  Legal-values: (high medium low)
  Default: medium
Miles per Gallon
  Value:
  Range: (0–100)
Year
  Value:
  Range: (1940–1990)
  If–changed: (error: value cannot be modified)
Owner
  Value:
  If–added: (apply-for-title and obtain-tag and pay-sales-tax)

These last three facets—all procedures—are also called **daemons** or *demons*. They represent the previously mentioned ability to incorporate procedural knowledge (functions) within the structure of the frame.

One problem with frames is that one can get carried away with defining attributes (slots) for the frame and assigning values. In many cases, these attributes have to be repeated if we want to define a frame for another specific automobile. This need led to the concept of *inheritance* as a way to minimize the attributes of frames. Let us look at this a bit further.

**TABLE 8-3  Coupe Frame**

*Generic **Coupe** Frame*
Specialization–of: **AUTOMOBILE**
Generalization–of: (**Suzie-Smith's-automobile,**
 **John-Doe's-automobile Avelino's-automobile**)
Doors
 Value: 2

When you examine the description for the coupe model in Table 8-3, you are immediately struck with its simplicity. Because this frame describes a generalized subclass of automobiles, it does not need to represent all features shared by all automobiles and coupes. It only needs to identify those characteristics that distinguish it from a generic automobile. This indicates the concept of *inheritance* and it shows how inheritance provides significant economy within the overall representation. The concept of inheritance originated with Minsky's frames, and has since been adopted as a central feature of OOP. This inheritance feature of frames is illustrated by the *Generalization–of* slot in the more general frame. Likewise, this general frame is in turn a specialization of an even more general frame, the **VEHICLE** frame. This is indicated by the *Specialization–of* slot. Particular automobiles (objects or instances of classes in OOP) can be created using a general frame even if they are different in some features (one has a V-6 engine whereas the other has a V-8).

The inheritance hierarchy is described in Figure 8-4. The child frames inherit from the parent frame, which in turn, inherit from its parent frame. Note that multiple inheritance—the ability to inherit from more than one parent frame—is allowed in many frame systems. However, it is heavily frowned upon because of the complexities it introduces.

The MUSTANG frame is shown in Table 8-4. Avelino's new Ford Mustang might be described, for example, by the frame shown in Table 8-5. Note that this instance-level frame is a *Specialization–of* a **COUPE**, which in turn is a *Specialization–of* an **AUTOMOBILE**, which in turn is a *Specialization–of* a **VEHICLE**. Most of the information describing Avelino's Mustang is *inherited* from the generic **AUTOMOBILE** frame with the **COUPE** frame adding a slot called *Doors*. Should information about Avelino's car not be explicitly listed in the frame slot (e.g., the *Country–of–Manufacture*), the daemons associated with the frame system may be able to define precisely how this information should be determined. In this example, it looks at the parent frame (MUSTANG) to see whether it can inherit the value of *Country–of–manufacture*. Note that the MUSTANG frame does not specify the country of manufacture. The frame system then goes up to its parent frame (COUPE), and finds nothing of use there either. It then continues to AUTOMOBILE where it sees an *if–needed* daemon called *get-origin*. Although also not explicitly defined, this function can associate the manufacturer with the country of manufacture. In our case, it knows that the manufacturer is Ford, so it returns a value of USA.

Other information (i.e., the number of doors on Avelino's car) is not explicitly stated in his Mustang's instance-level frame's representation. Instead, it is inherited

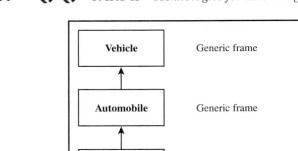

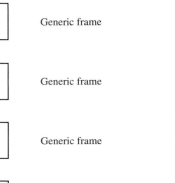

FIGURE 8-4 Inheritance Hierarchy for Example Frame System

from the more general frame **COUPE** by using the first explicit value found in the search up through the hierarchy. Thus, we can see that with inheritance, we do not need to represent the values at all levels, but instead, assign them to the most general frame possible for "distribution" to all its descendant frames. This greatly simplifies the process of defining a frame system.

Frames attempt to represent general knowledge about classes of objects or concepts, knowledge that is true for a majority of cases. Often, the specific objects or concepts represented as instances of a frame violate properties contained in the general frame. This allows frame systems to represent the complexities of the real world, where boundaries between classes are often fuzzy (e.g., a penguin is a bird yet it does not fly—a characteristic otherwise associated with all birds). An important concept of frames is that properties associated with higher level, or more general,

TABLE 8-4   Generic Frame Mustang

Generic **Mustang** frame
   Specialization-of: Coupe
   Generalization-of: Avelino's-automobile
Manufacturer
   Value: Ford
Engine
   Value:
   Legal-values: (3.0L-V6, 4.6L-V8)

**TABLE 8-5   Specific Frame for an Automobile**

*Avelino's-Automobile Frame*
Specialization-of: Mustang
Manufacturer
    Value: Ford
Vehicle ID No.
    Value: 12345AJG67890
Country-of-manufacture
    Value:
Color
    Value: red
Reliability
    Value: medium
Miles per gallon
    Value: 19.7
Year
    Value: 2002
Owner
    Value: Avelino
Doors
    Value:

frames are considered to be fixed, whereas the lower-level frames may vary but follow the general framework described by the ancestor frames. When a conflict in values occurs (e.g., birds fly, but a penguin does not), the more specialized value takes precedence over the general value.

One should note that when a frame is created as a child of another, it does not immediately add the inherited information to all its slots. That is, the parents' slot values are not actually assigned to the new child frame. This would have a negative effect on memory usage in the frame system because we would be repeating information unnecessarily. Instead, when a value of a slot in a frame is requested, and it is not present, the frame system can seek it out from its parent frames automatically, and return the inherited value when found. This process is quite complex, because it also must coordinate the retrieval process with the *IF-NEEDED:* facet daemon and the *DEFAULT:* facet as well. These also have the ability to return a value not found in the slot of the frame addressed. This is further discussed below.

Frame-based systems have gained increasing acceptance because they allow the packaging of declarative knowledge (the basic structure of the frame) with procedural knowledge (the *IF–NEEDED:*, *IF–ADDED:*, and *IF–CHANGED:* facets of the slots). This general approach has been used to develop other knowledge representation schemes (e.g., scripts [Schank, 1977]), several general knowledge representation languages (e.g., KRYPTON [Brachman, 1983], and FRL [Goldstein, 1977]) as well as expert system shells (e.g., KEE [Fikes, 1985]).

Keep in mind that we have abstracted many of the intricate details of how to make the changes to the frames or how to ask the questions. However, this example is quite realistic in showing the power of a frame-based KB system. It resembles a database management system in many ways. However, it represents the associations between concepts (in our case, cars) by writing functions (daemons), instead of linking directly as typically done in databases. This allows great flexibility in representing knowledge.

At this point, you have been introduced to rules and frames as the basic ways to represent knowledge. Frames are presented in a simple as well as in a more detailed form. However, how that knowledge is manipulated remains to be described, which we do in the next section.

## ◇◇ ◇◇ ◇◇ Automated Reasoning Process

The other part of understanding how KB systems work involves knowing how they manipulate the knowledge in the knowledge base to achieve their objective. The automated reasoning process is closely associated with the inference engine. It defines how the knowledge is exercised to yield the desired results. From the preceding discussion, we see and understand the two main knowledge representation paradigms—rules and frames. They are distinctly different in nature. Therefore, they are exercised in fundamentally different ways. How these types of knowledge are exercised is the main topic of this section. We start with the easier one, frame-based reasoning.

### Frame-Based Reasoning

The reasoning process for a frame-based system typically consists of answering questions about a particular concept represented by a frame or set of frames with inheritance relationships and daemons. This means accessing the value of the *VALUE:* facet of the slot in question, either directly if it has a value, or indirectly through inheritance or derived from associations. For example, if we want to know the color of Avelino's car, we may be able to directly retrieve the value by asking the frame **AVELINO'S-AUTOMOBILE** However, if the value of the *VALUE:* facet of its *color* slot is empty, then we can try to inherit it from parent frames (**MUSTANG, COUPE,** or **AUTOMOBILE**). Lacking that, we may be able to derive it through the *IF−NEEDED*: daemons. Finally, if the value cannot be retrieved, inherited, or derived, it may be obtained as a default value if the slot has a *DEFAULT :* facet. This facet can contain values for the slot that can be used if all else fails—in our case, it may return red because that may be the most popular color for mustangs.

The *RANGE:* and *LEGAL-VALUES:* facets can be used to ensure that any values added to the *VALUE:* facet are legal. In our example, if a value of 2.3L-4-Cyl, is to be placed in **AVELINO'S-AUTOMOBILE** Engine slot's *VALUE:* facet in Table 8-4, it will be rejected, because Mustangs do not offer a 2.3-liter, 4-cylinder engine option.

The questions asked of a frame system can be used in a simple response to a user's query, or internally by the system for further inferences in the solution of a problem. Although the daemons can be used for any purpose, they have been traditionally used only for deriving values not found in the *VALUE:* facets of slots, as well as for maintaining consistency among the various slots and facets in the frame system. Therefore, the use of frames with their traditional functionality is rather straightforward. Furthermore, few systems are solely composed of frame-based reasoning. Frames are typically used as part of some other type of reasoning mechanism.

Any further discussion of frames would inevitably lead us into much more detail than is truly warranted in this chapter. Those desiring further information should see Gonzalez and Dankel [1993]. Nevertheless, let us finalize this discussion by saying that frames are indeed a powerful means of representing knowledge, and have an important place in KM. They are the primary means of representing cases in case-based reasoning systems. We see this in the next chapter.

## Rule-Based Reasoning

Rule-based reasoning, on the other hand, is a bit more complex but also a bit more formalized. In this subsection, we discuss how a rule-based inference engine uses the knowledge in the knowledge base to solve problems or answer questions. We do so without delving too deeply into the foundations of automated reasoning, which can be found in formal logic and traced back to the ancient Greeks.

The objective of the reasoning process of rule-based systems is to derive a value (and often, also a measure of certainty) for a conclusion. How this is done, however, can vary significantly. In many situations, humans find it most natural to progress from the initial data to a final answer. This approach makes good sense whenever relatively few data are required, or there are many possible conclusions. This is in fact the approach used in our little thunderstorm prediction example shown previously in this chapter.

Alternatively, applications exist where much data are available and only a small portion of them is relevant. It would be highly inefficient to consider all the data, most of which would be irrelevant anyway. A good example of this is that when we go to the doctor, we tell the physician only about our abnormal symptoms (e.g., headache, nausea). We do not tell her all the things that are okay (e.g., my neck doesn't hurt and my back feels fine). A good doctor determines a possible diagnosis based on the limited initial data we provide and then tries to prove the hypothesis by asking additional questions.

Thus, there are two means of deriving conclusions:

1. Start with all the known data and progress naturally to the conclusion (called *data driven, forward chaining,* or *forward reasoning*).
2. Select a possible conclusion and try to prove its validity by looking for supporting evidence (*goal driven, backward chaining,* or *backward reasoning*).

Let us illustrate these ideas through examples. Suppose we have a task of identifying different items of fruit presented to us (classification). We might describe the knowledge used in this identification process through a set of rules that examine the physical characteristics of the fruit. The knowledge about fruit classification has already been described in a graph in Figure 8-3. The rules depicted in that graph, now written in plain English, are as follows:

| | | |
|---|---|---|
| Rule 1 | *IF* | *Shape = long* |
| | | *Color = green or yellow* |
| | *THEN* | *Fruit = banana* |
| Rule 2 | *IF* | *Shape = round or oblong* |
| | | *Diameter > 4 in.* |
| | *THEN* | *Fruitclass = vine* |

| Rule 3 | *IF* | *Shape = round* |
| | | *Diameter < 4 in.* |
| | *THEN* | *Fruitclass = tree* |
| Rule 4 | *IF* | *Seedcount = 1* |
| | *THEN* | *Seedclass = stonefruit* |
| Rule 5 | *IF* | *Seedcount > 1* |
| | *THEN* | *Seedclass = multiple* |
| Rule 6 | *IF* | *Fruitclass = vine* |
| | | *Color = green* |
| | *THEN* | *Fruit = watermelon* |
| Rule 7 | *IF* | *Fruitclass = vine* |
| | | *Surface = smooth* |
| | | *Color = yellow* |
| | *THEN* | *Fruit = honeydew* |
| Rule 8 | *IF* | *Fruitclass = vine* |
| | | *Surface = rough* |
| | | *Color = tan* |
| | *THEN* | *Fruit = cantaloupe* |
| Rule 9 | *IF* | *Fruitclass = tree* |
| | | *Color = orange* |
| | | *Seedclass = stonefruit* |
| | *THEN* | *Fruit = apricot* |
| Rule 10 | *IF* | *Fruitclass = tree* |
| | | *Color = orange* |
| | | *Seedclass = multiple* |
| | *THEN* | *Fruit = orange* |
| Rule 11 | *IF* | *Fruitclass = tree* |
| | | *Color = red* |
| | | *Seedclass = stonefruit* |
| | *THEN* | *Fruit = cherry* |
| Rule 12 | *IF* | *Fruitclass = tree* |
| | | *Color = orange* |
| | | *Seedclass = stonefruit* |
| | *THEN* | *Fruit = peach* |
| Rule 13 | *IF* | *Fruitclass = tree* |
| | | *Color = red or yellow or green* |
| | | *Seedclass = multiple* |
| | *THEN* | *Fruit = apple* |
| Rule 14 | *IF* | *Fruitclass = tree* |
| | | *Color = purple* |
| | | *Seedclass = stonefruit* |
| | *THEN* | *Fruit = plum* |

Note that each rule describes some characteristic of the different fruits through a series of *parameters*. In the above example, parameters include *Fruit*, *Fruitclass*, *Seedclass*, etc. When used in the rule premises, these parameters identify the values whose existence is necessary for the rules to execute. When used in the conclusions, these parameters identify values derived when the rules execute. In this regard, parameters are similar to variables in programming languages with each having a specific set of values that are acceptable. Parameters that represent the final answer are called *conclusions* or *goals*. The others are called *intermediate parameters* or *intermediate conclusions*. A combination of parameter and value that is considered true is called a *fact*. To refresh your memory, the workspace contains all the facts at any point in time during the execution of the KB system. In our example, the parameter *Fruit* is the only conclusion. By assigning it a value (e.g., Fruit = apple), we solve the problem of classifying a specific instance of a fruit. We use this example to show the differences between forward and backward reasoning.

## Forward Reasoning

Forward reasoning moves from the inputs toward the conclusions. Inputs are used to satisfy the premises of certain rules. This allows them to be executed (fired), and values to other intermediate (or final) parameters set. These newly derived facts, in turn, may cause the premises of other rules to be satisfied and to be fired. This progressive process forms the rule chaining mentioned earlier in this chapter. It ultimately results in a value (and possible certainty) assigned to a conclusion.

More specifically, in forward reasoning, a rule is selected for execution when its premises (i.e., the rule's *if's* or conditions) are satisfied. If a rule is satisfied, the rule is executed, deriving new facts that might then be used by other rules to derive additional facts. This process of checking the rules to see whether they are satisfied is called **rule interpretation.**

This reasoning approach is ideally suited for problem domains involving synthesis, such as design, configuration, planning, and scheduling. In these problem domains, the data drive the solution approach. When using forward reasoning to solve our fruit classification problem, we would start with an initial set of data, gathered from observing a piece of fruit, and progress toward the final classification of the fruit.

The inference engine performs the rule interpretation in a KB system. Rule interpretation, or inference, in forward reasoning involves the repetition of the basic steps shown in Figure 8-5 [Davis, 1983]:

1. *Matching.* In this step, the rules in the knowledge base are compared with the known facts to decide which rules are *satisfied*. By satisfied we mean that all the situations, premises, or antecedents of the rule have been found true.
2. *Conflict resolution.* It is possible that the matching phase can find multiple rules that are satisfied. Conflict resolution involves selecting the rule with the highest priority from the set of all rules that have the potential to be executed (i.e., those whose premises have been satisfied).
3. *Execution.* The last step in rule interpretation is the execution (or *firing*) of the rule. This execution can result in one of two possible outcomes. A new fact (or facts) can be derived and added to the workspace, or a new rule (or rules) can be added to the set of rules (the knowledge base) that the system considers for execution.

In this manner, execution of the rules proceeds in a forward manner (from the *IFs* to the *THENs*) toward the final goals.

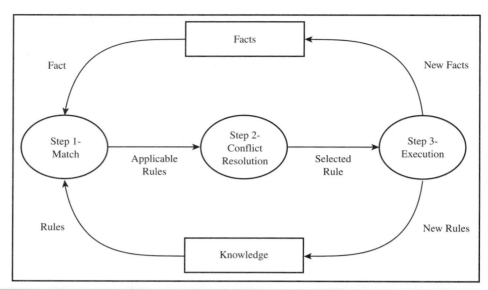

◆◇ ◆◇ ◆◇ FIGURE 8-5 Forward Reasoning Rule Interpretation Process

To illustrate this process, let us consider the fruit identification rules. For this example, we must specify a particular interpreter that clarifies the process of conflict resolution. This interpreter consists of the following steps:

1. **Matching.** Find all rules whose premises are true and mark them as applicable.
2. **Conflict resolution.** If more than one rule applies, then deactivate any whose actions add a duplicate result to the database. If more than one remain, then pass forward the lowest-numbered applicable rule.
3. **Action.** Execute the action of the rule passed forward by the conflict resolution step. If none applies, then halt execution.
4. **Reset.** Reset the applicability of all rules and return to step 1.

Note that the matching phase of the inference engine involves examining the knowledge base to see whether the specified parameters have been given the values shown within the rule.

Again, refer to the fruit classification system in Figure 8-3. For this example, let us say the workspace contains the following facts, *a priori* observed by a human and entered into the system though the keyboard:

| Facts in the Workspace (Inputs) |
|---|
| Diameter = 1 in. |
| Shape = round |
| Seedcount = 1 |
| Color = red |

**TABLE 8-6   Trace of Rule-Based Execution**

| Execution Cycle | Applicable Rules | Selected Rule | Derived Fact |
|:---:|:---:|:---:|:---|
| 1 | 3, 4 | 3 | Fruitclass = tree |
| 2 | 3, 4 | 4 | Seedclass = stonefruit |
| 3 | 3, 4, 11 | 11 | Fruit = cherry |
| 4 | 3, 4, 11 | — | — |

Table 8-6 details a trace of the execution of this system. In each execution cycle, one rule is selected for execution and its specified conclusion is derived and added to the workspace. In execution cycle 1 the inference process finds that two rules are applicable, rules 3 and 4. Because both rules can derive new facts, the lowest numbered of these rules is selected and executed, thereby deriving the new fact *Fruitclass = tree*. Note that for illustration purposes, only the newly derived facts are shown in Table 8-6 when a rule executes, instead of the entire workspace. In cycle 4, we discover that all the applicable rules have been executed (i.e., their conclusions are already derived and present within the workspace). Consequently, no new rules are selected and execution halts. The final conclusion derived by the system is that the fruit must be a cherry.

### Backward Reasoning

In backward reasoning, on the other hand, a goal (i.e., intermediate or final conclusion) is selected, and the system looks for ways to set a value for it by finding supporting evidence. Therefore, the inference process can begin without any inputs specified. The inputs can be requested from the user or otherwise sought internally, only as they become necessary to derive a value for the selected goal. This approach is ideally suited for diagnostic problems that have a small number of possible conclusions. The system requests inputs only when they are needed. When it finds the answer, it can stop the execution or go on to satisfy another goal. This process is known as **tracing a goal**.

The rule interpreter for backward reasoning differs significantly from that of forward reasoning. Although both processes involve an examination and application of rules, backward reasoning starts with a desired conclusion and decides whether the existing facts support the derivation of a value for this conclusion. The system typically starts with an empty workspace of known facts.

*Known Workspace: ()*

A list of goals (or conclusions) is provided for which the system attempts to derive values. These goals are specified in the order that the developer believes is best to pursue. There is only a single top-level goal in our fruit identification problem—the type of fruit. This is indicated by the goal *Fruit*.

*Goals: (Fruit)*

Backward reasoning uses this list of goals to coordinate its search through the rule base. This search consists of the following steps:

1. Form a list initially composed of all top-level goals defined in the system. The top-level goals are predefined by the developer.

2. Consider the first goal from the list. Gather all rules capable of deriving a value for this goal.

3. For each of these rules, in turn examine its premises:

   a. If all its premises are satisfied (i.e., each premise has its specified value contained as a fact in the workspace), then execute this rule to derive its conclusions. Remove this goal from the list and return to step 2. This is done because a value has been derived for the current goal.

   b. If a premise of a rule is not satisfied because of the absence of a fact to satisfy one of its premises (i.e., one of the premise's values does not exist as a fact in the workspace), look for rules that derive the specified value for this premise. If any can be found, then consider this premise to be a subgoal, place it on the beginning of the goal list, and go back to step 2.

   c. If step b cannot find a rule to derive the specified value for the current premise, then query the user for its value and add it to the workspace as a fact. If this value satisfies the current premise, then continue with this rule's next premise. If the premise is not satisfied, then consider the next rule.

4. If all rules that can satisfy the current goal have been attempted and all have failed to derive a value, then this goal remains undetermined. Remove it from the list and go back to step 2. If the list is empty (i.e., all top-level goals have been processed), then halt and announce completion.

To illustrate backward reasoning, let us now trace the execution of the rules to see what they derive as the value for *Fruit*. The trace of execution begins with the single top-level goal: *Fruit*.

Step 2 specifies that all rules that can derive this goal should be gathered. This list of rules consists of rules 1, 6, 7, 8, 9, 10, 11, 12, 13, and 14, because they all are able to set a value for the conclusion *Fruit*. Execution starts with the first of these rules, rule 1. The first premise of this rule (*Shape = long*) is examined and no value for *shape* is found in the workspace. Because no rules can derive a value for the premise *shape*, the inference mechanism asks the user for its value:

**What is the value for shape?**

We respond with the value of *round,* which is added to the workspace:

Current Workspace
| |
|---|
| ((Shape = round)) |

Rule-based systems generally follow the closed-world assumption. This means that if a fact specifically asserting something is not present, it is assumed to be false. Therefore, absence of a particular fact makes it false by definition. Because the proper value for this premise is not found in the workspace, this value causes rule 1 to fail. Execution then proceeds to rule 6. The first premise of this rule (*Fruitclass = vine*) is examined and no value for this parameter is found in the workspace. A search of the rules determines that rules 2 and 3 are capable of deriving values for *Fruitclass*, so we temporarily suspend our processing for *Fruit* and add this parameter to the list as a subgoal:

### Goals: (Fruitclass Fruit)

After collecting the two rules (rules 2 and 3) that can derive values for *Fruitclass*, we examine the first of these to see whether it is satisfied. The first premise of rule 2 asks whether the value of *Shape* equals *round* or *oblong*. Because the *Shape* does exist in the workspace and does have a value of *round*, we proceed to the next premise. A value for *Diameter* does not exist and no rules can derive its value so the system asks the user for a value:

### What is the value of diameter?

The user responds with *1 in.,* which changes the workspace to:

|  Current Workspace  |
| :--- |
| ((Shape = round) |
| (Diameter = 1 in.)) |

Rule 2 fails because its second premise is not satisfied. The interpreter now examines rule 3. Both premises of this rule are satisfied by the values in the workspace so this rule derives *Fruitclass = tree,* which is added to the workspace:

|  Current Workspace  |
| :--- |
| ((Shape = round) |
| (Diameter = 1 in.) |
| (Fruitclass = tree)) |

Because a value for *Fruitclass* has been found, this subgoal is removed from the goal list and we return to the goal *Fruit*, continuing with rule 6. Then because the value derived for *Fruitclass* does not satisfy the first premise of this rule, we proceed to the next rule, rule 7.

   Both rule 7 and rule 8 fail because both their first premises (i.e., *Fruitclass = vine*) are not satisfied. The next rule, rule 9, has its first premise (*Fruitclass = tree*) satisfied, so we examine its next premise, *Color = orange*. The value for *Color* is not in the workspace and no rules can derive it so the inference process asks the user for its value:

### What is the value of Color?

to which the user responds *red.* This value causes rules 9 and 10 to fail.

Finally, we reach rule 11. The first two premises are satisfied by values in the workspace so we proceed to the third premise, *Seedclass = stonefruit*. Because no value exists in the workspace for this parameter and no rules can derive it, the inference engine asks the user for a value:

### What is the value of seedclass?

This question triggers a response of *stonefruit*. This new fact satisfies rule 11 and allows it to fire; thus, deriving *cherry* as the value for *Fruit*, our final workspace is now:

| Final Workspace |
|---|
| ((Shape = round) |
| (Diameter = 1 in.) |
| (Fruitclass = tree) |
| (Color = red) |
| (Seedclass = stonefruit) |
| (Fruit = cherry)) |

Because *Fruit* has a value, it is removed from the goal list. The list is now empty, so the backward reasoning process halts with the appropriate value derived for *Fruit*.

Note how the inputs were requested only as they became necessary for the inference process. This presents a significant advantage to forward reasoning in problems where there are many inputs, not all are needed, and they are not easy to obtain.

## ◇ ◇ ◇ Developing Knowledge-Based Systems

Development of a KB system differs greatly from that of standard software. Although the latter's requirements can be rather easily defined, in most cases this is not as readily done for problems suitable for solution by KB systems. If we agree that intelligent systems simulate human intelligence, then it is conceivably only necessary to point to one task (or set of tasks) performed by a human, and merely specify that it be replicated in a computer. That may be an oversimplification, because there may be aspects of that task or tasks that are more important than others, and the interface with the user always needs to be very carefully specified. Nevertheless, specifications in intelligent systems have traditionally been of secondary importance, and this may be the reason why.

Human expertise is difficult to define and even more difficult to elicit. Thus, it is incumbent on the developer of a KB system to maintain close contact with the experts throughout the entire development process. It is this constant and almost continuous interaction that separates KB systems development from that of conventional software.

The desirable qualities for KEs are also quite different. Instead of solely possessing knowledge of computers and programming languages, the developers of KB systems must depend equally on intuition and personal qualities to be successful, such as the ability to get along well with others. The developers' knowledge of computers and languages is not to be discounted; however, many of the techniques they employ are different from those used in developing standard software.

Whereas the conventional software developer has been given the name of software engineer, the KB systems developer is a KE, and the development process for KB systems has been dubbed knowledge engineering. A definition of the knowledge engineering process found in Gonzalez and Dankel [1993] follows:

> The acquisition of knowledge in some domain from one or more non-electronic sources, and its conversion into a form that can be utilized by a computer to solve problems that, typically, can only be solved by persons extensively knowledgeable in that domain.

From a KM standpoint, therefore, knowledge engineering is basically the elicitation, capture, and storage of tacit or explicit knowledge for later application. All other aspects of knowledge engineering equate fairly closely with software engineering.

During the development of a KB system, KEs face many challenges unlike those seen by their counterparts in software engineering. As the name implies, knowledge engineering is heavily related to knowledge.

Note that this definition of knowledge engineering makes no mention of the development of the underlying program utilizing the knowledge to solve the problem. The job of a KE, like that of other engineers, is to use existing and available tools to solve a problem. Nevertheless, should an adequate tool not be available, the KE should possess the appropriate skills to develop one. Tools are discussed in the following section.

Knowledge engineering, however, involves more than merely translating the knowledge from human terms to a machine-readable form. Knowledge engineering expertise involves recognizing what knowledge is in use to solve a problem, categorizing this knowledge, and determining the best way to represent it. This last step is important because improperly represented knowledge may ultimately doom a KB system development project. One problem is that the impact of a poor representation may not be immediately felt. The developer may expend significant effort creating a system that, ultimately, must be completely redeveloped because of the use of a poor knowledge representation paradigm.

The methodology of knowledge engineering is rapidly progressing. In Chapter 10, we present some of the practical aspects of this evolving field. Further explorations and refinements within this field will hopefully one day transform these techniques from their current state of an art into a true science.

## ◇ ◇ ◇ Knowledge-Based System Tools

Generally, two types of infrastructures are available for developing a KB system. These are (1) using a commercial *KB system tool*, or (2) developing one from scratch. We discuss these alternatives briefly below.

### Commercial Knowledge-Based System Tools

A commercial KB system tool is a software package containing some or all the components and features we describe in the KE's view of a system—except, of course, for the knowledge. The KE uses this package to develop a knowledge base and possibly a specialized user interface. Such tools are commonly called *expert system shells*. However, we do not particularly like the term *expert system*, because it limits the scope of KB systems to applications where expert-level knowledge is represented. Thus, we refer to these tools as *knowledge-based system shells* or simply *shells*.

There are many commercially available shells, and their prices range from less than $100 to tens of thousands of dollars. They also range widely in the number of features they offer. It is not our intent to make a commercial comparison of the various shells. Instead, we roughly classify them according to the knowledge representation paradigms that they support, and their means to inference. KB system shells are classified as follows:

1. Inductive shells
2. Rule-based shells
3. Hybrid shells
4. Special purpose shells

Inductive shells are the simplest. In these systems the KE specifies example cases as a table of known data (or premises) and their resulting effects (or conclusions). This table is then converted into a decision tree and subsequently to a set of *IF-THEN* statements. The advantage of inductive systems is that knowledge acquisition is performed through the specification of these examples. This is an important consideration in KM. Inductive techniques are covered in detail in Chapter 11. Although not all problems lend themselves to this approach, for those that do, the main system development task is that of selecting the proper examples to present to the inductive tool. This is often simpler than distilling the knowledge from these examples. Nevertheless, inductive shells tend to be relatively simplistic in their capabilities. Furthermore, it is often difficult to build an extensive knowledge base purely through examples. Finally, expertise is rarely exhibited through such examples.

Rule-based shells are the most common of shells. They can range from the very simple to the highly complex. Some simple rule-based shells are really nothing more than decision trees with good user interfaces. These types of shells are limited to solving relatively simple problems. Other rule-based shells can be quite sophisticated. They structure the rules into subsets and provide extensive rule-editing features. Regardless of their degree of sophistication, the knowledge within these shells is expressed as *IF-THEN* rules describing situations that may occur and conclusions that can be drawn if the situations become true. Rule-based shells contain an inference engine (either forward or backward reasoning), an empty workspace, an empty knowledge base, and a development environment to assist the KE in developing the knowledge base. These shells liberate the developer from having to program the inference engine and all other functions.

The more sophisticated shells, called *hybrid shells*, support multiple knowledge-representation paradigms, as well as various reasoning schemes. These systems allow the KE to represent knowledge not only as rules but also as frames. This gives the KE great latitude in developing a proper knowledge structure. Because these various representation paradigms require different reasoning schemes, these systems are typically quite complex, as well as powerful.

CLIPS is a highly sophisticated hybrid shell. It is naturally a forward-reasoning system, but permits limited backward reasoning. CLIPS has been in existence since the early 1980s, thus making it a mature product. Yet, this shell is powerful and easy to use. Furthermore, CLIPS is free. The latest version of CLIPS can be easily obtained from various Internet sites. A Web search with the keyword "CLIPS" will identify these sites.

*Special-purpose shells* also exist that were specifically designed for particular types of problems. For example, one type of special-purpose shell specializes in the diagnosis of process control systems. However, it should be noted that just because these were designed for a highly specialized domain does not mean that they cannot be comfortably used for many other types of problems.

### Developing a System from Scratch

Developing a system from scratch (in a programming language) is certainly a large effort to undertake. However, it can have several advantages. The system can include exactly what is necessary to manage the knowledge therein—no more and no less. Furthermore, the developer cannot be subservient to the whims and business practices of the shell vendor, who may choose to discontinue the product, upgrade it, or simply refuse to add any custom features required by the KB system developer. However, we do not encourage any but the most sophisticated of programmers to attempt to develop a system from scratch. This involves significant programming effort, well beyond the scope of this book. It is preferable to carefully select a reliable and reputable vendor who is willing to work with the developer's organization to provide a satisfactory product for the life of the KB system. There are many that fit that description.

## SUMMARY ◆◇ ◆◇ ◆◇

This chapter serves to describe KB systems, how they work, and how they are built. They are problem-solving systems that rely heavily on human knowledge for their power. They attempt to emulate the problem-solving prowess of an expert.

KB systems are composed of several different parts, depending on the standpoint of the viewer. The most important ones, however, are the knowledge base and the inference engine. The former holds the domain-specific knowledge whereas the latter contains the functions to exercise the knowledge in the knowledge base. Knowledge can be represented as either rules or frames. Rules are a natural choice for representing conditional knowledge, which is in the form of *if–then* statements.

Inference engines supply the "motive power" to the knowledge. There are several ways to exercise the knowledge, depending on the nature of the knowledge. Rule-based systems can be either forward chaining or backward chaining. Forward-chaining systems move from inputs toward conclusions (also called goals or solutions). They are used when the number of inputs is limited, or when the inputs are gathered automatically. Backward-chaining systems, on the other hand, work backward from the conclusions to the inputs. These systems attempt to validate the conclusions by finding evidence to support them. In this process, they only request the inputs necessary to validate a particular conclusion, thereby limiting the number of requests necessary. This can be significant if the inputs must be entered by a human user through the keyboard.

Frames serve to represent structured knowledge—that which consists of things or concepts and the relationships between their components. For example, frames can easily describe a business organization, and how it is structured internally. It can clearly depict how the different departments and people within them interact with each other.

This chapter also defines the term *knowledge engineering*—the process for development of KB systems. Knowledge engineering is an emerging discipline, with its own techniques and tools to undertake this difficult task successfully. Knowledge engineering is different than the conventional software engineering process followed to develop conventional software. Although the two processes have been merging as of late, they still maintain some very different characteristics.

Finally, we should reiterate the importance of KB systems for KM. Before KM became a discipline, KEs had already been struggling with how to formalize the knowledge of experts in a KB system. The KEs were, in fact, the first knowledge managers.

## Key Terms ◇◆ ◇◆ ◇◆

- backward reasoning—p. 135
- bidirectional reasoning—p. 135
- daemons—p. 142
- developer's interface—p. 135
- development environment—p. 132
- facets—p. 141
- forward reasoning—p. 135
- frame—p. 133

- inference chain—p. 138
- inference engine—p. 132
- intelligent program—p. 130
- knowledge acquisition tool—p. 135
- knowledge base—p. 132
- knowledge-based systems—p. 129
- knowledge engineering—p. 130

- pattern matching—p. 138
- problem-specific database—p. 130
- rule interpretation—p. 149
- slots—p. 141
- structured knowledge—p. 136
- test case database—p. 135
- tracing a goal—p. 151
- user interface—p. 130

## Review Questions ◇◆ ◇◆ ◇◆

1. State in your own words the difference between backward and forward chaining. What are the advantages and disadvantages of one versus the other?
2. State in your own words when one should use rules as opposed to frames when considering the development of a knowledge-based (KB) system.
3. What are some advantages of inductive shells compared with rule-based shells? What are the disadvantages?
4. For each of the following, state why or why not a forward-reasoning approach would be suitable.
   a. A monitor for the printing of a newspaper for problems with the printing press.
   b. A diagnostic system for ignition problems in an automobile.
   c. A monitoring system that makes corrections to the process of producing gasoline in a refinery. Note that this is a continuous process where raw materials flow in one end of the refinery and gasoline and waste products flow out the other.
   d. An automatic pilot for a low-altitude aircraft flying over unknown terrain. This system is able to monitor the terrain though radar, sonar, and visual input.
   e. A diagnostic system for a printer problem with your personal computer. You issue the print command and nothing happens.
   f. A system to determine why your lawn mower cannot start.
   g. A system to determine the appropriate action for a weapons officer to take in a nuclear attack submarine.
   h. An air traffic controller, which provides the appropriate directions to aircraft.
   i. A design system that helps with the process of designing a bicycle.
   j. A scheduling system for games in a Little League baseball season.

k. A financial investment advising system.

    l. A system for driving an automobile automatically.

    m. A system for evaluating employee performance in a small company.

    n. A system for auditing the financial records of a major corporation.

    o. A system for determining the desirability of hiring job applicants.

    p. A system for deciding whether to make a formal proposal to a solicitation. Keep in mind the expense of making such a proposal.

    q. A system for deciding whether to rent or to own a fleet of small vehicles for a small corporation.

    r. A system to determine sales strategy for a large corporation.

5. For each subproblem mentioned in Problem 4 above, state why or why not a backward-reasoning approach would be suitable.

## APPLICATION EXERCISES ◇ ◇ ◇

1. Using the CLIPS tool, implement the fruit classification knowledge-based (KB) system described in this chapter.
2. Using the CLIPS tool, develop a small KB system for finding the best route to your place of employment or university.
3. Develop a frame system describing a typical college of business administration in a typical public university.
4. Develop a frame system to describe the organization of a small company. Do the same for a large company.
5. Develop a frame system to describe your family tree.

## REFERENCES ◇ ◇ ◇

Brachman, R.J., Fikes, R.E., and Levesque, H.J. 1983. KRYPTON: A functional approach to knowledge representation. *IEEE Computer,* 16(10) October, 67–73.

Davis, R., and Rich, C. 1983. Expert Systems: Part I-Fundamentals, Tutorial No. 4, 3rd Nat'l. Conf. on Artificial Intelligence, AAAI.

Fikes, R., and Kehler, T. 1985. The role of frame-based representation in reasoning. *Communications of the ACM,* 28(9) September, 904–920.

Goldstein, I.P., and Roberts, R.B. 1977. NUDGE: A Knowledge-Based Scheduling Program, 5th

Int. Joint Conf. on Artificial Intelligence, pp. 257–263.

Gonzalez, A.J., and Dankel, D.D. 1993. *The Engineering of Knowledge-Based Systems: Theory and Practice,* Prentice Hall, Englewood Cliffs, NJ.

Minsky, M. 1975., A framework for representing knowledge. In Winston, P.H. (Ed.), *The Psychology of Representing Knowledge,* McGraw-Hill, New York, pp. 211–277.

Schank, R.C., and Abelson, R.P. 1977. *Scripts, Plans, Goals and Understanding,* Lawrence Erlbaum, Hillsdale, NJ.

CHAPTER

# Using Past History Explicitly as Knowledge

## *Case-Based Reasoning Systems*[1]

### ❖ ❖ ❖ Introduction

The reader has learned about artificial intelligence (AI), knowledge-based (KB) systems, and in particular, rule-based systems. An alternative to expressing knowledge as rules based on the heuristic knowledge of an expert is to express it explicitly in terms of historical problems that were once solved, and their solutions. Such an approach is called *case-based reasoning (CBR)*. This chapter describes the essence of CBR. The chapter also discusses the weaknesses of rule-based systems that CBR systems attempt to address. Finally, it provides an in-depth analysis of the strengths and weaknesses of CBR systems.

### ❖ ❖ ❖ Weaknesses of Rule-Based Systems

As we saw in Chapters 7 and 8, KB systems that derive their knowledge from experts (i.e., expert systems) effectively represent the experts' "compiled" experience as heuristics. Over several years of experience, experts may be exposed to many instances of a particular problem (and their subsequent solutions). Their knowledge, therefore, is an accumulation and a combination of these experiences. They may not be able to identify specifically when they learned a particular bit of knowledge that permits them to solve a current problem. It is like scrambled eggs—once you scramble three eggs, it is hard to tell which one is where.

---

[1]This chapter is written in collaboration with Douglas D. Dankel.

In reality, there is absolutely nothing wrong with this scenario from a problem-solving standpoint. The (true) experts know their business, and can solve problems very effectively when asked to do so. The difficulties arise when trying to manage that knowledge. First, we must elicit it from the expert. Then we must represent or formalize it in a form consistent with the computing paradigm we are using. Furthermore, we must validate and verify this knowledge. Only at this point can it be finally managed to provide organizational advantages. Obviously, all these processes have pitfalls.

The first of these pitfalls is that we are relying on these experts to interpret the domain for us. The knowledge we elicit, represent, and manage is, in fact, the experts' personal interpretation of the domain. Expertise is a spectrum—some experts are very knowledgeable; others are only minimally so. Furthermore, different experts may see the same domain from different perspectives, and they may all in fact be correct. Thus, the source of the knowledge can have an impact on the knowledge gathered.

Second, as we can see in the next chapter, sometimes transferring this codified knowledge can be difficult and error-prone. Experts can provide erroneous knowledge when answering ill-posed questions, or the knowledge engineer (KE) can misinterpret an expert's correct answer. Furthermore, developers can misrepresent correct knowledge in the system code. These all contribute to invalid systems.

Third, rules have several inherent disadvantages that emerge when we develop large rule-based systems. For instance, many rules may be needed to properly represent one domain. The pioneering expert system GenAID mentioned in Chapter 7, when initially deployed, had somewhere in the neighborhood of 10,000 rules. Although it was later modified to condense some of the rules, resulting in a reduction to approximately 3,000 rules, it was still a large system by any definition. Systems with such a large number of rules have two distinct disadvantages: (1) the rules have to be coded, verified, validated, and maintained; and (2) they have to be executed by the inference engine, the rule-firing process we saw in Chapter 8. These factors affect the efficiency of the system.

It is safe to say that the less voluminous the system is, the easier it is to develop, test, and maintain. Computational algorithms have been developed to make the rule-firing process more efficient—see Srinivasa [1999]. However, the fewer rules to fire, the faster the system can run.

One alternative approach to addressing these difficulties is to capture the knowledge directly from the same source from which the experts learn. In other words, look at the individual experiences seen by the experts, and do not combine them into a mass of compiled knowledge. Instead, keep the **cases** that might have led to the learning by the experts, and reason through them. This precludes the personal influence of the individual experts. In fact, we bypass the expert and look at the information that allowed them to learn and acquire their expertise. We no longer need their interpretation, with its associated drawbacks. This approach is the subject of this chapter. CBR is an essential technology for developing knowledge application systems, to be discussed in Chapter 16.

# ❖ ❖ ❖ Basic Concepts in Case-Based Reasoning

CBR came about partly as an attempt to address some of the drawbacks of rule-based expert systems, mainly the problem of knowledge acquisition and maintenance. This technique originates from Schank's concept of **remindings** [Schank, 1982], which states that when people are thinking (e.g., solving problems), they are merely recalling past experiences that somehow remind them of the current situation. If the current and historical situations are sufficiently similar, it can be inferred that the solutions to both situations are the same. Therefore, people apply solutions of past problems to current problems that are similar in nature.

Consider the following examples that illustrate this process [Klein, 1985]:

> ***Example 1.*** A fire ground commander was coordinating his crew as they combated a fire at a four-story apartment building. He looked up and noticed billboards on the roof, and recalled an earlier incident where the flames had burned through the wooden supports of the billboards, sending them crashing to the street below. He then ordered that the spectators be moved farther back to prevent injury from falling billboards.
>
> ***Example 2.*** Another fire ground commander noticed some peculiar properties in a cloud of smoke at a fire. He recalled an incident in which toxic smoke had been given off showing the same features of density, color, and heaviness as the cloud he saw. He ordered his crew to use breathing support systems.

CBR uses explicit historical experiences to solve new problems. It assumes that problems recur, and that ". . . similar problems have similar solutions" [Leake, 1996, p. 3]. It is an intuitive and simple concept that most users find very natural and easy to understand. Furthermore, it provides a natural form of learning by merely adding any newly solved problem to its database of cases.

In both of these examples, the decision makers use previous explicit experiences (the cases), to help them solve the current problem. They retrieved the appropriate cases from a larger set of cases. The similarities between the current problem and the retrieved case were the basis for the selection.

In its simplest, most basic form, CBR consists of:

1. A repository of historical cases called the **case library;**
2. A means to find and retrieve a similar case from the case library, and use its solution to solve the current problem;
3. A means to add the newly solved problem and solution to the case library as a new case.

However, what happens when the most similar case is not deemed similar enough to the current problem? In such a situation, the solution of the most similar case may not be applicable. Do we then throw up our hands and punt? CBR provides for such circumstances with techniques to *adapt* the solution of the most similar case to the current problem, such that it becomes applicable. This process is called **adaptation.** There exist a few suggestions for how to do adaptation, but there is no theory or common body of knowledge to help system developers. It is mostly a domain-specific process. In many systems, adaptation has been abandoned altogether, opting for making improvements on searching and learning. Combining CBR systems with other types of systems to close this gap has also been studied. This is particularly the case with using rules to make the adaptations.

Furthermore, how can we add a new case to the case library without determining whether it succeeded or failed? Certainly, failed solutions can provide as much, if not more, useful information that those that succeeded. Nevertheless, the system needs to know how to treat them. Therefore, some form of feedback is necessary to categorize new cases.

Finally, developing a robust application in CBR implies overcoming several real-world problems before claiming success. We look at these in this section and provide a more in-depth view of CBR.

Real-world, case-based systems are significantly more complex than the simple system described earlier. Much of the complexity comes as a result of the peculiarities of the problem domain. A typical system consists of the following processes:

1. ***Search the case library for similar cases.*** This implies utilizing a search engine that examines only the appropriate cases, and not the entire case library, because it may be quite large. This implication gives rise to *indexing* the cases, and organizing the case library to maximize efficiency. These topics are discussed shortly.
2. ***Select and retrieve the most similar cases.*** This implies having a means to compare each examined case with the current problem, quantify their similarity, and somehow rank them in decreasing order of similarity. Several techniques exist to accomplish this, and selecting an appropriate one is very domain dependent.
3. ***Adapt the solution for the most similar case.*** If the current problem and the most similar case are not similar enough, then the solution may have to be adapted to fit the needs of the current problem. However, this is not considered by many to be a necessary step in CBR [Leake, 1996].
4. ***Apply the generated solution and obtain feedback.*** Once a solution or classification is generated by the system, it must be applied to the problem. Its effect on the problem is fed back to the CBR system for classification of its solution (as success or failure).
5. ***Add the newly solved problem to the case library.*** This implies having determined that the case is in fact worth adding to the case library—a potentially difficult task. It also implies placing the new case in the appropriate location in the case library—hardly trivial for the more complex library organizations.

The next sections discuss some of the issues involved in implementing these five steps. Please keep in mind that we only present a basic treatment of these issues. Refer to Kolodner [1993] and Leake [1996] for more details.

## ⬦ ⬦ ⬦ Indexing and Case Library Organization

Indexing is the labeling of data items in such a way that they are easily retrieved. For example, when you go to a library, how do you find one book amid the thousands upon thousands of books in the endless canyons of shelves? Well, you look for an index that maps something interesting about the book to its location in the stacks. Its title, its author, or its subject could be some of these interesting aspects of a book. Indexing, therefore, can be advantageous in case libraries as well. The indices could be used to map something important about a case (its goal, its most important attribute, etc.) to the part of the library where it can be found. Therefore, indexing the cases may make the search more efficient by limiting the search space to a group of cases that somehow share something of importance with the current problem (as well as possibly among themselves). This group may be clustered in a specific part of the library, or the search engine may first examine the index of a case to determine its relevance before examining its (possibly many) other attributes. If the index is irrelevant, it skips to the next one. Indexing can be done by hand, automatically, or not at all, depending on the specifics of the application.

Nevertheless, how these indices are expressed is an important issue. If they are defined too broadly, an unnecessarily large number of cases may be retrieved for examination. Conversely, if they are expressed too narrowly, there may be some truly similar cases not examined for similarity. One way to approach this problem is to use *explanation-based indexing* [Barletta, 1988]. This technique addresses the indexing problem by providing a set of *observables* (features) of the problem description, both before and after an action. This set is coupled with an explanation of why they were given and a description of the goal for which the action was taken. Refer to Kolodner [1993] for additional ways to index a case library.

The organization of a library of cases is also a critical task. The effect of retrieving an improperly matched case [Barletta, 1988] is often more computationally expensive than selecting the wrong rule to execute in a rule-based system. Inefficient searches through the case library because of its poor organization can result in unacceptable performance. To address this, the case library may be organized as a flat database or hierarchically, based on some organizational structure with inputs and goals.

**Flat case libraries** are the simplest. The cases can be placed in a list, an array, or a file, possibly ordered in some way. For small case libraries, this is typically the preferred organization. Flat organizations may work properly even for larger libraries containing simple cases that can be quickly examined. The library can be searched in sequence or in parallel.

For larger libraries with complex cases, sequential search of a flat library may be too inefficient for the needs of real-world applications. In such cases, indexing can be very useful. As discussed above, its use may improve the efficiency of a sequential search of a flat library by partitioning the library, or by simplifying the examination of the cases. For example, we are interested in organizing a case library for a system that determines the creditworthiness of loan applicants based on loans previously made to individuals or companies with similar asset and income attributes. Certainly, the first thing the system should look for is the context of prospective borrowers. Are they individuals or businesses? The two are subject to vastly different criteria, and there is no point in comparing historical cases of loans to individuals when the current applicant is a corporate entity. Therefore, we index the case library such that all individual borrowers are in one side of the library and all corporate or business borrowers are in the other. This serves to prune the search space.

Alternatively, if the case library is not organized in such a way that the related cases are physically clustered, then the search engine could do a sequential search but simply compare the most relevant attribute first. If the value of the attribute does not match the desired value, the comparison with that case ends and the search engine goes on to the next case. This would reflect a flat case library, but facilitated by a sort of virtual indexing. For example, assume all cases are arbitrarily distributed in a flat case library. However, the search engine knows that the current problem (the loan applicant on whom it has to make a decision) is a limited partnership. The search engine first checks the TYPE attribute for all cases it compares sequentially. Any value other than *limited-partnership* for that attribute would cause the search process to abandon that comparison and continue to the next one.

Other more complex organizations are *shared feature networks* and *redundant shared feature networks.* Shared feature networks are hierarchical organizations that segregate the cases by what features they have in common. Those that have one feature in common can reside together at one level of the tree (e.g., the root level). The next level contains two or more groups of cases that share another feature besides all having shared the one at the root level. The same happens at the next level with a third feature and so on. The shared feature network attempts to cluster the cases as much as possible, choosing the feature most universally shared for the root node. The search process now merely follows the path on the tree that matches the features of the current problem. The lower it goes in the tree, the more similar the case is to the current problem. One disadvantage is, of course, that determining a clustering method is not trivial. Additionally, when a new case is added to the library, its insertion location must be carefully considered to be consistent with the current clustering of cases. Furthermore, depending on the indexing, several of these networks may be necessary, with each case possibly occupying several different clusters.

Following our example of loan applications, we already have seen that determining the context of the applicant (whether the applicant is an organization or an individual) would serve to prune the search space. However, we could do even better if we distinguished between corporate entities and limited partnerships. Furthermore, we could distinguish between employed and self-employed individuals. The amount requested could also serve to distinguish cases, because different rules may apply to different levels of lending. Another distinguishing feature for both, businesses and individuals, could be their income or assets. It is obvious that this would create a tree with each feature (attribute) residing at each level of the tree. Figure 9-1 depicts a tree representing a shared feature network. The cases applicable to each path on the tree are clustered together at the leaf level.

 **FIGURE 9-1  Shared Feature Network for a Loan Application Example**

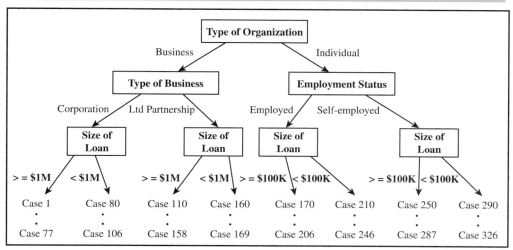

The problem with both structuring methods is that if the definition of the current problem is incomplete (e.g., we do not know the passive income of the applicant), no direction is provided for how to continue traversing the tree [Kolodner, 1993]. This can lead to a dead-end or to a sequential search—exactly what we were trying to avoid. The redundant shared feature nets address this problem by constructing several shared feature nets, each with a different priority. That way, if information on an attribute is missing, we choose the net that has it closest to the leaf level, so that the roadblock comes in at the latest possible stage in our search. This, obviously, is the sledgehammer approach. Unfortunately, there are no better ways to do it. Consequently, it is best to use such hierarchical organizations only when there is little reason for having incomplete information. Property appraisal is one of these domains, where the houses are typically well documented in Multiple Listing Service (MLS) databases. Entries in the MLS database are uniform, each displaying the living area, the number of bedrooms, bathrooms, garage size, etc. Each case most likely has values assigned to each attribute. On the other extreme are diagnostic cases, where often data are not recorded or are otherwise unavailable.

## ◇ ◇ ◇ Matching and Retrieval

**Retrieval** is merely returning the most similar (or the few most similar) cases for further processing. We have already discussed the **problem space** to be searched (the case library), and how it is to be organized and indexed. Assuming a well-organized and indexed case library, we only need to discuss the matching and ranking procedures that precede retrieval of the best cases.

Matching procedures are very domain and problem dependent. Certainly, some attributes are more important than others, and they should weigh more heavily than others. Attributes may take on discrete values or continuous numerical values. Beyond considering the values, one must often consider:

- The context of the current problem and how it differs from those of the cases retrieved, for example, the type of borrower (either individual or organization);
- Satisfaction of requirements by an attribute, for example, boulders serving as a place to sit (as compared to chairs) [Kolodner, 1993, p. 349];
- Specificity of value, for example, an eagle is closer to a bird-of-prey than to a bird;
- Comparison of asymmetric cases; for example, when comparing houses, the current problem may have an attribute stating its lakefront location, whereas the historical cases do not address this issue.

The matching functions can use one of several techniques, but one thing they all have in common is that they seek to compute the "distance" between each historical case and the current problem. However, distance can be defined very differently for different domains. In cases where the attributes have numerical values (e.g., income), distance is often easier to conceive. For example, if the current applicant has an income of $89,000 and the historical case's income is $100,000, then obviously, the distance is $11,000. Attributes with symbolic values (e.g., high, low, hot, or cold) often make it more difficult to measure the distance. Furthermore, the distance of each attribute must somehow be "scrambled" together to compute the overall distance between the historical case and the current problem. Clearly, some attributes are more important than others, and small distances in important attributes can compensate for large distances in less important ones. Given the heavy domain dependence of distance, we do not attempt to further characterize any techniques for matching.

The retrieval process takes the most similar cases and passes them on for further processing. In some domains, the solutions of the best cases can be somehow integrated (e.g., averaged) to arrive at a best solution. In other domains, the one single best case offers its solution for further processing (adaptation).

## ◇ ◇ ◇ Evaluation and Adaptation

The CBR system is now charged with determining the adequacy of the retrieved historical solution for the current problem. The process of **evaluation** may involve implementing the solution in a simulator of some sort, or in real life under test conditions. However, that is not always possible. It may also partly involve looking for negative cases — those whose solution did not solve the current problem when applied.

It is realistic to believe that even very similar cases are not identical to the current problem. Do these differences invalidate the historical solution? If the answer is yes, then the historical solution may be modified (*adapted*) to make it valid. This optional step compensates for any remaining differences.

Adaptation is one of the most complex procedures in CBR. In some domains, adaptation is not even possible, or so difficult that it is neglected by the system developers. For example, the nature of a prefilmed video clip is that it does not (reasonably) permit any changes to it. Therefore, it is considered invalid as a historical solution if it were to require adaptation — you cannot modify existing film clips [Leake, 1996, p. 11]. Many developers have replaced the search–retrieve–adapt cycle with **search–retrieve–propose,** where the solution of the most similar case is presented to a human user for consideration [Leake, 1996, p. 11].

Nevertheless, some domains do allow for adaptability of historical solutions. In such instances, some techniques exist to adapt historical solutions. These are discussed below.

### Reinstantiation

*Reinstantiation* instantiates an old solution with new objects. The historical solution may include objects that are not relevant to the solution when applied to the current problem. These may be substituted in the new solution with new, relevant objects. Kolodner [1993, p. 395] uses the example of planning a menu for a dinner party. She uses old cases of successful dinner parties to help in the menu planning process. However, for the current party (current problem), one of the guests does not eat red meat. Adaptation means substituting chicken as the meat and snow peas as the vegetable in a meal plan. These replace beef and broccoli in the problem, and satisfy the guest who does not eat red meat. Chicken and snow peas are the new objects that substitute beef and broccoli in the historical solution.

## Parameter Adjustment

This technique simply adjusts parameters in the historical solution when its original values make it invalid for the current problem. Heuristics can be used for making these adjustments. Rules may be a good way to represent these heuristics. In our running example, let us say that our creditworthiness system finds a case where an individual was lent $60,000 for a home improvement loan. This individual had an income of $60,000 per annum. The current problem is very similar to this historical case—the requested loan amount is also $60,000, with similar assets and employment. However, the applicant's annual income is only $50,000. The rules prohibit loans for less than an applicant's annual income. Then, the solution for the historical case can be adapted by reducing the loan amount to $50,000.

## Search

**Search** searches a knowledge structure (frame, semantic net) or a problem space for a substitute for the part of the historical solution that causes invalidity. For example, it has been determined that a leak exists in the car's vacuum system. The historical solution involves replacing the hose where the leak resides. However, the current problem's leak is not in the same location. Adaptation may involve searching the description of the automobile's vacuum system representation to find the exact location of the leak. Local search may also consist of searching a hierarchical structure upward (more abstract) to find another path parallel to the invalid attribute value. Kolodner [1993, pp. 407–413] describes three variants of this concept, called *local search, query memory,* and *specialized search.* These variants arise from domain-dependent issues.

## Case-Based Substitution

**Case-based substitution** can be used in some problem-solving situations, in which the solution may represent several largely independent subprocesses or values. If one of these is invalid, we only need to replace that subprocess or value, instead of the entire solution. In such instances, we can use a case-based approach to find a substitute for that particular invalid subprocess or value. The key is that the item to be substituted must already exist, and it only remains to be found and substituted.

## Transformation

*Transformation* is similar to case-based substitution except that the subprocess to substitute does not exist per se. It must be built through some knowledge. Generally, heuristic rules are employed. Therefore, it can be said that the element to be used as a substitute must be transformed from other solutions.

## Model-Guided Repair

**Model-guided repair** is an interesting approach, making use of a causal model to determine the appropriate transformation. It focuses on finding the *differences* between the current problem and the most similar case. Once found, these differences are evaluated utilizing the causal model, and are characterized. In other words, what effect do they have on the historical solution? Subsequently, for each difference, repair heuristics are applied to repair the historical solution [Kolodner, 1993]. Of course, this approach assumes a causal model exists, thereby precluding weak-theory domains by definition.

These methods of substitution and transformation are general approaches. One must put them in the context of their application to determine their relevance. Mostly, they come from applications in the literature where the techniques originated. In our opinion, these are domain-specific methods devised by the developers to address the needs of their particular application. We shall not discuss these any further here.

##  Learning

In our opinion, **learning** is by far the most significant feature of CBR systems. The ability to update and maintain a knowledge base by merely adding new cases is a tremendously advantageous and elegant feature. Although not without caveats, this ability compares very favorably with the rather painful and expensive knowledge acquisition and maintenance process for rule-based systems.

Because CBR makes explicit use of specific historical cases, addition of new cases can seamlessly and easily add more knowledge to the knowledge base—at least in theory. Let us now define the problem space as an amorphous $n$-dimensional space, with each dimension representing an attribute that partially describes each potential problem. In Figure 9-2, we give a two-dimensional version of this concept. The squares represent a conceptual case, each occupying a certain position in the space, and each case providing a solution. You can easily imagine cases adding to the library such that they progressively cover more and more of the problem space. Many of the cases overlap, but

**FIGURE 9-2** Pictorial Representation of Two-Dimensional Problem Space

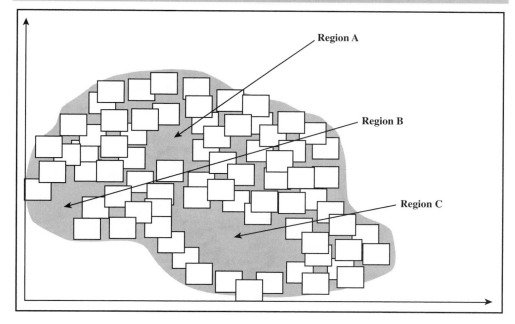

as long as their solutions are consistent, this is not a serious problem. In general, the more cases there are in the library, the better the coverage of the problem domain. However, too many cases overlapping can result in more cases than necessary, thereby clogging the search and retrieval process unnecessarily. Furthermore, if the newly solved problems are not sufficiently diverse, the process may leave some significant gaps in coverage. Regions A, B, and C in Figure 9-2 represent such gaps.

Thus, the learning process has to be selective. It may not be desirable to add every potential new case to the library. Only those that cover a previously uncovered gap in the problem space should be added. Moreover, when using structured organizational schemes, it is necessary to determine where the new case should be inserted in the library.

Another issue to consider is the solution of each case. To further develop this idea, let us again imagine a second space similar to that in Figure 9-2. This space consists of the solution space (i.e., the solutions prescribed by each case in the library). Each case in the problem space (Figure 9-2) is mapped to a solution in the solution space. This is shown in Figure 9-3. The CBR system associates the current problem with a case in the problem space. This historical case is then mapped to a solution in the solution space. This solution, either directly or after adaptation, is then assigned to the solution of the current problem. If the problem domain (1) is based on a natural process, (2) is well understood, and (3) all cases are completely defined, it is likely that the solutions provided by neighboring cases in the problem space are also neighbors in the solution space. That is, we say they are *consistent* with each other.

What happens, however, if the domain is poorly understood, or based on the foibles of human endeavors (e.g., stock market or home prices), or simply incompletely defined? The result may be that solutions may conflict with each other. That is, solutions to nearly identical cases may be radically different. We refer to this as an inconsistent situation, and adding new cases to such a case library must be carefully

 **FIGURE 9-3 Problem and Solution Spaces and the Mapping Between Them**

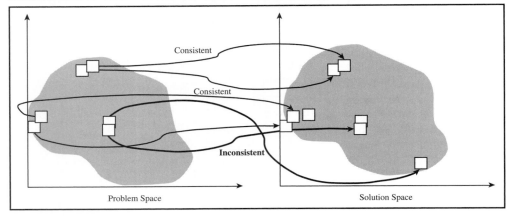

considered. In case of inconsistency, the new case must be discarded; or the existing cases must be deleted from the library, to be replaced by the new case. Otherwise, an inconsistent case library can result, providing conflicting solutions for minimally different problems. This situation is further discussed in the next section.

## ◆◇ ◆◇ ◆◇ Example of a Case-Based Reasoning System

CBR is an excellent technique to use when many well-documented histories of past problems and their solutions exist. For example, the legal profession thrives on judicial precedent, where a decision about a current case can be dependent on a landmark decision on a similar case. The similarities as well as the differences between the present and the landmark case have to be carefully considered by the plaintiff and defendants before a judge makes a decision, or before they make an appeal. As an example, the HYPO system [Ashley, 1988] is designed to assist in the analysis of court cases dealing with trade secret laws by using other cases that have been previously decided. In this application, historical court cases are used as precedence, and the attributes of the current court case are compared with historical court cases to determine a verdict. The legal process functions in much the same way, so application of CBR to this domain only seems natural.

Property appraisal is in many ways similar to judicial precedence. It is a time-consuming task designed to place a value (price) on a piece of property. There are three basic methods for appraising the value of real estate: (1) the cost approach, (2) the market data approach (also called sales comparison), and (3) the income approach.

The cost approach is based on the reproduction cost of the building plus the value of the land. The market data approach is based on the selling price of similar properties in the market. The income approach is based on the amount of net income the property can produce. For a more detailed description of these methods, see Creteau [1974], AIREA [1988], or Boyce [1984]. Although an appraiser uses a combination of these methods to make a property valuation, the most popular is the market data approach, especially in the appraisal of residential properties that do not produce income.

The market data approach for property appraisal operates on the premise that an informed buyer would pay for a property no more than the cost of acquiring another existing property with the same features [Boyce, 1984]. The sales price in a transaction is then a reflection of the knowledge that both the seller and the buyer have of the market. This justifies the use of similar properties that have been sold recently (called *comparables*) to determine the market value. The principle involved is that each factor or element of comparison in a property has a contribution to value, and this contribution may be reflected in a sales price differential.

To illustrate the process of CBR in a real-world application, we use the market data method of property appraisal. The value of a property is generally determined by the property's market price in the area where the property is located, at the time of the appraisal. A recently sold property similar in size, function, and features must be found in the same area to serve as evidence of value. A large and reliable database of sold properties (a case library) is readily available from the local realty association or local government.

The property appraisal domain is characterized by having a single parameter in its solution—the estimated value of the appraised property. This makes it different from most other CBR applications whose solution may be composed of several variables. Furthermore, because of the heuristic nature of the domain, different experts may reach somewhat different answers while having the same data at their disposition.

A knowledge application system called the *property appraisal system* was developed to automatically estimate the appraised value of a property using CBR [Gonzalez, 1992]. This system uses the following elements of comparison in a home (called *features*):

- Living area in square feet
- Number of bedrooms
- Number of bathrooms
- Architectural style of the house
- Age of the house
- Location (neighborhood)
- Date of sale
- Type of cooling equipment
- Type of heating equipment
- Type of garage
- Site or lot size
- Availability of a swimming pool

The first step in the process is, of course, case retrieval. The property appraisal system looks in a case library of recently sold properties, retrieves the ten best cases, and ranks them in order of decreasing similarity. The evaluation of a case is performed by assigning weights to each feature and determining how to evaluate differences in these features.

The next step is case adaptation. Because the values of the features of the retrieved properties are not precisely the same as those of the property being appraised, even if the degree of similarity is high, each retrieved case must be adapted to compensate for its differences with the appraised property. This is done using **critics.** A critic is a rule that increases or decreases the actual sold price of a retrieved property based on the differences between it and the property being appraised.

For example, let us assume that house A is the appraised property and house B is a recently sold case that the system retrieved as one of the top ten matches. The property appraisal system adapts the sales price of B based on how well it resembles A. For example, if A has a swimming pool, but B does not, this represents a difference for which B must be compensated. The swimming pool critic might indicate that the resale value of a pool is $5,000. Thus, if B sold for $75,000, its adapted sales price would now be $80,000. These critics were obtained by interviewing appraisal experts, and they are fairly standard in the field.

The adaptation process is cumulative and is done for all the elements of comparison. For instance, the critic for living area might specify a compensation of $500 for every 50 square ft of difference. If A has 2,100 square ft. and B has 2,000 square ft., then the adaptation process would decrease the adapted sales price of B by $1,000, now making it $79,000.

However, too many adaptations to the cases can result in inaccuracies. The property appraisal system penalizes each case for the extent of adaptations made. The more adaptations are made, the higher the penalty incurred. This leads to computing a *comfort factor* that tells the system which of the ten adapted cases was least extensively adapted. The system ranks the ten adapted cases in order of decreasing comfort factor and selects the top three, because that is the traditional number of comparisons used in the appraisal business. Finally, it takes the average of the three and uses that value as the expected sales price of the appraised property.

The property appraisal system provided some excellent results when tested on actual appraised values for real estate properties. Tests were done with the assistance of a real estate agent who specialized in appraisals. This was done to ensure realism in the process as well as in the answers. For more information on this system and the testing performed, see Gonzalez [1992] and Laureano-Ortiz [1991]. Details of other knowledge application systems based on CBR technology are presented in Chapter 16.

## ❖❖❖ Discussion on Case-Based Systems

Case-based systems provide a highly intuitive and natural way to solve problems. They can be effective, efficient, and relatively easy to build. The technique developed significant momentum in its early years because of the strong conviction among some researchers that it could overcome the drawbacks of rule-based systems. Specifically, it was thought to be able to relieve the knowledge acquisition bottleneck by replacing the knowledge of an expert with a database of historical cases. Improvements in performance would then naturally result from its built-in learning ability. Furthermore, its maintenance would likewise be considerably easier than for an equivalent rule-based system. Although much of this is true, one must carefully consider when and how to apply CBR in lieu of rule-based systems. CBR systems have significant drawbacks as well—something not loudly proclaimed by the CBR proponents. Let us begin this discussion by placing rule-based systems and CBR in context.

As we have mentioned several times before, CBR is based on the idea that problem solvers remember past experiences *explicitly* and draw on them for solutions. In reality, rule-based systems are founded on a rather similar tenet. Experts' experiences result from them having seen, and solved, not only one but also probably several cases similar to the current problem. Such experiences have allowed experts to "compile" this knowledge into heuristics that they use to solve future problems. These heuristics form the rules and frames that make up traditional expert systems. The heuristics are remembered, but the specific instances that were used to compile them are forgotten or discarded (for the most part). This makes it more difficult to modify the compiled rules, because experts would first have to modify their own knowledge before it was reflected in the knowledge base. Additionally, a new knowledge engineering effort, albeit more modest, would have to be started.

In our earlier narrative example of a fire ground commander, had the commander been an expert, he would have relied on his personal rule of thumb that spectators always be moved back from the building whenever billboards reside atop the burning building. Likewise, the presence of a cloud of smoke of a certain color and dispersion at a fire would prompt him to order his men to don breathing apparatus.

One difference, therefore, is that although CBR takes the experience explicitly and specifically, rule-based systems filter the experience through the eyes of an expert. There are advantages to filtering the experiences through an expert. The expert can provide many insights that a sterile case library cannot, no matter how detailed the cases are. On the other hand, developing a knowledge base is typically more difficult and costly than an equivalent case library. This is because for many applications, the historical cases are already documented or similarly expressed in a formal manner. It only remains to place them in a properly designed and organized case library. On the other hand, an expert's knowledge must be elicited, and the rules painstakingly coded.

It has been said that CBR uses specific examples, whereas rule-based system generalize the knowledge found in the historical examples [Kolodner, 1993]. This tends to provide a wider coverage of problems, at the cost of specificity. Many cases would be necessary to cover the same problem space equally covered by a few rules. Specific cases, on the other hand, may provide a more accurate solution.

Let us return to the issue of coverage of the problem space (see Figures 9-2 and 9-3). If cases map regularly and consistently into solutions in the solution space, we can say that the solutions are in the same neighborhood relative to the cases from which they originate. Thus, neighboring cases can ideally provide neighboring solutions. This makes for a good application of CBR. This is generally the case in domains based on natural phenomena, such as diagnosis of well-understood systems. Nature works very predictably if we truly understand the phenomena. On the other hand, other domains such as the stock market and property appraisal depend on less predictable human considerations. For example, two nearly identical, equivalently maintained houses next to each other may have sold for significantly different amounts. House A sold for $150,000, whereas the nearly identical House B sold for $200,000. Certainly, any minimal difference between them (e.g., 500 sq. ft. difference, fireplace) does not merit a 33% price difference. The reason may have been that the male buyer of House A liked something about the house that reminded him of his boyhood home. He absolutely had to have this house, regardless of cost. Alternatively, he may just have had more money to spend than the buyer of House B, and consequently paid the asking price to avoid hassles. Nevertheless, the selling prices (i.e., solutions) of these two neighboring cases are not consistent with each other, and they map into widely different solutions for very similar problems. These two cases are clearly inconsistent with each other. The property appraisal system addresses this problem by taking the best three cases, and averages their adapted cost. This effectively spreads out the influence of such a situation.

Even in consistent domains, incomplete descriptions of the problems may lead to problems in the solutions. In our property appraisal system example, if the aesthetic condition of the house is not somehow reflected in the case definition (e.g., handyman's special), two otherwise equivalent houses may sell for widely varying prices. The property appraisal system acknowledges that this is indeed possible, and only uses the best cases that are within a certain range of each other. Outliers are typically disregarded; however, because in some situations there may not be enough similar cases to provide three solid cases, the ultimate solution's confidence is degraded.

Adaptation also has limits. Going back to Figure 9-2, small gaps such as those labeled as regions A and B could conceivably be covered, by adapting the solutions of some of the nearby neighboring cases. However, region C is comparatively large and possibly not covered by adapting solutions of neighboring cases. Furthermore, because rules are the most common means of implementing adaptation, the same problem of knowledge engineering (albeit to a smaller degree) is faced as well.

Building a CBR system involves the development of a fairly robust and well-indexed set of cases. Ideally, the case library would be composed of documented, complete historical cases that are already in electronic form. In many domains, this is exactly the case (e.g., property appraisal). However, in many other domains, the documented cases are ad hoc, incomplete, inconsistent, or poorly understood. In others, they are nonexistent. In such domains, experts can be called on to develop a case library or to interpret a poorly defined one, based on their experiences. This clearly defeats the purpose of facilitating initial knowledge development. However, maintenance of the case library, once built, can be significantly improved as the case library grows with time. Although Kolodner [1993] states that CBR systems only need a seed set of cases to start, we do not believe this is realistic for large, complex domains.

Having discussed the issues on CBR systems, let us continue by concisely summarizing the advantages and disadvantages of CBR, as discussed in the above paragraph.

### Advantages and Disadvantages of Case-Based Reasoning

The following is a discussion on the advantages and disadvantages of CBR systems.

### Advantages

In light of our earlier discussion, some advantages of CBR over rule-based systems are:

1. The knowledge acquisition process is considerably simplified in many applications, especially where the case library may already exist as corporate documentation, possibly even in an electronic database.
2. The knowledge maintenance process is greatly facilitated by the learning ability of CBR systems.
3. CBR is modeled after human reasoning. There is significant evidence to believe that CBR is a cognitive problem-solving model [Kolodner, 1993].
4. CBR performs better than rule-based systems in so-called **weak-theory domains.** That is, these are domains where experts may not exist, or if they exist, they do not fully understand the intricacies of the domain.
5. The base of experience used can be that of an entire organization, instead of that of a single individual. This can multiply the breadth of a knowledge base in CBR.

In many cases, CBR systems are much more efficient than rule-based systems. This is especially true for problems where knowledge is highly tacit and hard to codify. Furthermore, it is also applicable when the domain theory is weak, such as when humans do not fully understand the phenomena involved. Finally, this efficiency applies to domains where the historical cases are already documented, and preferably in electronic form. However, some features of CBR systems—distance metric, need to search, adaptation, and learning—can often impede the execution of CBR systems. For each application, the potential user must decide which technique is more appropriate based on the characteristics of the actual domain.

### Disadvantages

There are several disadvantages associated with CBR.

1. Just as efficiency is seen as an advantage, it can also be a disadvantage for large systems with poorly organized or indexed case libraries. Moreover, the matching process, if complex, can add computational cost to the CBR system, regardless of how well designed the case library may be.

2. In many cases, distance calculations between the desired and actual solution can be difficult to make. This is from a conceptual as well as a computational standpoint.

3. Adaptation may be quite difficult or impossible in many domains. In others, it is done with rules.

4. Learning, although natural and intuitive, demands some careful considerations as to which cases are added to the case library, and how.

5. Building a case library may not be easy in some situations, and it may approach the difficulty of building a rule base. This may be the case where cases do not already exist or are poorly documented. In such cases, experts can be asked to create the cases from their experiences. This may be as difficult as implementing the knowledge in a conventional rule-based system. We argue that this neutralizes one otherwise major advantage of CBR.

In summary, CBR is a great technique for those applications where it fits well. Many such applications clearly exist. One must resist, however, the temptation to apply CBR to all problems. It is clearly not the proper approach for many problems. The reader should be sure to carefully analyze the intended application before deciding which technique to use.

## ◈ ◈ ◈ Variations of Case-Based Reasoning

As a point of interest to the reader, there are variants of CBR, such as exemplar-based reasoning, instance-based reasoning, memory-based reasoning, and analogy-based reasoning. Some of these different variations of CBR are described below [Aamodt and Plaza, 1994; Leake, 1996]:

1. *Exemplar-based reasoning.* These systems seek to solve problems through classification, that is, finding the right class for the unclassified exemplar. Essentially the class of the most similar past case then becomes the solution to the classification problem, and the set of classes are the possible solutions to the problem [Kibler and Aha, 1987].

2. *Instance-based reasoning.* These systems require a large number of instances (or cases) that are typically simple; that is, they are defined by a small set of attributes vectors. The major focus of study of these systems is automated learning, requiring no user involvement [Aha et al., 1991].

3. *Memory-based reasoning.* A variation of CBR only in name, this virtually shares all the functionality and processes of CBR.

4. *Analogy-based reasoning.* These systems are typically used to solve new problems based on past cases from a different domain [Aamodt and Plaza, 1994; Veloso and Carbonell, 1993]. Analogy-based reasoning focuses on case reuse,

also called the *mapping problem,* that is, finding a way to map the solution of the analogue case to the present problem.

## SUMMARY

In this chapter, we cover a different way to represent knowledge—through explicit historical cases. This approach differs greatly from the rule-based approach because the knowledge is not compiled and interpreted by an expert. Instead, the experiences that possibly shaped the expert's knowledge are directly used to make decisions.

This approach provides some advantages, such as a reduced knowledge engineering effort, and seamless learning. Obtaining rules from an expert or other sources is no longer the bottleneck in the KB system development effort. This is because CBR systems use historical, documented cases to reflect knowledge as past experiences. Rules are no longer the knowledge representation paradigm of choice. Instead, frames with their ability to hold attribute and value pairs are typically used to express each historical case.

Learning is an important issue in CBR, because with the mere addition of new cases to the library, the system learns. This can be a very valuable feature of CBR systems, but only if it is well understood and properly used. An improperly used learning facility can actually serve to disrupt the consistency of a case library by permitting cases to be added that are not consistent with the cases therein. At its worst, improper learning can cause conflicts with other cases; at best, it can cause duplication of cases and, therefore, inefficient searching and matching.

## KEY TERMS

- adaptation—p. 162
- case—p. 161
- case-based substitution—p. 168
- case library—p. 162
- critic—p. 172
- comfort factor indexing—p. 173

- evaluation—p. 167
- flat case libraries—p. 164
- learning—p. 169
- model-guided repair—p. 168
- parameter adjustment—p. 168
- problem space—p. 166

- remindings—p. 161
- retrieval—p. 166
- search—p. 168
- search–retrieve–propose— p. 167
- weak-theory domains—p. 175

## REVIEW QUESTIONS

1. List five general features common to applications that would be suited for solution through case-based reasoning (CBR).
2. List five problems that would make excellent applications of CBR. Justify your answers.
3. List five applications that would make poor fits with CBR. Justify your answers.
4. The property appraisal system we describe in this chapter used a flat case library. This was justified by the relatively small number of cases employed (21). How would you design the case library if instead of the 21 cases it had 21,000? Justify your answer. Discuss the indexing, as well as the organization.
5. Would the stock market represent a good application for CBR? Explain why or why not.

## APPLICATION EXERCISES ◇ ◇ ◇

1. For 1 week, keep track of what you eat for breakfast, lunch, and dinner. Also record any special attribute that contributed to you ordering or preparing each specific meal. Were you particularly hungry? Did you have a special hanker for something? Were you eating out? Were you celebrating some good news? By looking at these cases, decide how you can index the case library to achieve the most efficiency in searching.

2. For the problem of deciding what to eat for the following week, design a distance metric to determine similarity in cases.

3. Pose a problem to a hypothetical case-based system dealing with what to eat for Thursday night of next week. Identify the special characteristics or circumstances of the meal.

4. Is there an opportunity for adaptation of the most similar cases? If there is, how would you do it?

5. Build a case on the results in step 4 above. If realistic, then assume that you in fact ate that meal on the determined day, and add the new case to the case library. Now run the same problem again.

## REFERENCES ◇ ◇ ◇

Aamodt, A., and Plaza, E. 1994. Case-based reasoning: Foundational issues, methodological variations, and system approaches. *AI Communications,* 7(1), 39–52.

Aha, D., Kibbler, D., and Albert, M. 1991. Instance-based learning algorithms. *Machine Learning,* 6(1).

AIREA — American Institute of Real Estate Appraisers. 1988. *Appraising Residential Properties.* AIREA, Chicago, IL.

Ashley, K.D., and Rissland, E.L. A case-based approach to modeling legal expertise. *IEE Expert,* (Fall), 70–77.

Barletta, R., and Mark, W. 1988. Explanation-based Indexing of Cases, Proc. 7th Int. Conf. on Artificial Intelligence, AAAI, pp. 541–546.

Boyce, B.N., and Kinnard, W.N. 1984. *Appraising Real Property.* Heath and Co., Lexington, MA.

Creteau, P.G. 1974. *Real Estate Appraising (Step by Step),* 2nd ed. Castle Publishing, Portland, ME.

Gonzalez, A.J., and Laureano-Ortiz, R. 1992. A case-based reasoning approach to real estate property appraisal, expert systems with applications. *An International Journal,* 4(2), 229–246.

Klein, G., and Calderwood, R. 1985. How Do People Make Analogues to Make Decisions.

Proc. 1988 Case-Based Reasoning Workshop, pp. 209–223.

Kolodner, J. 1993. *Case-Based Reasoning.* Morgan Kaufman Publishers, San Mateo, CA.

Kibler, D., and Aha, D. 1987. Learning representative exemplars of concepts: An initial study. Proceedings of the 4th Int. Workshop on Machine Learning, UC-Irvine, June, pp. 24–29.

Laureano-Ortiz, R. 1991. A Case-Based Appraisal System, Master's Thesis. Department of Computer Engineering, University of Central Florida, Orlando, FL.

Leake, D.B. 1996. *Case-Based Reasoning — Experiences, Lessons and Future Directions.* AAAI Press, Menlo Park, CA.

Srinivasa, R. 1999. Parallel Rule-Based Isotach Systems. University of Virginia, Computer Science Department, Report No. CS-99-04, February 5.

Schank, R. 1982. 1982. *Dynamic Memory: A Theory of Learning in Computers and People.* Cambridge University Press, New York.

Veloso, M., and Carbonel, J. 1993. Derivational analogy in PRODIGY. *Machine Learning,* 10(3), 249–278.

# Knowledge Elicitation

## Converting Tacit Knowledge to Explicit Knowledge[1]

### ◇ ◇ ◇ Introduction

As we see in previous chapters, knowledge can be either tacit or explicit. By definition, explicit knowledge is already captured in an understandable form. This is not so for tacit knowledge. It is, therefore, important to elicit tacit knowledge and then capture it in a form that makes it easily manageable. This process is by no means a simple task.

Knowledge elicitation does not need to be limited to the process of developing knowledge-based systems. Humans seek and acquire knowledge in our everyday activities. We read books, magazines, and articles; and we observe others perform tasks. More significantly, we often ask questions of knowledgeable people, for example, at the auto parts store, the computer store, the hardware store, and the travel agency. We occasionally take classes to accelerate our learning process. All these activities are part of the process of managing knowledge. Developing case studies for instruction is also very much akin to knowledge elicitation. It is clear from Chapter 8 that knowledge can be represented in many ways for retrieval and reuse. In this chapter, we are less interested in the representation of the knowledge, and more interested in the ways to elicit the knowledge from experts.

In this chapter, we discuss several ways to capture tacit knowledge from human sources. Currently, the most commonly used knowledge elicitation process is a manual one. It consists of interviewing knowledgeable individuals and eliciting their knowledge via several question-and-answer sessions. This process typically requires too many sessions, making it slow and difficult. Typically, competent knowledge engineers

---

[1]This chapter is written in collaboration with Douglas D. Dankel.

(KEs) who work with knowledgeable, patient, and communicative experts can make a big difference in the success of this process. However, it is still a long and difficult process for any but the most trivial of systems. Nevertheless, the traditional interview process is destined to remain the primary method of knowledge elicitation for the foreseeable future. This is primarily because it permits capturing important tacit knowledge expressed in the subject's body language, in a way that no machine is able to do.

In this chapter we also discuss alternative methods to (partially) automate the knowledge elicitation process. These programs interact directly with a subject matter expert to help experts structure their knowledge appropriately. These methods can be used alone or in combination with the more traditional interview method, thereby facilitating the capture of domain-specific knowledge. These techniques are essential for developing the knowledge capture systems described in Chapter 14. We first begin with the manual elicitation process.

## ◆◇ ◆◇ ◆◇ Manual Knowledge Elicitation

We discuss in this section the manual process of **knowledge elicitation.** It specifically addresses elicitation of tacit knowledge from human sources, and not from documents. We specifically focus on eliciting the knowledge from a knowledgeable human and representing it in some machine understandable way for storage and application. Therefore, we define the term **knowledge capture** as the combination of knowledge elicitation and representation of the knowledge in a machine-readable form. Figure 10-1 depicts these concepts.

Knowledge capture is an iterative process consisting of knowledge elicitation, representation, and confirmation that could seemingly continue forever. It is, therefore, important that this be done competently, risking failure otherwise. Therefore, we concentrate on this step in this section. We cover the chronology or sequence of events that occurs when a single person interfaces with one domain expert to elicit knowledge

◆◇ ◆◇ ◆◇ FIGURE 10-1 Knowledge Elicitation and Knowledge Acquisition

Knowledge Elicitation

Knowledge Capture = Knowledge Elicitation + Knowledge Representation

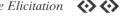

from that expert. We discuss the different types of techniques used during these knowledge elicitation meetings called **interviews.** We also cover team interviewing and the special considerations taken in such contexts.

The main vehicle for knowledge elicitation is face-to-face discussions between the subject matter experts (SMEs) who possess the domain knowledge, and the KEs who ask questions, observe the expert solving problems, and determine what knowledge is used. These interviews occur repeatedly over several weeks or months, making this a rigorous and tedious process. Thus, care should be taken to perform it efficiently.

The following sections discuss the interview process. Interviewing is first described as a sequence of different types of interview sessions, each having separate and distinct objectives. We then concentrate on other issues in the process, for example, techniques for eliciting knowledge from the experts.

## Basic Unstructured One-On-One Interview Process

Interviews can take many different formats, as presented below. The basic interview is conducted between one KE and one expert. This simply means that one KE and one expert meet and interact to allow the KE to elicit the knowledge. All other interview contexts are variations of this theme. Ideally, the **one-on-one interview** process consists of a series of interview sessions, each possibly of a different type, having slightly different objectives. These are described below.

### Kickoff Interview

The main objective in this first meeting, **the kickoff interview,** is to establish good rapport with the expert. If this is the first extensive meeting with the expert, the KE should attempt to make a good first impression.

This can be achieved by demonstrating to the expert that an honest attempt has been made by the KE to gain familiarization with the domain before the meeting. Therefore, when preparing for this initial interview, the KE should become acquainted with the discipline. Extensive familiarization is not required or desired because the expert's guidance should be used in learning about the domain and significant prior knowledge might cause important relationships to be ignored (they might appear to be obvious facts or relationships about the domain to both the expert and KE).

A typical agenda for the initial interview consists of:

1. An introduction and light conversation.
2. An explanation of what the objectives of the elicitation process are.
3. A discussion of the importance of the project (if applicable).
4. A discussion of what is expected of the expert as well as what the expert can expect from the KE.
5. An identification of what reading materials the expert recommends for the KE to review and to become familiar with the domain.
6. The scheduling of the next meeting.

We now discuss each of these critical agenda items in greater detail.

A key to this meeting is getting the expert familiar with *what* is going to happen, not the specifics of *how* it can be done. The discussion should include defining the material that the KE should review to become somewhat knowledgeable with the domain. This allows the KE to use documentation familiar to the expert (i.e., textbooks, reports, and illustrations). The advantage of reading material familiar to the expert is that it provides a common set of concepts, terminology, and vocabulary with the expert. This can greatly assist the knowledge elicitation process.

Finally, it is important that the expert and KE clearly identify each other's roles so their working relationship is firmly established early in the process. If the expert, because of other commitments, cannot or does not want to make the required commitment toward this project, then it is better to know this early in the process so alternatives can be explored. Included within these discussions should be a description of the interview process, and an explanation of the concepts of incremental development.

It is important that the length of the kickoff interview be kept short (i.e., to not more than 1 hour). Remember that the most significant accomplishment of the kickoff session is establishing ground rules and mutual understanding of expectations. All other goals should be secondary.

### General Knowledge-Gathering Sessions

The so-called *knowledge elicitation sessions,* following the kickoff interview, begin the actual knowledge elicitation process. We can classify them into one of two categories by the types of knowledge gathered: (1) **general knowledge-gathering interview sessions** and (2) **specific problem-solving, knowledge-gathering interview sessions.**

KEs use the first type of session to learn general principles about the domain from the expert. The knowledge they gather, although important and educational, probably is not explicitly expressed because it is primarily used to gain a basic understanding of the domain. They use this knowledge to understand the more specific knowledge that is to be elicited in later sessions.

KEs use the second kind of session to understand and gather the specific knowledge used by the expert. This is the knowledge that the engineer must capture and represent. In the next two subsections we describe these sessions in more detail as well as some useful techniques in extracting knowledge.

The first few sessions after the kickoff interview are general knowledge-gathering sessions. The main objectives for the KE at this point are to:

1. Better understand the subject matter.
2. Better understand the expert's opinions and viewpoints on the domain.

Before the first of these sessions, the KE should be well read in the domain, having not only reviewed the literature suggested by the expert, but also other documents that could be located that may not have been mentioned by the expert. At this point the KE knows the vocabulary and has a basic understanding of the domain. This enables the engineer to converse with the expert and understand the replies to the engineer's questions. This relieves some of the burden from the expert by not requiring a continual definition of every term used. It also facilitates the major task of these sessions: knowledge gathering through **open-ended questions.**

Open-ended questions are similar to essay questions on an examination. They require discussion and cannot be answered simply with a yes, a no, a simple term, or a number. Using these questions is effective because they give the expert an opportunity to talk freely about the domain. This can serve as a concentrated learning experience for the KE. Experts generally enjoy an opportunity to speak openly about their domain and show how much they know. An astute KE benefits from such dialogues by gaining insight into the expert's tacit knowledge base. This verifies and strengthens the KE's understanding of the domain. If the KE does not understand certain concepts or terminology, this is the proper time to ask questions.

Interviews such as these may range from 1 to 2 hours in duration. It is often difficult and undesirable to schedule longer periods with the expert. Concentration decreases quickly after 2 hours. Open-ended questioning should continue for as many sessions as are needed to satisfy the objectives of obtaining a good understanding of the problem domain, and the expert's opinions and viewpoints on the domain. During this time the KE should also be identifying subareas that are appropriate for further examination.

### Specific Problem-Solving, Knowledge-Gathering Sessions

Once the KE understands the basics of the domain, the process should continue by selecting a subarea that can serve as the first chunk of knowledge to be extracted from the expert and represented explicitly. Specific subareas can be difficult to identify because a definition of what is appropriate for further examination can depend greatly on issues such as the development schedule or customer preferences. However, subareas should involve issues or areas that are:

1. Well understood by the particular expert interviewed.
2. Reasonably well understood by the knowledge engineer.
3. Of sufficient breadth and depth to truly represent the difficulties of this domain.
4. Small enough to require only 2 to 3 months of development effort without trivializing the scope of this domain's problems.

It is now time to shift the focus of the interviews from general learning and fact gathering to more specific knowledge elicitation. Whereas the previous interviews were of a wide-ranging nature, the next several ones are to be highly directed, emphasizing depth instead of breadth of coverage. The objective of these interviews is to explore how the expert solves specific problems or answers questions in the domain. More specific questions are asked, many of which result in yes, no, or numeric answers. Such questions are called **close-ended questions.**

### Knowledge Elicitation Sequence

One technique commonly used in knowledge elicitation is the **output–input–middle method**. This technique consists of the following sequence:

1. Identifying the answers or solutions to the problem under discussion—the *outputs* of the expert. These represent the goals that the expert reaches when searching for an answer. In the case where more than one exists, they should all be defined with their subtle differences clearly identified. These differences should be understood by the KE.

2. Identifying the sources of information that the expert uses to deduce the solution or the answer—the *inputs*. How these inputs are identified, determined, and generated should also be known and understood by the KE.
3. Finally and most important, determining the links between the inputs and the outputs—the *middle*. These connections represent the core of the expert's knowledge. Some inputs may not be required initially, but may be requested later after the initial inputs are interpreted. For example, initial analysis may indicate the need for more inputs to resolve an ambiguity. Additionally, intermediate goals or hypotheses may be required to complete the connections.

The example in Vignette 10-1 illustrates this concept for automotive diagnostics knowledge.

The input–output–middle process gives the KE, a means to effectively organize the knowledge elicitation sessions.

### Other Knowledge Elicitation Techniques

The unstructured question-and-answer interview described above is the most common means of eliciting knowledge from an expert. However, it is not always the most efficient. There are other knowledge elicitation techniques besides the simple question-and-answer interview that can be more effective under certain circumstances. In some domains, considerable expertise is documented in instruction manuals or books. For example, in automobile diagnosis there are literally dozens of maintenance manuals published for every type of automobile. Some are published by the manufacturer, whereas others are written by third parties. A significant portion of knowledge about automobile diagnosis can be obtained from such manuals by someone who understands the basics of that domain.

Some experts, cooperative as they may be, often have a hard time articulating their expertise. Part of the reason is that they perform the tasks so automatically and subconsciously that they do not really know how they do it. They do, however, know what to do when it comes time to solve the problem. A good analogy to this is when Tom asks Joe for directions to a location to which Joe has often been. Joe's answer often is something like, "I know how to get there, but I can't explain it to you."

In cases such as this, alternative techniques must be used that do not rely as heavily on the question-and-answer routine. These can be broken down into two different methods:

1. **Observational elicitation** involves the KE observing the expert at work and trying to understand and duplicate the expert's problem-solving methods.
2. **Role reversal** involves the KE attempting to become a pseudoexpert and implementing this pseudoknowledge about the problem domain.

Both techniques are applied in an iterative fashion. We next discuss each of these methods in more detail.

The technique of observation simply means looking over the shoulders of an expert doing the job. This provides an indication of the process the expert uses to solve a particular (and real) problem. There are many variations of the observation technique, some of which are discussed in the following subsections.

 VIGNETTE 10-1

## An Output – Input – Middle Example

An expert mechanic system is designed to allow motorists to call and obtain a diagnosis of their automobile's cooling system malfunction. The motorist is assumed not to be mechanically inclined and, therefore, unable to inspect obvious parts like hoses or belts. All communication with the motorists takes place over the telephone. The KE first compiles a list of all the possible problems that may occur with the cooling system of an automobile.

### OUTPUTS

The possible outputs expected in this domain are:

- Leak in radiator.
- Broken fan belt.
- Defective water pump.
- Loss of coolant through evaporation due to a loose radiator cap.
- Broken or cracked water hose.
- Frozen coolant.

Then the KE determines the various inputs used to discover these problems.

### INPUTS

The inputs necessary for an expert mechanic to diagnose the cooling system malfunction are:

- Temperature indicator on the dashboard.
- Steam coming out of the hood.
- Weather conditions.
- Puddles of coolant underneath engine compartment.

Finally, the expert determines the relationships between the inputs and the outputs.

This may require some intermediate goals or states that the expert may have to define. If the objective of this exercise is to build an expert system to perform automotive diagnosis, then these relationships are translated into the rules of the system. A few sample rules for diagnosing cooling systems are provided below. Note that these rules are just a representative sample and not a complete set of rules.

### MIDDLE

Because the knowledge of this domain is mostly heuristic, the appropriate format for representing it is rules. Some rules determined to be applicable are:

- *Rule 1.* The presence of a "hot" reading on the dashboard temperature gauge generally implies that at least one problem exists.
- *Rule 2.* The absence of a hot reading on the temperature gauge does not necessarily imply absence of a problem.
- *Rule 3.* A large pool of coolant under the engine compartment can indicate radiator leaks, broken hoses, or defective water pump.
- *Rule 4.* A relatively small pool of coolant under the engine compartment, not accompanied by a hissing sound, usually implies a defective water pump.
- *Rule 5.* The absence of a pool of coolant under the engine compartment, and a hot reading on the dashboard temperature gauge indicates a broken fan belt.
- *Rule 6.* An ambient temperature below 10°F implies that the coolant is frozen.
- *Rule 7.* The presence of a hissing sound accompanied by a small pool of coolant under the front of the engine compartment indicates a radiator or a hose leak.

 **VIGNETTE 10-2**

## Observation

Pattie, a graduate student in biology, was interacting with an agricultural extension agent to build an expert system that would offer advice about when pesticides should be applied to a crop. The expert explained that performing a field survey and counting the number of insects fell into five size categories. Based on the number of insects in each category and the age of the crop, the expert determined whether pesticides were economically warranted.

Pattie gathered knowledge from this expert and built a series of rules that described this approach. Because there were several cases not covered by the examples that they discussed, she prepared a simple written test that would uncover additional rules.

When this test was administered to the expert, Pattie discovered that the expert was reducing the five categories used, to three, by adding several insect counts together. This quiet on-site observation of the expert's problem-solving process allowed Pattie to uncover the true technique in use, and not the technique that the expert thought was being used.

### Quiet On-Site Observation

This type of observation does not permit KEs to question the experts while they are solving a real problem. Because the experts' train of thought is not continually interrupted by questions, they are able to proceed at their most effective as well as realistic form. There is clearly something to be learned from this.

The disadvantage to this technique is that the lack of interaction leaves the KE wondering about the solution approaches taken by the expert. Consequently, the technique of quiet observation should be used only when there is a need simply to get a feel for the total magnitude of the problem-solving process or to verify that a hypothesized approach is in use (Vignette 10-2 gives an example). It is usually not a good technique for obtaining details about the process. A second disadvantage to this technique occurs if the experts are asked to think out loud about what they are doing. Thinking aloud might make experts self-conscious about their approach, causing them to alter it or to create a verbalization that is much more complex than what they are actually doing.

### On-Site Observation with Discussion

This is, of course, the process of observation described above without a gag order on the KE. Although this interaction does not allow the experts to be themselves, thereby clouding full visibility of the problem-solving process, the inclusion of questions does permit the KE to better probe the process observed. The danger is that the expert may become distracted by the questions and not follow the normal procedure in solving the problem.

If the observed task does not significantly challenge the expert's problem-solving abilities (i.e., the problem is routine for the expert), the expert can be free to devote significant time and effort toward providing a detailed explanation of the approach. A perceptive KE can acquire significant knowledge from this exercise, because the expert feels quite at ease and performs the task relatively uninhibited.

If the problem is significantly more difficult, then the expert may struggle to reach a solution. Some symptoms of this are uneasiness, hesitation in making a decision, or simply refusing to create a solution in front of the KE. This approach may not work with an uncooperative expert. With a cooperative expert, however, such situations can provide a wealth of information. The expert typically verbalizes the problem-solving process because the problem and its solution approach are so uncertain. The various alternatives are overtly explored. It is important that a question-and-answer session follow so the KE can satisfy whatever questions were raised during the exercise, whether the observation period included questions or not.

### Exercising the Expert

One disadvantage of the pure observation method is that real problems have to be used. Although experts in some domains solve several problems every day, in other domains problems arise only seldom and unpredictably. Even in domains where problems are abundant, the difficulty level of these problems may not be sufficiently high, limiting their usefulness.

One method to alleviate this difficulty is to prepare cases of varying difficulty from historical data. These can then be presented to the expert in an "off-line" environment to observe the expert's methodology. In effect, we "exercise" experts by asking them to solve artificial (albeit realistic) problems off-line, and observe how they solve the problem presented.

One way to improve the elicitation process is to provide what Hoffman [1987] calls **limited information tasks** and **constrained processing tasks.** He defines them as follows:

> *Limited information tasks.* A routine task is performed, but the expert is not provided certain information that is typically available.
> *Constrained processing tasks.* A routine task is performed, but the expert must execute it under some constraint, for example, within a limited amount of time.

These techniques examine experts' abilities to provide additional information about their problem-solving talents. Both require observation, making them special cases of the techniques described above.

### Problem Description and Analysis

This category does not consist of posed problems, whether real or historical, but instead classical problems. These problems are best characterized as ones typically discussed and analyzed by instructors in a classroom situation. Their importance is demonstrated by their use in the teaching environment—they illustrate important or significant relationships within the domain that every problem solver should possess. Normally, experts select these, because they have been exposed to them during their careers. Occasionally, however, the KE can select them when questioning the approach of the expert.

In examining these problems, the expert explains the rationale behind distinguishing these problems as classics. Why are they used for teaching purposes? What are the important relationships and features that make each of these problems significant? This examination is typically performed as a case study where the expert describes the setting and then identifies the significant features that are present that make this problem important. This methodical approach clearly illustrates to the KE what is significant and important.

### Role Reversal Techniques

Role reversal is ideally suited for situations where the KE already has a significant understanding of the problem-solving process and wishes to verify its correctness. These techniques are generally not used for eliciting knowledge, but instead for verifying knowledge previously obtained.

KEs using role reversal attempt to become pseudoexperts in the domain. They study the techniques and approaches used by the expert, and build a set of protocols on how to attack problems. Then with the aid of the expert, they test their abilities using the concept of *role-playing*.

Role-playing employs the idea of role reversal, where the KE acts as the expert. The pseudoexpert attempts to solve a problem in the presence of the true expert who questions the pseudo-experts about what they are doing and why. In effect, this is the process of observation with questions where the roles have been reversed. With the right expert and appropriate topic of discussion, this process can clarify and modify approaches that were thought to be appropriate and can provide significant new knowledge not previously uncovered by the KE.

### Team Interviewing

All the discussions about knowledge elicitation interviews in a previous subsection are based on one-on-one interviews between a single expert and one knowledge engineer. Another option, however, does exist—team interviewing—which under certain circumstances can be quite beneficial. There are three types of team interviews:

1. One KE and multiple experts (one-on-many).
2. Multiple KEs and one expert (many-on-one).
3. Multiple KEs and multiple experts (many-on-many).

Each has its own advantages and disadvantages.

### One-on-Many Interviews

**One-on-many interviews** are common when several experts work closely together. If the experts are compatible, such meetings can be very fruitful because of the synergism of the situation. Each expert may be specialized in slightly different areas, thereby complementing each other and ensuring that the most complete set of knowledge is captured. If differences in opinion arise during a discussion, chances are good that they can be resolved at that point. Usually, differences of opinion resolved amicably result in the uncovering of a higher level of knowledge, benefiting both the KE and the experts. If circumstances exist for the use of one-on-many interviews, it is highly encouraged.

Problems can arise, however, if the experts do not get along. Some disagreements can be very useful and productive because they help to clarify subtle issues within the domain, but a lack of cooperation can undermine the productivity of the team interview. Furthermore, one-on-many interviews are not appropriate in some situations. One of these is a generic knowledge-gathering session. This would be analogous to attending a lecture on college algebra with two or more instructors present. All are simply not needed. The second situation is when the KE is inexperienced or introverted, and can easily feel overwhelmed by multiple experts. Finally, such interviews can be mentally taxing to KEs because their concentration is required for the entire length of the meeting. Although an individual expert can drift in and out of the conversation, the KE must maintain continual attention to not only the topic discussed, but also the multiple sources of knowledge (experts).

## Many-on-One Interviews

**Many-on-one interviews** are normally not as advantageous as one-on-many, because the single expert may feel overwhelmed by the multitude of KEs and may thus be more defensive. There is also little chance for synergism because no one else is present with the expert's level of understanding of the domain.

One advantage to this approach, however, is that multiple sets of eyes and ears are most always better than one. The junior KEs can observe the expert carefully and can identify many subtle issues that a single one might miss. Each can provide an alternative perspective about what happened during the interview, thereby clarifying the meeting's results.

One must be careful not to overextend the expert in the same way that the KE can become mentally exhausted in a one-on-many interview.

## Many-on-Many Interviews

**Many-on-many interviews** can range from massive interviews with a roomful of experts and KEs to simple two-on-two meetings. We unequivocally do *not* recommend the former, because the larger the group, the harder it is to accomplish anything. Nevertheless, there are times when large interviews are unavoidable due to pressures from external sources (i.e., management). More advantageous are few-on-few meetings (e.g., two-on-two or two-on-three) where the advantages of synergism and multiple observers combine.

## Some Concluding Remarks

In many instances, tacit knowledge simply cannot be converted into explicit knowledge via interview sessions. As we discuss earlier, some experts turn knowledge into reflex action; that is, they do not know what they know. They simply use the knowledge. Although observational techniques are helpful in this situation, they are by no means foolproof. One example is judging the distance of another car when we try to pass a slow truck in a two-lane country road. An experienced driver instinctively knows when to pull out into the oncoming lane and pass the truck before the oncoming car gets too close. However, trying to tell someone learning how to drive how that is done is impossible, no matter how articulate one might be.

## ❖❖ ❖❖ ❖❖ Facilitating the Knowledge Elicitation Process: Repertory Grids

The participants in the time-consuming process of manual knowledge elicitation are the KEs and the knowledge sources. Both are required to successfully capture the knowledge from the source. It would be a great saving in cost if the process could be reduced to just one (set of) participants—the knowledge sources. This is the objective behind the *automated knowledge capture* systems. These systems aim to greatly reduce the participation of the KEs by designing systems that provide a vehicle for the knowledge sources to "dump" their knowledge about a particular domain. Most of these systems accomplish this through an intelligent question-and-answer dialogue with the "interviewed" expert. The expert's responses are accumulated and stored as explicit knowledge. We discuss one technology that makes this possible—**repertory grids.**

Efforts to facilitate the knowledge capture process have been primarily based on Kelly's [1955] theory of personal constructs in clinical psychology. This theory was designed to improve the effectiveness of clinical sessions with a patient. Because individual persons perceive the world from a different and changing perspective, a model is built for particular persons that represents their views of the world. As persons change their perspectives of the world, their models are modified to represent their revised beliefs about the world.

Kelly proposed a tool called *repertory grids* for the implementation of the Personal Construct Theory. Shaw and Gaines [1987] adapted the repertory grids for use as an aid in knowledge elicitation and demonstrated its use in a system called PLANET [Shaw, 1982]. Other systems were developed in subsequent years, including Expertise Transfer System (ETS) [Boose, 1984], MORE [Kahn, 1985], SALT [Marcus, 1985], Auto-Intelligence [Parsaye, 1988], and ICONKAT [Ford et al., 1991]. More recent work in repertory grids extends the concept of relationships to include those among several grids. These are called *tracked repertory grids* [Delugach, 1998] and provide multiple dimensions to the conventional two-dimensional grid. Delugach and Skipper [2000] furthered the concept of tracked repertory grids by using conceptual graph schema to represent the relationships among the grids. They used it to represent tactical knowledge for modeling human behavior in battle situations.

These systems ask questions of the knowledge source about the domain of interest, with the goal of assisting in developing a more adequate knowledge structure. Some claim that this process often leaves the experts thinking that they have learned more about their own knowledge [Parsaye, 1988].

A repertory grid is a list of specific characteristics of a domain that are to be evaluated by an expert or some knowledgeable person. These domain characteristics, also called the *elements* of the domain, represent features of the domain whose value ranges between two extremes. For example, elements of basketball players may include their outside shooting ability, ball-handling skills, rebounding effectiveness, free-throw percentage, etc. Each element is identified with opposing extreme values. Individual players can then be rated for their abilities with respect to each element. For example, basketball players' outside shooting abilities can be designated as somewhere between "never misses" or "heaves bricks."

Each element with its respective labels and rating is called a *construct.* The set of constructs makes up the repertory grid. The rating assigned by the expert to an element for a given construct can be either binary (0 or 1) or range of values. The range of values can indicate the degree of membership in a fuzzy set expressed by one of the extremes [Boose, 1985] and [Shaw, 1987]. The meaning of these sets simply depends on how developers of the repertory grid decide to organize it and the results they seek from its use. This provides experts with greater flexibility in expressing their knowledge about the domain.

The repertory grid shown in Table 10-1 represents the personal construct for a typical staff consisting of ten subordinates [Shaw, 1987]. Individual members of the staff are characterized by their managers through 14 categories, each of which has two extreme and diametrically opposed characteristics (i.e., intelligent—dim; creative—uncreative). This is done by assigning a number that accurately describes the person's standing in relation to the opposing extremes. In this example, a value of 1 could indicate strong tendency to the left-most characteristic, whereas 5 would relate strongly to the right-most characteristic. For example, employee 1 would be considered intelligent, willing, neutral reliability, mildly self-starter, and rather unhelpful among other things.

How this can be employed in knowledge capture is best illustrated through an example. This example uses repertory grids to automatically elicit and represent expert knowledge involving the classification of various types of automobiles according to their characteristics. We indicate the system queries in CAPITAL LETTERS and the user responses in *italics*. This is depicted in Vignette 10-3.

**TABLE 10-1   Repertory Grid**

|  | *Staff Member No.* | *1* | *2* | *3* | *4* | *5* | *6* | *7* | *8* | *9* | *10* |  |
|---|---|---|---|---|---|---|---|---|---|---|---|---|
| 1 | Intelligent | 1 | 1 | 4 | 5 | 3 | 3 | 5 | 2 | 3 | 5 | Dim |
| 2 | Willing | 1 | 2 | 4 | 5 | 1 | 1 | 4 | 3 | 1 | 2 | Unwilling |
| 3 | New boy | 1 | 2 | 3 | 5 | 4 | 4 | 4 | 1 | 4 | 3 | Old sweats |
| 4 | Little supervision | 3 | 1 | 4 | 5 | 2 | 1 | 5 | 2 | 2 | 3 | Needs supervision |
| 5 | Motivated | 1 | 1 | 4 | 5 | 2 | 2 | 5 | 3 | 3 | 2 | Unmotivated |
| 6 | Reliable | 3 | 2 | 2 | 5 | 1 | 1 | 5 | 1 | 2 | 3 | Unreliable |
| 7 | Mild | 3 | 4 | 5 | 2 | 2 | 3 | 1 | 5 | 4 | 5 | Abrasive |
| 8 | Idea person | 1 | 1 | 5 | 4 | 2 | 3 | 1 | 3 | 4 | 4 | Staid |
| 9 | Self-starter | 2 | 1 | 5 | 5 | 1 | 3 | 5 | 3 | 4 | 5 | Needs a push |
| 10 | Creative | 1 | 1 | 5 | 5 | 2 | 3 | 4 | 3 | 4 | 5 | Uncreative |
| 11 | Helpful | 4 | 3 | 4 | 2 | 3 | 5 | 1 | 4 | 5 | 5 | Unhelpful |
| 12 | Professional | 1 | 2 | 3 | 3 | 2 | 1 | 5 | 2 | 4 | 4 | Unprofessional |
| 13 | Overall rating high | 2 | 1 | 3 | 4 | 1 | 2 | 5 | 2 | 3 | 4 | Overall rating low |
| 14 | Messer | 2 | 2 | 5 | 4 | 3 | 5 | 1 | 5 | 3 | 1 | Tidy |
|  | *Staff Member No.* | *1* | *2* | *3* | *4* | *5* | *6* | *7* | *8* | *9* | *10* |  |

 **VIGNETTE 10-3**

## Automobile Classification

Initially, the system queries the user about the problem domain and the objective of the knowledge base. This is followed by a request for a list of the automobiles and the typical places where these could be found. Alternatively, the list could be pre-determined and provided to the user. In this example, we assume that the user has been asked to supply the list of cars. We pick up the dialogue at this point with the user's response (this example is based on an example found in Parsaye [1988]):

| Porsche 911 | Road Racing |
|---|---|
| Dodge Caravan | Family vacations |
| Cadillac ETC | Golf club parking lot |
| Ford Focus | Factory parking lot |
| Mazda Miata | Sunday drive |
| Mercedes Benz | Estate entrance |
| Jeep Grand Cherokee | Dirt roads |
| BMW 5-Series | University faculty parking lot |
| Chevy S-10 truck | Farmhouse |

PLEASE THINK OF:

| PORSCHE 911 | ROAD RACING |
|---|---|
| CADILLAC ETC | GOLF CLUB PARKING LOT |
| DODGE CARAVAN | FAMILY VACATIONS |

IS ONE OF THEM SOMEHOW DIFFERENT FROM THE OTHER TWO?
*Yes, Porsche 911*
WHAT IS A TRAIT THAT CHARACTERIZES THIS DIFFERENCE?
*High performance*
WHAT IS THE OPPOSITE TRAIT OF HIGH PERFORMANCE?
*Flat performance*

PLEASE THINK OF:

| DODGE CARAVAN | FAMILY VACATIONS |
|---|---|
| CADILLAC ETC | GOLF CLUB PARKING LOT |
| FORD FOCUS | FACTORY PARKING LOT |

IS ONE OF THEM SIGNIFICANTLY DIFFERENT FROM THE OTHER TWO?
*Yes, Ford Focus*
WHAT IS THE TRAIT THAT CHARACTERIZES THIS DIFFERENCE?
*Small*
WHAT IS THE OPPOSITE OF SMALL?
*Large*

PLEASE THINK OF:

| PORSCHE 911 | ROAD RACING |
|---|---|
| MAZDA MIATA | SUNDAY DRIVE |
| MERCEDES BENZ | COUNTRY ESTATE |

IS ONE OF THEM SOMEHOW DIFFERENT FROM THE OTHER TWO?
*Mercedes Benz, Sedan*
WHAT IS THE OPPOSITE OF SEDAN?
*Coupe*

This question-and-answer process may continue for a longer period, taking three cases at a time. If three at a time is not effective in distinguishing some types of automobiles from each other, the system reverts to two at a time comparisons. For example,

PLEASE THINK OF:

| PORSCHE 911 | ROAD RACING |
|---|---|
| DODGE CARAVAN | FAMILY VACATIONS |

IS THERE A TRAIT THAT DISTINGUISHES THEM?
*Yes, functional*
WHAT IS THE OPPOSITE TRAIT OF FUNCTIONAL?
*Fun to drive*

Once these traits have been identified, the system allows the user to specify how well each automobile matches the characteristics defined above. The system performs this step by presenting a template to the user that must be filled with relative weights. We again pick up the dialogue:

PLEASE THINK OF A FORD FOCUS. PLEASE PROVIDE A NUMBER BETWEEN 0 AND 100 SHOWING HOW WELL IT MATCHES (100 MEANS A COMPLETE MATCH AND 0 MEANS NO MATCH AT ALL):

HIGH PERFORMANCE: *20*

INEXPENSIVE: *80*

SMALL: *90*

FUNCTIONAL: *60*

SEDAN: *40*

FUEL-EFFICIENT: *80*

FAST: *40*

LUXURIOUS: *10*

PLEASE THINK OF PORSCHE 911. PLEASE PROVIDE A NUMBER BETWEEN 0 AND 100 SHOWING HOW WELL IT MATCHES (100 MEANS A COMPLETE MATCH AND 0 MEANS NO MATCH AT ALL):

HIGH-PERFORMANCE: *100*

INEXPENSIVE: *10*

SMALL: *40*

FUNCTIONAL: *20*

SEDAN: *0*

FUEL-EFFICIENT: *70*

FAST: *95*

This type of questioning continues until all the automobiles and traits are correlated. This information can be represented in a grid, as shown in Table 10-2, where each automobile defines a row and each trait defines a column. Pattern matching can be utilized to apply this represented knowledge to the classification of a particular automobile.

**TABLE 10-2  Automobile Selection Grid**

| Car | High-Performance? | Cost | Size | Functional? | Type | Fuel-efficient? | Speed |
|-----|-------------------|------|------|-------------|------|-----------------|-------|
| P-911 | Yes | High | Small | No | Coupe | No | Fast |
| Van | No | Medium | Large | Yes | Van | Yes | Slow |
| Caddy | No | High | Large | Yes | Sedan | No | Medium |
| Focus | No | Low | Small | Yes | Sedan | Yes | Slow |
| Miata | Yes | High | Small | No | Coupe | Yes | Fast |
| M-B | Yes | High | Large | Yes | Sedan | No | Fast |
| BMW | Yes | High | Medium | Yes | Sedan | No | Fast |
| Jeep | No | Medium | Small | No | SUV | No | Slow |
| S-10 | No | Low | Medium | Yes | Truck | Yes | Slow |

◆◇ ◇◆ ◆◇ ◇◆

Although the knowledge represented within this grid is not sufficient to build a complete knowledge-based system, it provides an excellent starting point from which to proceed in its development. KEs may still be necessary, but their tasks would be greatly simplified to be one of refinement, instead of bulk knowledge capture.

Repertory grids are excellent means of acquiring knowledge that has the following characteristics:

1. It is easily characterized as attribute–value pairs.
2. The values can vary over a range covering two extremes.
3. Certain characteristics of the object of knowledge can be easily identified.
4. The knowledge centers about knowing how an object fits within this template.

## ◇◇ ◇◇ ◇◇ Automating the Knowledge Capture Process

There are many instances where human knowledge is buried in documents or other media. One example of this is the design process. The design process performed by human designers, engineers, architects, or designers is typically reflected in the drawings and specifications of the system they designed. It is often important to be able to elicit this knowledge from a nonhuman source. Whereas the automated knowledge capture systems described above query a human expert, other techniques exist to query nonhuman sources. In some cases, these can result in a near automatic capture of knowledge. These systems make use of knowledge embedded in databases. In some cases, such as the one described below, it may still be necessary for someone to refine the knowledge base. However, there is no need to interact with an expert, because the source of the knowledge is not the expert but the database.

Consider, for example, the development a model of an engineered system [Towhidnejad, 1993]. The process of engineering design generally uses both algorithmic and heuristic knowledge to formulate a design. When a device is designed, it is typically represented as a drawing in a computer-aided design (CAD) system with knowledge about the device largely embedded within its graphic representation. If the design representation (drawing) is performed on a CAD system, then the knowledge already exists in an electronic form. Sometimes, knowledge about how the device was designed is shown explicitly (e.g., the formula used to derive parts of the design is shown in the drawing). Other times, it is tacit (e.g., no justification of any of the components comprising the design exists on the drawing).

Unfortunately, the majority of engineering designs are representations of implicit knowledge. This makes the automated capture of knowledge about the device or system considerably more difficult, because some background knowledge of general engineering design must exist to understand the new knowledge expressed within the representation.

The knowledge extracted from a CAD database can be said to be a *model,* a description of the engineering system in question (e.g., a chemical process system or an electronic circuit). Knowledge about the components that compose such systems and how these components are interconnected can be used to diagnose any mis-operations or faults within the target system. Such a model constitutes the knowledge base for a **model-based reasoning system.** Model-based systems are knowledge-based systems using the deep causal knowledge contained in these models to overcome some of the deficiencies of the uncertain associative knowledge-based systems.

More generally, the systems applicable to model-based reasoning include those that can be represented in a **one-line diagram** or a *schematic drawing*. These drawings depict systems from a functional perspective, showing all the general features of the components as well as their connections, while skipping over their detailed connections (i.e., which wire goes to which terminal). Systems that lend themselves to such representations include hydraulic, pneumatic, gas, or chemical process systems as well as electrical or electronic circuits. The model can be described using frames, where each frame represents a component in the system.

The knowledge required by a model to enable diagnostic reasoning consists of:

1. *System connectivity.* This defines how each component in the system is connected to the other system components.
2. *Functionality.* A specification of the functionality of the various components in the system allows each component to be modeled. Typically this functionality includes the component's transfer function, units, tolerance, range of operation, time delay in reacting (if any), etc.

System connectivity can be obtained from the CAD system database. Usually each component is represented as an object with connection terminals (input and output ports) defining the object's location within the system. This is done by identifying its neighbors—those other devices or components to which it is connected via inputs or outputs.

Because connectivity data are typically easily found in a CAD system database, it is normally unnecessary to know the nature of a component to establish its connectivity. Nevertheless, to completely define a model, information not typically present in the CAD system database must be integrated into a model generated by an automated knowledge capture system. Such information must therefore be retrieved from an external database of generic components and their attributes. This database is called the *component knowledge base* and can be quite extensive.

The knowledge base on components is continually growing as new components are included. This knowledge base is generally updated by a human, although some updates can be made by the knowledge capture system automatically, with the help of a human. Included in the form of constraints is information about how a component would be applied in the model of the extracted system. For example, this database would know that a valve or filter could be connected to the output of a water pump, whereas an electrical transformer could not; or that a three-way valve would have three ports and, therefore, three connections.

Identifying the proper information within this database may be trivial in cases where the component is adequately labeled. A program is written to examine the description information contained in the CAD database and extract the component's identity from its description. Once the component is identified, a search is made of the component knowledge base to locate an entry closely matching the component's description. A certainty factor can be assigned to this description to reflect how well it matches the actual component.

Frequently, however, a component description is inadequately specified in the CAD database. This may occur when an abbreviation or a synonym is used, making the identification process much more difficult. On rare occasions a component within the database may be incorrectly specified or not described at all. These situations generate conflicts within the knowledge capture system, which must be resolved before a consistent and correct knowledge base can be generated. Ultimately, a human can assist in this resolution, but there are some actions that the system can take before requesting assistance. For example, let us assume that the system has knowledge of the connectivity of the unknown components as well as the existing constraints applicable to all known components as found in the component database. All components can be assigned a certainty factor describing the certainty of their identification, based on the various sources of information described above. Working from known components (i.e., those with high certainty factors) and using the *relaxation labeling* technique [Price, 1985; Thathachar, 1986], the system can begin to propagate the constraints from these *islands of certainty,* thus narrowing the number of possibilities for the unknown components. This process is very similar to that followed by a process engineer in identifying unknown components in the drawing.

Another technique that can be used to identify the components is to utilize icons representing the components within the drawing. The American National Standards Institute (ANSI) provides definitions and interpretations for standard icons. A knowledge capture system can search the library used by the CAD system in creating the drawing or can interpret the shape of the icon directly in an attempt to correctly identify it. Unfortunately, this approach is not always foolproof either because not all companies use the standard library of icons.

As an example of automated knowledge capture from CAD databases, let us look at extracting the model description from the electronic circuit shown in Figure 10-2 [Gonzalez, 1991]. The CAD system database stores a set of lists that (usually) identify each component and how it is connected to other components (its *connectivity*). For our example, the first is called the *component* list and is shown in Table 10-3 [Gonzalez, 1991].

◆◇ ◆◇ ◆◇ **FIGURE 10-2 Electronic Circuit**

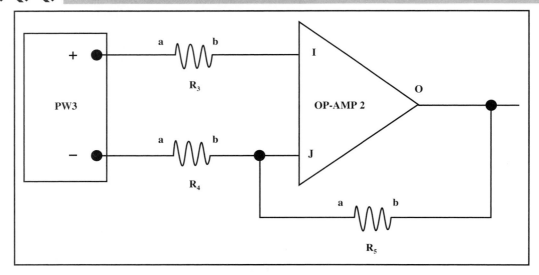

**TABLE 10-3  Component List Obtained for Example Problem**

| Component Name | Description | Units |
|---|---|---|
| PW3 | Power supply | VDC |
| OP-AMP2 | Operational amplifier | Volts |
| R3 | Resistor | Ohms |
| R4 | Resistor | Ohms |
| R5 | Resistor | Ohms |

This list supplies the component name, its description (which is often optional and at the whim of the person doing the drawing—the *draftsperson*), and the units that are often not specified by the draftsperson. Table 10-4 [Gonzalez, 1991] depicts the *to–from* list that details the connections for each component listed in the component list. A third list, the *node list,* indicates the connection points for each component (Table 10-5). Other sources of information are available from the CAD system, but the ones described here are the most important.

The objective of the automated knowledge capture system is to create a set of frames, each representing a system component, which contains the structural as well as the functional description of the applicable component. Thus, some slots that need to be filled correspond to:

1. Input
2. Output
3. Transfer function
4. Description
5. An-instance-of
6. Units
7. Delay
8. Tolerance
9. Current-value

**TABLE 10-4  To–From List for the Example Problem**

| Component Name | Connect Point | Component Name | Connect Point |
|---|---|---|---|
| PW3 | + | R3 | A |
| PW3 | − | R4 | A |
| R3 | b | OP-AMP2 | I |
| R4 | b | OP-AMP2 | J |
| R4 | b | R5 | A |
| OP-AMP2 | O | R5 | B |

**TABLE 10-5  Node List for the Example Problem**

| Net No. | Component Name | Connect Point |
|---------|----------------|---------------|
| 026 | PW3 | + |
| 026 | R3 | A |
| 027 | R3 | B |
| 027 | OP-AMP2 | I |
| 028 | OP-AMP2 | O |
| 028 | R5 | B |
| 029 | R5 | A |
| 029 | OP-AMP2 | J |
| 029 | R4 | B |
| 030 | R4 | A |
| 030 | PW3 | – |

⟨·⟩ ⟨·⟩ ⟨·⟩ ⟨·⟩

Of these, the *input* and *output* slots deal mainly with the connectivity of the system. As mentioned above, these can be generally obtained from the CAD database rather easily. Conversely, the *transfer function, delay,* and *tolerance* slots represent the functional description of the component, which must be obtained from the component knowledge base. The *description* and the *unit* slots are some of the means through which the component is identified and a match within the component knowledge base is made.

In our example, the components have been properly documented by the draftsperson, thus easing the problem of identification. A challenge exists when the description for some components is either incorrect or nonexistent. In such cases, the automated knowledge capture system tries to find *islands of certainty* within the target system and, uses constraints to propagate the belief outwardly to "discover" the nature of other, unknown components without having to resort to human intervention.

To accomplish this, the process consists of two phases:

1.   The *parser* involves a module that interprets the natural language using keywords to isolate the name of the component from a possibly erroneous, mislabeled, or nonexisting textual description entered by the draftsperson doing the drawing. The parser refers to a predefined knowledge base of components typically used in that context to compare the selected keywords and identify the component at the right level of specificity. This knowledge base is called, aptly enough, the *component knowledge base.* Developing it is part of the knowledge engineering process, but once developed, it is reusable for automatically generating models of other systems in the same context. Some of the descriptions may be sufficient to identify the component with high certainty, whereas other descriptions may not be.

2.   If the description, as isolated by the parser and the component knowledge base, is not sufficient to identify the component in question, then the second phase comes into effect. This phase uses constraint programming to identify an unknown component. It

relies on the likelihood that not all components in the system can emerge from the parser as unknown. Instead, some components can be easily identified by the parser, and form islands of certainty, such as shown in Figure 10-3. By using these islands of certainty, the constraints can help isolate the possible legal identities of the unknown components. By iterating on the uncertain elements in the presence of certain ones, the constraint identifier, as this module is called, can identify most unknown components, at least to a reasonable degree of certainty. It is then up to the human KE to verify its identity. Figure 10-3 shows a graph of the electronic circuit of Figure 10-2 assuming some of the components are known and others are unknown.

In Figure 10-3, suppose that resistor R4 was not labeled, giving its identity a low certainty factor, whereas the power supply PW3 and the OP-AMP2 components are properly described, making their identity and acquired functional attribute values highly certain. Looking at the component knowledge base entry for resistors, we see that one of a resistor's constraints is that it is an electrical component, which our unknown component is. Another characteristic is that a resistor is used to limit electric current in a circuit; that is, it can be connected to a power source. Using such constraints, heuristics, and supporting facts (units of the unknown component are ohms), the conflict resolution algorithm can determine that the most likely identity of the unknown component is a resistor and endow the unknown component with all the functional characteristics of the resistor entry in the component knowledge base. A detailed description of this *resolver* algorithm is beyond the scope of this book. See Myler [1993] for details.

Tests of the system with CAD databases of designs for systems at the National Aeronautics and Space Administration (NASA) Kennedy Space Center showed that it was effective in correctly capturing a high percentage (up to 90%) of the model for well-defined systems, and up to 50% of the model for poorly defined designs. The latter design representations contained inconsistencies, as well as scant or nonexistent descriptions with many misspellings.

**FIGURE 10-3 Graphic Representation of Electronic Circuit**

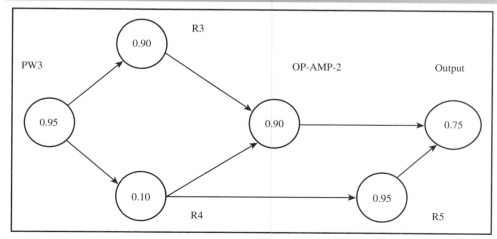

In summary, this system acquires the knowledge from a database and places it into a different format, one usable for diagnosis. Humans, however, already know this knowledge. In Chapter 12, we examine other techniques that can sift through databases to discover knowledge unknown to humans. This is referred to as *data mining* (DM). DM is a field commonly associated with statistics and machine learning.

## SUMMARY ◇ ◇ ◇

In this chapter, the reader learns the techniques available for knowledge elicitation. The purpose is twofold: (1) to show the reader the rigorous and difficult process of eliciting knowledge manually from an expert through a series of face-to-face interviews, and (2) to show how some technologies can be used to make the process easier and more effective for all involved. In the process, we discuss:

1. Knowledge elicitation techniques (including the way to plan and conduct an interview) and a way to sequence the tasks.
2. The facilitation of the elicitation technique consists of asking questions of the expert through a dialogue with an automatic knowledge capture tool. The most popular technique for implementing this is the repertory grid, a template of the expert's thinking on the domain. This grid can assist in the early stages of the knowledge capture process when the knowledge structure is designed.
3. The automated capture of knowledge from databases technique can be used to build models of engineered systems from CAD drawings. It comprises the examination of a design database for a schematic of a system, the identification of the components included therein, the resolution of any conflicting information, and the final creation of a knowledge base (i.e., a model) for use in a model-based reasoning system. It employs a constraint propagation and an external knowledge base of domain elements to carry out the task. The automated acquisition of knowledge from a CAD design database can be powerful, although limited in its applications.

Although methods 2 and 3, in general, do not replace the traditional interview method, they provide useful alternatives for some problem domains at various stages of the knowledge capture process. Research is continuing in these topics, and we expect that significant advances can be made in the area in the near future.

## KEY TERMS ◇ ◇ ◇

- close-ended questions—p. 183
- constrained processing tasks—p. 187
- general knowledge-gathering interview sessions—p. 182
- interviews—p. 181
- kick-off interview—p. 181
- knowledge elicitation—p. 180
- knowledge capture—p. 180

- limited information tasks—p. 187
- many-on-one interview—p. 189
- many-on-many interview—p. 189
- model-based reasoning—p. 194
- observational elicitation—p. 184
- one-line diagram—p. 195
- one-on-many interview—p. 188

- one-on-one interview—p. 181
- open-ended questions—p. 182
- output–input–middle method—p. 183
- repertory grids—p. 190
- role reversal—p. 184
- specific problem-solving, knowledge-gathering interview sessions—p. 182

## REVIEW QUESTIONS ◇ ◇ ◇

1. Describe in your own words the concept of a repertory grid. What concepts from clinical psychology inspired this idea?
2. Describe the difference between a general knowledge-gathering session and a specific problem-solving, knowledge-gathering session.
3. What are the advantages and disadvantages of a many-on-many interview?
4. What are the advantages and disadvantages of a many-on-one interview?
5. Describe in your own words the input–output–middle method.

## APPLICATION EXERCISES ◇ ◇ ◇

1. Team up with a classmate or peer who is an expert at some task (almost everybody is expert in something) and try to elicit your partner's knowledge, even if it does not represent a good application for knowledge-based systems. Employ the basic one-on-one interview techniques discussed in this chapter. Begin with general knowledge capture. List what worked and what did not. What was the greatest difficulty faced? How did you get around it?
2. Conduct specific problem-solving knowledge capture with the same partner. Use the output–input–middle method to organize the elicited knowledge. How does this differ from general knowledge capture? List what worked and what did not. What was the greatest difficulty faced? How did you get around it?
3. Team up with another classmate or peer who is an expert at some task and quietly observe how your partner solves problems or makes decisions in that domain. Do not ask questions during the problem-solving process. How does this technique compare in effectiveness to the question-and-answer interview?
4. Repeat the process described in Problem 3, except now allowing questions to be asked during the problem-solving process. Does this improve your ability to elicit the knowledge? What effect does it have on the expert's ability to concentrate?
5. After interviewing your expert using any or all of the above techniques, try solving a problem supplied to you by your expert partner. Does solving this problem provide you with a greater insight into what the expert's thinking process is? Justify your answer.
6. Reverse roles with your partner. List all actions that the knowledge engineer (KE) partner did that were effective in eliciting your knowledge. Also, list those that were not.
7. Use the input–output–middle method to document the important knowledge in the following transcript of an interview.

> There can be many reasons why an automobile won't start. The most basic one is that it is out of fuel. This is also the simplest one to detect and recognize, but depending on where you are, it is not always the easiest one to fix. By looking at the fuel gauge, you can easily determine whether this is the problem or not.
>
> From this point on, it gets somewhat more complicated. A weak or dead battery is typically the most likely cause of the problem. If the engine turns over, but does so weakly, then that is a good indication that you have a battery problem. The lights can confirm this if they are dim because a weak battery will result in either dim lights or no lights at all.
>
> Occasionally, however, the battery may be too weak to crank up the engine properly, but it will have enough residual capacity to turn on the lights, brightly, for a short period of time. While this will happen only rarely, the presence of the bright lights might seem to contradict the dead battery assumption. What you have to consider in this case is the age of the battery. An old battery will have significantly decreased capacity, whereas a new battery should be quite vigorous. If the battery is two years old or less, then I would consider that a new battery. If the age of the

battery is between two and four years, then I still say that it is new, but I say that much less confidently. On the other hand, any battery older than four years is approaching the end of its life.

The ambient temperature also has an effect. The hotter it is, the better the battery will operate. Thus, if the temperature is below 20°F, then you can be surer of the battery problem, even though there may not be anything really wrong with the battery. The ultimate test, if you happen to have a voltmeter handy, is to measure its voltage. If the voltage across the posts is 13 volts or greater, then your battery is in good shape. Between 8 and 13, it is probably normal, but it is less so as you get closer to 8. Any voltage less than 8 means that the battery is for all practical purposes dead.

If the engine turns over and the battery does not appear to be dead, then it could be fuel starvation. This could be the result of carburetor flooding. If the carburetor is flooded, a strong smell of gasoline will be noticeable. A defective solenoid could also prohibit the car from starting. The symptoms involved here would be either a clicking sound when the ignition is operated, or no sound at all. The latter could also be due to a totally dead battery, so you have to eliminate the latter before you can be sure of the former. Nevertheless, a totally dead battery is not likely unless you left the lights on for two days straight, and I think you would probably know if you did. The last possibility is the starter motor. A good indication of a bad starter motor is if the car tries to turn over and a screeching sound comes from the motor. It could fail in other ways, but this is the most likely one.

8. Pick a classmate who has expertise in some topic (almost everyone has expertise in some area). Interview this classmate and draw a repertory grid from the results of the interview.
9. Using the members of your family, your teammates, or co-workers, draw up a repertory grid describing their television viewing habits.

## REFERENCES ◇ ◇ ◇

Boose, J.H. 1985. A knowledge acquisition program for expert systems based on personal construct theory. *International Journal of Man-Machine Studies,* 23(5) November, 495–525.

Delugach, H.S. 1998. Repertory Grid Graphs: A Hybrid of Repertory Grids and Conceptual Graphs. Proc. 11th Knowledge Acquisition Workshop (KAW-98), Banff, Alberta, Canada.

Delugach, H.S., and Skipper, D.J. 2000. Knowledge Techniques for Advanced Conceptual Modeling. Proc. 9th Conf. Computer Generated Forces and Behavioral Representation, Orlando, FL, May.

Ford, K.M., Stahl, H., Adams-Webber, J.H., Canas, A.J., Novak, J., and Jones, J.C. 1991. ICONKAT: An integrated constructivist knowledge acquisition tool. *Knowledge Acquisition,* 3, 215–236.

Gonzalez, A.J., and Myler, H.R. 1991. Issues in automating the extraction of a systems model from CAD databases for use in model-based reasoning. *International Journal of Expert Systems, Research and Applications,* 4(1), 29–50.

Hoffman, R.R. 1987. The Problem of Extracting the Knowledge of Experts from the Perspective of Experimental Psychology. *AI Magazine,* 8(2) Summer, 53–67.

Kahn, G., Nowlan, S., and McDermott, J. 1985. MORE: An Intelligent Knowledge Acquisition Tool. *Proc. 9th Int. Joint Conf. on Artificial Intelligence,* Vol. 1. Morgan Kaufmann, San Mateo, CA, pp. 581–584.

Kelly, G.A. 1955. *The Psychology of Personal Constructs, Vol. 1-A Theory of Personality.* W.W. Norton, New York.

Marcus, S.J., McDermott, J., and Wang, T. 1985. Knowledge Acquisition for Constructive Systems. *Proc. 9th Int. Joint Conf. on Artificial Intelligence,* Vol. 1. Morgan Kaufmann, San Mateo, CA, pp. 581–584.

Myler, H.R., Gonzalez, A.J., and Towhidnejad, M. 1993. Constraint mechanism for knowledge acquisition from computer-aided design data. *Journal of Artificial Intelligence in Engineering, Design and Manufacturing,* 7(3), 181–188.

Parsaye, K. 1988. Acquiring and verifying knowledge automatically. *AI Expert,* 3(5) May, 48–63.

Price, K.E. 1985. Relaxation matching techniques— a comparison. *IEEE Transactions on Pattern Analysis and Machine Intelligence,* PAMI-7(5) September, 617–623.

Shaw, M.L.G. 1982. PLANET: Some experience in creating an integrated system for repertory grid application on a microcomputer. *International Journal of Man-Machine Studies,* 17(3), 345–360.

Shaw, M.L.G., and Gaines, B.R. 1987. An interactive knowledge elicitation technique using personal construct technology. In Kidd, A.L. (Ed.), *Knowledge Acquisition for Expert Systems.* Plenum Press, New York, pp. 109–136.

Thatachar, M.A., and Sastry, P.S. 1986. Relaxation labeling with learning automata. *IEEE Transactions on Pattern Analysis and Machine Intelligence,* PAMI-8(2) March, 256–267.

Towhidnejad, M., Myler, H.R., and Gonzalez, A.J. 1993. Constraint mechanism in automated knowledge generation. *International Journal of Applied Artificial Intelligence,* 7(2), 113–134.

CHAPTER 11

# The Computer
# as a Medium
# for Sharing Knowledge

## ◇ ◇ ◇ Introduction

Much of knowledge management (KM) involves communicating knowledge among people. Certainly, knowledge must be applied to be useful. The wider the application of knowledge is, the more beneficial it is for the organization fostering that interchange of knowledge. Such widespread application comes from communicating the knowledge in its natural or electronically represented form. Furthermore, knowledge bases benefit from widespread contributions that are only possible through wide-ranging communications. In the several previous chapters, we discuss some of the leading technologies for representing, storing, exercising, and acquiring knowledge. Now let us look at some of the communications technologies that permit and enhance this communication.

In the modern preinformation age, two-way communication was typically best done via the telephone. The telephone's advantage was its synchronous capability—the communicants were speaking to each other at the same time in real time, as if they were face to face. This provided an improvement over the asynchronous communication means available prior to that time, such as the telegraph, and prior to that, the physical conveyance of written letters. However, there is one significant advantage to the asynchronous communication means prevalent prior to that time—the communicants did not have to communicate at the same time. In today's hyperactive business environment, to actually get persons on the phone when you call them is practically impossible. Phone mail services and answering machines became popular as a reaction to this problem, but these limited the exchange of information to something short, such as "call me back." Furthermore, the telephone was not able to facilitate communication of nonhuman information (documents, photos, drawings, films, etc.). Therefore, for all the advances made in the 20th century, communications were still very limited until the emergence of the digital computer. The **Internet** and the **World Wide Web (WWW)** have revolutionized the concept of communications. This chapter discusses briefly the WWW and some techniques for sharing knowledge via this communication link. A basic discussion of computer networking can be found in Appendix A. We describe these technologies for knowledge-sharing systems in Chapter 15.

# World Wide Web

As significant as the impact of electronic mail (e-mail) and file transfer have been on companies managing knowledge, they pale in comparison to the impact of the WWW. Often, the Internet and the WWW are erroneously considered to be the same thing. The Internet is the underlying infrastructure that permits communication between computers in different and **heterogeneous networks.** The Internet provides the services that enable the transport of information packets, and the security and reliability required for a robust communication medium. In the early days of the Internet, information was merely made available to clients in anonymous file transfer protocol (FTP) directories. If one knew the address of the computer holding the desired documents, one would log in anonymously and be permitted to download the desired documents. Although this is still used today, it is highly limiting in terms of exchanging information. A radically better, more interactive means of sharing information was sought, and the WWW resulted.

The WWW is not a network, but instead, a format that enables large-scale storage of documents to be easily accessed by a user via a specialized software package called the *browser*. In effect, it is a hypermedia system, distributed over the entire Internet. An individual user seeking specific information utilizes the browser to request information from a particular server offering its documents to inspection and possible download by outsiders. To fully understand the WWW, we must learn about WWW servers, browsers, **Hypertext Markup Language (HTML),** and the **Java** computer language.

We discuss these in this section, followed by how these can be used to facilitate KM.

## Accessing Documents in the World Wide Web

WWW servers are computers whose main objectives are to serve as repositories of documents, files, photos, drawings, videos, programs, databases, and other such potential holders of knowledge; and to make them available to others via the Internet. On the other end of the communication is the *client*—a computer that requests the information from the WWW server. The servers communicate their contents to their clients through *Web pages*. These Web pages are hypermedia documents that express the contents of the server in an organized and often highly artistic and dynamic fashion.

A Web page consists of a file expressed in HTML. HTML is a standard representation for text and graphics that allows the browser to interpret the intentions of the Web page designer. The browser displays the file containing the Web page description on the client computer requesting the information of the server. This page identifies to the requester the information about the company or organization sponsoring the Web site, and how to acquire the desired information. HTML is a markup language and does not strictly specify the format of the text and graphics. This is because the heterogeneity of the Internet requires that the page be displayed in many different types of computers. This precludes the ability to strictly constrain such things as font size, color, or type. HTML merely provides the designer with the ability to determine the relative size of the font. Each individual computer then decides what font type, color, and size to employ. HTML also facilitates the display of images in the pages. However, it does so indirectly by indicating where the image display is to be positioned in the Web page, and where the image file can be found. An HTML file does not include the graphics file.

HTML files (Web pages) are accessed in this fashion. First, the client computer invokes the browser. Netscape Communications' Navigator and Microsoft's Internet Explorer are the dominant browsers in the market today. The browser acts as a client process that requests the **Uniform Resource Locator (URL)** of a server to be accessed. The URL is of the form [Comer, 2001]:

### *protocol://computer_name:port/document name*

The computer name is the address of the computer acting as the server. The protocol is the format used by the Web page. This is typically **Hypertext Transfer Protocol (HTTP),** which appears as http. The browser sends a packet to that address asking for the Web page indicated by the user. The default page is the *homepage* or *portal* for that Web site. On receipt, the server responds by sending the requestor an HTML file containing the Web page requested. The file then is displayed in the client computer and the connection between the client and the server is closed. The Web page, in fact, runs on the client computer without any link to the server.

The server, therefore, has a simple function—it sends the requested files to the client making the request. The browser, on the other hand, must not only make the requests but also display the files received. In some interactive Web sites (accessing a database or an on-line application form), the browser must also interpret mouse clicks and text entries. It must also enable links to other Web sites to which users may want to shift their attentions. All these functions require the browser to contain other processes to accomplish these functions.

One important aspect of Web pages is that they provide the ability for the client to download documents. This is a critical aspect of KM, where documents can be easily shared among a knowledge community. Web pages handle this by providing click operations that invoke the FTP protocol automatically. It only remains for clients to ask the users where they wish the downloaded file to be stored and the process begins.

### Dynamic and Active Web Documents

The above section describes the basic way in which a client computer can obtain Web pages from a server through a browser. The pages involved, however, were **static Web documents.** This section describes how **dynamic Web documents** (weather maps, live video feeds, etc.) are transferred through the Web browser interface.

There are three basic types of documents:

1. *Static.* The contents of the document (Web page) is determined at the time the document is created by its designer and it does not change. When a static document

is requested, the server sends the same document all the time. These are the kinds of documents discussed in the previous section.

2. ***Dynamic.*** These Web documents are not predefined. The document is created automatically by the Web server when the document is requested. A program in the server creates the Web page on request by the client, and sends the file via the Internet. As a result, subsequent pages sent by the server may not be identical. One possible application is a Web site that sends the time at the moment the request is received, or the hit count at any one time. Nevertheless, once the page is created and sent, it does not change. A widely used technology for building dynamic Web pages is called the *Common Gateway Interface (CGI)*. It provides guidelines to the developer on how to build dynamic pages.

3. ***Active.*** Active pages include computer programs that run on the client computer and while interacting with the client, may change their displays. In effect, the Web page is indeed created when the request is filled. However, its nature is active and can change once it gets to the client computer and runs therein.

We now further discuss **active Web documents** (pages). One type of quasi-active Web pages in reality is nothing more than a continuously updated dynamic page sent by the server. These pages can be used to continuously display the time at the client computer, sending an update every minute. Weather radar maps with storms showing can also be one of these types of pages. These quasi-active pages represent an early form of active pages and are still in use today.

Nevertheless, active pages are not continuously updated, but instead, their appearance is actively modified by running a program on the client computer. For this to happen, the program must be written in such a way that it runs on any computer. Executable programs must be sent via the Internet in binary form, and immediately executed in the client computer. However, this is in reality a formidable task for conventional computer programs, because they are very specific to operating systems, and somewhat less so to processor type and compiler version. Thus, it is clear that they could not be written and compiled with conventional languages and compilers. The language Java was designed to address this issue.

Java was developed by Sun Microsystems as a way to interface with and control household appliances such as refrigerators, toasters, and coffee machines. It was not long after development began that the developers began to see the much greater potential for this language. Java is a general-purpose, high-level, object-oriented language whose syntax resembles C++ in many ways. It is interpreted, instead of compiled. For this reason, it tends to be a bit slower than C or C++. However, its advantage is that it is translated into what is called Java byte code. This byte code is interpreted by the Java interpreter resident in the client computer. Each type of computer has a different interpreter, but the Java byte code is the same. This allows the server to send a machine-independent binary program to the client, who can run it by simply interpreting the byte code. This eliminates the need to compile the code with its attendant difficulties. Java also has a built-in *socket* library for easy access to the Internet. Sockets provide the means for programs to access the Web. Java has in its own right become a popular programming language for non-Web-related programs. Its object-oriented nature and high portability tend to overcome its relatively low speed of execution for non-real-time applications. It also has a well-developed graphics library.

## ◇ ◇ ◇ Web Search Engines

The standard browser interface requests the URL of the server that the client would like to "visit." Oftentimes, users are not certain of where to look for something. Other times, the objective of their search may not be not completely defined. Given the cryptic names of all but the most common of servers, looking for something ill-defined is not a practical task, unless the user knew the exact address of the server desired. It thus becomes practically impossible to search the billions of Web sites in existence, one at a time. Search engines are utilized to assist this process.

Search engines permit a user to enter relatively unconstrained terms that roughly or exactly describe the objective of their search, and return a set of Web sites that can potentially meet their requirements. The client can then access the Web sites identified through links provided in the returned information. This has become one of the most indispensable tools of the Web nowadays.

Search engines, of course, do not actually search the Web (actually, the servers connected to the Internet) in real time while clients await the results of their search requests. This would take entirely too long and clutter the Internet with unnecessary traffic. They, instead, search an index or a directory that contains information relevant to all (or most) sites in the Web. This index (or directory) and how it is populated, is very important, because it provides a map to the Web and its contents. The more complete and detailed this database is, the more thorough the search can be. There are many search engines in existence today. There is also great competition among the search engine designers to be the one most used by the clients. This permits the Web engine authors to charge fees to advertisers on their search engine Web site, or to sell the search engine to organizations for proprietary intranet search activities. Although there are many engines in existence, they all do basically the following:

1. They compile an index (or directory) of the contents of the Web. How they accomplish this is very important, and is discussed in more detail below.
2. They compile the information found in this index into a database that can be accessed in real time to provide indication of Web sites relevant to the client request.
3. Search engines provide access to this database to the clients by providing them an interface—the search engine itself. Through this interface, the client can enter words, phrases, terms, or other identifiers of the subject about which they are interested in finding a Web site. The search engine then searches the database for the Web sites having some level of relationship to the requested keywords.
4. They provide results that are useful to the client. This involves algorithms to rank the Web sites found in the database search according to how likely they are to meet the desires of the client. These algorithms are closely guarded secrets by the engine developers and are the subjects of cat-and-mouse games between the Web site designers and search engine developers. These also are discussed in more detail below.

There are two principal ways to compile an index. A few years ago, the only way to do it was through deliberate, manual development of the database. Web designers contacted the search engine organization and provided them with the URL and some keywords that described their Web site. The search engine operators would then add this information to their databases, and made it available for searching. This approach is still used today, and the resulting databases are called *Web directories*. An open directory is an example of databases obtained through such manual means [Sullivan, 2002]. The Yahoo search engine makes use of these directories [Atlantic Telephone, 2000]. The main drawback is that the Web page designers must expressly contact the search engine operators and describe in their own words the purpose and contents of their Web site. Updating these directories is not always done in a regular or timely fashion. As a result, abandoned Web sites can linger long after they are no longer maintained or useful, or even exist. However, the information is supplied by a human, with its (presumably) careful consideration in what information it carries.

A newer, more powerful way to create listings for databases is through **Web crawlers,** or *spiders*, as they are also often called. These software agents "traverse" the Web, going from site to site through the links found therein, and inspecting all the Web pages they visit. As they visit the different Web sites, they extract the required information from them, and move on to the next Web site. Google was the first crawler-based engine, and it began as an academic search engine. Using four Web crawlers, the original system could crawl 100 pages per second, creating 600 KB of data per second [Franklin, 2002]. Other search engines now employ the same crawler techniques to populate their database with listings. These spiders visit Web sites continually, day and night, visiting sites on a regular basis to reflect any changes. This keeps the database current, at least within the time frame of their repeat visits—typically a month or two. Furthermore, there may be a time lag between the time of the site visit by the crawler and the time the information is made available to the database.

The Web crawling process typically begins with a popular Web site, and branches out from it through its links to other Web sites. This means that a new Web site may not be visited until such a time as it is linked to by other known Web sites. This can often be several months. As an alternative, the Web designer can contact the search engine operators and provide them with the URL to enable the Web crawler to initiate a visit. Web designers may also keep out a crawler if they do not want to have it visit their Web page. This may be done for privacy reasons or for practical reasons. A robot exclusion protocol permits the designer to do this [Franklin, 2002].

Some search engines are hybrid systems—they populate their databases via human contact as in the previously mentioned directories, as well as through Web crawlers. These provide the best of both worlds.

However, what do these crawlers look for in Web pages? What do they extract from them? Technically, the crawler agents do not extract the information. They merely do the legwork. They pass on the pages to indexing software that performs this function. This is how they are able to extract these massive amounts of information per second. The indexing software systems are all different, depending on the engine operator. Generally, they look for words found in the page, and consider these an indication of the material content of the page. Most indexing systems strip away the unimportant words such as articles, pronouns, and possibly adjectives, which typically do not add meaning to the contents. The software also records the location of the words selected as keywords. The closer the keywords are to the top, the more important they are deemed to be. The frequency of a word appearance may also affect its importance. The indexing software also looks for metatags in the Web page. These metatags are provided by the Web page designer as keywords.

A fourth kind of search engine is called a metasearch engine. These engines make use of other search engines for their work. They provide the client requests to several other search engines and somehow collect their results in a common format to present to their user.

The last issue to consider is how to rank the Web sites whose pages indicate some relation to the search request based on the matching of words, keywords, or metatags. This ranking is important, because there may be several dozen hits on the search, but they may not all be relevant. The search engine wishes to place the sites most likely to satisfy the search request at the top of the list of sites. The extracted information from a Web page is used by the search engine to rank the sites that can potentially respond to a search request. Once again, each search engine uses a different algorithm, and the algorithm is not publicly described. However, in general, the location of the key word in the Web page, and its frequency of appearance are the most important weighing factors in the ranking of the page. The higher in the page the key word appears, the more likely it is to be in a title or subtitle. Likewise, the more often it appears, the more likely it is to be significant. Using these factors to weight their rankings, the results can be listed in descending order of desirability.

The above leads to the previously mentioned cat-and-mouse game. To increase the number of hits or increase the ranking of their Web sites, Web page designers often include important words repeatedly, but unreasonably so. Furthermore, they include metatags that are unrelated to the true contents of the Web site to appear in more lists and, consequently, to acquire more hits. The search engine companies respond by correlating word content to the metatags, and neglecting any metatags that are not supported by word content. User feedback is also often considered when irrelevant sites keep appearing in search results.

More advanced search engines such as Ask Jeeves[1] allow clients to express their search needs through natural language. The interface is designed for simple questions, but it is quite different than keyword-based request interfaces. Although this technology still has a long way to go, it is indeed the wave of the future.

Needless to say, it is important to (legitimate) Web site designers to describe the contents of their Web sites in such a way so as to fairly and accurately reflect the contents of their sites. Understanding how these search engines work can help immeasurably in this regard.

## ◇◆ ◇◆ ◇◆ Network Security

One important aspect of managing knowledge is keeping it secure and safe from inadvertent loss, or from malicious intrusion by unauthorized parties. Security was not an issue in the early days of the Internet and the WWW. More recently, however, it has been the conduit for significant malfeasance. It is used to hack into computers at safety critical agencies and organizations. It has also been used as the means to commit financial crimes such as identity theft as well as the medium for dissemination of pornography. This has resulted in an overriding need to provide secure channels for transactions

---

[1]www.askjeeves.com

performed via the Internet. In this section, we briefly discuss some of the issues related to Internet security. What exactly is meant by security is one issue to be discussed.

Security can mean many things to different organizations. One interpretation of security might be that no one outside the organization may access certain data or knowledge contained in a particular computer. Another might be that only authorized outsiders can access it. Another level may be that outsiders can download the information or knowledge, but cannot change it. In yet other cases, outsiders may be asked to provide input to the Web site, and in the process change its content. When making sales transactions on the Internet, the preferred form of payment is the credit card. Of course, knowing others' credit card numbers may provide someone with evil intentions with the opportunity to make illegal purchases charged to the card number pilfered. Although it is more difficult than commonly thought, intercepting messages in the Internet can indeed serve as a way to illicitly learn about credit card numbers. Therefore, it is in the interest of the merchants that secure means exist for executing electronic sales transaction. Let's now look at some ways this can be done [Comer, 2001].

### Passwords and Access Control

Passwords have been used for many years as a way to control access. Web sites can be password controlled. However, eavesdroppers can learn passwords relatively easily as they are passed around a network, from a client trying to access a Web site to the server hosting the secure site. Local area networks (LANs) are particularly susceptible to eavesdropping because several types of networks permit sniffers to easily work within their networks. This is exacerbated in wireless networks more and more commonly found in offices and public locations. Additionally, hackers have been defeating password-controlled access to computers for a long time, even before the advent of networks and Internets. Nevertheless, for some low-security applications, this approach may be sufficient.

### Encryption

Like the Germans and Japanese did in World War II, messages can be encrypted to allow no one but the intended recipient to understand the message. Several algorithms exist that can encrypt a message using a key. The recipient, having access to the same key, can decode the message into an understandable form using the same algorithm. Some of these algorithms are very complex, such as those used for military and governmental communications. Others are less so.

Encryption techniques can serve to disguise the packets containing the credit card numbers of the customers making on-line purchases. Messages containing passwords can likewise be encrypted to thwart network eavesdroppers. On-line applications that require the submission of personal data such as social security numbers, health history, bank account numbers, and such can also be encrypted to disguise the critical information or knowledge. Although encryption techniques can be defeated, it takes a serious and concerted effort by evildoers, making it more attractive for them to pursue easier targets.

### Digital Signatures

In some cases, e-mail messages are used as legal authorization for many critical transactions. It is commonly assumed that only the person with the authority to sign has access to that mail account. Thus, if the message comes with the correct sender address, it is assumed to be legitimate. In reality, this is not always safe. Intruders may access the signer's account, either physically or electronically, and forge electronic communications to gain an illicit advantage. Digital signatures are often used to verify the author's identity. These signatures are encrypted with a key known only to the legitimate sender. The recipient knows the key and can verify the identity of the signatory. Those involved in a project in Germany to make electronic cash available to on-line customers (in lieu of using credit cards) have made this secure signature a keystone of their work [Jantke, 2000].

### Firewall Software

Firewalls are software systems that filter the traffic going in and out of the protected computers from the Internet. This is done to keep out undesired intruders who present a security risk as well as to keep aggravating promotional e-mails (spam) and pop-ups from cluttering the internal network and storage devices. A firewall runs on a gateway computer connected directly to the Internet. All messages coming into the organization's computers must first pass through this firewall. Messages not adhering to the organization's security policy are to be kept out by the firewall. Firewalls are very important in modern computer network security. Like everything else, firewalls are not perfect and they can be breached. However, they add another significant barrier to discourage all but the most determined intruder.

## ❖ ❖ ❖  Workflow Systems

Traditional information systems are based on an interpretation based on the company's business culture and management's needs. Computer-generated information typically does not lend itself to interpretation that produces action, and knowledge implies action based on the information. Today the fast-paced, highly competitive business world forces the need for variety and complexity in the interpretation of information generated by computer systems.

Group decision-making tools can help companies make better decisions by capturing the knowledge from groups of experts. Furthermore, companies that capture their customer's preferences can improve their customer service, which translates to larger profits [Becerra-Fernandez et al., 1998]. Organizations are now concentrating their efforts not only in gathering documentation but also in capturing the knowledge embedded in their business processes. In its purest sense, workflow represents the automation of a business process.

A **workflow management (WfM) system** is a set of tools that support defining, creating, and managing the execution of workflow processes [Workflow Management Coalition, 1999]; in other words, this system provides a method for capturing the steps that lead to the completion of a project within a fixed time frame. WfM systems have been around on factory assembly lines for some time. By automating many of their routine business processes, companies are able to save time and valuable human resources. WfM systems can serve as the basis for collaborative computing, as evidenced by their growing popularity. Workflow systems provide a mechanism for the analysis and optimization of the entire process that make up a project. One benefit of using a WfM system is that it provides the user with an audit of necessary skills and resources prior to project initiation. Workflow systems also provide a platform for the replication and reuse of stored processes. Finally, WfM systems can also serve as a training tool because they provide a broad overview with detailed operations of tasks as well as an identification of possible "weak links" in a process.

A workflow tool provides a method of capturing the steps that lead to the completion of a project within a fixed time frame, and in doing so, provides a method of illustrating such steps. Workflow systems can be useful for projects by enacting their elemental tasks, as well as by providing a mechanism, for the analysis and optimization of the entire processes detailing the project.

The Web provides a readily available communications infrastructure for the building of WfM systems. Many existing WfM systems provide Web interfaces but only a few make use of the underlying communications mechanisms that the Web offers. WfM systems that provide only a Web interface are referred to as Web-enabled, whereas Web-based WfM systems use Web technology as their underlying infrastructure.

## Document Management via the Web

Another technique frequently touted under the auspices of KM is document management. At the core of a document management system is a centralized repository, an electronic storage medium with a primary storage location that affords multiple access points. **Document management systems** essentially store information. A document management system unifies an aggregate of relevant information conveniently in one location through a common interface. Document management builds on the central repository by adding support to the classification and organization of information, and unifying the actions of storage and retrieval of documents instituted over a platform-independent system. The document management collaborative application increases communication, thus allowing the sharing of organizational knowledge.

A collaborative environment (which allows the informal exchange of ideas) combined with a detailed workflow (which captures process steps) is an efficient method of streamlining business practices. A document management system unifies an aggregate of relevant information conveniently in one location through a common interface. Categorizing and processing information for search purposes provide a detailed knowledge warehouse. The collaborative application increases communication, thus allowing the sharing of organizational knowledge. Although there are benefits of using these three tools (document management, workflow, and groupware) independently of one another, their integration augments their individual contributions. The document management system essentially stores information. The electronic documents are usually organized and relevant to its hierarchical structure. The workflow, which details the steps involved in completing a project, combined with a central repository that contains information relevant to a project, provides added benefits. The most important benefits, according KM theory, are the elicitation and capture of the organizational know-how that typically is not captured by most information systems, as well as an obvious user interface to access and reuse this organizational know-how. Collaborative computing provides a common communication space, improves sharing of knowledge, provides a mechanism for real-time feedback on the tasks performed, helps to optimize processes, and results in a centralized knowledge warehouse.

## SUMMARY ◆ ◇ ◆

The WWW is a giant information depository linked by the Internet. Servers containing information to be made available to the requesting public await requests received through the Internet and respond to them by giving the client access to their information, in the form of Web pages. The Web pages, expressed in HTML, provide access to files and other downloadable information, as well as serve to send programs executable in the client's own machine. Internet search engines allow clients to search the content of the WWW to find the specific information they seek.

The chapter discusses the techniques behind the Web search engines. This includes how they acquire the information contained in their indexing databases, and how they rank the sites whose content partially matches the requests.

This chapter covers network security. This is an issue causing growing concern in network managers. As the amount of data, information, and knowledge placed on the Web grows, the danger of breaching the network security and obtaining illicit access to these sources can be devastating to an organization highly dependent on competitive edges over the competition. Therefore, a knowledge manager must weight the advantages of common availability of the knowledge, information, and data, with the inherent dangers of doing so. In this chapter, we provide a brief discussion of some of the technology available to thwart such breaches.

Some tools that are collectively called collaborative computing are briefly discussed in this chapter. They include workflow management tools and document management systems. Both are best used through the Web.

## KEY TERMS ◆ ◇ ◆

- active Web documents—p. 207
- document management systems—p. 213
- dynamic Web documents—p. 206
- heterogeneous networks—p. 205

- Hypertext Markup Language (HTML)—p. 205
- Hypertext Transfer Protocol (HTTP)—p. 206
- Internet—p. 204
- Java—p. 205
- static Web documents—p. 206

- Uniform Resource Locator (URL)—p. 206
- Web crawlers—p. 209
- workflow management (WfM) systems—p. 212
- World Wide Web (WWW)— p. 204

## REVIEW QUESTIONS ◆ ◇ ◆

1. What is the difference between a directory-based search engine and one that uses Web crawlers?
2. List and describe the three basic types of Web documents.
3. What are the major differences between these three document types?
4. What are the means available to protect sensitive computer systems from malicious intrusion? Describe them in your own words.
5. Define collaborative computing. How does it help in the knowledge management (KM) process?

## APPLICATION EXERCISES ◇◆ ◇◆ ◇◆

1. Design (on paper) a static Web page serving as a sales medium for a company selling suntan lotion in Canada.
2. Do the same for a dynamic Web page.
3. Do the same for an active Web page.
4. What are the relative benefits and disadvantages of each of the above Web pages?
5. Imagine the task of a mail carrier. Develop a workflow structure for her daily routine of delivering mail in a suburban residential neighborhood.

## REFERENCES ◇◆ ◇◆ ◇◆

Anonymous. 2000. How Search Engines Work. Atlantic Telephone Membership Corp., www.atmc.net.

Becerra-Fernandez, I. 1998b. NASA Project Corporate Memory–Final Report, grant No. NAG10-0232, August.

Comer, D.G. 2001. *Computer Networks and Internets,* 3rd ed. Prentice Hall, Upper Saddle River, NJ.

Franklin, C. 2002. How Internet Search Engines Work, www.howstuffworks.com.

Langenstein, B., Vogt, R., and Ullmann, M. 2000. The use of formal methods for trusted digital signature devices. Proceedings of the Thirteenth International Florida Artificial Intelligence Research Society Conference, May, pp. 336–340.

Sullivan, D. 2002. How Search Engines Work. http://searchenginewatch.com, October 14.

Workflow Management Coalition. 1999. *Terminology and Glossary*.

CHAPTER

# Discovering
# New Knowledge:
# Data Mining[1]

## ❖ ❖ ❖ Introduction

In Chapter 10, we learned how to elicit tacit knowledge from human sources. By definition, the tacit knowledge elicited was already known by humans. Our task, therefore, was merely to elicit it from the human knowledge source, and codify and capture it in its explicit form for proper management. We also looked at capturing human knowledge, found embedded in the design of an engineered system, directly from the electronic representation of the design. Again, humans already possessed this knowledge. In a very basic way, our task was just a question of converting existing knowledge from tacit to explicit form, or from one form of explicit knowledge to another form of explicit knowledge.

However, there are considerable limitations to human knowledge. Enormous "gold mines" of knowledge are buried in databases, and heretofore unknown to humans. Knowing, understanding, and using this knowledge can give an organization significant competitive advantage. Therefore, it is important that organizations be able to harvest this knowledge effectively. One example of this is how to design better and more efficient products based on data about product performance and customer preferences. Another example is finding out how to better serve existing customers based upon information about their buying habits or the problems they typically face.

The reference to gold mines was intentional. Techniques currently exist that can "dive" into databases and look for patterns in the data that may be of great value to an enterprise. Such patterns can be indicative of previously unknown relations between variables. Knowing about these relations can be very valuable indeed. These techniques, or rather, families of techniques, refer to *knowledge discovery in databases* (KDD) or more commonly, *data mining* (DM). KDD as a discipline began in the mid-1980s when the first workshop on KDD was held. However, it should be noted that the natural and social

---

[1]This chapter is written in collaboration with Douglas D. Dankel.

science fields have been using these techniques for years as the basis for investigation with the scientific process. An edited book resulted from that workshop [Piatetsky-Shapiro and Frawley, 1991]. This book is considered by many to be the first text on the subject.

There are numerous techniques for mining databases for knowledge. Many books have been written on the topic since the original by Piatetsky-Shapiro and Frawley. Therefore, an exhaustive survey of all techniques is clearly beyond the scope of this chapter. We instead concentrate on the more popular DM techniques, and treat them in-depth. We believe our readers can be better served in this manner.

## ❖ ❖ ❖ Objectives of Data Mining

In general, the goals of a DM study can be seen to answer one of two main questions: to *describe* what has happened, or to *predict* what can happen. *Descriptive* DM seeks patterns in past actions or activities to affect these actions or activities. For example, in looking for criminal activity in financial transactions such as money laundering, one would look for unusual behaviors on the part of depositors. Once these unusual patterns are discovered, a criminal can be arrested and brought to justice. Techniques to accomplish this include affinity (or association) and clustering techniques.

*Predictive DM*, on the other hand, involves looking at past history with the intent to predict future behavior. There is no intent to do anything about the prior cases as in descriptive DM. Techniques to do this include the **classification** and prediction (or estimation) techniques to be discussed later in this chapter. These terms are further defined below.

1. ***Classification.*** DM techniques in this category serve to classify a discrete outcome variable, such as *customers*, into discrete predefined categories. A goal of the DM study could be "... to identify the customers who are most likely to buy a new product offering." Classification can be descriptive or predictive. Classification can be used to learn how to classify groups of people or objects according to some attributes. These criteria could then be used to predict how new instances of the data are to be classified. This may provide significant advantage in how we deal with the new instances. For example, if it is discovered that there is a clear relationship between certain employment aspects of past loan holders and their subsequent loan defaults, a loan applicant meeting that employment criteria could be labeled as a "bad risk," and, therefore, be denied the loan. In another example, the goal of the DM study could be "to predict how much money, on average, people who are late in paying their taxes owe the IRS."

2. ***Affinity or association.*** Association serves to find items closely associated in the data set. Techniques falling in this category include *market basket analysis* and *link analysis*. For example, a goal of the DM study could be "to identify the products that customers are likely to purchase together." The type of model required is a descriptive model. It can help a supermarket develop marketing campaigns targeting all the items historically purchased together.

3. ***Clustering.*** This can also be used to describe natural groupings of data not obvious through a casual inspection. The aim of this category of techniques is to

create clusters of input objects, instead of an outcome variable. For example, a business goal could be "to identify the Medicare billing records that look unusual." The type of model required is a descriptive model.

The many DM techniques fall under one of three underlying approaches: (1) symbolic and inductive, (2) connectionist, and (3) statistical. Although several techniques exist within each approach, we only discuss the few most common ones.

Relations among variables can be expressed in several forms: decision tables, decision trees, rules, functions, or clusters of related data. Decision tables are multidimensional data structures, where each row contains one *example* of data, and the columns are attributes of each example. The value of each attribute is designated for each row and column combination. The last of the columns typically represents the classification of the example. Table 12-1 in this section depicts a simple decision table of examples consisting of four attributes, the last of which is the class to which each belongs. Decision tables are rudimentary and the least intuitive means of reflecting newly found patterns or relations.

Decision trees are much better suited for reflecting relationships. Their graphic representation makes them easier to understand, and their hierarchical organization permits representation of more complex concepts. A tree is a hierarchical, acyclical (i.e., has no closed cycles) network of *nodes* and *links*. Nodes are elements that contain information. They are associated with other nodes via the links (also called *arcs* or *edges*). A rooted tree is hierarchically organized into levels and has the *root node* as its only node at the top level. The nodes at the level below the root node are called the *children* of the root node. The *leaf* nodes, on the other hand, have no children. Leaf nodes most often populate the lowest level of a tree, but this is not always the case. The nodes at all levels in between have both parents and children.

Decision trees are also commonly used as a problem-solving paradigm. In such a context, decisions are expected of the user at every node in a decision tree, for each problem solved. Depending on the answer given, the problem solver follows a particular path down the tree, ultimately finishing at a leaf node. The leaf node reached contains the desired solution. In classification problems, leaf nodes hold the desired classification for the item classified. The structure of the tree per se incorporates the mined relations, leading to a solution (the class or final answer). A small decision tree can be seen in Figure 12-1 below. The leaf nodes are shown as circles whereas the root node is shown as an octagon. Intermediate nodes (those with parents as well as children) are seen as rectangles.

Rules are the most intuitive of the knowledge representation means. People feel very comfortable expressing certain types of knowledge as conditionals. They are also

**TABLE 12-1  Data Samples**

| Name | Outlook | Temperature | Humidity | Class |
|------|---------|-------------|----------|-------|
| Data sample 1 | Sunny | Mild | Dry | Enjoyable |
| Data sample 2 | Cloudy | Cold | Humid | Not enjoyable |
| Data sample 3 | Rainy | Mild | Humid | Not enjoyable |
| Data sample 4 | Sunny | Hot | Humid | Not enjoyable |

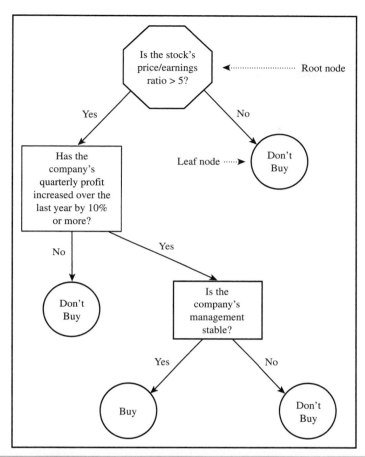

**FIGURE 12-1  Simple Decision Tree on Purchasing Stock**

quite easy to understand in a casual way. Chapter 8 describes rules at length, so we assume the reader's current familiarity with them. Some authors (e.g., Witten and Frank [2000]) define several types of rules that can be mined, such as association rules, classification rules, rules with exceptions, and rules involving relations.

Developing functions that mathematically describe the patterns formed by the relationship has been the goal of statistical techniques for years. If an equation that accurately describes the relations and patterns in the database can be identified, it can also help predict behavior of situations similar to what is found in the database.

Finally, clusters are groups of data examples that are somehow naturally related to each other. By knowing that these examples have something in common, they could be assumed to be of the same class. In a later section, we discuss the topic of data clustering in the context of neural networks.

DM has been closely linked to machine learning. In fact, the two are typically mentioned in the same breath. It is obvious why—the computer actually learns by sifting through the data in an organized fashion. The distinction is that DM is strictly limited to uncovering new relationships from data, whereas machine learning is a more general field in which learning per se is the main focus, regardless of whether what is learned is already known by humans or not, or whether it is from data or otherwise. DM techniques are essential for knowledge discovery systems, as we discuss in Chapter 13.

Now that we know the various goals for which one would undertake a DM study, let us now look in detail at the techniques available to accomplish our goals. We start with the symbolic approaches.

# ◆▸ ◆▸ ◆▸ Symbolic Approach: Induction Learning Rules from Examples

We briefly discuss inductive reasoning tools in Chapter 8. There we treat induction as an inference method. In this chapter, we shall see how it also serves as a learning strategy. In fact, **inductive learning** is one of the primary techniques for machine learning. It has become one of the most popular DM techniques

According to Webster's dictionary, induction is defined as "reasoning from particular facts or individual cases to general conclusion." Induction is said to be the basic element in scientific discovery. The general conclusion derived is the relationships discovered, which can be represented as rules or functions. The individual cases are the results of the observation of a natural or man-made phenomenon.

An inductive strategy learns by presenting to a machine a series of data samples and the conclusion that should be drawn from each data sample. The machine, through a set of predefined induction heuristics, analyzes each data sample and builds an internal representation of the characteristics of the domain.

Winston [1992], an early researcher in machine learning, defined these inductive heuristics to be rules examining a series of data samples to capture the presence or absence of specific features that identify the important relationships and features from these data samples. This technique is especially well suited to classification problems. In Winston's approach, a series of true data samples (features that support a specific classification) and *near misses* (negative data samples whose features fail to support a specific classification but come close) are presented to the learner one at a time. By applying the inductive heuristics and observing the features of all data samples, Winston's system learns which features distinguish true data samples from near misses.

## INDUCTIVE ALGORITHMS

A second, and much more popular, inductive approach, originally called the ID3 algorithm [Quinlan, 1983], provides a way to systematically extract rules from a set of data samples. ID3 has since evolved into more advanced algorithms called C4.5 and, currently, C5.0. [Quinlan, 1983; 1993] We refer to the work described here as C5.0, although its roots date back to the ID3, and an earlier *concept learning system (CLS)* algorithm [Hunt, 1966].

The C5.0 algorithm extracts rules from data samples by first generating a decision tree, called an **induction tree,** from the presented data samples. The data samples are composed of slightly constrained features (attribute and value pairs) having the following features:

1. Exactly the same pair of attributes and values must be used for each data sample—no more and no less.
2. The attribute values must be discrete. They must be enumerated and defined *a priori.*
3. Each data sample must unequivocally indicate to what class it belongs.

The induction tree is likened to a decision tree. It is built progressively, adding nodes and links as they become necessary to segregate the data samples. To begin, one of the predefined attributes is assigned to a node of the emerging induction tree. We start with the root node of the tree, which is all there is at the start of the process. Assigning an attribute to a node is analogous to attaching a question to a node in the simple decision tree of Figure 12-1. Then links from the node are created that lead to children nodes at the next level of the tree. The different values of an attribute are assigned to each of these links emanating from the node assigned that attribute.

The next step is to "distribute" the entire set of data samples down the emerging induction tree. Initially, all data samples "reside" at the root node. Then the feature of each data sample defined in the node on which it resides is examined for its value. Depending on its value, the data sample is then "moved" to the child node connected to the parent node via the link whose value coincides with the value of that data sample. This is done for all data samples in the node.

If, after the distribution of all data samples, all data samples residing in each child node have the same classification, the process stops. If any one child node contains data samples with more than one classification, then another feature is selected for that node, and the same process is started.

Figure 12-2 depicts a two-level induction tree for a simple set of data samples dealing with the weather. The data samples are shown in Table 12-1 above. They are used to classify days as either *enjoyable* or *not enjoyable.* Three features (attributes) are used, *Outlook, Temperature,* and *Humidity. Outlook* has three possible values: *sunny, cloudy,* and *rain. Temperature* has also three values: *hot, mild,* and *cold.* Finally, *humidity* has two values, *humid* and *dry.*

 **FIGURE 12-2** Simple Induction Tree

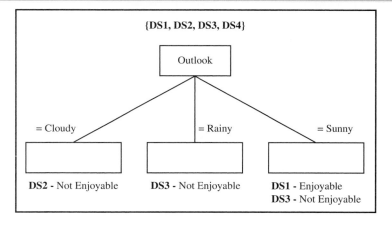

The tree of Figure 12-2 does not complete the classification, because data samples DS1 and DS4 fall into the same node, yet have different classification (DS1 is *enjoyable* whereas DS4 is *not enjoyable*). A new level of the tree must now be created to try to disambiguate the situation. In this case, we use the *Temperature* attribute and extend the tree another level, but only from the node containing the ambiguous data samples. This is shown in Figure 12-3.

Before describing the inductive algorithm that, in a modified version, is now C5.0, let us first define some terminology, and relate it to our simple example above. We assume a classification problem, which is most typical of applications of inductive learning.

We are given a set of data samples with a predefined classification. These data samples are described in terms of a fixed collection of features (shown in Table 12-1). Let $C$ be the set of all such data sample instances, $C = \{c_1, c_2, c_3, \ldots, c_n\}$. For the sake of simplicity, we assume that each $c_i$ is associated with a classification of either $A$ or $B$. Each data sample has a fixed set of features (attributes) $F$, where $F = \{f_1, f_2, f_3, \ldots f_m\}$. Each feature $f_j$ has a set of possible discrete values $V = \{v_1, v_2, v_3, \ldots, v_k\}$. Relating these definitions to the data samples of Table 12-1:

$$C = \{c_1: DS1, c_2: DS2, c_3: DS3, c_4: DS4\}$$
$$A = enjoyable\ B = not\ enjoyable$$
$$F = \{f_1: Outlook, f_2: Temperature, f_3: Humidity\}$$
$$Outlook = \{v_1: sunny, v_2: cloudy, v_3: rain\}$$
$$Temperature = \{v_1: mild, v_2: cold, v_3: hot\}$$
$$Humidity = \{v_1: humid, v_2: dry\}$$

❬◆❭ ❬◆❭ ❬◆❭   **FIGURE 12-3** Resolution of Simple Data Sample

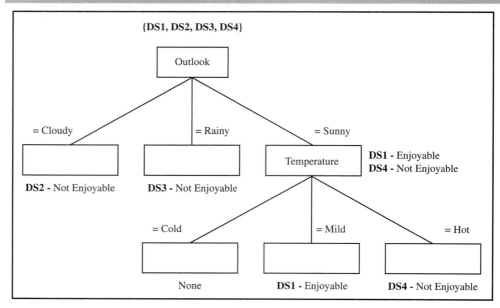

Note that the number of values (the value of $k$ in the set $V$) can vary for each feature. Furthermore, each feature $f_j$ for each data sample $c_i$, where $j = 1, \ldots, m$, has one of its respective possible values. The associated value $v_i$ for $f_j$, of course, may and will probably be different from one data sample to another.

In the C5.0 algorithm, the trainer (user or expert) determines which feature to select at each point in the process.

In summary, we select a feature and partition $C$ into disjoint sets $C_1, C_2, C_3, \ldots,$ $C_n$, where each partition contains the members of the original set that have the same value for the chosen feature. Each of these subcollections is then examined to see whether all its members belong to the same class. If they do not, another attribute is selected and the process is repeated. The resulting leaves of the tree carry the name of each class, although some classes may be repeated across more than one leaf node.

Rules are written by traversing the tree exhaustively in a depth-first fashion from root node to each leaf node. A rule antecedent is composed of all the decisions faced by the traversing agent, with the values depending on which branch the agent took. In our simple data sample in Figure 12-2, we could write the following rules:

> ***Rule 1.*** If *Outlook* is *cloudy*, then the *Weather* is *not enjoyable*.
> ***Rule 2.*** If Outlook is *rainy*, then the *Weather* is *not enjoyable*.

No further rule can be written, because the third branch in our partial tree contains two data samples with different classifications. We would have to select another feature to resolve this ambiguity, as shown in Figure 12-3. This extension would allow for the following two additional rules to be written:

> ***Rule 3.*** If the *Outlook* is *sunny* and *Temperature* is *mild*, then the *Weather* is *enjoyable*.
> ***Rule 4.*** If the *Outlook* is *sunny* and *Temperature* is *cold*, then the *Weather* is *not enjoyable*.

This process can easily be extended to handle the case where the original set of objects, $C$, contains objects from several classes. This is illustrated by the following, more complex example.

Suppose that we are attempting to select a knowledge-based (KB) system shell for some application. Each shell is designed with particular features (i.e., development language, memory requirements, monetary cost, reasoning schemes, or external interfaces) that help us classify the shell as *acceptable* or *unacceptable* for the application. Our original set of objects (i.e., the shells) can be described by a set of vectors. Each vector describes one combination of features associated with a particular KB system shell. Note that because each shell can have multiple reasoning schemes and external interfaces, a particular shell might be described by more than one vector.

For this example, suppose that we are considering the following (hypothetical) KB system shells: ThoughtGen, Offsite, Genie, SilverWorks, XS, and MilliExpert. The attributes with their possible values are

Development language: {java, C++, lisp}
Reasoning method: {forward, backward}
External interfaces: {dBase, spreadsheetXL, ASCII file, devices}
Cost: Any positive number
Memory. any positive number

The collection, *S*, is shown in Table 12-2. Note that an asterisk is used to signify that all the values for this attribute are acceptable. Because all objects do not all belong to the same classification, we must apply the partitioning method.

The first step in the algorithm is to select an attribute and form a tree with the name of the attribute at its root. If we select *Language* as our attribute, we have three branches emanating from this root, each labeled for one of the three possible values of that attribute. All the objects having the same value for the selected attribute are placed at the end of the corresponding branch. This results in the tree shown in Figure 12-4.

Note that all the leaf nodes in the tree shown in Figure 12-4 have data sets with multiple associated classes. This is not acceptable. Therefore, the process must be

**TABLE 12-2  Collection of Objects Described by Vectors of Attributes**

| Language | Reasoning Method | Interface Method | Cost | Memory | Classification |
|---|---|---|---|---|---|
| Java | Backward | SpreadsheetXL | 250 | 128 MB | MilliExpert |
| Java | Backward | ASCII | 250 | 128 MB | MilliExpert |
| Java | Backward | dBase | 195 | 256 MB | ThoughtGen |
| Java | * | Devices | 985 | 512 MB | OffSite |
| C++ | Forward | * | 6500 | 640 MB | Genie |
| LISP | Forward | * | 15,000 | 5 GB | Silverworks |
| C++ | Backward | * | 395 | 256 MB | XS |
| LISP | Backward | * | 395 | 256 MB | XS |

◈ ◈ ◈ ◈

*, All values acceptable.

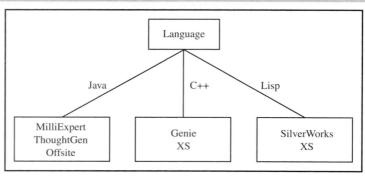 ◈ ◈ ◈ **FIGURE 12-4 Resulting Decision Tree from Selection of the Language Attribute**

repeated on all these nodes with a new attribute. Suppose that we now select the attribute *Reasoning Method* for all nodes on this level. This results in the tree shown in Figure 12-5. Note that all but the leftmost leaf node contain the names of only one system (unique classifications), so they need not be considered further.

Further refinement is still necessary for the left side of the tree. At this point we have three attributes from which to select for further refinement—*Interface Method*, *Cost,* and *Memory Requirements*. Suppose that the *Interface Method* attribute is selected. Making this last application of the classification algorithm, we discover that each leaf node contains single objects; therefore, the process halts. Figure 12-6 displays the final resulting tree that can easily be used to derive a set of rules to assist us in selecting a particular KB system for some application or for identification of its characteristics.

The rules resulting from these data samples are generated by traversing the tree depth first, starting from root node and visiting the left-hand side first. The rules would be as follows:

> **Rule 1.**  *If* Language = Java and Reasoning Method = Backward, and Interface = SpreadsheetXL, *then* Answer = MilliExpert.
> **Rule 2.**  *If* Language = Java and Reasoning Method = Backward, and Interface = ASCII, *then* Answer = MilliExpert.
> **Rule 3.**  *If* Language = Java and Reasoning Method = Backward, and Interface = dBase, *then* Answer = ThoughtGen.
> **Rule 4.**  *If* Language = Java and Reasoning Method = Backward, and Interface = Device *then* Answer = OffSite.
> **Rule 5.**  *If* Language = Java and Reasoning Method = Forward, *then* Answer = OffSite.

**FIGURE 12-5 Resulting Decision Tree from the Addition of the Reasoning Method Attribute**

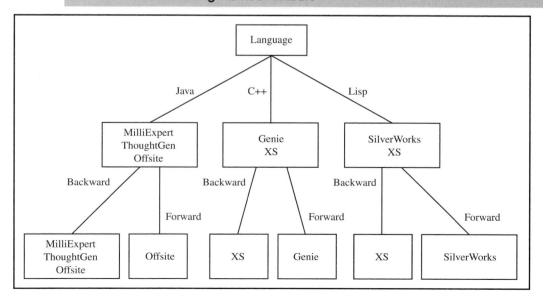

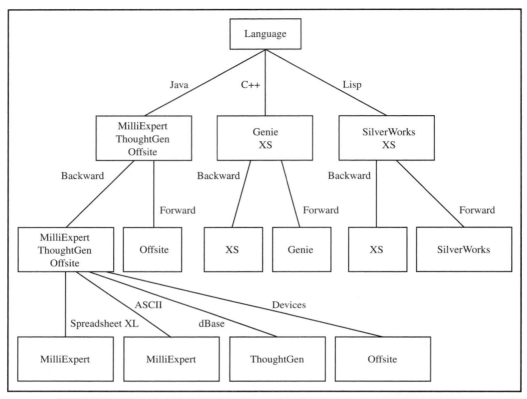

◇ ◇ ◇ **FIGURE 12-6 Final Resulting Tree**

> ***Rule 6.*** *If* Language = C++ and Reasoning Method = Backward, *then* Answer = XS.
> ***Rule 7.*** *If* Language = C++ and Reasoning Method = Forward, *then* Answer = Ginie.
> ***Rule 8.*** *If* Language = Lisp and Reasoning Method = Backward, *then* Answer = XS
> ***Rule 9.*** *If* Language = Lisp and Reasoning Method = Forward *then* Answer = Silverworks.

Note, however, that the structure of an induction tree varies according to which attribute is chosen first, second, etc. For example, in the earlier example about the weather being *enjoyable,* it is easy to see that if we had selected *Humidity* first, instead of *Outlook,* then we would not have needed to go any further than the first level. This is because had we selected *Humidity* as the first attribute to employ in the segregation of the data samples, all data samples residing at the same leaf node would have had the same classification. This would allow us to restructure the induction tree as shown in Figure 12-7 and derive the following rules:

> ***Rule 1.*** *If Humidity* is *humid, then Weather* is *not enjoyable.*
> ***Rule 2.*** *If Humidity* is *dry, then Weather* is *enjoyable.*

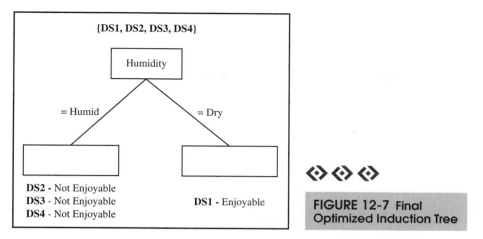

{DS1, DS2, DS3, DS4}

Humidity

= Humid          = Dry

DS2 - Not Enjoyable
DS3 - Not Enjoyable          DS1 - Enjoyable
DS4 - Not Enjoyable

**FIGURE 12-7** Final
Optimized Induction Tree

The decision on which attribute to select first, therefore, has a distinct effect on how the rules need to be written. Naturally, derivation of a minimal decision tree minimizes the complexity of the rules because the number of tests (premises) required to classify an object using the rules derived from the induction tree may be the fewest possible. Therefore, our objective when selecting the attribute to use in partitioning the remaining cases might be to derive the minimal tree.

C5.0 extends the original CLS algorithm to permit it to develop a minimal tree by using an informational–theoretical approach [Quinlan, 1993]. The path through a decision tree, which an object follows when classified, can be viewed as a message. The measure of the information content of this message determines how the object is classified. C5.0 bases the selection of the best attribute to use on the plausible assumption that the complexity of the decision tree is strongly related to the amount of information conveyed by this message [Quinlan, 1983]. By determining the amount of information that can be gained by testing each possible attribute and selecting the one containing the largest amount of information, our tree can be optimized. To do this, we first need to calculate the overall information content of the final messages. We then compare this number to that calculated in a similar fashion from the partial trees created when a particular attribute is tested. This is a complex process well beyond the scope of this book. See Gonzalez and Dankel [1993] for details. Suffice it to say, however, that this feature permits C5.0 to optimize the size of the resulting decision tree, making the rules derived from the tree minimal in terms of the number of premises they contain.

## OTHER INDUCTION ALGORITHMS

Another less publicized but equally important inductive learning algorithm is CART [Breiman, 1984]. CART was developed at approximately the same time as and independently of ID3. CART was created by statisticians, whereas ID3 originated in the machine-learning community. They share many concepts—including the idea of representing the learned knowledge in the form of induction trees. One difference is that CART was designed to work with problems that use continuous values, whereas ID3 could only handle discrete induction. C5.0, however, is likewise able to handle variables with continuous ranges of values.

Another algorithm used to build induction trees—called CHAID—was developed by J.A. Hartigan in 1975, and is a statistical technique for constructing decision trees. CHAID is similar in nature to CART and C5.0, but differs from them in some ways, namely, CHAID stops growing the tree before over fitting occurs; and its use is restricted to discrete variables. For more information on CHAID refer to Berry and Linoff [1997].

### SOME FINAL COMMENTS ON INDUCTION

In summary, inductive DM mining is well suited for finding relations in the data. These relations are typically expressed as induction trees or rules. Because rules are typically derived from the induction trees by traversing them exhaustively, they are really two very similar forms of knowledge representation.

The key to inductive techniques, of course, is that the user must ensure that all relevant attributes be considered in the analysis. Otherwise, good correlation may be impossible to achieve. One anecdotal incident illustrates the importance of including the relevant attributes in a kind of DM exercise. In this real-life incident, an electric utility power generating station on the shores of Lake Michigan experienced vibrations in one of its generator subsystems. These vibrations initially dumbfounded all diagnosticians, because the vibrations began just as suddenly as they stopped, and no obvious malfunction of the system was evident. After a while, someone noticed a correlation between the vibrations and the way the wind was blowing. If the wind blew in from the lake, the vibrations would increase. If the wind blew out to the lake, the vibrations would cease. After some analysis, it was found that the cool wind from the lake would cool the lubricating oil to a temperature lower than designed, thereby causing the vibrations. A wind blowing out would not do so, therefore causing no vibrations. Had a DM algorithm been applied without including the wind direction as a potentially relevant attribute, this problem would not have been solved.

## ◇ ◇ ◇ Connectionist Approach: Artificial Neural Networks

The second most popular approach to DM is the family of connectionist techniques. These are embodied by **artificial neural networks (ANNs)**. ANNs take an entirely different approach than the symbolic ones presented by CART, CHAID, and C5.0. ANNs represent a computer implementation of the human brain's physiological structure in an attempt to duplicate its functionality. The main advantage of neural networks is their innate ability to learn when presented with sufficient data samples. Another advantage is their ability to identify clusters of information that are somehow related. This ability can be useful in a tool for DM. Clusters can be thought of as data samples linked by some similar attributes. This similarity is not obvious to a human observer because of the complexity or the volume of the data. First, let us look into the neural network architecture and training methods.

ANNs originated with the pioneering work of McCulloch and Pitts in the early 1940s. In their seminal paper, McCulloch and Pitts [1943] described the calculus of neural computation. Minsky wrote his doctoral dissertation on neural computation as a means to model the human brain [Minsky, 1954]. A subsequent paper by Minsky

[1961] contained descriptions of what are now considered modern neural networks. Ironically, it was Minsky who, along with Pappert, published a book that severely dampened the enthusiasm for neural networks [Minsky and Papert, 1969]. They pointed out the limitations of the single layer perceptron architecture, one of the important neural network structures at that time. This opinion persisted until the 1980s, when the concept of neural computation was reborn as a result of the seminal papers by Hopfield [1982] and Rumelhart and McClelland [1986], and the so-called artificial intelligence boom. Today neural networks have become a viable, if contentious, technology. An excellent historical account of neural networks can be found in Haykin [1994].

## NEURONS AS THE BASIC PROCESSING ELEMENT IN NEURAL NETS

In brief, neural networks work by simulating the human brain in that it is a strongly connected group of simple processing elements called *neurons*. These neurons "fire" when their input is higher than some threshold value. When neurons fire, they communicate their value to the downstream neuron, which performs the same function. Figure 12-8 depicts a simple model of a neuron [Haykin, 1994].

The inputs enter a neuron either from external sources, or in multilayered networks (defined later), from the output of neurons in a previous layer. These are indicated by $x_n$. The weights are values that signify the strength of the connection. The inputs for each neuron are multiplied by their respective weight to form the input into the summing junction. The summing junction, indicated by the summation symbol $\Sigma$, adds all the inputs into the neuron, and forwards the result to the activation function. The latter decides whether the total strength of its inputs merits forwarding its computed value to the next neuron (or to the output), and if so, what the value should be. This is called *firing* the neuron.

The purpose of the activation function, beyond determining whether the neuron fires, is to cap the value of the output. The output of the activation function, when the neuron fires, is normally constrained in the range between 0 and 1.0. This has the effect of limiting the influence of any one neuron when it gets a disproportionately large input, thereby preventing it from unfairly skewing the final output. There are three

 **FIGURE 12-8 Simple Model of a Neuron**

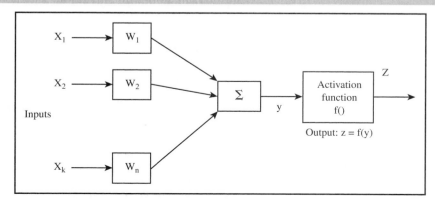

commonly used activation functions: (1) *threshold*, which is a step function (yes or no) depending strictly on the scalar value of the summing junction; (2) *piecewise linear*, which instead of a very steep drop, has a more gradual one, from 0 to 1.0; and (3) *sigmoid*, which like the piecewise linear, gradually goes from 0 to 1.0. However, it does so much more softly than the piecewise linear—it looks like an s-curve. For all three activation functions, the *y*-axis is a number from 0 to 1.0—this is the limit of what the neuron can pass on to its output. In Figure 12-9, we see diagrams of these activation functions. These functions can compute an output value for a neuron based on the value computed by the summing junction.

## NEURAL NETWORK ARCHITECTURES

The individual neurons are very simple processing elements. One neuron alone cannot accomplish much. However, when connected with other neurons, significant computational power can be gained. Neural network architectures define how the neurons are interconnected to provide solutions. Two of the most popular neural network architectures are the *single layer* and the *multilayer* network. Other popular neural network architectures, such as recurrent networks and adaptive resonance theory nets, as well as many others, are beyond the scope of this discussion.

In most instances, the structure of many neural network architectures is the same: an *input layer*, a (usually distinct) *output layer*, and some (possibly zero) number of *hidden layers* in between. In general, the greater the number of hidden layers, the more complex is the function or relationship that the network might be able to discover from the training data. Note that too many hidden layers may result in computational intractability or "overtraining." Overtraining means that the resulting network is not likely to generalize well when presented with data sets that it did not see during training.

Figure 12-10 shows a single-layer network. Figure 12-11 depicts a two-layer network. A *fully connected network* is one where *all* neurons in one layer are connected to all neurons in the next layer. A *weakly connected* network is one where *not* all neurons of one layer are connected to all the neurons in the next layer. The networks shown in Figures 12-10 and 12-11 are both strongly connected.

◆❯ ❮◆❯ ❮◆❯ **FIGURE 12-9 Three Common Activation Functions**

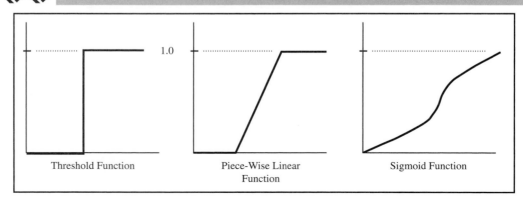

| Threshold Function | Piece-Wise Linear Function | Sigmoid Function |

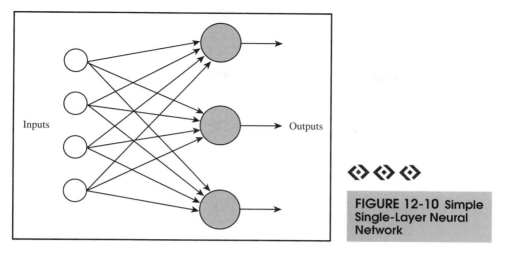

◆❯ ◆❯ ◆❯

**FIGURE 12-10 Simple Single-Layer Neural Network**

The number of neurons used and the number of layers are determined by the designer, depending on the characteristics of the problem. They are compromises between effectiveness in solving the problem and the efficiency in training.

## TRAINING NEURAL NETWORKS

The most significant aspect of neural networks is their ability to be trained to solve problems by virtue of exposing them to a set of examples. In effect, the weights (or strengths) of the network, defined in Figure 12-12, are set by the *learning* or *training process*. The learning algorithm employed is the third characteristic that differentiates neural networks. The other two, of course, are the neuron model and the neural network

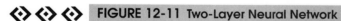

◆❯ ◆❯ ◆❯    **FIGURE 12-11 Two-Layer Neural Network**

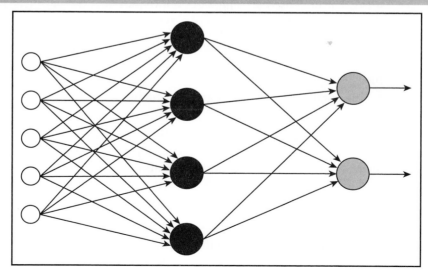

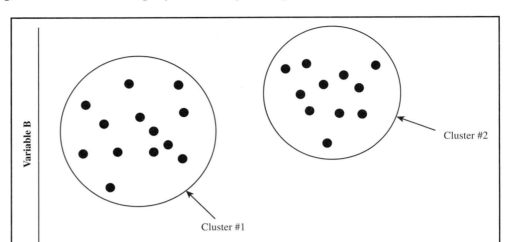

❖ ❖ ❖  **FIGURE 12-12**  Clusters of Related Data in Two-Dimensional Space

architecture. The learning ability of a neural net, in turn, is determined by its architecture (the number and the connectivity structure of the neurons) and by the method chosen for training. We now briefly discuss how training of neural networks is accomplished.

Neural network learning techniques can be classified as one of two types: (1) supervised learning, and (2) unsupervised learning. Supervised learning requires that a set of examples be available to the individual training the neural network. Each of these examples consists of an input pattern and the expected output. This type of learning is considered supervised learning because the examples play the role of a teacher, so to speak. Unsupervised learning does not require that the data sets used have an explicit classification (solution). There are several techniques in each of these categories.

It is not important that the reader be familiar with these specific algorithms for the purposes of this book. Therefore, we skip most of them and refer the reader to several excellent books for those that would like to learn further about neural nets [Haykin, 1994]. Nevertheless, we present below a description of one of the most elementary (as well as popular) supervised learning techniques.

### Supervised Learning: Back Propagation

In this approach, training is done by assigning a randomly generated initial value for the network weights, and then presenting the network with an example. The network output is compared with the expected output, and an error is computed. This error propagates back from the output nodes and assigns credit or blame to the appropriate neuron, modifying the value of its weight in response. This process continues iteratively, as several examples are presented in sequence to the network. The process stops when the training process converges (i.e., the error values stabilize below an acceptable threshold). Alternatively, the process also stops if it is determined that it cannot converge (i.e., the error is not yet within an acceptable threshold and it is not improving with additional iterations). This **back propagation** learning method for multilayer networks is composed of three phases: (1) presentation of the examples (input patterns with outputs) and feed forward execution of the network; (2) calculation of the associated errors when the output of the previous step is compared with the expected output and back propagation of this error; and (3) adjustment of the weights. The weights are modified by applying an adjustment based on the prediction errors associated with this neuron. This increments or decreases the old value of the weight. Through this process, the network attempts to synthesize a function capable of classifying the training patterns correctly, and thus to predict output for new patterns.

Several other factors can affect this algorithm. Initial weights are often not set randomly, but through an algorithm. Furthermore, a momentum factor ($\alpha$) can be introduced which takes into account the previous changes to determine the current change in value of weights. The momentum factor allows for appropriate acceleration or deceleration of learning, so that the network can converge to a solution faster. Alternatively, the learning rate ($\eta$) can also be adjusted to accelerate the learning or slow it down, as needed A designer must carefully consider the values of these parameters to achieve acceptable results.

Back propagation has proved highly successful in the training of multilayered neural nets. This is because in back propagation, unlike in some learning schemes for single-layer networks, the network is given not just reinforcement for how it is doing on a task. Information about errors is also filtered back through the system and is used to adjust the connections between the layers, thus improving performance.

## Unsupervised Neural Networks: The Kohonen Network

In many cases, it can be desirable to determine how complex data records are similar to each other. For simple records, a person using standard database functions can find this similarity rather easily. This process becomes much more difficult, however, when the records become complex (*n*-dimensions). It thus becomes a good candidate for advanced computational methods.

Clustering is a process by which natural grouping among data records are sought. These records contain no information about their own classification, so the clustering is determined on the basis of the attributes of the records and their values. The central concept in **cluster analysis** is to determine a *distance* among the records. The records in one cluster should be close to each other and distant from those in other clusters. This would indicate some commonality among the members of the cluster that is not readily obvious. A class can then be established for the members of each cluster. Figure 12-12 depicts two clusters in two-dimensional space. It shows how the members of a cluster are conceptually close to each other and far from those of the other cluster. This is described later in this chapter. It should be noted that not all data cluster naturally. The clustering process is sometimes not successful, regardless of what technique is employed.

Because we are dealing with multiple dimensions (several attributes), the distance in *n*-dimensional space can be difficult to describe and compute. This process is somewhat similar to case-based reasoning (CBR), where the distance between the current problem and each historical case must be computed as an expression of similarity. As mentioned in Chapter 9, this is often not easy to do in CBR systems. A special kind of neural network called the *Kohonen network*, or the *Kohonen self-organizing map*, is able to do this very effectively.

In the second type of learning method, *unsupervised learning*, the hidden neurons must find a way to organize themselves without help from the outside. In essence, the neurons are compelled to compete among themselves for the job of responding to a particular input. Eventually, the neuron or group of neurons best suited for particular tasks assumes that role. In this approach, no sample outputs are provided to the network against which it can measure its predictive performance for a given vector of inputs. Instead, the vectors of inputs are merely grouped into *similarity clusters* representing classes for purposes of categorizing any new examples that are later encountered outside the training set.

The Kohonen network is a well-known unsupervised learning neural network [Kohonen, 1990]. It is typically composed of a grid or map of neurons. Each neuron is connected to every input applied to the network, and each connection has a weight assigned to it. When a new pattern (data record) is presented to the Kohonen network during training, it compares the input vector to the weight vector of each cluster unit in the grid. The one cluster unit whose weight pattern most closely matches the current input vector "takes" the input and modifies its weights to better reflect this input. All clusters near the winning unit likewise adjust their weights to better match the neighboring winning cluster. The Kohonen network continues this competition process until the weights reflect a natural clustering of the input data. When used to classify, the input pattern is assigned to one of the cluster units. It should be noted, however, that the weights in the connections are *not* multiplied by its inputs, as is the case in other networks. They are merely used to reflect the input patterns naturally clustered around this neuron.

Kohonen nets do not have output per se. They are not typically predicting anything in DM applications, so outputs are not necessary. Their contribution is the distribution of the input records throughout the map; in other words, the final state of the neuron weights is the output. A human then must label the clusters as classifications. Figure 12-13 shows a simple Kohonen map.

Note that a connection weight is only shown for one connection at the lower left-hand side of Figure 12-13. This is done merely for simplification of illustration. In reality, each connection has a similar weight.

In summary, neural networks perform DM primarily in two ways: (1) predictive mode, which aims to develop models to predict outcome on the basis of input variables; (2) unsupervised mode, specifically used to identify clusters of data based on a set of attributes. However, some projects that have used neural nets to discover patterns in data and have built nets to predict are reported in the literature. For example, neural networks have been used to predict stock market variations, managing $200 million in institutional assets without human intervention with astonishingly accurate results [Fishman, 1991a]. Furthermore, varied simulations of the human neural physiology have been successful in learning rules for synthesizing speech from text [Tesauro, 1989]; in playing backgammon [Tesauro, 1989]; and even for making decisions in that most grail-like of all nonlinear dynamic systems, the stock market [Fishman, 1991b].

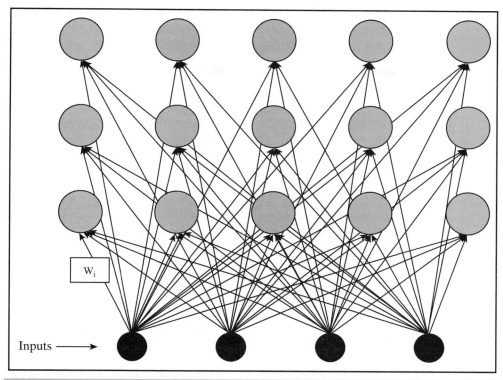

Inputs ⟶

❖❖ ❖❖ ❖❖ **FIGURE 12-13** Kohonen Self-Organizing Map

## ❖❖ ❖❖ ❖❖ Statistical Methods for Data Mining

We have now seen techniques that discover knowledge and express it in terms of rules, decision trees, neural networks, and clusters. Certainly neural networks can be thought of as functions in the sense that they map a set of inputs to outputs. However, they are considered black boxes, in that it is very difficult to visualize the effect that each input variable plays on the output, or how significant the impact of that input variable is on the output. On the other hand, rules and decision trees present results in a more intuitive manner; therefore, they are called *transparent* or *white boxes*. However, rules and trees are not representations of exact functions in the traditional mathematical sense. Now let us examine techniques that express the knowledge as transparent functions. These are based on statistical methods for DM.

One of the objectives of statistical analysis is to find correlation between variables. This has been traditionally done by examining the data. It is for this reason that statisticians often look askance at the field of DM and shrug, knowing that they have been doing exactly that for a long time. In fact, they have come up with the following equation to describe DM [Witten and Frank, 2000]:

$$\text{Statistics} + \text{Marketing} = \text{Data Mining}$$

Although not totally accurate, there is some truth to that view.

Statistical analysis seeks to determine how two or more variables are related to each other. This would certainly represent knowledge about relations between variables, and this relationship could be exhibited by the data observed. The question is whether these variables are somehow related, and if so, exactly how?

The most common method of statistical analysis is **curve fitting.** This technique (or families of techniques) seeks to identify a mathematical equation that can accurately describe the relationship between variables and their associated values as observed in the data. It is one of the earliest techniques for data mining, even before the term was coined. Of course, one important limitation is that the data must be expressed numerically. Attributes with symbolic values cannot be (easily) handled by such techniques.

For a simple two-dimensional problem space, curve fitting seeks to find a mathematical expression that closely predicts the value of the $y$ variable based on given values of $x$. We assume a two-dimensional problem where data are described by a set of $n$ ordered pairs $(x_i, y_i)$, where $i = 1, 2, 3, \ldots, n$. Furthermore, this procedure assumes $x$, the input or independent variable, is fixed and the $y$ is the output or dependent variable. The data is assumed to have a normal distribution with a variance of $\sigma^2$.

### CURVE FITTING WITH THE LEAST SQUARES METHOD

This function can be learned from the data provided. Curve fitting attempts to compute coefficients for a predetermined template of a function. The most popular method for finding the appropriate curve is called the *method of least squares*. In least squares, the curve that best fits the data is that which " ... minimizes the sum of squares of deviations of the observed values of $y$ from those predicted" [Mendenhall, 1971]. In this definition, $y$ is the variable to which the function maps the inputs. Mathematically, the square of the differences we wish to minimize is expressed as:

$$\Sigma_{i-1 \text{ to } n} (y_i - y_i')^2$$

Where $y_i$ is the value of $y$ for the $i^{th}$ pair of observed data, and $y_i'$ is the value of $y$ obtained from the curve selected to express the relationship, for the $i^{th}$ value of $x$. The curve that results in the above expression being minimal is the best fit for the data.

Showing the above pictorially, Figure 12-14 depicts the data plotted on a two-dimensional graph, whereas Figure 12-15 depicts the deviations, the sum of whose squares must be minimized. By squaring the deviation, the issue of whether it is positive or negative disappears.

If a constant relationship is suspected, a straight-line function can be used as the basis of the curve. This straight line is shown on Figure 12-15, and is in the general form of:

$$y = b_0 + b_1 x$$

It is then up to the curve-fitting procedure to find the values of $\mathbf{b}_0$ and $\mathbf{b}_1$ that best permit the function to predict the data. The method of least squares permits a closed form solution for these values, sets up the following two equations, and solves for $b_0$ and $b_1$. The process used to obtain these equations uses advanced calculus and is rather complex, placing it beyond the scope of this book. Therefore, we skip the discussion of this derivation altogether and go on directly to the result which is

$$nb_0 + b_1 \Sigma x_i = \Sigma y_i$$

$$b_0 \Sigma x_i + b_1 \Sigma x_i^2 = \Sigma x_i y_i$$

The values of $x_i$ and $y_i$ are, of course, the ordered pairs in the data. The unknowns are $b_0$ and $b_1$. Isolating these unknowns:

$$b_1 = \frac{[n\Sigma x_i y_i - \Sigma x_i \Sigma y_i]}{[n\Sigma x_i^2 - (\Sigma x_i)^2]}$$

$$b_0 = y_{\text{ave}} - b_1 x_{\text{ave}}$$

Where $y_{\text{ave}}$ and $x_{\text{ave}}$ are the averages of the values of $x$ and $y$ found in the data.

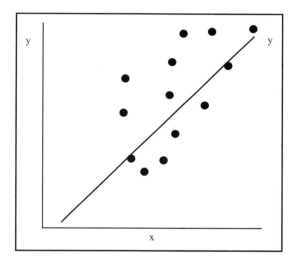

**FIGURE 12-14** Data Plotted on Graph

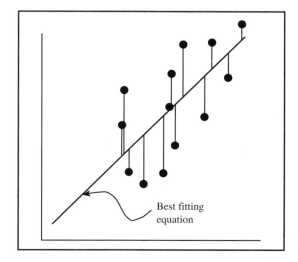

**FIGURE 12-15** Data and Deviations

### Probabilistic Model of Curve

The function determined by the least squares method is a deterministic function. That means that it provides a specific value of $y$ for a value of $x$. If the data collected were not normally distributed, but instead, perfectly collected (no measurement error), and the result of an expression defined by a deterministic physical phenomenon (i.e., $F = ma$ or $= iR$), this would be correct as is. However, the curve fit is realistically never perfect (we assume normal distribution of data). Therefore, to better model the observed data, we should provide some clue as to the probabilistic validity of predictions made with the newly fitted curve. Thus, the equation can now be modified somewhat to be:

$$y = b_0 + b_1 x + \varepsilon$$

where $\varepsilon$ is a random variable with a variance of $\sigma^2$ and an expected value of zero. $\varepsilon$ is also the amount by which the values of $y$ observed in the data can deviate positively and negatively from the curve defined by $b_0$ and $b_1$. Furthermore, the value of $\varepsilon$ selected for one value of $y$ (say, $y_i$) will be different and independent of the value of $\varepsilon$ selected for another value of $y$ (say, $y_j$).

### Measuring the Strength of the Correlation

It is often important to determine whether a linear relationship exists for a set of observed data points, and if so, the strength of the relation. To do that, we need to compute the coefficient of relation between $x$ and $y$, called $r$. This coefficient is described by the following expression:

$$r = \frac{[\Sigma (x_i - x_{\text{ave}})(y_i - y_{\text{ave}})]}{\sqrt{[\Sigma (x_i - x_{\text{ave}})^2][\Sigma (y_i - y_{\text{ave}})^2]}}$$

Interestingly enough, $r$ can assume the same sign as the estimated value of $b_1$ (called $b_1$'). A positive value for $r$ implies a rising curve (positive slope), whereas a negative value of $r$ implies a falling curve (negative slope). If $r = 0$, this indicates that $b_1$' $= 0$, thus saying there is no relationship at all.

To interpret the magnitude of the nonzero values of $r$, $r$ would have values of $+1$ or $-1$ if and only if all the observed points exactly coincided with the curve (i.e., fell right on top of it). However, it has been found that mathematically $r^2$ is more meaningful than $r$. The value $r^2$ can also fall in the range between 0 and 1.

One last point to note is that $r$ is only a measure of the strength of a linear relationship. A low value of $r$ does in no way indicate that a nonlinear relation would not fit the data well.

### Nonlinear Correlation

As mentioned above, in many cases, the data may not always be adequately described by a straight-line function. In that case, a polynomial function or exponential function may be better suited. Under these circumstances, a polynomial equation can be proposed as the function that accurately describes this data. The prototype for this equation is:

$$y = b_0 + b_1 x + b_2 x^2 + b_3 x^3 + \cdots + b_m x^m$$

The task is the same—calculate $b_0, b_1, b_2$, etc. using least squares. The set of simultaneous equations becomes:

$$nb_0 + b_1\Sigma x_i + b_2\Sigma x_i^2 + b_3\Sigma x_i^3 + \cdots + b_m\Sigma x_i^m = \Sigma y_I$$

$$b_0\Sigma x_i + b_1\Sigma x_i^2 + b_2 x_i^3 + b_3\Sigma x_i^4 + \cdots + b_m\Sigma x_i^{m+1} = \Sigma x_i y_I$$

$$b_0\Sigma x_i^m + b_1\Sigma x_i^{m+1} + b_2\Sigma x_i^{m+2} + b_3\Sigma x_i^{m+3} + \cdots + b_m\Sigma x_i^{2m} = \Sigma x_i^m y_I$$

This set of equations is not as easy to compute in a mathematically closed form. However, several computer algorithms exist that can approximate the desired values of $b_0, b_1, b_2, \ldots b_m$ iteratively.

Finally, if the relation is suspected to be exponential, the following equation prototype can be proposed:

$$Y = ab^x$$

This equation can be more easily solved by taking logarithms, thus converting the exponential into a linear relation. The equation to be solved is now much simpler:

$$\text{Log } y = \log a + b \log x$$

Then $b$ and $\log a$ can be easily obtained by fitting a straight line onto the data set converted to $(\log x_i, \log y_i)$. Nevertheless, computer algorithms can effectively estimate this through iterative techniques, instead of solving the closed form equation.

### Multivariate Correlation

In other cases, the relation may be strong, but only if several variables are considered. This is called **multivariate correlation.** This is different from a **nonlinear correlation** between two variables in that the correlation is still expected to be linear, but the problem space is now multidimensional. In this case, the set of independent variables becomes $\{x_1, x_2, x_3, x_4, \ldots, x_k\}$.

The expression computed by the least squares method would become the form:

$$y = b_0 + b_1 x_1 + b_2 x_2 + b_3 x_3 + b_4 x_4 + \cdots + b_k x_k + \varepsilon$$

The error to be minimized by the least squares method can be expressed as we do for the two-dimensional system, as follows:

$$\Sigma(y_i - y_i')^2$$

However, if we replace $y_i'$ by the above function, we get:

$$\Sigma[y_i - (b_0 + b_1 x_1 + b_2 x_2 + b_3 x_3 + b_4 x_4 + \cdots + b_k x_k)]^2$$

The solution of this equation, while conceptually simple, is actually quite difficult to execute, and is typically solved with the aid of iterative approximation algorithms.

### K-Means Clustering

Clustering can also be accomplished through statistical means. One technique capable of this is called **K-means.** The K is for the index k, used to indicate k number of clusters to be defined. The means is for the mean of the clusters to be defined.

K-means is more interactive than the Kohonen networks described earlier. The user can interject prior knowledge, either from intuition or from prior analysis, to guide the process. For example, users must define the number of clusters sought. Additionally, they can add an approximation of the mean value for the variables of every cluster. Having this initial estimate, the algorithm can examine the data and assign each data sample to the cluster whose estimate is closest.

The addition of each new data sample to the cluster affects its mean value, thereby causing the cluster to slightly drift toward the influence of the newly added data samples. Once the first pass of the data is complete, the means (center) of each cluster becomes different from its original estimate. Then the algorithm performs a second iteration through the data to ensure that each data sample belongs to the cluster that is closest. If not, the data sample can be moved to the closest cluster and the means can be recomputed. After a number of such iterations, the reassignments stabilize to near zero, thereby indicating the end of the process.

### Other Statistical Data Mining Techniques

There are other techniques worth mentioning that have been used for a long time. We describe these briefly in this section.

**Market Basket Analysis (MBA)**   This analysis was developed to determine buying patterns of people. Its output is expressed in rules that describe associations between products that people purchase together. For example, a resulting rule could express the following:

***If beer is purchased, then chips and dip are also purchased 75% of the time.***

There is advantage to be gained from this knowledge, because the merchandiser could promote one of the products and increase the sales of the other automatically.

The MBA technique begins by presenting data consisting of actual purchases made by a monitored group of customers over a period of time. Each data sample can include information of the purchases made and the date. The MBA technique proposes a rule based on two items to be purchased. It then evaluates the validity of the rule against the data available. Rules that demonstrate a measure of validity can be saved. The saved rules can then have one new item added to them and they may once again be evaluated by the data. Once again, those demonstrating validity can be saved and presented to the user.

Although MBA was originally used to identify buying habits for grocery shoppers, it can be used to identify any patterns, which associate two or three variables. For example, it can be used to identify what banking services or telephone services customers tend to purchase together. Health insurers can use this approach to associate diagnostic services prescribed by doctors for specific diseases. In this way, they can flag service requests that deviate from this norm and possibly question the validity of the diagnosis.

**Discriminant Analysis**   This is very similar to linear regression described in detail earlier in this chapter. In a way, discriminant analysis also seeks to form clusters of related data. It assumes that there are different and distinct populations at play in the data, and that several variables can be used to discriminate between the populations. It then seeks to find the combinations of values of the variables that provide separation between the populations (clusters). Unlike clustering algorithms, which seek to identify the clusters themselves, discriminant analysis is already aware of the clusters, and only has to find which variables separate them from each other. It is a fine distinction, yet an important one. Discriminant analysis assumes that the populations all adhere to a normal distribution for each associated variable.

**Logistic Regression**   The technique of **logistic regression (LR)** is a variation of discriminant analysis and linear regression. Remember that discriminant analysis assumes clusters, instead of continuity. Unlike discriminant analysis, LR assumes continuity in the description of the data. By assuming continuity, LR seeks to define a linear function that separates two classifications.

Recall that LR attempts to find a linear function that best predicts the data examined. In LR, linear separation is the goal, not the prediction of data. LR is used to find a variable that is able to separate two categories. Furthermore, the resulting line may not always be linear per se; it can look like an S-curve.

## ◇ ◇ ◇ Guidelines for Employing Data Mining Techniques

Once the purpose of the study is understood, the characteristics of the data can play the deciding role as to which technique is most appropriate. Input variables (also called *predictors*) and output variables (also called *outcomes*), could be continuous or discrete (also called *categorical*). Table 12-3 summarizes the different *inferential* statistic techniques and their applicability pertaining to the characteristics of the input and output variables. Inferential statistical techniques are differentiated from *descriptive* statistics. Inferential statistics are used to generalize from data and thus develop models that generalize from the observations, whereas descriptive statistics are used to characterize data that have already been collected and directly measured.

The key difference between using statistical techniques and nonstatistical techniques is that the former requires a hypothesis to be specified beforehand. In addition, statistical techniques often are subject to stringent assumptions, such as normality of the sample data, uncorrelated error, or homogeneity of variance. However, statistical techniques provide for a more rigorous test of hypotheses. Table 12-4 summarizes the predictive nonstatistical techniques, and their applicability pertaining to the characteristics of the input and output variables. *Memory-based reasoning* (MBR) is a DM technique that looks for the nearest neighbors of known data samples, and combines their

**TABLE 12-3   Summary of Applicability of Inferential Statistical Techniques**

| *Goal* | *Input Variables (Predictors)* | *Output Variables (Outcomes)* | *Statistical Technique* | *Examples [SPSS, 2000]* |
|---|---|---|---|---|
| Finding linear combination of predictors that best separate the population | Continuous or Dummies | Discrete | Discriminant analysis | • Predict instances of fraud<br>• Predict whether customers remain or leave (churners or not)<br>• Predict which customers respond to a new product or offer<br>• Predict out comes of various medical procedures |
| Predicting the probability of outcome in a particular category | Continuous or Dummies | Discrete | Logistic and multinomial regression | • Predict insurance policy renewal<br>• Predict fraud<br>• Predict which product a customer may buy<br>• Predict that a product is likely to fail |
| Obtaining output that is a linear combination of input variables | Continuous or Dummies | Continuous | Linear regression | • Predict expected revenue in dollars from a new customer<br>• Predict sales revenue for a store<br>• Predict waiting time on hold for callers to an 800 number.<br>• Predict length of stay in a hospital based on patient characteristics and medical condition |
| Doing experiments and repeated measures of the same sample | Most inputs must be discrete | Continuous | Analysis of variance (ANOVA) | • Predict which environmental factors are likely to cause cancer |
| Predicting future events whose history has been collected at regular intervals | Continuous | Continuous time | Time series analysis | • Predict future sales data from past sales records |

◇ ◇ ◇ ◇

Dummies is a transformed variable coded as 0 or 1 to represent the absence or presence of a characteristic.

**TABLE 12-4  Summary of Applicability of Noninferential Predictive Techniques**

| *Goal* | *Input (Predictor) Variables* | *Output (Outcome) Variables* | *Statistical Technique* | *Examples [SPSS, 2000]* |
|---|---|---|---|---|
| Predicting outcome based on values of nearest neighbors | Continuous, discrete, and text | Continuous or discrete | Memory-based reasoning (MBR) | • Predict medical outcomes |
| Predicting by splitting data into subgroups (branches) | Continuous or discrete (different techniques used based on data characteristics) | Continuous or discrete (different techniques used based on data characteristics) | Decision trees | • Predict which customers may leave<br>• Predict instances of fraud |
| Predicting outcome in complex nonlinear environments | Continuous or discrete | Continuous or discrete | Neural networks | • Predict expected revenue<br>• Predict credit risk |

values to assign classification or prediction values for new data samples. It is very similar to CBR, as described in Chapter 9. Like CBR, MBR uses a distance function to find the nearest element to a new data sample, and a combination function to combine the values at the nearest neighbors to make a prediction. For more information on MBR refer to [Berry and Linoff, 1997].

Different decision tree and rule induction methods are applicable depending on the characteristics of the data. Table 12-5 summarizes the various methods.

Table 12-6 summarizes the different descriptive techniques, including both association and clustering methods, and their applicability pertaining to the characteristics of the input variables. Note that for all these techniques, the output variable is not defined. Market basket or association analysis can include the use of two techniques: Apriori is an association rule algorithm that requires the input fields to be discrete. Apriori is generally faster to train than generalized rule induction (GRI). Apriori allows only the specification of logical (or dichotomies) for the input variables, such as (true, false) or (1, 0) to indicate the presence (or absence) of the item in the market basket. GRI is an association rule algorithm, capable of producing rules that describe associations between attributes to a symbolic target, and capable of using continuous or logical data as its input.

Typically, several methods could be applied to any problem with similar results. The knowledge discovery process is an iterative process. Once the model has been developed the results must be evaluated. Special attention must be paid to errors. This next section discusses the important issue of errors.

**TABLE 12-5 Summary of Applicability of Decision Tree Techniques**

| Goal | Input (Predictor) Variables | Output (Outcome) Variables | Statistical Technique | Examples [SPSS, 2000] |
|---|---|---|---|---|
| Predicting by splitting data into more than two subgroups (branches) | Continuous, discrete, or ordinal | Discrete | Chi-square automatic interaction detection (CHAID) | • Predict which demographic combinations of predictors yield the highest probability of a sale<br>• Predict which factors are causing product defects in manufacturing |
| Predicting by splitting data into more than two subgroups (branches) | Continuous | Discrete | C5.0 | • Predict which loan applicants are considered a "good" risk<br>• Predict which factors are associated with a country's investment risk |
| Predicting by splitting data into binary subgroups (branches) | Continuous | Continuous | Classification and regression trees (CART) | • Predict which factors are associated with a country's competitiveness<br>• Discover which variables are predictors of increased customer profitability |
| Predicting by splitting data into binary subgroups (branches) | Continuous | Discrete | Quick, unbiased, efficient, statistical tree (QUEST) | • Predict who needs additional care after heart surgery |

◈◈ ◈◈ ◈◈ ◈◈

# ◈◈ ◈◈ ◈◈ Errors and Their Significance in Data Mining

The cost of errors must be carefully evaluated when the model is examined. For example, Table 12-7 presents the results of a study to predict the diagnosis of patients with heart disease based on a set of input variables. In this table, the columns represent predicted values for the diagnostic and the rows represent actual values for diagnostic of patients undergoing a heart disease examination. Actual values are coded in the cells, with percentages coded in parenthesis along the actual values. In Table 12-7, the predictions made along the shaded quadrant (*Actual no disease/Predicted no disease*) represent patients that were correctly predicted as healthy. That means that 118 patients (or 72% of a total of 164 patients) were diagnosed with *No disease* and they were indeed healthy. On the other hand, looking at the shaded quadrant (*Actual presence of disease/Predicted presence of disease*) 96 patients (or 69.1% of a total of 139 patients) were diagnosed with *Presence of* disease and they were indeed sick. So for the patients in these two quadrants, the

**TABLE 12-6  Summary of Applicability of Clustering and Association Techniques**

| Goal | Input Variables (Predictor) | Output Variables (Outcome) | Statistical Technique | Examples [SPSS, 2000] |
|---|---|---|---|---|
| Finding large groups of cases in large data files that are similar on a small set of input characteristics | Continuous or discrete | No outcome variable | K-means cluster analysis | • Group customer segments for marketing<br>• Group similar insurance claims |
| Creating large cluster memberships | | | Kohonen neural networks | • Cluster customers into segments based on demographics and buying patterns |
| Creating small set associations and look for patterns between many categories | Logical | No outcome variable | Market basket or association analysis with *a priori* | • Identify which products are likely to be purchased together<br>• Identify which courses students are likely to take together |
| Creating small set associations and look for patterns between many categories | Logical or numeric | No outcome variable | Market basket or association analysis with GRI | • Identify which courses students are likely to take together |
| Creating linkages between sets of items to display complex relationships | Continuous or discrete | No outcome variable | Link analysis[1] | • Identify a relationship between a network of physicians and their prescriptions |

classification algorithm correctly predicted their heart disease diagnosis. However, the patients whose diagnosis falls off this diagonal (the quadrants that are not shaded) were incorrectly classified. In this example, 46 patients (or 28% of a total of 164 patients) were diagnosed with the disease, when in fact they were healthy. Furthermore, 43 patients (or 30.9% of a total of 139 patients) were incorrectly diagnosed with no disease when in fact they were sick.

Summarizing this example, 70.6% of the patients were correctly classified with the prediction algorithm. Note that in this example, the cost of incorrectly giving patients a

**TABLE 12-7  Classification Table Results**

| Heart Disease Diagnostic | Predicted No Disease | Predicted Presence of Disease |
|---|---|---|
| Actual—no disease | 118 (72%) | 46 (28%) |
| Actual—presence of disease | 43 (30.9%) | 96 (69.1%) |

sound bill of health, when in fact they are sick, is considered much higher than incorrectly predicting patients to be sick, when in fact they are healthy. The former may cause the patient to die without the proper care, whereas the latter may give the patient an unpleasant jolt, but further tests are likely to exonerate them.

## SUMMARY ◆ ◆ ◆

DM is a very important issue in KM. By discovering trends in the data that were not known previously, business organizations can optimize their product offerings, streamline their organization, and make any marketing campaign maximally effective. DM provides a competitive advantage over competitors not engaged in such discovery. This chapter describes the major techniques used for DM. They are divided into three general families of approaches:

1. *Symbolic techniques.* The most popular and important of these is rule induction. Several algorithms exist to do this. The most popular ones are C5.0 and CART. In this chapter, we describe in detail the C5.0 inductive algorithm. C5.0 examines data and builds decision trees based on the attributes and their values. They were originally used for classification, but can be used for other purposes as well. Rules can be generated by traversing the decision tree. Alternatively, the tree can be used as a data structure from which knowledge can be recalled.

2. *Connectionist techniques.* The reason for this name is because these techniques consist of strongly connecting several simple processing elements called neurons to perform complex tasks. The result is a neural network. There are many kinds of neural networks. They are distinguished primarily by their architecture (connectivity), activation function, and learning process. As suggested by the last sentence, one major advantage of neural networks is that they can be trained. One popular way to do this (called supervised learning) is to present the network with data samples consisting of the values for each variable examined, and the final classification for that data sample. Using this information, the learning algorithm can assign a weight to each connection between neurons. These connections, when the network is used in a predictive mode, serve to identify an unknown pattern of data. For DM, however, Kohonen networks, which use unsupervised learning (i.e., no classification is provided for the example) are able to cluster the data into natural groups, if such exist.

3. *Statistical methods.* Statistical methods have been used to analyze data for a long time, even before the advent of computers. In fact, their use preceded the term data mining. The most popular of these methods is linear regression. This technique seeks to identify a linear function (a line) that best fits the data provided. This function can then be used to predict the performance or behavior of other new data samples. Other techniques described, albeit briefly, include K-means, market basket analysis, discriminant analysis, and logistic analysis.

The discussion in this chapter paves the way for further discussion of knowledge discovery systems in Chapter 13. Chapter 13 treats this topic in the context of systems that perform DM, and thus help discover new knowledge.

## KEY TERMS ◆ ◆ ◆

- artificial neural networks (ANN)—p. 228
- back propagation—p. 233
- classification—p. 217
- cluster analysis—p. 233

- curve fitting—p. 236
- discriminant analysis—p. 241
- induction tree—p. 220
- inductive learning—p. 220
- K-means clustering—p. 240

- logistic regression—p. 241
- market basket analysis—p. 240
- multivariate correlation—p. 239
- nonlinear correlation—p. 239

## REVIEW QUESTIONS ◆ ◆ ◆

1.  Describe the difference between supervised and nonsupervised learning in neural networks. Give an example of a learning algorithm for each.
2.  What is meant by a strongly connected neural network.
3.  List and describe the ways that relations among variables can be expressed. Give the advantage and disadvantage for each.
4.  What are some of the purposes for doing a data mining (DM) study?
5.  List the three most common types of activation functions for neural networks. Under what conditions would one use one versus another?

## APPLICATION EXERCISES ◆ ◆ ◆

1.  Develop a minimal tree from the set of examples shown below for the diagnosis of an automobile that does not start.

| Lights | Sound | Turnover | Fuel Gauge | Smell | Diagnosis |
|--------|--------|----------|------------|--------|-----------|
| Dim | Howl | Yes | Not empty | Normal | Battery |
| Normal | Screech | No | Not empty | Normal | Starter |
| Normal | Click | No | Not empty | Normal | Solenoid |
| Normal | Normal | Yes | Empty | Normal | Out of gas |
| Normal | Normal | Yes | Not empty | Gas | Flooding |

2.  Do the same as in Problem 1 for the set of examples shown below for the classification of certain types of trees in the southern temperate zone.

| Leaf Shape | Leaf Size | Fruit | Wood | Deciduous | Type of Tree |
|------------|-----------|-------|------|-----------|--------------|
| Broad | Large | Brown-balls | Hard | Yes | Sycamore |
| Needle | Short | Acorn | Fine | No | Pine |
| Thin | Long | Nut | Fibrous | No | Coconut |
| Simple | Small | Acorn | Hard | No | Live oak |
| Lobed | Large | Samara | Hard | Yes | Maple |

## REFERENCES ◆ ◆ ◆

Berry, M., and Linoff, G. 1997. *Data Mining Techniques for Marketing, Sales and Customer Support,* John Wiley & Sons, New York.

Breiman, L.1984. *Classification and Decision Trees,* Friedman, Ohlsen, & Stone (Eds.), Wadsworth Press, Belmont, CA, 1984.

Fausett, L. 1994. *Fundamentals of Neural Networks — Architectures, Algorithms and Applications.* Prentice Hall, Englewood Cliffs, NJ.

Fishman, M.B., and Barr, D.S. 1991a. A hybrid system for market timing. *Technical Analysis of Stocks and Commodities,* 9(8), 26–34.

Fishman, M.B., Barr, D.S., and Heavner, E. 1991b. A New Perspective on Conflict Resolution in Market Forecasting. In *Proceedings of the 1st International Conference on Artificial Intelligence Applications on Wall Street,* IEEE Computer Society Press, Los Alamitos, CA, pp. 97–102.

Gonzalez, A.J., and Dankel, D.D. 1993. *The Engineering of Knowledge-Based Systems: Theory and Practice.* Prentice Hall, Englewood Cliffs, NJ.

Haykin, S. 1994. *Neural Networks — A Comprehensive Foundation.* McMillan College Publishing, New York.

Hopfield, J.J. 1982. Neural Networks and Physical Systems with Emergent Collective Computational Abilities. *Proceedings of the National Academy of Scientists,* 79, 2554–2558.

Hunt, E.B., Marin, J., and Stone, P.J. 1966. *Experiments in Induction.* Academic Press, New York.

Kohonen, T. 1990. The self-organizing map. *Proceedings of the IEEE,* 78(9), 1464–1480.

McCulloch, W.S., and Pitts, W. 1943. A logical calculus of the ideas immanent in nervous activity. *Bulletin of Mathematical Biophysics,* 5, 115–133.

Mendenhall, W. 1971. *Introduction to Probability and Statistics,* 3rd ed. Wadsworth Press, Belmont, CA.

Minsky, M.L. 1954. Theory of Neural-Analog Reinforcement Systems and Its Application to the Brain-Model Problem, Doctoral Dissertation, Princeton University, Princeton, NJ.

Minsky, M.L. 1961. Steps towards artificial intelligence. *Proceedings of the Institute of Radio Engineers,* 49, 8–30.

Minsky, M.L., and Papert, S.A. 1969. *Perceptrons.* MIT Press, Cambridge, MA.

Piatestky-Shapiro, G., and Frawley, W.J. (Ed.), *Knowledge Discovery in Databases.* AAAI Press/MIT Press, Menlo Park, CA.

Quinlan, J.R. 1983. Learning efficient classification procedures and their application to chess games. In Michalski, R.S., Carbonel, J.G., and Mitchell, T.M. (Eds.), *Machine Learning.* Tioga Press, Palo Alto, CA, pp. 463–482.

Quinlan, J.R. 1993. *C4.5: Programs for Machine Learning.* Morgan Kaufmann Publishers, San Mateo, CA.

Rummelhart, D.E., and McClelland, J.L. (Eds.). 1986. *Parallel Distributed Processing, Explorations of the Microstructure of Cognition,* Vol. 1. MIT Press, Cambridge, MA.

SPSS. 2000. *Data Mining: Modeling.* SPSS, Chicago, IL.

Tesauro, G., and Sejnosky, T.J. 1989. A parallel network that learns to play backgammon, *Artificial Intelligence,* 39(3), 357–390.

Webster. 1960. *Webster's New World Dictionary of the American Language.* World, New York.

Winston, P.H. 1992. *Artificial Intelligence,* 3rd ed. Addison Wesley, Reading, MA.

Witten, I.H., and Frank, E. 2000. *Data Mining: Practical Machine Learning Tools and Techniques with Java Implementations.* Morgan Kaufmann Publishers, San Francisco, CA.

CHAPTER

# 13

# Knowledge Discovery Systems

*Systems That Create Knowledge*

## ❖❖❖ Introduction

In Part II, we discussed the underlying technologies that enable the creation of knowledge management (KM) systems. In this part of the book we present the different types of KM systems. In Chapter 13, we introduce knowledge discovery systems. Knowledge discovery dates back to the time before the existence of the word *researcher*. Certainly, popular lore contends that Galileo discovered knowledge while dropping objects from the Tower of Pisa, and observing the time each took to reach the ground. The Wright brothers, Alexander Graham Bell, Thomas Edison, and thousands of other less well-known researchers and inventors throughout history have discovered knowledge that has helped our understanding of how things work in nature. Cumulatively, their contributions have shaped our present lives in many ways. How is knowledge discovered? For the purposes of this chapter, we focus on two significant ways:

1. Synthesis of new knowledge through socialization with other knowledgeable persons.
2. Discovery by finding interesting patterns in observations, typically embodied in explicit data.

As we see in Chapter 3, knowledge discovery systems support the development of new tacit or explicit knowledge from data and information or from the synthesis of prior knowledge. Knowledge discovery systems rely on mechanisms and technologies that can support the **combination** and the socialization processes. For the purpose of the discussions in this chapter, we do not distinguish between knowledge creation and knowledge discovery; and we consider both to describe the same thing: the innovation and advancement of knowledge. We do distinguish knowledge creation from knowledge capture; the latter activity presumes that knowledge has already been created and may exist tacitly in the minds of experts. Knowledge creation assumes knowledge did not exist before the activity that catalyzed the innovation.

You may recall from Chapter 3 that *knowledge discovery mechanisms* facilitate **socialization** processes. In the case of tacit knowledge, socialization facilitates the synthesis of tacit knowledge across individuals and the integration of multiple streams for the creation of new knowledge, usually through joint activities instead of written or verbal instructions. For example, one mechanism for socialization is research conferences, which enable researchers to develop new insights through sharing their own findings. Also, when friends brainstorm and do *back-of-the-napkin diagrams,* leading to the discovery of new knowledge that did not exist individually before the group activity, knowledge is created or discovered by the team. We expand on the topic of socialization as a mechanism for knowledge discovery in the next section.

On the other hand *technologies* can also support knowledge discovery systems by facilitating *combination* processes. New explicit knowledge is discovered through combination, wherein the multiple bodies of explicit knowledge (data or information) are synthesized to create new, more complex sets of explicit knowledge. Existing explicit knowledge may be recontextualized to produce new explicit knowledge, for example, during the creation of a new proposal to a client that is based on existing prior client proposals. Knowledge discovery mechanisms and technologies can facilitate socialization and combination within or across organizations. Knowledge creation systems can be enabled by the use of **data mining (DM)** technologies, such as those discussed in Chapter 12. These may be used to uncover new relationships among explicit data, which in turn, can serve to develop models that can predict or categorize—highly valuable assets in business intelligence. We expand on this topic in a later section.

## ❖❖ ❖❖ ❖❖ Mechanisms to Discover Knowledge: Using Socialization to Create New Tacit Knowledge

Socialization, as defined in Chapter 3, is the synthesis of tacit knowledge across individuals, usually through joint activities instead of written or verbal instructions. Socialization enables the discovery of tacit knowledge through joint activities between masters and apprentices, or among researchers at an academic conference. Many Japanese companies, for example, Honda, encourage socialization through "brainstorming camps" to resolve problems faced in research and development (R&D) projects [Nonaka and Takeuchi, 1995]. The format for these meetings is outside the workplace, much like the one spearheaded at Westinghouse and presented in Vignette 13-1. The idea is to encourage participants to meet outside their normal work environment, perhaps at a resort, where they are able to discuss their problems in an informal and relaxed environment. These meetings serve not only as a medium for creativity to flourish but also as a way for sharing knowledge and building trust among the group members. Socialization as a means of knowledge discovery is a common practice at many organizations, pursued either by accident or on purpose.

Simple discussions over lunch among friends discussing their daily problems often lead to knowledge discovery. Cocktail napkins have been known to contain descriptions

 VIGNETTE 13-1

## The Westinghouse Innovation Group

George Westinghouse, considered by many as one of the world's leading inventor-engineers, founded Westinghouse Electric Corporation in 1886, and eventually 59 other companies; he received over 100 patents for his work. Westinghouse Electric Corporation[1] established one of the nation's first industrial research laboratories in 1886 with the invention of the transformer, which enabled the transmission of electricity over large distances by increasing the voltage of alternating current electricity.

The company had established a reputation for developing advanced technology products. Its Transmission and Distribution (T&D) business unit was a relatively small segment of the corporation's product range and sales volume, and was composed of several product divisions. These divisions were fairly independent. They manufactured products for electric utilities and large industrial complexes, and each division addressed different (noncompeting) product lines within the same industries. The products ranged from the world's largest power transformers, power circuit breakers, and electronic voltage regulators for large electrical generators, all the way to the more mundane pole-mounted transformers and standard house meters.

In 1979, those in the Westinghouse T&D Business Unit (comprising all the divisions that built and marketed products for the T&D market segment) realized that the unit's product offerings were rather mature and seriously needed upgrading. The president of the T&D Business Unit, in cooperation with the Westinghouse Headquarters technical staff, instituted and sponsored the T&D Innovation Group to foster innovation and creativity in its technical offerings. Its mission was to cre-

atively apply new ideas to solve old problems, and more specifically, to inject a measure of high technology into its product line. Furthermore, through this group, it sought to "upgrade the competence" (i.e., enhance the knowledge) of technical staff members at their home divisions. One senior engineer from each T&D division was selected to participate in this 12-member group. In addition, the sponsoring manager from corporate headquarters, who arranged the meetings, suggested the agenda and provided guidance to the group, and also served as the communication link to the T&D president and his staff. Individual selected engineers would communicate directly with their own division general managers, bypassing the three or four hierarchical levels in the chain of command. This communication involved briefing the general managers on the proceedings of the group, as well as obtaining from them any problems that they would like to have addressed by the group.

The T&D Innovation Group meetings took place once per quarter, and lasted for two and a half days (and three nights), typically in a resort hotel near one of the participating division headquarters or factories, which served as the host for that meeting. This location ensured freedom from interruptions from the members' daily responsibilities. Although some of the problems to be addressed were defined by the business unit staff or the division general managers, others originated within the group. In the early meetings, most of the problems addressed were of a technical nature. As the group matured and the operating procedures became more streamlined, the discussions shifted to problems of an

---

[1]www.westinghouse.com

*continued*

**VIGNETTE 13-1** *(cont.)*

organizational nature. The group always addressed each problem using the technique of *creative brainstorming* (described in Vignette 13-2), until a consensus was reached on a set of recommendations for the individual presenting the problem, typically during the same 2- or 3-hour meeting.

The T&D Innovation Group continued to meet for 3 years before reorganizations, divestitures, promotions, transfers, retirements, and such took a toll on those individuals who had a vested interest in this concept.

Nevertheless, in its relatively short existence, the group succeeded in generating a few dozen patent disclosures, many of which later became valuable corporate patents. In addition, several products were upgraded as a direct result of the group's work. Moreover, several recommendations were made to senior management, which were either implemented or (at the very least) seriously considered. Finally, the T&D Innovation Group had some success in injecting advanced technology into the technical staff of the divisions.

of critical new ideas. Organizations interested in fostering discovery of knowledge take steps to formalize this socialization among their employees. This process promotes innovation and creativity, which in turn leads to advances in knowledge. Vignette 13-1 presented earlier describes a formal mechanism instituted by a major U.S. corporation back before KM had become a household word.

Vignette 13-2 describes the use of the creative brainstorming process, which involves a customer (the person with the problem or need), a facilitator (the person controlling the process), and the innovators (who brainstorm solutions to the customer's problem or need). The process begins by having the facilitator establish the ground rules, which are not many. The main one is that one person speaks at a time, and there are no such things as crazy, dumb, wild, or silly ideas. The latter ensures the creative freedom of the innovators to generate solutions, which may at first glance appear silly or wild. Customers then take their turns explaining the problem briefly, without discussing what has already been tried. Then the main part of the process begins. The innovators voice ideas out loud to the facilitator. These ideas are described in one or two sentences. The facilitator displays them each in a way that is visible to the participants (a flip chart, a whiteboard, a computer with a projection device, etc.). This process runs unabated until the ideas cease to flow (typically 30 to 45 minutes depending on the size of the group and the complexity of the problem). Customers are then once again given the floor and asked to select a few (three to five) ideas that appeal to them. The appealing ideas are then further examined to make them viable. Finally, those ideas showing the greatest potential are even further examined and the potential drawbacks are identified. The process ends and the customers depart with some innovative potential solutions to their problems. It should be mentioned that the problem does not need to be technical or scientific in nature. Any kind of problem is eligible for this approach.

The process addresses two important aspects of problem solving and decision making. One is to identify the real problem. In many situations, problem solvers are not addressing the real problem, but a perceived one. Even if the perceived problem is

### Creative Brainstorming

Westinghouse Electric Corp. was a major manufacturer of home appliances before White Consolidated Industries acquired the product line in 1974 (now called White-Westinghouse). Once upon a time, they built washing machines that stood on four small metal legs on each corner at the bottom of the boxlike structure that we commonly recognize as a washing machine. The legs were fitted with built-in screws to stabilize the machine during operation and avoid vibrations. These small legs protruded from the basic boxlike design of the washing machine. Unfortunately, when these appliances were shipped in boxes, their movement (and often dropping of the boxes from trucks) caused these small legs to bend. Bent legs destabilized the washing machine and caused annoying as well as damaging vibrations when the machine was in operation. This resulted in significant warranty expenses to Westinghouse when a serviceman had to be called to fix the bent legs.

The manager of engineering at the product division that built the washing machines was told to solve the problem. He assembled his best design engineers and told them to go into a room and not come out until they had a solution. The lore goes that the engineers labored night and day for 3 days and finally emerged from the room proudly, with a new design that greatly strengthened the legs by adding steel thickness and additional bracing. The manager looked at the solution and saw that this would add significant cost to the product, which was deemed unacceptable. The leader of the group, angry that their 3 days of captivity had gone for naught screamed, "What do you want us to do, stand on our heads?" Immediately, another member of the group, one who apparently had gotten some sleep the night before, immediately said, "I've got it! We ship the washing machines upside down." They proceeded to do an analysis of whether the top of the box could withstand the shocks and whether there were any components that would be damaged by the upside-down shipment. They found out there were none. The problem was solved without adding any cost to the product.

This vignette shows that the engineering task force was solving the wrong problem. The problem was in the shipment of the washing machines, not in their design. The legs were well designed for their purpose. There was no need to design them for anything else. Furthermore, it shows how seemingly silly ideas can become realistic and provide a way to solve the problem in unintended ways. This, of course, is new knowledge.

solved, it does not address the real problem. Group thinking may be able to identify the real problem and address it. The second aspect is what is referred to as lateral thinking. This is when an entirely different approach is taken to solve a problem. Identifying wild, crazy, or silly ideas may trigger new ideas (new knowledge) in the other innovators that may be not be wild, crazy, or silly; these new ideas may actually solve the problem. Vignette 13-2 describes an anecdotal experience of the successful application of the collaboration process fostered in creative brainstorming.

## ❖❖❖ Technologies to Discover Knowledge: Using Data Mining to Create New Explicit Knowledge

We discussed in Chapter 12 the technologies that enable the discovery of new knowledge by examining data. *Knowledge discovery technologies* can be very powerful for organizations wishing to obtain an advantage over their competition. Recall that **knowledge discovery in databases (KDD)** is the process of finding and interpreting patterns from data, involving the application of algorithms to interpret the patterns generated by these algorithms [Fayyad et al., 1996]. Another name for KDD, as discussed in Chapter 12, is data mining. Although the majority of the practitioners use KDD and DM interchangeably, for some, KDD is defined to involve the whole process of knowledge discovery including the application of DM techniques.

Although DM systems have made a significant contribution in scientific fields for years, for example, in breast cancer diagnosis [Kovalerchuk et al., 2000], perhaps the recent proliferation of electronic commerce (e-commerce) applications, providing reams of hard data ready for analysis, presents us with an excellent opportunity to make profitable use of these techniques. The increasing availability of computing power and integrated DM software tools, which are easier than ever to use, have contributed to the increasing popularity of DM applications to businesses. Many success stories have been published in the literature describing how DM techniques have been used to create new knowledge. We briefly describe some of the more mature or specifically relevant applications of DM to KM for business.

Over the last decade, DM techniques have been applied across business problems.[2] Examples of such applications are as follows:

1. *Marketing.* **Predictive DM techniques,** like artificial neural networks (ANNs), have been used for target marketing including market segmentation. This allows the marketing departments using this approach to segment customers according to basic demographic characteristics, such as gender, age, and group, as well as their purchasing patterns. These techniques have also been used to improve direct marketing campaigns, through an understanding of which customers are likely to respond to new products based on their previous consumer behavior.
2. *Retail.* DM methods have likewise been used for sales forecasting. These, take into consideration multiple market variables, such as customer profiling based on their purchasing habits. Techniques like **market basket analysis** also help uncover which products are likely to be purchased together.
3. *Banking.* Trading and financial forecasting have also proved to be excellent applications for DM techniques. These are used to determine derivative securities pricing, futures price forecasting, and stock performance. **Inferential DM techniques** have also been successful in developing scoring systems to identify credit risk and fraud. An area of recent interest is attempting to model the relationships between corporate strategy, financial health, and corporate performance.

---

[2]For an extensive review of articles on DM techniques and applications to specific business problems see Bishop [1994]; Widrow et al. [1994]; Wong et al. [1997]; and Smith and Gupta [2000].

4. ***Insurance.*** DM techniques have been used for segmenting customer groups to determine premium pricing and to predict claim frequencies. Clustering techniques have also been applied to detecting claim fraud and to aid in customer retention.
5. ***Telecommunications.*** Predictive DM techniques, like neural networks, have been used mostly to attempt to reduce "churn," that is, to predict when customers may be lost through attrition to a competitor. In addition, predictive techniques can be used to predict the conditions that may cause a customer to return. Finally, market basket analysis has been used to identify which telecommunication products are customers likely to purchase together.
6. ***Operations management.*** Neural networks have been used for planning and scheduling, project management, and quality control.

Diagnosis is a fertile ground for mining knowledge. Diagnostic examples typically abound in large companies with many installed systems and a wide network of service representatives. The incidents are typically documented well, and often in a highly structured form. Mining the incident database for common aspects in the behavior of particularly troublesome devices can be useful in predicting when they are likely to fail. Having this knowledge, the devices can be preventatively maintained in the short range, and designed or manufactured in a way to avoid the problem altogether in the long term. Witten [2000] mentions a specific example where diagnostic rules were mined from 600 documented faults in rotating machinery (e.g., motors and generators) and compared with the same rules elicited from a diagnostic expert. It was found that the learned rules provided slightly better performance than the ones elicited from the expert.

In the electric utility business, neural networks have been used routinely to predict the energy consumption load in power systems. The load on a power system depends mostly on the weather. In hot weather areas, air-conditioners during the summer represent the biggest load. In cold regions, it is the heating load in the winters. Knowing the weather forecast, and how that maps to the expected load, can help forecast the load for the next 24, 48, and 72 hours; and thereby place the appropriate generating capacity in readiness to provide the required energy. This is particularly important because efficient power stations cannot be turned on and off within minutes if the load is greater than expected. Nuclear power stations (the most efficient) take several days or weeks to place on-line from a cold state. Coal- or oil-fired stations (the next most efficient) take the better part of one day to do the same. Although other types of generating equipment can be so turned quickly on and off, they are highly inefficient and costly to operate. Therefore, utilities greatly benefit if they can bring their efficient units on-line in anticipation of energy load increases; yet running them unnecessarily can also be expensive.

All major electric utilities have entire departments expressly dedicated to this load forecasting function. The expected temperature is the most influential factor. However, other attributes such as the day of the week, the humidity, and the wind speed have some influence as well. DM in this context consists of training neural networks to predict the energy load in a certain area for a specified period of time. This is considered supervised training. The relations are embedded in the weights computed by the training algorithm, typically, the **back propagation algorithm.** By mining a database containing actual recorded data on ambient temperatures, wind speed, humidity, day of the week (among others), and actual power consumed per hour, the network can be trained. Then, the forecast values can be fed for the same attributes and it can predict the load on a per hour basis for 24, 48, and 72 hours. Results have been very promising, leading the Electric Power Research Institute[3] to offer neural network-based tools to perform this specific function.

Witten [2000] describes an application of DM to credit applications. In this project, a credit institution undertook a project in DM to learn the characteristics of borrowers who defaulted on their loans, and thus to better identify those customers who were likely to do so. Using 1,000 examples and 20 attributes, a set of rules was mined from the data, which resulted in a 66% successful prediction rate. By 1996, 95% of the top banks in the United States were utilizing DM techniques [Smith and Gupta, 2000]. For example, in the mid-1990s, Bank of Montreal[4] was facing increased competition and the need to **target sell** to its large customer base. Earlier attempts to telemarketing had proved unsuccessful; therefore, the bank embarked on an attempt to develop a knowledge discovery system to determine a customer's likelihood of purchasing new products. As a result, the bank can now segment its customers for a more targeted product marketing campaign [Stevens, 2001].

Nevertheless, the most common and useful applications are in product marketing and sales, and in business operations. Every time someone purchases a product, a sales record is kept. Often, these records contain demographic information on the buyer, and other times they do not. In any case, obtaining a profile of the purchasers of the product can serve to better direct the product to this cross section of consumers, or expand its appeal to other cross sections not currently purchasing the product. This is true for not only hard products but also services, such as long distance, Internet service providers, and banking and financial services.

For example, Proflowers[5] is a Web-based flower retailer. Flowers perish quickly; therefore, Proflowers must level its inventory as the day progresses, in order to adequately serve its customers. Proflowers has achieved better management of its customer traffic via inventory optimization to downplay the better selling products on its Web storefront, while highlighting the slower selling ones. Based on its analysis of Web purchases, Proflowers is able to change its Web site throughout the day, and therefore effectively attract attention to lower selling items through its Web site [Stevens, 2001].

Another example is eBags,[6] a Web-based retailer of suitcases, wallets, and related products. Through the use of Web content mining, the company is able to determine which Web pages result in higher customer purchases. This information is used to adequately determine how Web content can drive the sales process. Finally, eBags uses the results from its Web content mining to help it personalize its retailing Web pages on the fly, based on customers' buying preferences and even geographic location. For example, capturing the Web visitor's zip code could be used to infer how affluent the on-line shopper is. If the shopper comes from an affluent neighborhood, the Web site may feature designer items. If the on-line shopper comes from a zip code marked by a large number of apartments, discounted offers would be made prominent in the users view of the Web store [Stevens, 2001].

---

[3]www.epri.com
[4]www.bmo.com
[5]www.proflowers.com
[6]www.ebags.com

   VIGNETTE 13-3

### Filling up the Grocery Cart at Safeway

Safeway Stores is one of Britain's leading food grocers, employing around 90,000 staff and owning more than 500 stores across Britain. Because the penetration of personal computers (PCs) in Britain is lower than in the United States, IBM[7] developed an application for Britain's Safeway Stores that enables customers to prepare their shopping lists on a personal digital assistant (PDA) and transmit their orders to the store for subsequent pickup without having to walk the aisles of the market. Shoppers quickly jumped on the convenience, which removes the marketer from the opportunity to suggest via attractive displays the spontaneous purchase of additional products that invariably fill up the shopping cart.

To provide for a means to suggest the purchase of additional products, Safeway turned to the use of DM as a means to recommend additional purchases to its clients. The idea of personalizing the recommendations was based on the prior successful implementations of such systems, which work by *filtering* a set of *items* (e.g., grocery products) through a **personal profile.** This filtering may be *content based*, which recommends based on what a person has liked in the past. Alternatively, the filtering may be collaborative, which recommends items that other people, similar to the one at hand, have liked in the past [Lawrence et al., 2001]. Safeway shoppers construct a shopping list via the PDA and electronic mail (e-mail) it to the grocer's server. Shoppers select products from lists residing in the personal catalog, the store's recommendations, and special promotions. Safeway customers are clustered based on their prior purchasing behavior, and a list of most popular products is generated to represent the preferred product purchases for the customers in each cluster. The *recommender* system at Safeway then ranks this list of products according to computed affinities with each customer, to produce a list of 10 to 20 highest-ranking products. When customers synchronize with the store server, they are presented with the recommended list, which in fact contains products that were not previously purchased by the customer.

Results demonstrated that using the recommender resulted in 25% of the orders including something from the recommendation list, and a 1.8% increase in revenue. The study demonstrates that DM can help improve the understanding of customer preferences, and thereby boost the revenue of the business. For more information on this study, see Lawrence et al. [2001].

[7] www.ibm.com

DM techniques have also been used in areas as diverse as facilitating the classification of a country's investing risk based on a variety of factors and identifying the factors associated with a country's competitiveness [Becerra-Fernandez et al., 2002]. For a quick overview of what knowledge discovery systems are and how they are used, let us look at Vignette 13-3 and how Britain's Safeway supermarkets are using DM techniques to recommend products to shoppers, and thus increase sales.

The KDD process is viewed as both an interactive and iterative process that turns data into information and information into business knowledge. In the following section we discuss the steps in the KDD process.

## ◆◆ ◆◆ ◆◆ Designing the Knowledge Discovery System

Discovering knowledge can be different things for different organizations. Some organizations have large databases, whereas others may have small ones. The problems faced by the users of DM systems may also be quite different. Therefore, the developers of DM software face a difficult process when attempting to build tools that are considered generalizable across the entire spectrum of applications and corporate cultures. Early efforts to apply DM in business operations faced the need to learn, primarily via trial and error, how to develop an effective approach to DM. If fact, as early adopters of DM observed an exploding interest in the application of techniques, the need to develop a standard process model for KDD became apparent. This standard should be well reasoned, nonproprietary, and freely available to all DM practitioners.

In 1999, a consortium of vendors and early adopters of DM applications for business operations—consisting of Daimler-Chrysler (then Daimler-Benz AG, Germany), NCR Systems Engineering Copenhagen (Denmark), SPSS/Integral Solutions Ltd. (England), and OHRA Verzegeringen en Bank Groep B.V. (The Netherlands)—developed a set of specifications called **Cross-Industry Standard Process for Data Mining (CRISP-DM)**[8] [Chapman et al., 2000; Two Crows, 1999; Brachman and Anand, 1996]. CRISP-DM is an industry consortium that developed an industry-neutral and tool-neutral process for DM. CRISP-DM defines a hierarchical process model that defines the basic steps of DM for knowledge discovery as follows:

1. *Business understanding.* The first requirement for knowledge discovery is to understand the business problem. In other words, to obtain the highest benefit from DM, there must be a clear statement of the business objectives. For example, a business goal could be "to increase the response rate of direct mail marketing." An economic justification based on the return on investment (ROI) of a more effective direct mail marketing may be necessary to justify the expense of the DM study. This step also involves an assessment of the current situation, for example:

> The current response rate to direct mail is 1%. Results of the study showed that using 35% of the current sample population for direct mail (the one that is likely to buy the product), a marketing campaign could hit 80% of the prospective buyers.

In other words, the majority of the people in a marketing campaign who receive a target mail do not purchase the product. This example illustrates how you could effectively isolate 80% of the prospective buyers by mailing only to 35% of the customers in a sample marketing campaign database. Identifying the most likely prospective buyers from the sample, and targeting the direct mail to those customers, could save the organization significant costs, mainly the costs associated with mailing a piece to 65% of the customers who are the least likely to buy the new product offering. The maximum profit occurs from mailing to the 35% of the customers that are most likely to buy the new product. Finally, this step also includes the specification of a project plan for the DM study.

---

[8]www.crisp-dm.org

2. ***Data understanding.*** One of the most important tenets in data engineering is "know thy data." Knowing the data well can permit the designers to tailor the algorithm or tools used for DM to their specific problem. This maximizes the chances for success as well as the efficiency and effectiveness of the knowledge discovery system. This step, together with preparation and modeling, consumes most of the resources required for the study. In fact, data understanding and preparation may take from 50% to 80% of the time and effort required for the entire knowledge discovery process. Typically, data collection for the DM project requires the creation of a database, although a spreadsheet may be just as adequate. DM does not require *data collection* in a **data warehouse;** and in case the organization is equipped with a data warehouse, it's best not to manipulate the data warehouse directly for the purpose of the DM study. Furthermore, the structure of the data warehouse may not lend itself for the type of data manipulation required. Finally, the construction of a data warehouse that integrates data from multiple sources into a single database is typically a huge endeavor that could extend a number of years and cost millions of dollars [Gray and Watson, 1998]. Most DM tools enable the input data to take many possible formats, and the data transformation is transparent to the user. The steps required for the data understanding process are:

   a. *Data collection.* This step defines the data sources for the study, including the use of external public data (e.g., real estate tax folio) and proprietary databases (e.g., contact information for businesses in a particular zip code). The data collection report typically includes the following: a description of the data source, data owner, who (organization and person) maintains the data, cost (if purchased), storage format and structure, size (e.g., in records, rows), physical storage characteristics, security requirements, restrictions on use, and privacy requirements.

   b. *Data description.* This step describes the contents of each file or table. Some of the important items in this report are number of fields (columns) and percentage of records missing. Also important for each field or column are data type, definition, description, source, unit of measure, number of unique values, list, and range of values. In addition, some other valuable specifics are some of the specifics about how the data were collected and the time frame when the data were collected. Finally, in the case of relational databases, it is important to know which attributes are the primary or foreign keys.

   c. *Data quality and verification.* In general, good models require good data; therefore, the data must be correct and consistent. This step determines whether any data can be eliminated because of irrelevance or lack of quality. In addition, many DM packages allow specifying which columns in a table can be ignored (for the same reasons) during the modeling phase. Furthermore, missing data can cause significant problems. Some DM algorithms (e.g., C5.0) can handle the missing data problem by automatically massaging the data and using surrogates for the missing data points. Other algorithms may be sensitive to missing values. In that case, one approach would be to discard the data sample if some of the attributes or fields are missing, which could cause a substantial loss of data. A better approach is to calculate a substitute value for the missing values. Substitute values could consist of the mode, median, or mean of the attribute variable, depending on the data type.

d. *Exploratory analysis of the data.* Techniques such as visualization and *on-line analytical processing (OLAP)* enable preliminary data analysis. This step is necessary to develop a hypothesis of the problem to be studied, and to identify the fields that are likely to be the best predictors. In addition, some values may need to be derived from the raw data; for example, factors such as *per capita income* may be a more relevant factor to the model than the factor *income.*

3. **Data preparation.**   The steps for this task include

a. *Selection.* This step requires the selection of the predictor variables and the **sample set**. Selecting the predictor variables is necessary because typically DM algorithms do not work well if all the variables (fields or database columns) are considered as *potential predictors.* In essence, that is why DM requires an understanding of the domain, and the potential variables influencing the outcome in question. As a rule of thumb, the number of predictors (columns) must be smaller than the number of samples (rows) in the data set. In fact, the number of simple observations should be at least 10 to 25 times the number of predictors. As the number of predictors increases, the computational requirement to build the model also increases. Selecting the sample set is necessary because when the data set is large, a sample of the data set can be selected to represent the complete data set. In selecting the sample, attention must be paid to the constraints imposed by sampling theory, for the sample to be representative of the complete data set.

b. *Construction and transformation of variables.*   Often, new variables must be constructed to build effective models. Examples include ratios and combination of various fields. Furthermore, some algorithms, such as market basket analysis, may require data to be transformed to categorical format (integer) when in fact the raw data exists in continuous form. This may require transformations that group values in ranges, such as *low, medium,* and *high.*

c. *Data integration.*   The data set for the DM study may reside on multiple databases, which would need to be consolidated into one database. Data consolidation may require redefinition of some of the data fields to allow for consistency. For example, different databases may relate to the same customer with different names; for example, one database may refer to the National Aeronautics and Space Administration, whereas other database fields may just use NASA, its acronym. These incompatibilities must be reconciled prior to data integration.

d. *Formatting.*   This step involves the reordering and reformatting of the data fields, as required by the DM model.

4. **Model building and validation.**   Building an accurate model is a trial-and-error process. The process often requires the DM specialist to iteratively try several options, until the best model emerges. Furthermore, different algorithms could be tried with the same data set, and the results then compared to see which model yields the best results. For example, both neural network and **rule induction algorithms** could be applied to the same data set to develop a predictive model. The results from each algorithm could be compared for accuracy in their respective predictive quality.

Following the model development, the models must be *evaluated* or *validated*. In constructing a model, a subset of the data is usually set aside for validation purposes. This means that the validation data set is not used to develop or train the model, but to calculate the accuracy of predictive qualities of the model. The most popular validation technique is **n-fold cross-validation,** specifically **ten-fold validation.** The ten-fold validation divides the population of the validation data set into 10 approximately equal sized data sets and then uses each of the 10 holdout sets a single time to evaluate the models developed with the remaining 9 training sets. For each of the 10 models (the last model includes using the whole data set), the accuracy is determined, and the overall model accuracy is determined as the average of each of the model samples.

5. *Evaluation and interpretation.* Once the model is determined, the validation data set is fed through the model. Because the outcome for this data set is known, the predicted results are compared with the actual results in the validation data set. This comparison yields the accuracy of the model. As a rule of thumb, a model accuracy of around 50% would be insignificant, because that would be the same accuracy as for a random occurrence.

6. *Deployment.* This step involves implementing the "live" model within an organization to aid the decision-making process. A valid model must also make sense in the real world, and a pilot implementation is always warranted prior to deployment. Also, following implementation, it's important to continue to monitor how well the model predicts the outcomes, and the benefits that this brings to the organization. For example, a clustering model may be deployed to identify fraudulent Medicare claims. When the model identifies potential instances of fraud, and these instances are validated as indeed fraudulent, the savings to the organization from the deployment of the model should be captured. These early successes will then act as champions, and will affect continued implementation of knowledge discovery models within the organization.

Figure 13-1 summarizes the CRISP-DM process methodology. Figure 13-2 illustrates the iterative nature of the CRISP-DM process.

CRISP-DM is only one of the institutions that have on-going efforts toward streamlining the KDD process. Other similar efforts include:

1. **Customer Profile Exchange (CPEX)**[9] offers a vendor-neutral, XML-based open standard for facilitating the privacy-enabled interchange of customer information across disparate enterprise applications and systems.
2. **Data Mining Group (DMG)**[10] is an independent, vendor led group, which develops DM standards, such as the Predictive Model Markup Language (PMML).

In general, the goal that these standards pursue is to facilitate the planning, documentation, and communication in DM projects, and to serve as a common reference framework for the DM industry. Many of these standards were developed based on practical experience resulting from the implementation of

---

[9]www.cpexchange.org
[10]www.dmg.org

| Business Understanding | Data Understanding | Data Preparation | Modeling | Evaluation | Deployment |
|---|---|---|---|---|---|
| **Determine Business Objectives** *Background* *Business Objectives* *Business Success Criteria* | **Initial Data Collection** *Initial Data Collection Report* | *Data Set* *Data Set Description* | **Generate Test Design** *Test Design* | **Evaluate Results** *Approved Models* *Assessment of Data Mining Results w.r.t. Business Success Criteria* | **Plan Deployment** *Deployment Plan* |
| **Situation Assessment** *Inventory of Resources* *Requirements* *Assumptions* *Constraints* *Risks and Contingencies* *Terminology* *Costs and Benefits* | **Data Description** *Data Description Report* **Data Quality Verification** *Data Quality Report* **Exploratory Analysis** *Exploratory Analysis Report* | **Selection** *Rationale for Inclusion/ Exclusion* **Cleaning** *Data Cleaning Report* **Construction** *Derived Variables* *Generated Records* *Transformation* | **Build Model** *Parameter Settings* *Models* **Model Evaluation** *Model Description* *Assessment* | **Review Process** *Review of Process* **Determine Next Steps** *List of Possible Actions* *Decision* | **Procedure Final Report** *Final Report* *Final Presentation* **Plan Monitoring and Maintanance** *Maintenance Plan* **Review Project** *Experience Documentation* |
| **Determine Data Mining Goal** *Data Mining Goals* *Data Mining Success Criteria* | | **Integration** *Merging* *Aggregation* | | | |
| **Procedure Project Plan** *Project Plan* | | **Formatting** *Rearranging Attributes* *Reordering Records* *Within-Value Reformatting* | | | |

❖❖ ❖❖ ❖❖ **FIGURE 13-1 CRISP-DM Data Mining Process Methodology**

*Source: SPSS, 2000.*

DM projects. In fact, the purpose is to help people, rather than software systems, communicate.

## ❖❖ ❖❖ ❖❖ Discovering Knowledge on the Web

As we see in Chapter 11, significant knowledge can be obtained from data on the Web. Business organizations can profit greatly from mining the Web. The business need for Web DM is clear:

> Companies venturing in e-commerce have a dream. By analyzing the tracks people make through their Web site, they'll be able to optimize its design to maximize sales. Information about customers and their purchasing habits will let companies initiate e-mail campaigns and other activities that result in sales. Good models of customers' preferences, needs, desires, and behaviors will let companies simulate the personal relationship that businesses and their clientele had in the good old days [Edelstein, 2001].

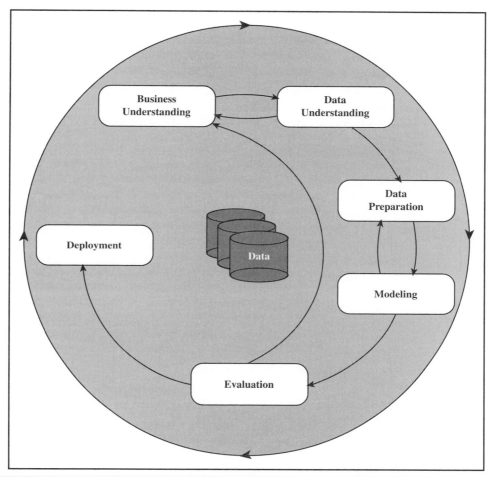

❖❖ ❖❖ ❖❖   **FIGURE 13-2** Iterative Nature of the KDD Process

*Source: SPSS [2000].*

Web-based companies are expecting to discover all this knowledge in the logs maintained by their Web servers. The expectation is that customers' paths through the data may enable companies to customize their Web pages, increase the average purchase amount per customer visit to the site, and in a nutshell increase profitability.

Certainly, e-business provides a fertile ground for learning market trends as well as what the competitors are up to. Therefore, learning to mine the Web can lead to a tremendous amount of new knowledge. Web pages and documents found on the Web can provide important information at minimal cost to develop or maintain. Text mining refers to automatically "reading" large documents (called *corpora*) of text written in natural language, and deriving knowledge from the process. *Web mining*, a relatively new term, is "Web crawling with on-line text mining" [Zanasi, 2000]. Zanasi reports about Online Analyst, a system that can mine the Web to provide *competitive intelligence,* a term that indicates knowledge leading to competitive advantages for a business organization. This system provides the user with an intelligent agent that surfs the Web in an intelligent fashion, reads, and quickly analyzes documents that are retrievable on-line. This system has the advantage that it can review many more documents than a human analyst can, even working 24 hours per day. Some of the documents may be well hidden (unintentionally or otherwise), whereas oftentimes the relevant information can be found deeply buried within one document. Zanasi does not describe the techniques behind Online Analyst, probably to protect its own secrets. The system was developed by IBM-Bologna in Italy, and is used as a tool for consulting.

Unfortunately, the information and data in the Web are unstructured. This can lead to difficulties when mining the Web. The conventional DM techniques described in Chapter 12 are not all applicable to Web mining, because by their nature, they are limited to highly structured data. There are several differences between traditional DM and Web mining. One significant difference is that Web mining requires **linguistic analysis** or **natural language processing (NLP)** abilities. It is estimated that 80% of the world's on-line content is based on text [Chen, 2001]. Web mining requires techniques from both information retrieval and artificial intelligence (AI) domains. Therefore, Web text mining techniques are rather different from the DM techniques described previously.

Web pages are indexed by the words they contained. Gerald Salton [1989] is generally considered the father of **information retrieval (IR).** IR indexing techniques consist of calculating the function **term frequency inverse document frequency (TFIDF).** The function consists of the product of a term frequency and its inverse document frequency, which depends on the frequency of occurrence of a specific keyword term in the text and the number of documents in which it appears. The *term frequency (TF)* refers to how frequently a term occurs in the text, which represents the importance of the term. The *inverse document frequency (IDF)* increases the significance of terms that appear in fewer documents, while downplaying terms that occur in many documents. TFIDF then highlights terms that are frequently used in one document, but infrequently used across the collection of documents. The net effect is that terms like *cryogenics,* which may occur frequently in a scientist's Web page, but infrequently across the whole domain of Web pages, result in a good indexing term.

Web mining techniques can be classified into four main layers [Chen, 2001]:

1. *Linguistic analysis and NLP* are used to identify key concept descriptors (the *who*, *what*, *when*, or *where*), which are embedded in the textual documents. In NLP the unit of analysis is the word. These functions can be combined with other linguistic techniques such as *stemming, morphological analysis, Boolean, proximity, range,* and *fuzzy search.* For example, a stemming algorithm is used to remove the suffix of a word. *Stoplists* are used to eliminate words that are not good concept descriptions, such as prepositions (*and, but,* etc.). Linguistic techniques can be combined with statistical techniques, for example, to represent grammatically correct sentences. **Semantic analysis** is also used to represent meaning in stories and sentences.

2. Statistical and co-occurrence analysis are like the TFIDF function mentioned above. For example, *link analysis* is used to create conceptual associations and

automatic thesauri for keyword concepts. Also, **similarity functions** are used to compute co-occurrence probabilities between concept pairs.

3. Statistical and neural networks clustering, and categorization, like the ones discussed previously in Chapter 12, are used to group similar documents together, as well as communities into domain categories. Kohonen NN techniques work well for large-scale Web text mining tasks and the results can be graphically visualized and intuitive.

4. Visualization and **human computer interfaces (HCI)** can reveal conceptual associations, which can be represented in various dimensions (one-, two-, and three-dimensional views). Furthermore, interaction techniques, such as zooming, can be incorporated to infer new knowledge.

There are three types of uses for Web DM. These are:

1. ***Web structure mining.*** Mining the Web structure examines how the Web documents are structured, and attempts to discover the model underlying the link structures of the Web. *Intrapage structure* mining evaluates the arrangement of the various HTML or XML tags within a page; *interpage* structure refers to hyperlinks connecting one page to another. Web structure mining can be useful to categorize Web pages, and to generate relationships and similarities between Web sites [Jackson, 2002].

2. ***Web usage mining.*** Web usage mining, also known as *clickstream analysis,* involves the identification of patterns in user navigation through Web pages in a domain. Web usage mining tries to discover knowledge about Web surfers' behaviors, through analysis of their interactions with the Web site, including the mouse clicks, user queries, and transactions. Web usage mining includes three main tasks: *preprocessing*, *pattern discovery*, and *pattern analysis* [Jackson, 2002]:

   a. *Preprocessing.* This task converts usage, content, and structure from different data sources into data sets ready for pattern discovery. This step is the most challenging in the DM process, because it may involve collecting data from multiple servers (including *proxy servers*), cleansing extraneous information, and using data collected by cookies for identification purposes.

   b. *Pattern analysis.* This step takes advantage of visualization and OLAP techniques, like the ones discussed in an earlier section to aid understanding of the data, notice unusual values, and identify possible relationships between the variables.

   c. *Pattern discovery.* This task is based on the different DM techniques discussed in Chapter 12, except certain variations may be considered. For example, in a market basket analysis of items purchased through a Web storefront, the click order for the items added to the shopping cart may be significant, which is not typically studied in brick-and-mortar settings.

3. ***Web content mining.*** Web content mining is used to discover what a Web page is about and how to uncover new knowledge from it. Web content data includes that used to create the Web page, including the text, images, audio, video,

hyperlinks, and *metadata*. Web content mining is based on text mining and IR techniques, which consist of the organization of large amounts of textual data for most efficient retrieval, an important consideration in handling text documents. IR techniques have become increasingly important, because the amount of semi-structured as well as unstructured textual data present in organizations has increased dramatically. IR techniques provide a method to efficiently access these large amounts of information.

Mining Web data is by all means a challenging task, but the rewards can be great, including aiding the development of a more personalized relationship with the virtual customer, improving the virtual storefront selling process, and increasing Web site revenues.

## ◇ ◇ ◇ Data Mining and Customer Relationship Management

Customer relationship management (CRM) includes the mechanisms and technologies used to manage the interactions between a company and its customers. Database marketers were the early adopters of CRM software, used to automate the process of customer interaction. CRM implementations can be characterized as operational or analytical. *Operational CRM* includes sales force automation and call centers. Most global companies have implemented such systems. The goal of operational CRM is to provide a single view and point of contact for each customer. On the other hand, *analytical CRM* uses DM techniques to uncover customer intelligence that serves to better understand and serve the customer.

In particular, the financial services, retailing, and telecommunications industry, facing increasing competitive markets, are turning to analytical CRM to do the following [Schwenk, 2002]:

1. *Integrate the customer viewpoint across all touchpoints.* Because many CRM solutions combine infrastructure components such as **enterprise application integration (EAI)** technology and data warehouses, as well as OLAP and DM. The CRM promise is to build an integrated view of the customer, to understand the customer touchpoints and resulting customer intelligence that enables organizations to better recognize and service the needs of the customer.

2. *Respond to customer demands in "Web time."* Because the Web has changed the dynamics of decision making, and competitive environments require organizations to react to increasingly complex customer requests at faster speeds. Also the analysis and interpretation of Web data can be used to enhance and personalize customer offerings. Analysis of Web data can uncover new knowledge about customer behavior and preferences, which can be used to improve Web site design and content.

3. *Derive more value from CRM investments.* Because DM analysis can be used to perform market segmentation studies that determine what customers could be targeted for certain products, to *narrowcast* (send out target e-mails) customers, and to perform other related studies such as market basket analysis.

For example, Redecard,[11] a company that captures and transmits MasterCard, Diners Club, and other credit and debit card transactions in Brazil, uses CRM to analyze transaction and customer data. The company performs market segmentation analysis to determine which customers to target for certain products [Lamont, 2002]. Also Soriana,[12] a Mexican grocery retailer, uses the market basket analysis capability of its CRM product to study promotion effectiveness and the impact of price changes on purchasing behavior [Lamont, 2002].

The first step in the CRM process involves identifying customer market segments with the potential of yielding the highest profit. This step requires sifting through large amounts of data, to find the "gold nuggets"—the mining promise. CRM software automates the DM process to find predictors of purchasing behaviors. In addition, CRM technology can typically integrate the solution of the DM study into campaign management software used to manage the targeted marketing campaign. The goal of campaign management software is to effectively manage the planning, execution, assessment, and refinement of myriad marketing campaigns at an organization. Campaign management software is used to manage and monitor a company's communications with its customers, including direct mail, telemarketing, customer service, point of sale, Web interactions, etc.

In CRM applications, the DM prediction models are used to calculate a *score*, which is a numerical value assigned to each record in the database to indicate the probability that the customer represented by that record may behave in a specific manner. For example, when using DM to predict customer attrition, or the likelihood that the customer may leave, a high score represents a high probability that the customer will indeed leave. The set of scores is then used to target customers for specific marketing campaigns.

Consider the following scenario: the result of a DM study at a large national bank revealed that many of its customers only take advantage of the checking account services it provides. Typical customers at this institution would deposit their checks, quickly moving the funds once they became available, to mutual funds accounts and other service providers outside the bank. Using the integrated capabilities for campaign management, the software automatically triggers a direct marketing piece for those customers with a sizable deposit, to encourage them to keep their money at the bank. DM and campaign management software can work together, to sharpen the focus of prospects, therefore increasing marketing response and effectiveness. For more details about the relationship between DM and CRM, please refer to Berson et al. [2000].

# ❬❭ ❬❭ ❬❭ Barriers to the Use of Knowledge Discovery Systems

Possibly two of the barriers that prevented earlier deployment of knowledge discovery in the business arena, versus what we have witnessed in the scientific realm, relate to the prior lack of data in business to support the analysis, and the limited computing power to perform the mathematical calculations required by the DM algorithms. Clearly, with the advent of more powerful computers at our desktops, and the proliferation of

---

[11]www.redecard.com.br
[12]www.soriana.com.mx/inicio.asp

relational databases, data warehouses, and data marts, these early barriers have been overcome. In fact, according to the **storage law** [Fayyad and Uthurusamy, 2002] the capacity of digital data storage worldwide has doubled every 9 months for the last decade, at twice the rate predicted by **Moore's law** for the growth of computing power. This growing capacity has resulted in phenomena called **data tombs** [Fayyad and Uthurusamy, 2002], or *data stores* where data is deposited to "merely rest in peace." This means there is no possibility that this data will be used, and the opportunity to discover new knowledge that could be used to improve services, profits, or products will be lost.

In addition, although many of the DM techniques have been around for more than 10 years for scientific applications, only in the past few years have we witnessed the emergence of solutions that consolidate multiple DM techniques in a single software offering. Probably one of the most significant barriers to the explosion of the use of knowledge discovery in organizations relates to the fact that today implementing a DM is still considered an art. Although a number of software packages exist that bundle DM tools into one software offering, adequately implementing the knowledge discovery models requires intimate knowledge of the algorithmic requirements in addition to familiarity of how to use the software itself, and a deep understanding of the business area and the problem that needs to be solved. In addition, a successful DM study typically requires a number of actors to partake in the activity, including the project leader, the DM client, the DM analyst, the DM engineer, and the information technology (IT) analyst [Jackson, 2002]. The project leader has the overall responsibility for the management of the study. The DM client understands the business problem, but in general does not have the adequate technical skills to carry the study. The DM analyst translates the business needs into technical requirements for the DM model. The DM engineer develops the DM model together with the DM client and analyst. The IT analyst provides access to hardware, software, and data needed to carry out the project. In some large projects, a number of DM analysts and engineers may be involved. Clearly, managing the number of actors involved in the study is indeed a challenging task that must be carefully coordinated by the project leader.

Perhaps one of the most interesting dilemmas facing KDD today is its basic definition as an "interactive" process versus the notion that for the technology to be successful it must become "invisible." KDD cannot be both interactive and invisible at the same time. Advocates of making KDD invisible argue that DM is primarily concerned with making it easy, convenient, and practical to explore very large databases without years of training as data analysts [Fayyad and Uthurusamy, 2002]. In fact, according to this view, this goal requires that the following challenges be addressed:

1. *Scaling analysis to large databases.* Current DM techniques require that data sets be loaded into the computer's memory to be manipulated. This requirement offers a significant barrier when very large databases and data warehouses must be scanned to identify patterns.
2. *Scaling to high-dimensional data and models.* Typical statistical analysis studies require humans to formulate a model, and then use techniques to validate the model via understanding how well the data fits the model. However, it may be increasingly difficult for humans to formulate models *a priori* based on a very large number of variables, which increasingly add dimension to the problem. Models that seek to understand customer behavior in retail or Web-based transactions may fall

in this category. Current solutions require humans to formulate a lower dimensional abstraction of the model, which may be easier for humans to understand.

3. ***Automating the search.*** DM studies typically require the researcher to enumerate the hypothesis under study *a priori.* In the future, DM algorithms may be able to perform this work automatically.

4. Finding patterns and models understandable and interesting to users. In the past, DM projects focused on measures of accuracy (how well the model predicts the data) and utility (the benefit derived from the pattern, typically money saved). New benefit measures, such as understandability of the model and novelty of the results, must also be developed. Also DM techniques are expected to incorporate the generation of meaningful reports resulting from the study.

Some of these current challenges are resolved today through the increasing availability of "verticalized" solutions. For example, in CRM software, KDD operations are streamlined through the use of standardized models, which may include the most widely used data sources. For instance, a standardized model for financial services would most likely include customer demographics, channel, credit, and card usage; as well as information related to the promotion and actual response. To streamline the KDD process, the metadata type for each table must be predefined (nominal, ordinal, interval, or continuous) whereas subsequent KDD operations are based on this information including the prespecification of algorithms that are appropriate to solve specific business problems [Parsa, 2000]. For example, based on the results presented earlier in Table 12-5, a verticalized application to predict which loan customers are considered a "good" risk, automatically implement the C5.0 algorithm if the input variables are continuous, and the outcome is discrete.

An additional limitation in the deployment of DM today is the fact that the successful implementation of KDD at any organization may require the integration of disparate systems, because there are few plug-and-play solutions. All these requirements translate into dollars, making many DM solutions sometimes quite expensive. Making the business case based on realistic estimations of ROI is essential for the success of the knowledge discovery initiative. Finally, effective application of the KDD to business applications requires the solution to be seamlessly integrated into existing environments. This requirement makes the case for vendors, researchers, and practitioners to adopt standards such as the CRISP-DM standard presented in an earlier section of this chapter.

## ❖❖❖ Case Study: Application of Rule Induction to Real Estate Appraisal Systems

In this section we describe an example of how rule induction can be used to discover specific values in databases. In this case, we seek specific knowledge that we know can be found in databases, but which can be difficult to extract.

In the world of real estate appraisal, it is important to know the incremental value that a particular feature may have on a property. For example, if a swimming pool, an in-law quarters, or a third garage is added to an existing house, by how much will the value of the house increase? Generally, the cost of constructing the new feature is not merely added on to the value of the house. It is the market that determines the incremental value.

For example, a new swimming pool in a house in a high-end neighborhood may increase the value of the house significantly. However, the same swimming pool in a retirement community of small homes may be perceived as an undesirable burden on the owner, and may negatively influence the value of the property.

Property appraisals are primarily done through a comparison of the target property to others recently sold. However, because no two homes are alike, and their locations and time of sale rarely ever coincide with the target property, it is difficult to make a one-to-one comparison. Typically, to do their job, property appraisers obtain their basis of comparison from a database of sold properties, used to collect the description of the sold properties and their sales price. Because the market changes very quickly in response to the state of the economy and the season of the year, it is important to understand the incremental value of these features on a regular and continuing basis.

The technique described here focuses on calculating either the *incremental* or *relative worth* of components of **aggregate sets.** An aggregate set represents a collection, assembly, or grouping of member components that have a common nature or purpose. A house is an aggregate set, and its components are its features, such as number of bedrooms, number of bathrooms, area, or number of garages. We use the term *worth* here generically to mean a real number representing the worth, weight, cost, price, or any other similarly quantifiable factor. In this application, we are trying to discover how much incremental worth a particular feature (e.g., an extra bathroom) may contribute to the overall worth of a house.

Calculating the incremental or relative worth of a feature is possible when a database contains many aggregate sets that are homogeneous (i.e., have the same attributes), but dissimilar (i.e., have different values). The induction algorithm finds aggregate sets in the database that exhibit minimal differences in their attributes' values, and strives to isolate the single differentiating attribute and value combination of nearly similar aggregate sets of individual houses. Any difference in worth between the houses can be attributed to this singular difference.

An aggregate set, H (in our case, a house) is therefore defined as a pair consisting of a set containing its components (called *attributes*, A), and the total worth of the house (worth). For example, one attribute could be the living area, or the number of bedrooms for each house. Furthermore, for each house attribute, we specify the value of the attribute (e.g., area = 1,500 sq. ft., or number of bedrooms = 4) and its individual worth. The individual worth of an attribute is the amount that this attribute contributes to the overall worth of the house in question. In these problems, each attribute's worth is typically not known.

Care should be taken not to confuse the terms *value* and *worth*. Value is the value associated with each attribute, much like the value of an attribute in a relational database. For example, the value of the attribute *number of bedrooms* could be 4. The value of an attribute can be either discrete or continuous. Discrete values can be binary, such as yes or no (e.g., for a swimming pool), or nonbinary, such as central heat, fireplace, and hot water radiators. Nonbinary discrete attributes (such as the number of bedrooms) typically have a relatively small set of possible values (2, 3, 4, or 5). They can be numerical or symbolic. Continuous attributes, on the other hand, such as the living area of the house, can take on a value from a much larger domain. To convert a continuous value into a discrete one, the range of the continuous domain values can be divided into several subintervals (i.e., <1,000; 1,000 to 1,500; and 1,500 to 2,000 sq. ft.). Worth, on the other hand, is measured in dollars for this example.

The procedure to create the decision tree based on the induction techniques presented in Chapter 12, is as follows:

1. ***Data preparation and preprocessing.*** Houses may exist in the database that, for a number of reasons, may not be consistent with the other sets. These could be because of attributes that are not reflected in the anomalous house (no value given for the air-conditioning attribute), or values of attributes that are not generally considered possible (a lakeside home). These examples need to be identified and eliminated from the database, because they could distort the final worth of the houses.

2. ***Tree construction.*** As the tree progressively expands by creating a new level — *tree construction* — the group of houses assigned to the nodes in the prior last level is further distributed to child nodes via branches originating in the parent node. For each node in a level, branches are created that represent each discrete value or range of values of the attribute represented in that node. The branch through which each house is routed depends on the value that each particular house has for the attribute represented in the parent node. All the houses populating every node are distributed through these branches to children nodes at the next lower level. This segregates the houses further. This process continues until all the attributes have been distributed through all the levels of the tree, and the leaf-level nodes are populated with identical houses.

3. ***House pruning.*** Heuristics are applied to identify and discard those houses whose worth are not consistent with those of other houses in the same leaf-level group. This can only be determined after the tree is built and the total worth of the houses populating a particular node can be compared with each other. If one deviates significantly from the others, it is removed from further consideration.

4. ***Paired-leaf analysis.*** This **paired-leaf analysis** is applied to the two sibling leaf nodes. All houses populating these leaves have identical values for all attributes except for the critical attribute (the parent nodes of the leaf-level nodes). Therefore, it can be inferred that any difference in worth between houses in two sibling leaves is directly caused by the difference in their values of the critical attribute. For example, if two houses are identical except for the fact that one has 3 bedrooms and the other 4. If the 4-bedroom house sells for $75,000 and the 3-bedroom one for $73,000, the difference of $2,000 can be attributed to the extra bedroom alone.

Figure 13-3 and Table 13-1 represent the partial decision tree resulting from the induction algorithm, based on a relatively small database of 84 sold homes. The incremental worth computed with the induction algorithm tracked relatively closely the opinions of experts in real estate appraisal in all but the number of bathrooms. Post facto analysis of the data indicated that there were very few houses with anything other than two bathrooms, thus skewing the results significantly. Although the differences in some of the other features appear to be unacceptably high, they are actually quite low compared with the sale price of the house. They were deemed quite acceptable by the expert validation panel.

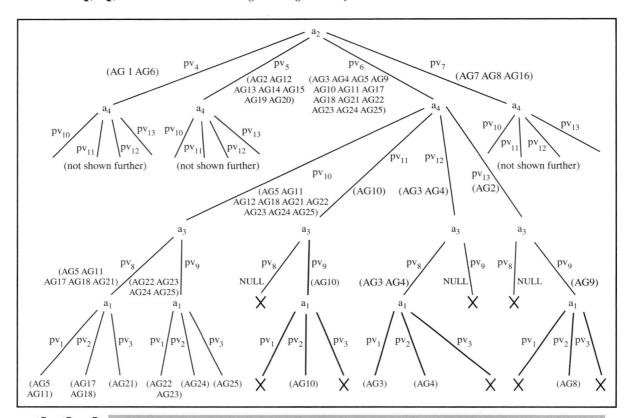

◆▸ ◆▸ ◆▸ FIGURE 13-3 Partial Decision Tree Results for Real Estate Appraisal
(Key: a = attribute, X = dead end.)

The ranges represent the maximum and minimum calculated values of the worth of the feature based on the several paired-leaf comparisons. The nature of the domain is such that the incremental worth of a feature is highly dependent on the sale price of a house. For example, the incremental worth of an additional bedroom is significantly

| **TABLE 13-1** | **Summary of Induction Results** | | |
| --- | --- | --- | --- |
| *Attribute* | *Induction Results* | *Expert Estimate* | *Difference* |
| Living area | $15–$31 | $15–$25 | 0–2.4% |
| Bedrooms | $4,311–$5,212 | $2,500–$3,500 | 49–72% |
| Bathrooms | $3,812–$5,718 | $1,500–$2,000 | 154–186% |
| Garage | $3,010–$4,522 | $3,000–$3,500 | 0.3–29% |
| Pool | $7,317–$11,697 | $9,000–$12,000 | 2.5–19% |
| Fireplace | $1,500–$4,180 | $1,200–$2,000 | 25–109% |
| Year built | 1.2–1.7% | 1.0–1.2% | 20–42% |

◆▸ ◆▸ ◆▸ ◆▸

greater when that bedroom represents the fifth bedroom in a house, as opposed to when it is the third one. More details on this case study can be obtained from Gonzalez et al. [1999].

##  Case Study: Application of Web Content Mining to Expertise-Locator Systems

To accompany the discussions presented in this section, please refer to the Expert Seeker Web Miner demo found in the CD included with this book.

One application of Web content mining methods is in the construction of **expertise-locator KM systems.** A KM system that locates experts based on published documents requires an automatic method for identifying employee names, as well as a method to associate employee names with skill keywords embedded in those documents. Although we discuss expertise locator systems in general in Chapter 15, we include in this section a discussion of the system's Web text mining component.

An example of an expertise-locator KM system is the NASA Expert Seeker Web Miner,[13] which required the development of a name-finding algorithm to identify names of NASA employees in NASA Web pages. Traditional IR techniques[14] were then used to identify and match skill keywords with the identified employee names. An IR system typically uses as input a set of inverted files, which is a sequence of words that reference the group of documents in which the words appear. These words are chosen according to a selection algorithm that determines which words in the document are good index terms. In a traditional IR system, the user enters a query, and the system retrieves all documents that match that keyword entry. Expert Seeker Web Miner is based on an IR technique that goes one step further. When a user enters a query, the system initially performs a document search based on user input. However, because the user is looking for experts in a specific subject area, the system returns the names of those employees whose names appear in the matching documents (excluding Webmasters and curators). The employee name results are ranked according to the number of matching documents in which each individual name appears. The employee information is then displayed to the user.

The indexing process was carried out in four stages. First, all the relevant data were transferred to a local directory for further processing. In this case, the data included all the Web pages on the NASA-Goddard Space Flight Center domain. The second stage identifies all instances of employee names by programmatically examining each HTML file. The name data are taken from the personnel directory databases (based on the X.500 standard). All names in the employee database are organized into a maplike data structure beforehand that is used in the Web content mining process. This map consists of all employee names referenced by their last name key. In

---

addition, each full name is stored in every possible form it could appear. For example, the name John A. Smith is stored as

- John A. Smith
- J. A. Smith
- J. Smith
- Smith, John A.
- Smith, J.A.
- Smith J.

An individual document is first searched for all last name keys. Subsequently, the document is again searched using all values of the matching keys. Name data organized in this way can increase the speed of the text search. Using one long sequence containing all names in every possible form as search criteria would slow down processing time.

The third stage involves identifying keywords within the HTML content. This is done using a combination of word stemming and frequency calculation. First, the text is broken up into individual words, through string pattern matching. Any sequence of alphabetical characters is recognized as a word whereas punctuation, numbers, and white space characters are ignored. The resulting list of words is processed to determine whether a word was included in a *stoplist*. The resulting list of words is then processed with a *stemming* algorithm. This is done to group together words that may be spelled differently but have the same semantic meaning. A person who types *astronomical* as a query term would most likely also be interested in documents that match the term *astronomy*. Once the stemming process is completed, the algorithm calculates the frequency of each term. Word frequency was used during the keyword selection process in the determination of good index terms. However, other indexing algorithms could have been used instead with comparable results.

It is important to note that the degree of relation between an employee name and a keyword within an individual document is not considered. Instead, expertise is determined based on the assumption that if an employee recurrently appears in many documents along with a keyword, then that person must have some knowledge of that term. Theoretically, a large document count for a search query should produce more accurate results.

The chosen keywords have a twofold purpose. First, they are used to quickly associate employees with recurring skill terms. These keywords can also be used in future work for clustering similar documents into topic areas. Finally, **knowledge taxonomy** can be constructed from the mined keywords, such that an appropriate query relevance feedback system can be developed to suggest query terms related to the query entered by the user. Details about the role of taxonomies on the development of expertise locator systems are presented in Chapter 15.

## SUMMARY ◇◆ ◇◆ ◇◆

In this chapter you learn about knowledge discovery systems, design considerations, and specific types of DM techniques that enable such systems. Also the chapter discusses the role of DM in customer relationship management. Two case studies that describe the implementation of knowledge discovery systems are presented, each based on different methodologies and intelligent technologies. The first system is based on the use of decision trees, or rule induction, as a knowledge-modeling tool, and is described in the context of a real estate appraisal system. The second system is based on the use of Web-content mining to identify expertise in an expertise locator system. Finally, the use of socialization in organizational settings is discussed as a mechanism to help discover new knowledge and catalyze innovation.

## KEY TERMS ◇ ◇ ◇

- aggregate sets—p. 270
- back propagation algorithm—p. 255
- combination—p. 249
- CRISP-DM—p. 258
- customer profile exchange (CPEX)—p. 261
- data mining—p. 250
- data mining group (DMG)—p. 261
- data preparation—p. 271
- data quality (DQ)—p. 259
- data tombs—p. 268
- data warehouse—p. 259
- enterprise application integration (EAI)—p. 266

- exploratory analysis of data (with OLAP)—p. 260
- expertise-locator (KM) systems—p. 273
- human computer interface (HCI)—p. 265
- inferential DM techniques—p. 254
- information retrieval (IR)—p. 264
- knowledge discovery in databases (KDD)—p. 254
- lateral thinking—p. 255
- linguistic analysis—p. 264
- market basket analysis—p. 254
- Moore's law—p. 268

- paired-leaf analysis—p. 271
- personal profile—p. 257
- predictive DM techniques—p. 254
- rule induction algorithms—p. 260
- sample set—p. 260
- semantic analysis—p. 264
- similarity functions—p. 265
- socialization—p. 250
- storage law—p. 268
- target sell—p. 256
- ten-fold cross-validation—p. 261
- term frequency inverse document frequency (TFIDF)—p. 264

## REVIEW QUESTIONS ◇ ◇ ◇

1. How do socialization techniques help to discover tacit knowledge?
2. Describe the six steps in the CRISP-DM process.
3. Why is understanding of the business problem essential to knowledge discovery?
4. Describe the three types of Web DM techniques. Which one is used in the Expert Seeker case study?
5. Describe some of the barriers to the use of knowledge discovery.

## APPLICATION EXERCISES ◇ ◇ ◇

Identify which DM techniques you would select to solve the following problems. Explain your answer. Include a description of the input and output variables that would be relevant in each case. Note that more than one technique may apply for each of these problems.

1. Predict fraudulent credit card usage based on purchase patterns.
2. Predict instances of fraud related to Medicare claims.
3. Predict which customers are likely to leave their current long-distance provider.
4. Predict whether a person will renew their insurance policy.
5. Predict who will respond to a direct mail offer.
6. Predict that a generator is likely to fail.
7. Predict which specialized voice services a person is likely to purchase from the local telecommunications provider.

8. Identify factors resulting in product defects in a manufacturing environment.
9. Predict the expected revenue from a customer, based on a set of customer characteristics.
10. Predict cost of hospitalization for different medical procedures.
11. Create customer segments in a marketing campaign.
12. Segment among university graduates those who are likely to renew their alumni membership.

## REFERENCES ◆ ◆ ◆

Becerra-Fernandez, I., Zanakis, S., and Walczak, S. 2002. Knowledge discovery techniques for predicting country investment risk. *Computers & Industrial Engineering*, 43(4), 787–800.

Berson, A., Smith, S., and Thearling, K. 2000. *Building Data Mining Applications for CRM*. McGraw Hill, New York.

Bishop, C. 1994. Neural networks and their applications. *Review of Scientific Instruments,* 65(6), 1803–1832.

Brachman, R. and Anand, T. 1996. The Process of Knowledge Discovery in Databases in *Advances in Knowledge Discovery and Data Mining*. AAAI Press, Menlo Park, CA/MIT Press, Cambridge, MA, pp. 37–57.

Chapman, P., Clinton, J., Kerber, R., Khabaza, T., Reinartz, T., Shearer, C., and Wirth, R. 2000. CRISP-DM 1.0 Step-by-step data mining guide. Technical Report. SPSS.

Chen, H. 2001. *Knowledge Management Systems: A Text Mining Perspective*. The University of Arizona, Tucson, AZ.

Edelstein, H. 2001. Pan for gold in the clickstream. *Information Week,* March 12.

Fayyad, U., Piatetsky-Shapiro, G., Smyth, P., and Uthurusamy, R. (Eds.) 1996. From data mining to knowledge discovery: An overview. In *Advances in Knowledge Discovery and Data Mining*. AAAI Press, Menlo Park, CA/MIT Press, Cambridge, MA, pp. 1–33.

Fayyad, U., and Uthurusamy, R. 2002. Evolving data mining into solutions for insights. *Communications of the ACM*, 45(8), 28–21.

Frakes, W., and Baeza-Yates, R. 1992. *Information Retrieval: Data Structures and Algorithms.* Prentice Hall, Upper Saddle, NJ.

Gonzalez, A.J., Daroszweski, S., and Hamilton, H.J. 1999. Determining the incremental worth of members of an aggregate set through difference-based induction. *International Journal of Intelligent Systems*, 14(3).

Gray, P., and Watson, H.J. 1998. *Decision Support in the Data Warehouse*. Prentice Hall, Upper Saddle River, NJ.

Jackson, J. 2002. Data mining: A conceptual overview. *Communications of the Association for Information Systems*, 8, 267–296.

Kovalerchuck, B., Triantaphyllou, E., Ruiz, J., Torvik, V., and Vityaev, E. 2000. The reliability issue of computer-aided breast cancer diagnosis. *Journal of Computers and Biomedical Research,* 33(4), 296–313.

Lamont, J. 2002. CRM around the world. *KM World*, 11(9) October.

Lawrence, R., Almasi, G., Kotlyar, V., Viveros, M., and Duri, S. 2001. Personalization of supermarket product recommendations. *Data Mining and Knowledge Discovery*, 5, 11–32.

Nonaka, I., and Takeuchi, H. 1995. *The Knowledge Creating Company*. Oxford University Press, New York.

Parsa, I. 2000. Data Mining: Middleware or Middleman, Panel on KDD Process Standards (Position Statement). Proceedings from the 6th ACM SIGKDD International Conference on Knowledge Discovery and Data Mining, Boston, MA, August 20–23.

Salton, G. 1989. *Automatic Text Processing*. Addison-Wesley, Reading, MA.

Schwenk, H. 2002. Real-time CRM analytics: The future of BI? *KM World*, 11(2), February.

Smith, K.A., and Gupta, J.N.D. 2000. Neural networks in business: Techniques and applications for the operations researcher. *Computers and Operations Research*, 27, 1023–1044.

SPSS. 2000. *Data Mining: Modeling*. SPSS, Chicago, IL.

Stevens, L. 2001. IT sharpens data mining's focus. *Internet Week,* August 6,

Two Crows. 1999. *Introduction to Data Mining and Knowledge Discovery*. Two Crows Corporation, Potomac, MD.

Widrow, B., Rumelhart, D.E., and Lehr, M.A. 1994. Neural networks: Applications in industry, business and science. *Communications of the ACM,* 37(3), 93–105.

Wong, B.K., Bodnovich, T.A., and Selvi, Y. 1997. Neural network applications in business: A review and analysis of the literature (1988–1995). *Decision Support Systems,* 19, 301–320.

Witten, I. 2000. Adaptive Text Mining: Inferring Structure from Sequences. Proceedings of the 34th Conference on Information Sciences and Systems, Princeton University, NJ, March 15–17.

Zanasi, A. 2000. Web mining through the Online Analyst. Proceedings of the First Data Mining Conference. Cambridge University, Cambridge, UK.

# CHAPTER 14

# Knowledge Capture Systems

## *Systems That Preserve and Formalize Knowledge*

### ◇ ◇ ◇ Introduction

In the previous chapter, we describe knowledge discovery systems. In this chapter, we discuss *knowledge capture systems*. These systems are designed to help elicit and store organizational and individual knowledge, both tacit and explicit. Knowledge can be captured using mechanisms or technologies, so that the captured knowledge can then be shared and used by others. Perhaps the earliest mechanisms for knowledge capture dates to the anthropological use of stories, the earliest form of art, education, and entertainment. **Storytelling** is the mechanism by which early civilizations passed on their values and their wisdom, from one generation to the next.

In this chapter, we first discuss issues about organizational storytelling, and how this mechanism can support knowledge capture. We then show how technology can enable the knowledge capture process. Specifically, we describe two types of knowledge capture systems. The first system presented serves best to support educational settings. Then a second system is presented, which serves best to capture *tactical* knowledge. Recall from Chapter 2 that tactical knowledge is defined as knowledge that pertains to the short-term positioning of the organization.

For a quick overview of how organizations can utilize strategic stories, let us look at a brief case study and how 3M[1] Corporation uses stories to embody its innovative culture.

---

[1] www.3m.com/

## ◆ ◆ ◆ What Are Knowledge Capture Systems?

As discussed in Chapter 3, knowledge capture systems support the process of eliciting either explicit or tacit knowledge that may reside in people, artifacts, or organizational entities. These systems can help capture knowledge existing either within or outside organizational boundaries, among employees, consultants, competitors, customers, suppliers, and even prior employers of the organization's new employees. Knowledge capture systems rely on mechanisms and technologies that support externalization and internalization. Both mechanisms and technologies can support knowledge capture systems by facilitating the knowledge management (KM) processes of externalization and internalization.

You may recall from Chapter 3 that *knowledge capture mechanisms* facilitate externalization (i.e., the conversion of tacit knowledge into explicit form) or internalization (i.e., the conversion of explicit knowledge into tacit form). The development of models or prototypes, and the articulation of stories are some examples of mechanisms that enable externalization. Learning by observation and face-to-face meetings are some of the mechanisms that facilitate internalization. **Technologies** can also support knowledge capture systems by facilitating externalization and internalization. Externalization through *knowledge engineering* (as we describe in detail in Chapter 10) is necessary for the implementation of intelligent technologies such as expert systems (see Chapter 8) and case-based reasoning (CBR) systems (see Chapter 9). Technologies that facilitate internalization include computer-based communication (see Chapter 11). Using such communication facilities, an individual can internalize knowledge from a message or its attachment, sent by another expert, an artificial intelligence (AI)-based knowledge acquisition system (see Chapter 10), or computer-based simulations. Both knowledge capture mechanisms and technologies can facilitate externalization and internalization within or across organizations.

## ◆ ◆ ◆ Knowledge Management Mechanisms to Capture Tacit Knowledge: Using Stories for Capturing Organizational Knowledge

The importance of using metaphors and stories as a mechanism for capturing and transferring tacit knowledge is increasingly drawing the attention of organizations. For example, as illustrated in Vignette 14-1, 3M[2] currently uses stories as part of its business planning to set the stage, introduce dramatic conflict, reach a resolution to the challenges the company is facing, and generate excitement and commitment from all the members of the organization [Shaw et al., 1998]. Stories are considered to play a significant role in organizations characterized by a strong need for collaboration. **Organizational stories** are defined as

> A detailed narrative of past management actions, employee interactions, or other intra- or extra-organizational events that are communicated informally within organizations [Swap et al., 2001].

---

[2]www.3m.com

VIGNETTE 14-1

### Using Stories to Build Effective Business Plans at 3M

Few companies rival 3M's 100 record years of innovation. From the invention of the sandpaper in 1904, to the invention of the masking tape in 1925, and Post-it Notes in 1980, 3M's culture is noted for its use of stories. Stories are part of the 3M sales representatives' training and award ceremonies, and in short are a "habit of mind. At 3M, the power of stories is recognized as a means to see ourselves and our business operations in complex, multidimensional forms—that we're able to discover opportunities for strategic change. Stories give us ways to form ideas about winning" [Shaw et al., 1998].

Recently, recognition about the power of stories transcended to 3M's board room. Traditionally at 3M, business plans were presented through bulleted lists. Cognitive psychologists have proved that lists are ineffective learning artifacts because item recognition decreases with the length of the list [Sternberg, 1975], and typically only items at the beginning or end of the list are remembered [Tulving, 1983]. As a contrast, a good story can better represent a business plan, because it includes a definition of the relationships, a sequence of events, and a subsequent priority among the items, which in turn causes the strategic plan to be remembered. Therefore, stories are currently used as the basic building blocks for business plans at 3M.

Shaw et al. [1998] defines an effective business plan to be a lot like a good story, and appropriately illustrates this with a narrative example. The strategic business plan must first *set the stage*, or define the current situation. For example:

Global Feet Graphics (a 3M division that makes durable graphic-marking systems for buildings, signs, and vehicles) was facing increasing demand from customers, at the same time that they were experiencing eroding market share due to diminishing patent advantages and competitors' low-cost strategies.

Next, the strategic story must *introduce the dramatic conflict*. Continuing with the same example:

The 3M division had to effect a quantum change in the production system that enabled the quick and competitive delivery of products. The solution included the development of innovative technologies that enabled this group's product offerings to differentiate from its competitors. In addition, sales and marketing skills had to appropriately match the new strategy.

Finally, the strategic narrative must *reach a resolution*. In other words, it must summarize how the organization can win, through effectively drawing on the diverse technological skills required to transform the business.

Studies at 3M have shown that the adequate use of narrative business plans has resulted in an improved understanding of the requirements for the plan to succeed. In addition, narrative strategy allows 3M employees to get excited as well as to generate commitment about the plan, as summarized by Shaw et al. [1998]:

When people can locate themselves in the story, their sense of commitment and involvement is enhanced. By conveying a powerful impression of the process of winning, narrative plans can motivate and mobilize an entire organization.

and typically include a plot, major characters, an outcome, and an implied moral. Stories originate within the organization, and typically reflect organizational norms, values, and culture. Because stories make information more vivid, engaging, entertaining, and easily related to personal experience, and because of the rich contextual details encoded in stories, they are the ideal mechanism to capture tacit knowledge [Swap et al., 2001]. Stories have been observed to be useful to capture and communicate organizational managerial systems (how things are done), norms, and values.

Snowden [1999], a long time proponent of storytelling at IBM Corporation, identifies the following set of guidelines for organizational storytelling:

1. Stimulate the natural telling and writing of stories.
2. Stories must be rooted in anecdotal material reflective of the community in question.
3. Stories should not represent idealized behavior.
4. An organizational program to support storytelling should not depend on external experts for its sustenance.
5. Organizational stories are about achieving a purpose, not entertainment.
6. Be cautious of overgeneralizing and forgetting the particulars. What has worked in one organization may not necessarily work in others.
7. Adhere to the highest ethical standards and rules.

Other important considerations in the design of an organizational storytelling program include [Post, 2002]:

1. For storytelling to be effective, people must agree with the idea that this could be an effective means of capturing and transferring tacit organizational knowledge.
2. Identify people in the organization willing to share how they learned from others about how to do their jobs.
3. Metaphors are a way to confront difficult organizational issues.
4. Stories can only transfer knowledge if the listener is interested in learning from them.

In fact, one of the strengths of stories is that they are clearly *episodic* in nature, which means related to events directly experienced. To the extent that the storyteller is able to provide a sufficiently vivid account for the listener to vicariously experience the story, many features of the story are encoded in the listener's memory and later available for retrieval [Swap et al., 2001]. In fact, the relatively recent emphasis on the use of case studies at most business schools is related to the effectiveness of stories as a pedagogical tool. Much like case studies, Denning [2000], who is best known for his efforts to implement communities of practice and storytelling at the World Bank, describes the importance of **springboard stories.** Springboard stories enable a leap in understanding by the audience to grasp how an organization may change, by visualizing from a story in one context what is involved in large-scale organizational transformations. Springboard stories are told from the perspective of a protagonist who was in a predicament, which may resemble the predicament currently faced by the organization.

An interesting question is what role does storytelling play with respect to analytical thinking. Denning [2000] supports the argument that storytelling supplements analytical thinking by enabling us to imagine new perspectives and new worlds. He sees storytelling as ideally suited to communicating change and stimulating innovation, because abstract analysis is easier to understand when seen through the lens of a well-chosen story and can of course be used to make explicit the implications of a story.

Finally, Denning [2000] describes the organizational areas where storytelling can be effective, including:

1. ***Igniting action in knowledge-era organizations.*** Storytelling can help managers and employees to actively think about the implications of change and the opportunities for the future of their organization. Listeners actively understand what it would be like if things were done a different way, re-creating the idea of change as an exciting and living opportunity for growth.

2. ***Bridging the knowing–doing gap.*** This view proposes that storytelling can exploit the interactive nature of communication, by encouraging the listener to imagine the story and to live it vicariously as a participant. Listeners perceive and act on the story as part of their identity.

3. ***Capturing tacit knowledge.*** Probably this line of reasoning is best captured in Denning's [2000] words: "Storytelling provides a vehicle for conveying tacit knowledge, drawing on the deep-flowing streams of meaning, and of patterns of primal narratives of which the listeners are barely aware, and so catalyzes visions of a different and renewed future."

4. ***Embodying and transferring knowledge.*** A simple story can communicate a complex multidimensional idea, by actively involving listeners in the creation of the idea in the context of their own organization.

5. ***Fostering innovation.*** Innovation is triggered by the interrelatedness of ideas. Storytelling enables listeners to easily absorb and relate knowledge, the same spark that triggers innovation.

6. ***Launching and nurturing communities.*** In many large organizations, the formation of communities of practice enables the grouping of professionals who come together voluntarily to share similar interests and learn from each other. These communities of practice may be known under different names: *thematic groups* (World Bank), *learning communities* or *learning networks* (Hewlett-Packard), best *practice teams* (Chevron), and *family groups* (Xerox). Denning explains how a storytelling program provides a natural methodology for nurturing communities and integrating them to the organization's strategy and structure because:

   a. Storytelling builds trust, enabling knowledge seekers in a community to learn from knowledge providers, through the sharing of candid dialogue.

   b. Storytelling unlocks passion, because it enables the members of the community to commit passionately to a common purpose, whether that is the engineering design of a new artifact or the sharing of discovery of a new medical remedy.

   c. Storytelling is nonhierarchical, because storytelling is collaborative, with the members of the community pooling resources to jointly create the story.

7. ***Enhancing technology.*** Most people agree that e-mail has made increasing demands in our lives, resulting in the expectation that we are available 24-7[3] to

---

[3]A term borrowed from the e-business domain, meaning 24 hours a day, each day of the week.

answer electronic requests that span from office memos to virtual garbage mail. Communities of practice and storytelling can enable us to interact with our neighbors and remain connected when we want to, providing us with "tranquility yet connectedness."

8. ***Individual growth.*** The world of storytelling is one that proposes avoiding adversarial contests, and win–win for all sides: the knowledge seeker and the knowledge provider.

## ❖ ❖ ❖ Techniques for Organizing and Using Stories in the Organization

The power of narratives or stories as a knowledge capture mechanism in an organization lies in the fact that narratives capture both the knowledge content as well as its context, and the social networks that define the way "things are done around here." To capture organizational knowledge through narratives, it is best to encourage storytelling in a work context. In addition to the knowledge elicitation techniques presented in Chapter 10, in this chapter we present knowledge elicitation techniques pertaining specifically to stories.

One technique described by Snowden [2000] for narrative knowledge capture is **anthropological observation,** or the use of naïve interviewers, citing an example where they used a group of school children to understand the knowledge flows in an organization. The children were naïve, therefore they asked innocent and unexpected questions, which caused the subjects to naturally volunteer their anecdotes; and they were also curious, which resulted in a higher level of knowledge elicitation.

Snowden also describes a second technique, **storytelling circles,** formed by groups having a certain degree of coherence and identity, such as a common experience in a project. Storytelling circles are best recorded on video. Certain methods can be used for eliciting anecdotes such as:

1. **Dit-spinning,** or *fish tales,* represent human tendencies to escalate or improve the stories shared previously.
2. Alternative histories are fictional anecdotes that could have different turning points, based, for example, on a particular project's outcome.
3. Shifting character or context are fictional anecdotes where the characters may be shifted to study the new perspective of the story.
4. Indirect stories allow disclosing the story with respect to fictional characters, so that any character similarities with the real life character are considered to be pure coincidence.
5. **Metaphors** provide common references for the group, to a commonly known story, cartoon, or movie.

Once a number of stories have been elicited and captured, the next problem is how the narratives are to be stored so people can find them. **Narrative databases** can be indexed by the theme of the story, by the **stakeholders** of the story, or by **archetypal** characters. The theme could be, for example, innovative stories. The stakeholders could be the scientists, the marketing group, or the customers. The archetypal characters represent well-known characters that represent a virtue, for example, the good father archetype represented by Bill Cosby in his role as Dr. Cliff Huxtable.

## ❖❖ ❖ Designing the Knowledge Capture System

Typically the documentation available in organizations is the result of applying expertise, instead of expertise itself. For example, radiologists interpreting high-precision functional images of the heart have the results of their diagnoses captured in documents, but the reasoning process by which they reach their diagnoses is not usually captured. In addition, consider the process of engineering for complex systems. Traditional methods for documenting and representing the engineered designs include creating engineering drawings, specifications, and computer-aided design (CAD) models. Often the decisions leading to the design choices, including the assumptions, constraints, and considerations, are not captured. Capturing these decisions not only is important, but also may lead to a more useful representation of the design, specifically when designing complex systems in an environment characterized by high uncertainty.

Knowledge elicitation techniques (Chapter 10) have been studied and used extensively in AI for the development of expert systems (Chapter 8). The purpose of these techniques is to assist the knowledge elicitation process, based on interview sessions between a knowledge engineer (KE) and the domain expert, with the goal of jointly constructing an expertise model. Although computers may understand the resulting expertise models, these models may not directly meet the objective of capturing and preserving the expert's knowledge so it can be transferred to others, in other words, so others can learn from it.

In the next sections we discuss how technology can facilitate capturing the knowledge of experts. We describe two such systems, based on different methodologies and intelligent technologies. The first system, discussed in the next two sections, is based on the use of concept maps as a knowledge-modeling tool. Then we describe the second system, which is based on the use of **context-based reasoning (CxBR)** to simulate human behavior. Each of these systems is best suited for certain specific situations. For example, the use of **concept maps** may be best suited to capture the knowledge of experts when supporting educational settings. On the other hand, CxBR is best suited to capture the tactical knowledge of experts, which requires assessing the situation, selecting a plan of action, and acting on the plan. Both of these knowledge capture systems can then be used to construct simulation models of human behavior.

## ❖❖ ❖ Knowledge Representation through the Use of Concept Maps

One type of knowledge capture system that we describe in the next section is based on the use of concept maps as a knowledge-modeling tool. Concept maps, developed by Novak [Novak and Gowin, 1984; Novak, 1998], aim to represent knowledge through *concepts,* enclosed in circles or boxes of some types, which are related via connecting lines, or **propositions.** Concepts are perceived regularities in events or objects that are designated by a label.

In the simplest form, a concept map contains just two concepts connected by a linking word to form a single proposition, also called a **semantic unit** or *unit of meaning.* For example, Figure 14-1 is a concept map that describes the structure of concept maps. Based on the concept map represented in Figure 14-1, the two concepts—*concept maps*

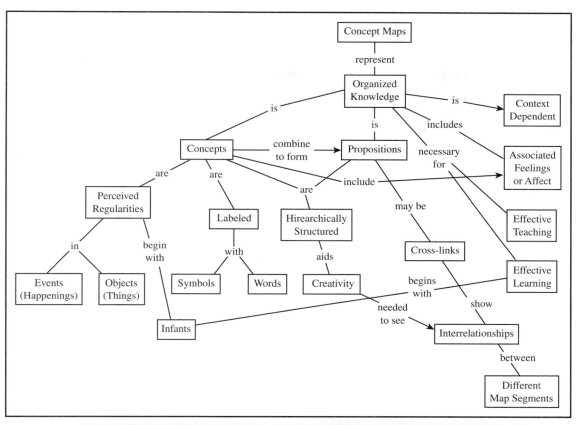

◇ ◇ ◇  **FIGURE 14-1** Concept Map about Concept Maps

*[Source: Novak].*

and *organized knowledge*—are linked together to form the proposition: *concept maps represent organized knowledge*. Additional propositions expand the meaning of concept maps, such as *concepts are hierarchically structured*.

In a concept map, the vertical axis expresses a hierarchical framework for organizing the concepts. More general, inclusive concepts are found at the top of the map, with progressively more specific, less inclusive concepts arranged below them. These maps emphasize the most general concepts by linking them to supporting ideas with propositions. Concept maps represent meaningful relationships between concepts in the form of propositions. In addition, relationships between concepts (propositions) in different domains of the concept map are defined as *cross-links*. These cross-links help to visualize how different knowledge domains are related to each other.

Sometimes the difference between concept maps and semantic networks could be a source of confusion. Semantic networks, also called associative networks, are typically represented as a directed graph, connecting the nodes (representing concepts) to show a relationship or association between them. This type of associative networks can be useful in describing, for example, traffic flow, in that the connections between concepts indicate direction, but directed graphs do not connect concepts through propositions. Furthermore, in a directed graph there is no assumption about the progression of generality to more specific concepts as the nodes are traversed from the top of the network. The same holds true for associative networks in general.

Concept maps were developed based on Ausubel's [1963] learning psychology theory. Ausubel's cognitive psychology research provides us with the understanding that learning takes place through the assimilation of new concepts and propositions into existing concept frameworks by the learner. Ausubel's studies uncovered the conditions for meaningful learning to include (1) a clear presentation of the material, (2) the learner's relevant prior knowledge, and (3) the learner's motivation to integrate new meanings into prior knowledge. Concept maps can be useful in meeting the conditions for learning by identifying concepts prior to instruction, building new concept frameworks, and integrating concept maps through cross-links.

In educational settings, concept-mapping techniques have been applied to many fields of knowledge. The rich expressive power of these techniques derives from each map's ability to allow its creator the use of a virtually unlimited set of linking words to show how meanings have been developed. Consequently, maps having similar concepts can vary from one context to another. Also, concept maps may be used to measure a particular person's knowledge about a given topic in a specific context. Concept maps can help formalize and capture an expert's domain knowledge in an easy to understand representation of an expert's domain knowledge. Figure 14-2 shows a segment of a concept map from the domain of nuclear cardiology.

## ◇ ◇ ◇ Knowledge Capture Systems Based on Concept Maps

To accompany the discussions presented in this section, please refer to the **CmapTools** demo found in the CD included with this book.

The goal of CmapTools,[4] a concept map-based browser, is to capture the knowledge of experts. The navigation problem, an important concern in hypermedia systems, is alleviated by the use of concept maps, which serve to guide in the traversing of logical linkages among clusters of related objects. The CmapTools extend the use of concept maps beyond knowledge representation, to serve as the browsing interface to a domain of knowledge.

Figure 14-3 shows the concept map-based browser as the interface for the explanation subsystem of a nuclear cardiology expert system [Ford et al., 1996]. Each of the concept nodes represents an abstraction for a specific cardiology pathology, which is fully described by the icons at the concept node. For the cardiologist, the image results of a nuclear medicine radionuclide ventriculogram[5] scan resembling a picture of

---

[4]CmapTools can be downloaded for free from cmap.coginst.uwf.edu/index.html

[5]This is a medical procedure to assess how well the heart is beating when at rest and also when exercising. It is also known as MUGA test. During the test, a small amount of radioactive material is injected into the patient so pictures can be taken of the blood in the heart. Experienced cardiologists are able to detect pathological conditions by abstracting a familiar shape from this image, which may resemble *asymmetric blue fingers*, a *ballerina's foot*, or an *ice cream cone*.

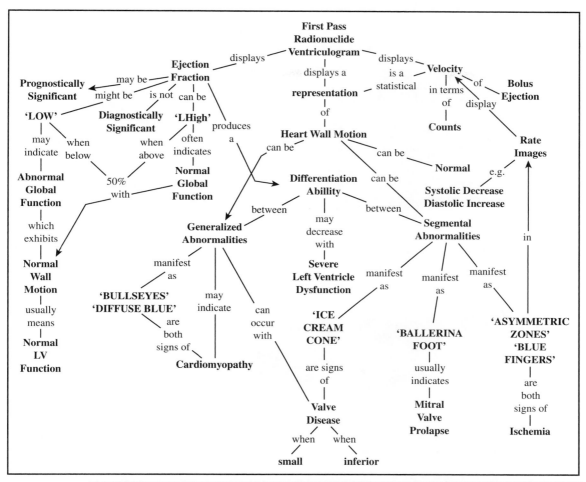

**◇ ◇ ◇   FIGURE 14-2  A Segment of a Concept Map from the Domain of Nuclear Cardiology**

*Source: Ford et al. [1996].*

*asymmetric blue fingers* (later depicted in Figure 14-4) is a sign of myocardial ischemia, or chronic heart failure. An image resembling a *ballerina foot* is usually a representation of a mitral valve prolapse. Clearly, the first patient needs to be quickly rushed to a hospital for emergency surgery, whereas the second may be given medication and a diet to relieve the symptoms.

The icons below the concept nodes provide access to auxiliary information that helps explain the concepts in the form of pictures, images, audio–video clips, text, Internet links, or other concept maps related to the topic. These linked media resources and concept maps can be located anywhere on the Internet [Ford et al., 1996].

The browser provides a window showing the hierarchical ordering of maps, highlights the current location of the user in the hierarchy, and permits movement to any

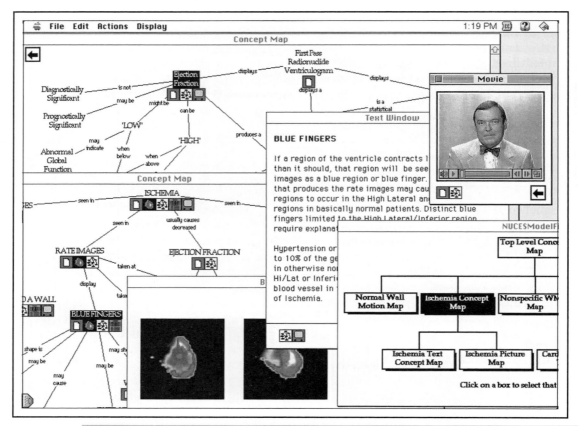

◆‹› ◆‹› ◆‹›  **FIGURE 14-3** Segment of a Concept Map from the Domain of Nuclear Cardiology, Represented Using Cmap Tools

*Source: Ford et al. [1996].*

other map by clicking on the desired map in the hierarchy. This concept map-based interface provides a unique way of organizing and browsing knowledge about any domain.

CmapTools provides a practical application of the idea of utilizing concept maps to capture and formalize knowledge resulting in context-rich knowledge representation models that can be viewed and shared through the Internet. CmapTools takes advantage of the richness provided by multimedia, providing an effective platform for aspiring students to learn from subject matter experts.

Concept maps provide an effective methodology to organize and structure the concepts representing the expert's domain knowledge. During the knowledge capture process, the KE and domain expert interact to collaboratively construct a shared conceptual model of the domain, which eventually becomes the concept map for the multimedia system. Users later browse this conceptual model through CmapTools. Browsing enables the learner to implicitly gain the expert's view of the domain. In general, this model for knowledge representation provides a broad view of the domain as understood by that particular domain expert.

Links in concept maps are explicitly labeled arcs, and usually connect two concepts to form a concept–link–concept relation that may be read as a simple proposition. CmapTools users learn about the domain by clicking on the small icons depicted at the nodes in the concept map and directly navigate to other contexts (or *subcontexts*) through hyperlinks, where other concepts are described. Figure 14-4 shows some of the different media windows opened from the windows in Figure 14-3.

Another advantage of using concept maps for knowledge representation is that, because of their hierarchical organization, concept maps can easily scale to large quantities of information. This particular characteristic can then enable the easy integration of domain concepts together.

In summary, concept-mapping tools, such as CmapTools, can be an effective way to capture and represent the knowledge of domain experts in representation models that can later be used by potential students of the domain. Practically speaking, the

❖❖ ❖❖ ❖❖  **FIGURE 14-4** Explanation Subsystem Based on the Concept Map in Figure 14-2

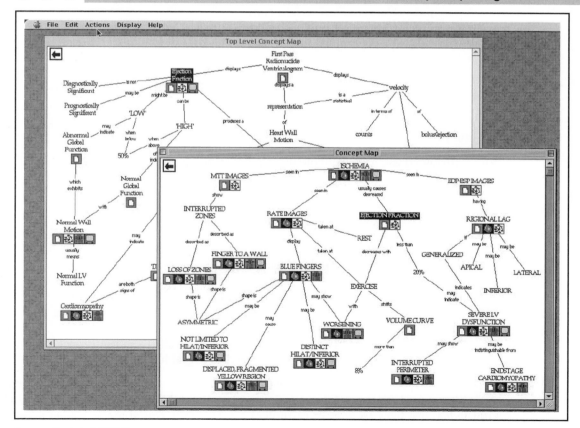

*Source: Ford et al. [1996].*

knowledge representation models illustrated in the previously mentioned Figures 14-2 to 14-4 could be used by students in the field of cardiology, to effectively learn the practical aspects of the domain from one of the best experts in the field.

## ❖❖❖ Knowledge Representation through the Use of Context-Based Reasoning

Recall from Chapter 2 that tactical knowledge is defined as pertaining to the short-term positioning of the organization relative to its markets, competitors, and suppliers and is contrasted to **strategic knowledge,** which pertains to the long-term positioning of the organization in terms of its corporate vision and strategies for achieving that vision. In the context of this example, tactical knowledge refers to the human ability that enables domain experts to assess the situation at hand (therefore short term) among myriad of inputs, to select a plan that best addresses the current situation, and to execute that plan [Gonzalez and Ahlers, 1998; Thorndike and Wescort, 1984]. Consider the following scenario:

> The commanding officer of the submarine is generally bombarded with a multitude of inputs when performing his job. He receives audio inputs such as engine noise, electronic noise, and conversations with others around him. He likewise receives visual inputs such as the radar and sonar screens, possibly the periscope, and tactile inputs such as vibrations of the submarine. He is able to cognitively handle these inputs rather easily when they are all in the normal expected range. However, if one of these should deviate from normal, such as abnormal noise and vibrations, the officer immediately focuses only on these inputs to recognize the present situation as, for instance, a potential grounding, collision, or engine malfunction. All other inputs received, meanwhile, are generally ignored during the crisis.

Alternatively, consider an example more relevant to our daily lives:

> The daily routine drive to and from work is marked by myriad of inputs while performing the task. Dads driving to work with their children receive audio inputs, such as the noise from babies, siblings vying for attention, pop music, their spouse's conversation, and who could forget, the cellular phone. In addition, he receives visual inputs like the gas gauge level (typically empty at this time), traffic signals (including those marking school zones), and the all too familiar police strobe lights. He is able to cognitively handle these inputs (even in the absence of coffee) when they are in the normal (albeit borderline chaotic) range. However, if any of these should deviate from normal (e.g., the strobe signal from police following the car, signaling to the driver that perhaps he has committed an infraction and needs to immediately pull over), at this point all other signals (including the screaming children) are ignored during the crisis at hand.

Tactical experts recognize and treat only the salient features of the situation, and thus are able to abstract a small, but important portion of the available inputs for general knowledge. Just like the nuclear cardiologist in Figure 14-3 is able to abstract a heart pathology that he describes as blue fingers, the commanding officer is able to abstract and treat the key features of the situation at hand, and act based on these features. CxBR helps to model this behavioral phenomenon. CxBR is based on the following basic tenets [Gonzalez and Ahlers, 1993]:

1. A tactical situation calls for a set of actions and procedures that properly address the current situation. In the case of a driver, for example, these actions could include maintaining the car in its proper lane, stopping at a stop sign, and not exceeding the speed limit (by much). The set of actions and procedures is described as the context.

2. As the situation evolves, a transition to another context, or set of actions and procedures, may be required to address the new situation. For example, when a driver exits an interstate highway onto a city street, a different set of functions and procedures are necessary to manage this new situation. In addition, one must be aware of cross traffic, traffic lights, etc. that would not have to be considered when driving on an interstate highway.

3. What is likely to happen in a context or current situation is limited by the context itself. Continuing with the same example, one would not have to worry about operating the cruise control while waiting at a traffic light. However, that could be a potential action while driving on the interstate.

CxBR encapsulates knowledge about appropriate actions or procedures, as well as compatible new situations, into hierarchically organized contexts. A sample hierarchy is depicted in Figure 14-5.

The *mission context* defines the scope of the mission, its goals, the plan, and the constraints imposed (time, weather, etc). The *main context* contains functions, rules, and lists of compatible subsequent main contexts. Identification of a new situation can be simplified because only a limited number of all situations are possible under the currently active context. Subcontexts are abstractions of functions performed by

 **FIGURE 14-5** Context Hierarchy

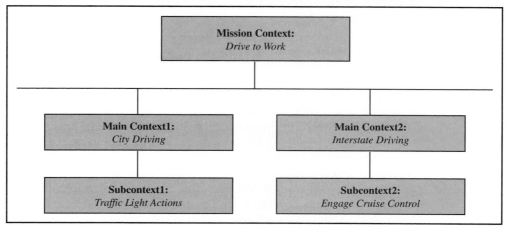

*Source: Gonzalez et al. [2002].*

the main context that may be too complex for one function, or that may be employed by other main contexts. This encourages reusability. Subcontexts are activated by rules in the active main context. They deactivate themselves on completion of their actions.

Decisions are heavily influenced by a sequence of main contexts, each of which, when active, controls behavior of an autonomous vehicle agent (either real or simulated) with an expectation for the future. Active main contexts change in response not only to external events or circumstances but also to actions taken by the agent itself. One example of a main context could be driving in city traffic, called *city driving.* Such a context would contain functions to maintain the vehicle on the road at a speed not to exceed the speed limit, know-how to handle intersections, pedestrians, school zones, etc. The context could call subcontexts to help it deal with traffic lights, school zones, and emergency vehicles.

One and only one specific main context is always active for each agent, making it the sole controller of the agent. When the situation changes, a transition to another main context may be required to properly address the emerging situation. For example, the automobile may enter an interstate highway, requiring a transition to another main context, called *interstate driving.* Transitions between contexts are triggered by events in the environment—some planned, others unplanned. Expert performers are able to recognize and identify the transition points quickly and effectively.

Any situation, by its very nature, can limit the number of other situations that can realistically follow. Therefore, only a limited number of things can be expected to happen within any one context. Using the domain of driving an automobile, a tire blowout is typically not expected while idling at a traffic light. However, getting rear-ended is a definite possibility. The converse is true when driving on an interstate highway. This can be used as an advantage in pruning the search space of the problem, because there is no need to monitor the simulation for blowouts when the driver is in the traffic light subcontext. If unexpected occurrences take place, they introduce the element of surprise into the agent's behavior, which is highly consistent with actual human behavior.

CxBR has proved to be a very intuitive, efficient, and effective representation technique for human behavior. As such, it provides the important hierarchical organization of contexts. Additionally, it has the ability to incorporate any programming paradigm within the control activity (e.g., neural networks, described in Chapter 12, have been used as subcontexts). The presence of a mission context to define the mission and provide global performance modifiers is also a notable difference. CxBR provides the ability to perform complex reasoning to dictate the transitions between main contexts if necessary for the application. Transitions can be coded through the use of rules (described in Chapter 8). This flexibility and representational richness distinguishes CxBR not only from the traditional state transition paradigms but also from other commonly used modeling paradigms for human behavior. CxBR can be used to adequately capture and represent tactical knowledge. Potential applications include the capture and representation of the knowledge of airline pilots and of air traffic controllers. In addition, it can serve to capture and represent the knowledge of commercial and bus drivers, as well as of subway and train engineers. Finally, CxBR can serve to represent knowledge related to military affairs. A full description of CxBR can be found in Gonzalez and Ahlers [1998].

#  Knowledge Capture Systems Based on Context-Based Reasoning

To accompany the discussions presented in this section, please refer to the **context-based intelligent tactical knowledge acquisition (CITKA)** demo found in the CD included with this book.

As we discussed in Chapter 10, eliciting the knowledge of experts is primarily done through detailed interview sessions with the subject matter expert by a knowledge engineer (KE). Furthermore, the success of the knowledge elicitation process depends on many nontechnical factors, such as the expert's personality, the KE's experience, and their preparation. Ultimately, one of the goals of the field of AI, which still remains unachieved, is to be able to build an expert's cognitive model directly via a query session between the expert and the intelligent system. Clearly, the advantages of accomplishing this would be many, most importantly the dramatic reduction in manpower required to capture the knowledge of experts, and a significant reduction in the logical errors coded in the system.

Because of its hierarchical and modular nature, CxBR lends itself well to automating the knowledge capture process. We describe a knowledge capture system based on CxBR known as CITKA. CITKA uses its own knowledge base to compose a set of intelligent queries to elicit the tactical knowledge of the expert.

CITKA composes questions and presents them to the expert. The questions are designed to elicit tactical knowledge and represent it in the underlying CxBR paradigm. On responding to the questions, the result is a nearly complete context base, which when used with a CxBR reasoning engine can be used to control someone performing the mission of interest in a typical environment (e.g., driving from New York to Boston, or flying an airplane from Houston to Dallas). CITKA can be used by the expert or the KE. It is likely that both may need to use it to complete the context base. The query sessions only take place with the expert. The KE is given direct edit access to the context base. Let us now look at how CITKA works.

The CITKA system consists of four modules of independent but cooperating subsystems. These modules are:

1. *Knowledge engineering database back-end (KEDB).* This is a data structure that holds the evolving context base as it gradually becomes developed, either by the KE or by the subject matter expert. The KEDB is subject to the hierarchical structure of mission, main, and subcontexts imposed by CxBR. To implement these data structures, a table is created for each context type.
2. *Knowledge engineering interface (KEI).* Maps into the KEDB module. Data entry in the KEI is provided by eight interacting dialogs: mission context, main contexts, subcontexts, entity objects, helping functions, memory variables, transition criteria, and action definitions. The KEI is designed in a table-driven fashion.
3. *Query rule-base back-end (QRB).* A rule-based system containing the rules for executing the intelligent dialog with the **subject matter expert (SME).** A rule is provided for each SME interface input screen. These query rules have to be mapped to buttons, checkboxes, and menus by the SME interface.
4. *Subject matter expert interface (SMEI).* The GUI for the QRB. This environment allows a great deal of flexibility: the SMEI dynamically produces interfaces that correspond to the questions and rules that are put forth in the QRB.

The CITKA system was evaluated for its effectiveness. There were two main issues: (1) estimating the reduction in person-hour effort to develop a context-based model for a particular mission, and (2) estimating the percentage of a context-based model that could conceivably be automatically developed through CITKA. The prototype was tested on a nontrivial mission, for a submarine to monitor a port and protect surface assets against underwater threats emanating from the monitored port. This context base was first developed through the traditional interview methods, and the hours spent developing it were carefully documented. It was then estimated how long it would take to develop the same model with the CITKA tool. Its developers report that there could be as much as an 80% reduction in person-hour effort to build with a context-based system as compared with the current manual means [Gonzalez et al., 2002]. Furthermore, they estimate that 50% to 80% of the context-based model could be developed directly through a query session in CITKA.

## ❖ ❖ ❖  Barriers to the Use of Knowledge Capture Systems

This section discusses the barriers to the deployment of knowledge capture systems from two perspectives. The first perspective describes that of KEs who seek to build such systems. The second perspective is that of subject matter experts, who would interact with an automated knowledge capture system to preserve their knowledge. First, let us consider the barriers to the development of knowledge capture systems.

As we discuss at the beginning of this chapter, there are two possible mechanisms to capture the knowledge of experts. The first mechanism is to simply ask the expert, through a knowledge elicitation process (described in Chapter 10) that must be properly managed to maximize the results of the process. This is the essence of the externalization process. The second mechanism is to observe a person's behavior or performance while they're executing their tasks. This method, *learning by observation*, is essentially the internalization process. Perhaps in the near future, we may be able to connect a device to a person's brain that could sense and capture the neural firings of the brain that constitute expertise, but clearly this is not yet a possibility. Undoubtedly, this futuristic possibility raises a host of ethical considerations as well. In fact, this possibility would clearly contradict the essence of KM that we describe in Chapter 1; that is, KM should not distance itself from the knowledge owners, but instead should celebrate and recognize their positions as experts in the organization.

One of the largest barriers to the automatic elicitation of expert's knowledge is that to effectively accomplish this task, the KE requires developing some idea of the *nature* and *structure* of the knowledge very early in the process. In Chapter 10, we discuss how KEs must attempt to become versed in the subject matter, or the nature of knowledge, prior to the interview process. Familiarization with the structure of knowledge is an additional requirement, often a fairly difficult proposition in the sense that the interviewer must quickly develop some idea of which paradigm would best represent the knowledge at hand. For example, while conducting the expert interviews, the KE observes that the expert's knowledge is very conditional; in other words, the expert describes it as "*if A then B*," this would be a good indication that the expert's knowledge would best be represented as rules. If the expert describes the knowledge in terms of connections, in other words, "*A* is related to *B*, *B* is related to *C*" (as in describing an architecture), then perhaps the most adequate representation is the concept map paradigm. Furthermore, if the expert's knowledge is based on recollections, such as "I remember when one such instance happened," then CBR is the most likely alternative. If experts describe their knowledge based on a schedule of events, "this happens on *A* after *B* event," then a constraint-based paradigm may be the best alternative. Finally, if the expert's knowledge is described in tactical terms, such as "how to drive a car," then CxBR would be the best representation.

Only if interviewers are able to develop an idea of the nature of knowledge early in the process, can they adequately represent it. In theory, we could replace the KE by an intelligent knowledge capture system that would develop a set of questions to adequately elicit the knowledge of the subject matter expert. The system would need to know the nature and structure of the knowledge, and how to ask such questions accordingly. In other words, the intelligent knowledge capture system and the expert would need to be in tune with each other. This is several generations ahead of the CmapTools and CITKA systems described above. On the other hand, if the end result is only to elicit the expert's knowledge to capture it in a document or a story, the structure requirement may not be necessary.

In summary, developing an automated system for knowledge capture, without *a priori* knowledge of the nature and structure of the knowledge in question, is essentially not possible. Furthermore, developing a multiparadigm tool, which could essentially define the appropriate knowledge capture technique, is almost impossible. The knowledge acquisition process must be tailored to the specific type of knowledge, and making that assessment ahead of time could be difficult.

From the point of view of the expert, who may be faced with the task of interacting with the knowledge capture system, this may pose additional barriers. The first one is that the expert needs to take the initiative of learning how to interact with the system, and may need to be coached through the first few sessions until reaching a certain comfort level with the technology. Naturally, some people may be resistant to trying new things, and the proposition of interacting with a machine may be one that many experts may not necessarily look forward to. This barrier can be overcome, with adequate training and the utilization of user-friendly interfaces. In the area of user interfaces, current research examines the impact that *talking heads*, even those that could portray emotion, could play on the user's feeling of ease with the technology.

## ◇ ◇ ◇ Research Trends: Using Learning by Observation to Capture Knowledge

In this section we discuss some research trends about how learning by observation could be used to capture knowledge. Without a doubt, humans and many animals, learn first by observation. Infants learn their language, what foods to eat and avoid, and what the signs of danger are, including distinguishing prey from predators. Many animals have been shown to learn by observation, including chimpanzees, dolphins, and some bird species. Research on how humans and animals learn through observation has been one important area of study in AI.

Just as humans can learn by observing others perform a task, robots could improve their effectiveness by doing the same thing. Providing robots with such ability implies they would need to be equipped with vision. In addition, the movements required for a specific task would need to be encoded to train the robot. Exact emulation of human movement has been happening since the 1970s. For example, a human could take a robot that paints automobile parts through the motions, and it could easily replicate exactly the same exact motions thereafter. What is much harder for the robot is to "understand" why the human is doing each task, so that it can extrapolate the learned tasks to slightly different situations. For example, if a robot has to only paint the doorknob in a door forthcoming on the assembly line, as long as the doorknob is in exactly the same location every time, learning dumb moves suffices. However, if the location of the doorknob varies with each door, and the robotic painting arm must look for it and paint it wherever it is, that is more difficult. Even more difficult is to understand when a door comes along that does not have doorknobs, which means the robot should not paint anything at all. Clearly the benefits for the robot arm to learn by observation would be significant, because it would allow the shortening of learning time, while decreasing the required programming effort.

Many recent developments in AI include the use of learning through observation to automate the knowledge acquisition task. For example, Sammut et al. [1992] used learning by observation (which they term as *behavioral cloning*) to obtain the knowledge required to fly a Cessna, through observation of a human using a flight simulator to fly a predefined flight plan. In their research, observation logs were kept from a large set of training examples that recorded the sensor inputs and appropriate actions, which were used to create decision trees describing the pilot's behavior. Also Pomerleau et al. [1994] developed an autonomous vehicle driving system that he titled Autonomous Land Vehicle in a Neural Network (ALVINN), using neural networks that were trained by observing how human drivers responded to diverse driving environments. ALVINN was trained to drive in a variety of conditions, including single-lane paved and unpaved roads; multilane roads; obstacle ridden on-road and off-road environments; and even under adverse environmental conditions like rain and snow, at speeds up to 55 mph. Wang [1995] also described another system that learned to produce machine parts through observation. OBSERVER recorded each step the expert performed to generate the machine part, and had the ability to learn operator preconditions and the corresponding actions for each step, even refining its actions through practice. Sidani and Gonzalez [1995] also captured the behavior of an expert automobile driver by observing the driver's actions in a simulated task. In their work, Sidani and Gonzalez built a system based on neural networks and symbolic reasoning that learned by observing the expert driver's behavior. The system successfully operated a car in a traffic light as well as in the presence of a pedestrian crossing in front of the vehicle. Later van Lent and Laird [1999] defined a system they called OBSERVO-SOAR, which combined behavioral cloning with OBSERVER's behavioral representation, to learn effectively in complex and dynamic domains, such as a flight simulator domain.

Learning by observation is beginning to show promise as a technique that may enable the automatic capture of expert's knowledge, in a format that enables computers to automatically learn. Although these systems are still in their infancy, the early success of these systems has proved the possibility of capturing knowledge from experts, through nonintrusive interaction and observation of the behavior of the human expert. Perhaps the science fiction idea of plugging in expertise through an electronic socket behind our ears is not such a remote possibility after all. Do you want to be a rocket scientist? Just put on your rocket scientist eyeglasses, and voilà.

## SUMMARY ❖ ❖ ❖

In this chapter you learn about knowledge capture systems, design considerations, and specific types of such systems. Specific attention is placed on the two knowledge capture systems, based on different methodologies and intelligent technologies. The first system is based on the use of concept maps as a knowledge-modeling tool, and is best suited to capture the knowledge of experts when supporting educational settings. The second system is based on the use of CxBR to simulate human behavior, and is best suited to capture the tactical knowledge of experts. Finally, the use of stories in organizational settings is discussed as a mechanism that can support knowledge capture.

## KEY TERMS ❖ ❖ ❖

- anthropological observation— p. 283
- archetypal—p. 283
- concept maps—p. 284
- CmapTools—p. 286
- Context-Based Intelligent Tactical Knowledge Acquisition (CITKA)—p. 293
- context-based reasoning (CxBR)—p. 284
- dit-spinning—p. 283
- metaphor—p. 283
- narrative databases—p. 283
- organizational stories—p. 279
- propositions—p. 284
- semantic unit—p. 284
- springboard stories—p. 281
- stakeholders—p. 283
- storytelling—p. 278
- storytelling circles—p. 283
- strategic knowledge—p. 290
- subject matter expert (SME)— p. 293

## REVIEW QUESTIONS ❖ ❖ ❖

1. What is a concept map?
2. What is context-based reasoning (CxBR)?
3. How would you describe the domains that are best suited to be captured by concept maps vs. CxBR?
4. Describe the two techniques for knowledge elicitation via the use of stories.
5. What types of knowledge can be acquired through automated knowledge by observation?

## APPLICATION EXERCISES ❖ ❖ ❖

1. Pick a sample domain of which you are knowledgeable and build a concept map to represent that domain.
2. Define using context-based hierarchy, the main contexts and subcontexts of the mission context that describes your particular driving pattern from home to work each day.
3. Define the rules that may cause the switch between main contexts and subcontexts in the previously mentioned context hierarchy.
4. Describe a story that adequately embodies your organization's corporate culture.
5. Describe a specific type of knowledge that could adequately be captured through automated knowledge by observation.

## REFERENCES ◆ ◆ ◆

Ausubel, D.P. 1963. *The Psychology of Meaningful Verbal Learning.* Grune & Stratton, New York.

Cañas, A.J., Coffey, J., Reichherzer, T., Suri, N., and Carff, R. 1997. El-Tech: A Performance Support System with Embedded Training for Electronics Technicians. 11th Florida Artificial Intelligence Research Symp., Sanibel Island, FL, May.

Denning, S. 2000. *The Springboard: How Storytelling Ignites Action in Knowledge-Era Organizations.* Butterworth-Heinemann, Boston.

Ford, K.M., Cañas, A.J., Jones, J., Stahl, H., Novak, J., and Adams-Weber, J. 1991. ICONKAT: An integrated constructivist knowledge acquisition tool. *Knowledge Acquisition,* 3, 215–236.

Ford, K.M., Coffey, J.W., Cañas, A.J., Andrews, E.J., and Turner, C.W. 1996. Diagnosis and explanation by a nuclear cardiology expert system. *International Journal of Expert Systems,* 9, 499–506.

Gonzalez, A.J., and Ahlers, R.H. 1993. Concise Representation of Autonomous Intelligent Platforms in a Simulation through the Use of Scripts. Proc. 6th Annual Florida Artificial Intelligence Research Symp., Ft. Lauderdale, FL, April.

Gonzalez, A.J., and Ahlers, R. 1998. Context-based representation of intelligent behavior in training simulations. *Transactions of the Society of Computer Simulation,* 15(4), 153–166.

Gonzalez, A.J., Gerber, W.J., and Castro, J. 2002. Automated Acquisition of Tactical Knowledge through Contextualization. Proc. Conf. on Computer Generated Forces and Behavior Representation, Orlando, FL, May.

Gonzalez, A.J., Georgiopoulos, M., DeMara, R.F., Henninger, A.E., and Gerber, W. 1998. Automating the CGF Model Development and Refinement Process by Observing Expert Behavior in a Simulation. Proc. 1998 Computer Generated Forces Conf., Orlando, FL, May.

Martin, J. 1982. Stories and scripts in organizational settings. In Hastorf, A., and Isen, A. (Eds.), *Cognitive Social Psychology.* Elsevier, New York, pp. 255–305.

Novak, J.D., and Gowin, D.B. 1984. *Learning How to Learn.* Cambridge University Press, New York.

Novak, J.D. 1998. *Learning, Creating, and Using Knowledge: Concept Maps as Facilitative Tools in Schools and Corporations.* Lawrence Erlbaum, Hillsdale, NJ.

Novak, J.D. The Theory Underlying Concept Maps and How to Construct Them, available on the Web at cmap.coginst.uwf.edu/info/. Accessed on July, 2003.

Pomerleau, D., Thorpe, D., Longer, J., Rosenblatt, K., and Sukthankar, R. 1994. AVCS Research at Carnegie-Mellon University. Proc. Intelligent Vehicle Highway Systems America 1994, Annual Meeting, pp. 257–262.

Post, T. 2002. The impact of storytelling on NASA and EduTech. *KM Review,* March/April.

Sammut, C., Hurst, S., Kedzier, D., and Michie, D. 1992. Learning to Fly. In Sleeman, D. (Ed.), *Proc. 9th Int. Conf. on Machine Learning.* Morgan Kauffmann, San Francisco, CA, pp. 385–393.

Shaw, G., Brown, R., and Bromiley, P. 1998. Strategic stories: How 3M is rewriting business planning. *Harvard Business Review,* May/June, 41–50.

Sidani, T.A., and Gonzalez, A.J. 1995. IASKNOT: A Simulation-base, Object-oriented Framework for the Acquisition of Implicit Expert Knowledge. Proc. IEEE Int. Conf. on System, Man and Cybernetics, Vancover, Canada, October.

Snowden, D. 1999. Three metaphors, two stories, and a picture. *KM Review,* March/April,

Snowden, D. 2000. The art and science of story or "Are you sitting uncomfortably?" Part 1: Gathering and harvesting the raw material. *Business Information Review,* 17(3), 147–156.

Sternberg, S. 1976. Memory scanning: New findings and current controversies. *Quarterly Journal of Experimental Psychology,* 27, 1–32.

Swap, W., Leonard, D., Shields, M., and Abrams, L. 2001. Using mentoring and storytelling to transfer knowledge in the workplace. *Journal of Management Information Systems,* 18(1), 95–114.

Thorndike, P.W., and Wescourt, K.T. 1984. Modeling Time-Stressed Situation Assessment and Planning for Intelligent Opponent Simulation. Final Technical Report PPAFTR-1124-84-1, Office of Naval Research, July.

Tulving, E. 1983. *Elements of Episodic Memory.* Oxford University Press, New York.

van Lent, M., and Laird, J. 1999. Learning Hierarchical Performance Knowledge by Observation. Proc. 16th Int. Conf. on Machine Learning, Morgan Kaufmann, San Francisco, CA.

Wang, X. 1995. Learning by Observation and Practice: An Incremental Approach for Planning Operator Acquisition. In Proc. 12th Int. Conf. on Machine Learning, Morgan Kauffman, San Francisco, CA

# CHAPTER 15

# Knowledge Sharing Systems

## *Systems That Organize and Distribute Knowledge*

## ◇ ◇ ◇ Introduction

In the last chapter we discuss knowledge capture systems. In this chapter, we consider what knowledge sharing systems are about, how they serve to organize and distribute organizational and individual knowledge, and their makeup; and provide examples of such systems. Knowledge sharing systems are designed to help users share their knowledge, both tacit and explicit. Most of the knowledge management (KM) systems in place at organizations are designed to share the explicit knowledge of individuals and organizations, and these are the focus of this chapter. These systems are also referred to as *knowledge repositories*. In this chapter, we also discuss some guidelines on how to design knowledge sharing systems for practical use. The two types of explicit knowledge sharing systems most widely discussed in the KM literature are lessons learned systems and **expertise-locator (EL) systems;** therefore, this chapter concentrates on those. Systems that support tacit knowledge sharing are those typically utilized by communities of practice (CoPs), particularly those that meet virtually. Finally, we discuss issues about CoPs and how KM systems can support tacit knowledge sharing.

**Corporate memory** (also known as an organizational memory) is made up of the aggregate intellectual assets of an organization. Corporate memory is the combination of both explicit and tacit knowledge that may or may not be explicitly documented, but which is specifically referenced and crucial to the operation and competitiveness of an organization. Knowledge management is concerned with developing applications that prevent the loss of corporate memory. Such loss often results from a lack of appropriate technologies for the organization and exchange of documents, a lack of adequate support for communication, and the proliferation of disparate sources of information. Often this results in the loss of explicit **organizational knowledge.** Another contributing factor to the loss of corporate memory is the departure of employees because of

 VIGNETTE 15-1

## Sharing Knowledge at the World Bank

In 1996 James Wolfensohn, then president of the World Bank,[1] outlined his vision for the *Knowledge Bank,* a partnership for creating and sharing knowledge, and making it a major driver of development. At the World Bank, KM is synonymous with sharing the experiences gained from staff, clients, and development partners; and creating linkages between groups and communities. The World Bank recognizes that "fighting poverty requires a global strategy to share knowledge effectively and to ensure that people who need that knowledge get it on time, whether from the World Bank or others." The World Bank has concentrated its KM efforts in becoming a global development partner, enabling the necessary knowledge exchange within and outside this organization.

Early on, the World Bank developed a matrix structure to combine local country knowledge with world-class technical expertise along five CoPs they called *thematic groups.* This number has subsequently grown to more than 100, and the role of these groups has been to bring together, on-line and face-to-face, experts from within and outside the World Bank, and across all its regions. The World Bank also implemented a number of advisory services that functioned as help desks, as an interface for connecting people and answers. The organization also launched a KM system for the purpose of sharing lessons and best practices.

Other KM initiatives at the World Bank included starting a global knowledge partner-ship conference, linking all its local offices to global communications, and establishing an innovation marketplace to share ideas, talents, and resources that address development challenges. This level of success would not have been accomplished if the organization had not rewarded knowledge sharing, which in 1998 became part of their annual performance evaluation system. In 2000, the World Bank launched the Global Development Learning Network, which provided 17 countries with simultaneous videoconferencing and Internet facilities for distance learning. Also, the World Bank established the Knowledge for Development program to help developing countries better understand how to exploit the knowledge revolution to help reduce poverty. For all its KM efforts, the American Productivity and Quality Center recognized the World Bank as a best practice partner.

Knowledge sharing at the World Bank is now a mainstream activity, which has required significant investments in infrastructure, CoPs, global networks, training, and understanding the role of knowledge in development. As a result, the role of the World Bank is now considered to be catalytic, ensuring effective integration of internal and client knowledge. The World Bank now understands that capacity building is about creating environments in which local and global knowledge can inform action and influence the change necessary to end poverty.

---

[1]www.worldbank.org

either turnover or retirement. The lost knowledge is typically the organization's tacit knowledge. A knowledge sharing system helps to organize and distribute an organization's corporate memory so that it can be accessed even after the original sources of knowledge no longer remain within the organization.

The standard communications medium on which KM applications are based is the World Wide Web (WWW), a medium that facilitates the exchange of information, data, multimedia, and even applications, among multiple distinct computer platforms. This characteristic of the Web is referred to as *platform independence.* Because the Web is pervasive and can interface with different computer platforms through a common user interface, it is often the base on which knowledge sharing systems are created.

For a quick overview of what knowledge sharing systems are and how they are used, let us look at two brief case studies and how these two organizations view knowledge sharing. These vignettes explain how two organizations, the World Bank (Vignette 15-1) and Ernest & Young (Vignette 15-2), successfully introduced knowledge sharing systems to share important knowledge, remain ahead of their competition, and create a knowledge organization.

Clearly, KM plays a significant role at the World Bank, an international organization funded by the governments of 184 countries. Vignette 15-2 discusses some of the KM experiences at a professional services organization, in the business of providing its clients with the knowledge they require to effectively compete and succeed.

E&Y KM initiatives specifically support knowledge sharing. These initiatives earned the firm many accolades for its leadership in KM, in addition to a competitive advantage.

## WHAT ARE KNOWLEDGE SHARING SYSTEMS?

**Knowledge sharing systems** can be described as systems that enable members of an organization to acquire tacit and explicit knowledge from each other. Knowledge sharing systems may also be viewed as *knowledge markets;* just as markets require adequate *liquidity*[2] to guarantee a fair exchange of products, knowledge sharing systems must attract a critical volume of knowledge seekers and knowledge owners to be effective [Dignum, 2002]. In a knowledge sharing system, knowledge owners may:

1. Want to share their knowledge with a controllable and trusted group;
2. Decide when to share and the conditions for sharing;
3. Seek a fair exchange, or reward, for sharing their knowledge.

By the same token, knowledge seekers may:

1. Not be aware of all the possibilities for sharing, thus the knowledge repository typically helping them through searching and ranking.
2. Want to decide on the conditions for knowledge acquisition.

---

[2] Liquidity refers to the number of trades made in the market—the greater the volume of trades, the greater liquidity.

◈ ◈ ◈ ◈ VIGNETTE 15-2 ◈ ◈ ◈ ◈

### Ernst & Young: The Creation of a Knowledge Organization

In 1995, Ernest & Young[3] (E&Y) underwent an important restructuring of its business strategy. This restructuring was designed to facilitate a move toward KM. It included capturing and leveraging knowledge from consulting engagements. Another aspect of the revised strategy was to use knowledge to accelerate the process of providing consulting solutions for clients. This strategy led to the creation of several different KM initiatives within the company.

One such KM initiative was the establishment of the Center for Business Knowledge (CBK), with the goal of harvesting the knowledge of the firm's employees. The CBK served as a library for consulting methods and techniques, as well as documents resulting from client engagements. Moreover, this center was created with the idea of distributing and integrating the knowledge of all the projects. E&Y's CBK used many tools and methods to assist its client-serving professionals. Some of those tools were:

1. *E&Y knowledge Web.* This tool is composed of individual knowledge databases that make up the collective organizational knowledge sharing system

2. *E&Y InfoLink.* This provides all E&Y client-serving and practice support professionals with electronic access to a set of business information products in three different ways:
   a. *Browsing.* This feature puts an electronic newsstand on the desktop of all company personnel.
   b. *Profiling.* This property provides company personnel information on selected topics (involving industries or companies).
   c. *Searching.* The search mode of E&Y InfoLink allows company personnel to initiate database searches to obtain the answers to specific questions.

3. *E&Y knowledge networks.* The E&Y knowledge networks are virtual teams of company personnel who focus exclusively on one area of business and who help ensure that the firm's intellectual capital and solutions are organized and accessible during engagement pursuits.

4. *E&Y knowledge bases.* The CBK is responsible for managing an electronic database to identify specific skills possessed by E&Y consultants.

[3]www.ey.com

A knowledge sharing system is said to define a learning organization, supporting the sharing and reuse of individual and organizational knowledge. Information technology (IT) tools—such as document management systems, groupware, e-mail, databases, and workflow management systems discussed in Chapter 11, and which historically were used for singular unrelated purposes—are now typically integrated into knowledge sharing systems. Although there are benefits of using document management, groupware, and workflow independently of each other, their integration in a knowledge sharing system augments their individual contributions.

Recall from Chapter 11 that one tool frequently emphasized under the auspices of knowledge sharing systems is *document management.* At the core of a document management system is a repository, an electronic storage medium with a primary storage location that affords multiple access points. This repository can be centralized or it can be distributed. Document management builds on the repository by adding support to the classification and organization of information, unifying the actions of storage and retrieval of documents over a platform-independent system. A document management system unifies an aggregate of relevant information through a common interface, typically Web based.

The document management application increases the sharing of documentation across the organization, thus assisting the sharing of organizational knowledge. Documents are typically organized or *indexed* following a standard hierarchical structure or classification taxonomy, much like the index catalog is used to organize the books in a library. Frequently, *portal* technologies are used to build a common entry into multiple distributed repositories, using the analogy of a door as a common entry into the organization's knowledge resources. Portals provide a common user interface, which can often be customized to the user's preferences, such as local news or weather.

Knowledge sharing systems are typically augmented with a collaborative environment. Collaborative environments, or groupware, is software that supports the communication and collaboration of two or more people. Collaborative environments include e-mail, electronic meeting systems such as discussion forums and chat, workflow, and videoconferencing communication technologies. Collaborative environments support the work of teams, which may not necessarily be at the same time or same place. Groupware allows the informal exchange of ideas, increasing organizational communication, and thus allowing the sharing of knowledge. Knowledge management mechanisms, discussed in Chapter 3, facilitate the use of knowledge sharing systems. For example, meetings and CoPs facilitate knowledge sharing, as illustrated in Vignette 15-2 earlier in the chapter. In a later section we also examine the use of KM mechanisms such as CoPs for sharing tacit knowledge.

A workflow tool provides a method for capturing the steps that lead to the completion of a project or a business process within a fixed time frame. In doing so, this tool provides a method for illustrating such steps. As we discussed in Chapter 11, workflow systems can be useful for projects by enacting the elemental tasks, as well as by providing a mechanism, for the analysis and optimization of the entire processes detailing the project. Another benefit of using a workflow system is that it provides the user with an audit of necessary skills and resources needed for the project, prior to project initiation. Workflow systems also provide a template for the replication and reuse of stored processes. Finally, workflow tools can also serve as a training tool because they provide a broad overview with detailed operations of tasks as well as identification of "weak links" in a process to streamline business processes.

In short, knowledge sharing systems integrate the capabilities of document management and collaborative systems along with KM mechanisms. A document management system unifies an aggregate of relevant information through a common, typically Web-based interface. Categorizing and processing organizational information for search and distribution purposes provides a detailed knowledge warehouse. A collaborative environment that includes workflow is an effective complement to a platform for sharing knowledge across the organization.

## ◇ ◇ ◇ Designing the Knowledge Sharing System

The main function of a knowledge sharing system is "to enhance the organization's competitiveness by improving the way it manages its knowledge" [Abecker et al., 1998]. The creation of a knowledge sharing system is based on the organization of digital media, including documents, Web-links, and the like, which represent the explicit organizational knowledge. Khun and Abecker [1997] identify the crucial requirements for the success of a knowledge sharing system in industrial practice:

1. *Collection and systematic organization of information from various sources.* Most organizational business processes require information and data including CAD drawings, e-mails, electronic documents such as specifications, and even paper documents. This requisite information may be dispersed and collected throughout the organization.

2. *Minimization of up-front knowledge engineering.* Knowledge sharing systems must take advantage of explicit organizational information and data, such that these systems can be built quickly, generate returns on investment, and adapt to new requirements. This information and data are mostly found in databases and documents.

3. *Exploiting user feedback for maintenance and evolution.* Knowledge sharing systems should concentrate on capturing the knowledge of the organization's members. This includes options for maintenance and user feedback so the knowledge can be kept fresh and relevant. Furthermore, knowledge sharing systems should be designed to support user's needs and their business process workflows.

4. *Integration into existing environment.* Knowledge sharing systems must be integrated into an organization's information flow, by integrating with the IT tools currently used to perform the business tasks. Humans, by nature, tend to avoid efforts to formalize knowledge (ever met a computer programmer that enjoys commenting on code?). In fact, as a rule of thumb, if the effort required in formalizing knowledge is too high, it should be left informal to be described by humans and not to be made explicit. For instance, consider the possibility of capturing the "how to" knowledge of how to ride a bicycle. Clearly, an understanding of the laws of physics can help explain why a person stays on the bicycle while it's moving, but few of us recall these laws while we ride. Other than the proverbial "keep your foot on the pedal," which does not explicate much about the riding process, most of us learned to ride a bicycle through hours of practice, and many falls, while we were kids. It would be impractical to try to codify this knowledge and make it explicit. On the other hand, it might be useful to know who's a good bicycle rider, in particular if one is looking to put together a cycling team.

5. *Active presentation of relevant information.* Finally, the goal of an active knowledge sharing system is to present its users with the required information when and wherever it is needed. These systems are envisioned to become intelligent assistants, automatically eliciting and providing knowledge that may be useful in solving the current task, whenever and wherever it's needed.

## ◇ ◇ ◇ Barriers to the Use of Knowledge Sharing Systems

Many organizations, specifically science- and engineering-oriented firms, are characterized by a culture known as the **not-invented-here (NIH) syndrome.** In other words, solutions that are not invented at the organizational subunit are considered worthless. Organizations suffering from this syndrome tend to essentially reward employees for inventing new solutions, instead of reusing solutions developed within and outside the organization. Organizations who foster the NIH syndrome discourage knowledge seekers from participating in the knowledge market, because the organizational rewards are tied to creating knowledge and not necessarily to sharing and applying existing knowledge. Furthermore, organizations that do not reward their experts for sharing their knowledge, or that try to disassociate the knowledge from those that create it may also discourage knowledge owners from participating in the knowledge market. The necessary critical volume can only be accomplished through adequate rewards to both knowledge creators and knowledge seekers to participate in the sharing of knowledge.

One of the impediments to nurturing the human component of KM is the lack of institutionalized reward systems for knowledge sharing in most organizations. Typically, rewards exist at the individual level. When a group is rewarded, the reward is usually tied to contributions in *strong tie networks,* such as when people collaborate as a team to develop a new product. It is much more difficult to reward people who contribute in *weak tie networks,* for example, someone who pops into one discussion group and says something that makes people think a bit differently, but who is not working in those groups on a long-term basis. Thus, organizations with significant intellectual capital recognize the importance of not only capturing knowledge for later reuse but also ensuring that adequate reward systems are in place to encourage the sharing of ideas, and the life-long learning by their employees.

## ◇ ◇ ◇ Specific Types of Knowledge Sharing Systems

Knowledge sharing systems are classified according to their attributes. These specific types of knowledge sharing systems include:

1. Incident report databases
2. Alert systems
3. Best practices databases
4. Lessons-learned (LL) systems
5. Expertise-locator (EL) systems

In this section we briefly describe the differences among the first four systems. Specific attention is placed on the two knowledge sharing systems most frequently discussed in the KM literature: (1) lessons learned systems and (2) expertise locator systems, which are described in detail in later sections of this chapter.

**Incident report databases** are used to disseminate information related to incidents or malfunctions, for example, of field equipment (such as sensing equipment outages) or software (such as bug reports). Incident reports typically describe the incident together with explanations of the incident, although they may not suggest any recommendations. Incident reports are typically used in the context of safety and accident investigations. As an example, the U.S. Department of Energy (DOE) disseminates chemical mishaps through their Chemical Occurrences Web page (www.dne.bnl.gov/etd/csc/).

**Alert systems** were originally intended to disseminate information about a negative experience that has occurred or is expected to occur. However, recent applications also include increasing exposure to positive experiences. Alert systems could be used to report problems experienced with a technology, such as an alert system that issues recalls for consumer products. Alert systems could also be used to share more positive experiences, such as www.thescientificworld.com, which alerts registered users of funding opportunities that match a set of user-specified keywords. Alert systems could be applicable to a single organization or to a set of related organizations that share the same technology and suppliers.

**Best practices databases** describe successful efforts, typically from the reengineering of business processes [O'Leary, 1999] that could be applicable to organizational processes. Best practices differ from lessons learned in that they capture only successful events, which may not be derived from experience. Best practices are expected to represent business practices that are applicable to multiple organizations in the same sector, and are sometimes used to benchmark organizational processes. For example, Microsoft offers a Web page that describes best practices for the use of its products (msdn.microsoft.com/library/), which can provide helpful tips, for example, to prevent database corruption. Also, the Federal Transit Administration publishes a Best Practices Procurement Manual on the Web (www.fta.dot.gov/library/admin/BPPM/). This manual describes procedures and practices for organizations wishing to pursue procurement opportunities with this agency.

With **lessons learned (LL) systems** the goal is "to capture and provide lessons that can benefit employees who encounter situations that closely resemble a previous experience in a similar situation" [Weber et al., 2001]. LL systems could be pure repositories of lessons or sometimes intermixed with other sources of information (e.g., reports). LL systems are typically not focused on a single task (e.g., pure knowledge representations as discussed in Chapter 8). In the future, enhanced document management systems are expected to continue to support distributed project collaborations and their knowledge sources, while actively seeking to capture and reuse lessons from project report archives. We discuss LL systems in detail later.

The differences among these types of knowledge sharing systems are based on:

- *Content origin.* Does the content originate from experience as in LL systems, or from industry standards and technical documentation as in best practice databases?
- *Application.* Do they describe a complete process, or perhaps a task or a decision?
- *Results.* Do they describe failures, as in incident report databases or alert systems; or successes, as in best practices database?
- *Orientation.* Do they support an organization or a whole industry?

Table 15-1 contrasts these knowledge sharing systems based on these attributes.

**TABLE 15-1   Types of Knowledge Repositories**

| Knowledge-Sharing System | Originates from Experiences? | Describes a Complete Process? | Describes Failures | Describes Successes? | Orientation |
|---|---|---|---|---|---|
| Incident reports | Yes | No | Yes | No | Organization |
| Alerts | Yes | No | Yes | No | Industry |
| Lessons Learned System | Yes | No | Yes | Yes | Organization |
| Best Practices Databases | Possibly | Yes | No | Yes | Industry |

❖❖❖❖

*Source:* Weber et al. [2001].

## ❖❖❖ Lessons Learned Systems

LL systems[4] have become commonplace in organizations and on the Web.[5] The most complete definition of what constitutes a lesson learned is currently used by the American, European, and Japanese Space Agencies [Weber et al., 2001]:

> A lesson learned is knowledge or understanding gained by experience. The experience may be positive, as in a successful test or mission, or negative, as in a mishap or failure. Successes are also considered sources of lessons learned. A lesson must be significant in that it has a real or assumed impact on operations; valid in that it is factually and technically correct; and applicable in that it identifies a specific design, process, or decision that reduces or eliminates the potential for failures and mishaps, or reinforces a positive result [Secchi et al., 1999].

The purpose of LL systems is to support organizational processes. Figure 15-1 describes the essential tasks of LL systems as *collect, verify, store, disseminate,* and *reuse* [Weber et al., 2001]:

1. **Collect the lessons.** This task involves collecting the lessons (or content) that may be incorporated into the LL system. There are six possible lesson content collection methods:

   a. *Passive.* The most common form of collection. Contributors submit lessons through a paper or Web-based form.
   b. *Reactive.* Where contributors are interviewed by a third party for lessons. The third party may submit the lesson on behalf of the contributor.
   c. *After-action collection.* Where lessons are collected during a mission debriefing, for example, in military organizations.
   d. *Proactive collection.* Where lessons are automatically collected by an expert system, which may suggest that a lesson exists based on analysis of a

---

[4] For a comprehensive survey of LL systems, including capabilities, limitations, design issues, and role of artificial intelligence in the creation of these systems, please refer to Weber et al. [2001].
[5] For a comprehensive list or LL systems maintained by various government and nongovernment organizations, visit the Web page created by David Aha and Rosina Weber published at www.aic.nrl.navy.mil/~aha/lessons/.

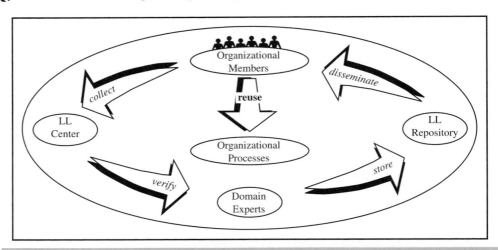

◆ ◆ ◆ **FIGURE 15-1** Lesson Learned Process

*Source:* Weber et al. [2001].

specific content. For example, an expert system could monitor individuals' e-mail and prompt them when it understands that a lesson is described.
   e. *Active collection.* Where a computer-based system may scan documents to identify lessons in the presence of specific keywords or phrases.
   f. *Interactive collection.* Where a computer-based system collaborates with the lesson's author to generate clear and relevant lessons.

2. ***Verify the lessons.*** Typically a team of domain experts performs the task required by this component, which requires the verification of lessons for correctness, redundancy, consistency, and relevance. The verification task is critically important, but sometimes introduces a significant bottleneck in the inclusion of lessons into the LL system, because it's a time-consuming process. Some systems, for example, Xerox's Eureka LL system, provide a two-staging process. The Eureka LL system, described in Vignette 15-3 in this section, supports field engineers in solving hard-to-fix repair problems with the company's printers. Contributors can enter fixes into the Eureka LL system. At that point, a team charged with the verification task receives an alert, prompting the test of the solution to ensure that it works. If everything checks out, the fix is made available to the rest of the field engineers.

3. ***Store the lesson.*** This task relates to the representation of the lessons in a computer-based system. Typical steps in this task include the indexing of lessons, formatting, and incorporating into the repository. In terms of the technology required to support this task, LL systems could be based on structured relational or object-oriented databases as well as case libraries (case-based reasoning) or semistructured document management systems. LL systems can also incorporate relevant multimedia such as audio and video, which may help illustrate important lessons.

4. ***Disseminate the lesson.*** This task relates to how the information is shared to promote its reuse. Five different dissemination methods have been identified:

 VIGNETTE 15-3

### Eureka: A Lessons Learned System for Xerox

In the mid-1990s, Xerox's[6] customers reported the lowest customer satisfaction in the company's history. This prompted the company to look at the way the copier field technicians serviced the machines. Xerox researchers realized field technicians would frequently share fixes over company provided radios originating from a set of notes that each technician carried with them.

Researchers developed Eureka in 1996, the first LL system designed to help service technicians detect and solve problems on the road, by integrating each of these original sets of notes. Eureka allows Xerox technicians to share their knowledge about how to better fix Xerox's copy machines. Each service technician is provided with a notebook computer that contains the subset of the Eureka database that is pertinent to each technician's area of expertise.

Eureka has an alert system that delivers new fixes according to the subscriber's profile. When technicians uncover a problem that is not addressed by Eureka, they submit the fix to the system, including their point of contact. At this point the fix is sent to a team tasked with verifying the solution, to ensure it works. The team then rates and publishes the solution in Eureka. Useless tips were discarded; others were certified as valuable or edited as necessary.

It was agreed that tips would be validated within a few days, and the submitter's name would appear alongside the tip as both a reward and an incentive [Mitchell, 2001]. The system currently supports field technicians in 71 countries and stores about 50,000 fixes, which have helped solve about 350,000 problems and saved Xerox approximately $15 million in parts and labor [Roberts-Witt, 2002].

[6]www.xerox.com

a. *Passive dissemination.* Where users look for lessons using a search engine.
b. *Active casting.* Where lessons are transmitted to users that have specified relevant profiles to that particular lesson.
c. *Broadcasting.* Where lessons are disseminated throughout an organization.
d. *Active dissemination.* Where users are alerted to relevant lessons in the context of their work (e.g., by a software help wizard that alerts a user of related automated assistance).
e. *Proactive dissemination.* Where a system anticipates events used to predict when the user may require the assistance provided by the lesson.
f. *Reactive dissemination.* When users launch the LL system in response to a knowledge need, for example, when they launch a *Help* system in the context of specific software.

5. **Apply the lesson.** This task relates to whether the user has the ability to decide how to reuse the lesson. There are three categories of reuse:

a. *Browsable.* Where the system displays a list of lessons that match the search criteria.
b. *Executable.* Where users might have the option to execute the lesson's recommendation (like when the Word processor suggests a specific spelling for a word).

    c. *Outcome reuse.* When the system prompts users to enter the outcome of reusing a lesson, to assess whether the lesson can be replicated.

Today, many commercial as well as government organizations maintain LL systems. Future LL systems are expected to integrate advanced intelligent technologies that can alert the decision maker of available support in the form of explicit lessons in the context of the decision-making process. Furthermore, LL systems are expected to integrate e-mail systems. E-mail messages could be a source for lesson extraction, because many contain historical archives of communications often composed of specific case problems, and their solutions that could be mined for organizational lessons. Next we see how Xerox successfully developed LL systems to support the work of its technicians, with a return on investment of about $15 million to the company.

## ◆ ◆ ◆ Expertise-Locator Knowledge-Sharing Systems

Several different business organizations have identified the need to develop EL systems to help locate intellectual capital. The intent of these systems is to catalog knowledge competencies, including information not typically captured by human resources systems, in a way that could later be queried across the organization. Vignette 15-4 illustrates a sample of EL systems developed across different industries.

Although EL systems across organizations serve a similar purpose, a number of characteristics differentiate these systems:

1. *Purpose of the system.* An EL system may serve a different purpose across organizations. One purpose could be to identify experts to help solve technical problems or staff project teams, to match employee competencies with positions within the company, or to perform gap analysis that point to intellectual capital inadequacies within the organization. Also, if a specific expertise domain is a critical knowledge area for an organization, and the EL system points to only three experts, it might serve to identify the need to hire or internally train additional experts in that area.

2. *Access method.* Most company EL systems are accessed via a company's intranet. However, interorganizational systems, such as SAGE (described in a later section) are accessed via the Web. Systems accessed via the Web provide experts with an increased level of visibility, but organizations may fear that such increased visibility may lure their experts into outside job opportunities.

3. *Self-assessment.* Most of the EL KM systems in place today rely on each employee completing a self-assessment of competencies, which is later used when searching for specific knowledge areas. Clearly, there are some advantages to this approach, mainly that it allows building a repository of organization-wide competencies quickly. On the other hand, using self-assessment as the way to identify expertise presents an inherent shortcoming, in that the results are based on each person's self-perception, and thus could be hard to normalize. Furthermore, employees' speculation about the possible use of this information could skew the results. Employees have been known to either exaggerate their competencies for fear of losing their positions, or downplay their duties so as not to have increasing responsibilities. For example, one particular organization conducted a skills self-assessment study during a period of downsizing. This resulted in employees'

  VIGNETTE 15-4

### Examples of Industry Expertise-Locator Systems

Hewlett-Packard developed CONNEX, an EL KM system [Davenport, 1996]. The goal of the project was to build a network of experts, available on-line, to provide a guide to human knowledge within Hewlett-Packard. CONNEX consists of a centralized database of user knowledge profiles, with a Web browser interface that allows users to find profiles in multiple ways. Users' profiles contain a summary of their knowledge and skills, affiliations, education, interests, and contact information. CONNEX users can easily find experts within Hewlett-Packard by searching the database using any combination of profile fields; or by browsing through the different areas of knowledge, geographies, or names. To support a large user base with high volume of transactions, CONNEX was built using Sybase database and Verity's Topic search engine, on a Hewlett-Packard platform.

The National Security Agency (NSA) has also taken a step toward the implementation of a system to locate experts [Wright and Spencer, 1999]. The NSA is part of the intelligence community, and its two missions are foreign signals intelligence and national information system security. The goal of the implementation of the Knowledge and Skills Management System (KSMS) is to catalog the talent pool within NSA to allow the precise identification of knowledge and skills,

and to take advantage of IT. The NSA went through the development of the system by applying database engineering to solve the complexities of implementing an adequate, workable, and successful KM system. NSA also divided the execution of this project into several work tasks including the development of knowledge taxonomy applicable to its workforce.

The goal of Microsoft's Skills Planning und [and] Development (SpuD) EL system was to develop a database containing job profiles available on-line across the IT group, and to help match employee's competency with jobs and work teams. The following are the five major components of the SPuD project [Davenport, 1997]: (1) developing a structure of competency types and levels; (2) defining the competencies required for particular jobs; (3) rating the employees' performance in particular jobs by the supervisors; (4) implementing the knowledge competencies in an on-line system, and (5) linking the competency models to learning offerings. The system was created based on a Structured Query Language (SQL) server as the database for Microsoft Access, as well as a Web front end. Note that the validation of the data in this model rests with individual supervisors, who essentially assign the competency criteria to each of the employees under their supervision.

exaggeration of their competencies, for fear they might be laid off if they did not appear maximally competent. On the other hand, another organization made it clear the self-assessment would be used to contact people with specific competencies to answer related questions. This resulted in employees downplaying their abilities to avoid serving as consultants for the organization. One EL system in place at Microsoft [Davenport, 1996] addresses this problem by requiring supervisors to ratify their subordinates' self-perceptions, and assigning a quantifiable value to each one. Although this can be successful if adhered to, many organizations would find this requirement too taxing on their supervisors.

**TABLE 15-2 Summary of Characteristics of Expertise-Locator Knowledge Management Systems**

| ELS Name | CONNEX(HP) | KSMS (NSA) | SPuD (Microsoft) |
|---|---|---|---|
| Purpose of the system | To share knowledge, for consulting and to search for experts | To staff projects and match positions with skills | To compile the knowledge and competency of each employee |
| Self-assessment | Yes | Yes, supervisors also participate in data gathering | No, supervisors rate employee's performance |
| Participation | Only those who are willing to share | Whole personnel | Whole personnel in the IT group |
| Knowledge taxonomy | U.S. Library of Congress INSPEC Index Own | Department of Labor (O*NET) | Own |
| Levels of competencies | No | Yes | Yes |
| Data maintenance | User (nagging) | User and supervisor | Supervisor |
| Company culture | Sharing, open | Technology, expertise | Technology, open |
| Platform | HP-9000 Unix Sybase Verity | OS/2, VMS, and Programming Bourne shell | SQL MS Access |

❖ ❖ ❖ ❖

*Source:* Becerra-Fernandez [2000a].

4. *Participation.* This defines whether the system represents expertise across the organization like the one at NSA, a department like the one at Microsoft, or merely volunteer experts willing to share their knowledge with others.

5. *Taxonomy.* This refers to the specific taxonomy used to index knowledge competencies within the organization. Some organizations like Microsoft developed their own knowledge taxonomy; NSA's is based on O*NET, a standard published by the U.S. Department of Labor; and Hewlett-Packard based its taxonomy of an existing standard published by the U.S. Library of Congress augmented by its own knowledge competencies.

6. *Levels of competencies.* This refers to expressing expertise as capability levels. Levels of competencies could be defined according to Wiig's [1993] levels of proficiency classifications that follow:

- Ignorant—totally unaware
- Beginner—vaguely aware, no experience
- Advanced beginner—aware, relatively unskilled
- Competent—narrowly skilled
- Proficient—knowledgeable in selected areas
- Expert—highly proficient in a particular area, generally knowledgeable
- Master—highly expert in many areas, broadly knowledgeable
- Grand master—world-class expert in all areas of domain

Other differentiating characteristics for EL systems may include technological differences, for example, the type of underlying database, the programming language used to develop the system, or the specifics about how the data is maintained current. Table 15-2 summarizes some of the major characteristics that differentiate the EL system described in Vignette 15-4.

## ◇ ◇ ◇ Role of Knowledge Taxonomies and Data Mining in the Development of Expertise-Locator Systems

A significant challenge in the development of EL systems, knowledge repositories, and digital libraries deals with the accurate development of **knowledge taxonomies.** Taxonomy is the study of the general principles of scientific classification. Taxonomies, also called classification or categorization schemes, are considered to be knowledge organization systems that serve to group objects together based on a particular characteristic. Knowledge taxonomies are used to organize knowledge (or competencies) relevant to the organization. In the case of EL systems, the knowledge taxonomy is used to describe the organization's critical knowledge areas used to index people's knowledge. The development of adequate knowledge taxonomies could be time consuming and complex—time consuming because typically this exercise requires the consensus of a cross-functional group tasked with defining the organization's most significant knowledge areas. The development could be complex because these decisions could play on organizational politics, and lack of representation in the knowledge taxonomy could be considered threatening to some subunits.

Many EL systems in place have addressed this consideration, keeping in mind that:

1. Taxonomies should easily describe a knowledge area.
2. Taxonomies should provide minimal descriptive text.
3. Taxonomies should facilitate browsing, not complicate it.
4. Taxonomies should have the appropriate level of granularity and abstraction. If the taxonomy is too granular and the specificity is too high, then it may be too complicated for the user. However, if the taxonomy is too abstract and the specificity level is too low, it may not properly describe the knowledge areas.

As we saw in the previous section, there exist a number of work classification standards that could be used to organize knowledge areas, such as the U.S. Library of Congress, INSPEC database, or the U.S. Department of Labor's O*Net. Using these standards may aid the development of knowledge taxonomies, but it may not be simple to apply any of these standards directly, without some thought and further development of the taxonomy.

Other related knowledge organization systems include **semantic networks, ontologies,** and **authority files.** Semantic networks serve to structure concepts and terms in networks or Webs vs. the hierarchies typically used to represent taxonomies. Ontologies are relevant to KM in that they are used to represent complex relationships between objects as rules and axioms, which are not included in semantic networks. Authority files are lists of terms used to control the variant names in a particular field, and link preferred terms to nonpreferred terms. Authority files are used to control the taxonomy vocabulary, in particular, within an organization. In other words, authority files are used to ensure that everyone in the organization uses the same terms to organize similar concepts.

The use of Web text data mining (DM) can mitigate some of the problems inherent to relying on biased self-reporting required to keep employee profiles up to date, or the need to develop an accurate knowledge taxonomy *a priori*. This technique draws from an existing pool of information that provides a detailed picture of what employees know, based on what they already publish as part of their jobs, including their Web pages. Web DM makes use of DM techniques to extract information from Web-related data. An approach based on Web DM requires minimal user effort to maintain the accuracy of the records, eliminating the need for "nagging" systems that prompt users to maintain their profiles up to date. Through Web DM, the collection of expertise data is based on published documents, eliminating the need for possibly biased self-reporting. Using Web DM, this information can be collected automatically, and employee skill information can be kept up to date through periodic reprocessing of the document body for documents that are new or have been updated. In Chapter 13, we discuss Web DM in detail.

## ◆▷ ◆▷ ◆▷  Case Study: Overview of the Searchable Answer Generating Environment (SAGE) Expert Finder in Locating University Expertise

This section presents insights and lessons learned from the development of the **Searchable Answer Generating Environment (SAGE)** Expert Finder, which is in the category of EL systems [Becerra-Fernandez, 1999, 2000a]. To accompany the discussions presented in this section, please refer to the SAGE demo found in the CD accompanying this book.

The motivation to develop SAGE was based on the National Aeronautics and Space Administration (NASA)–Kennedy Space Center (KSC) requirement to partner with Florida experts, as the agency looks to develop new technologies necessary for the continuation of space exploration missions. The purpose of SAGE is to create a searchable repository of university experts in the state of Florida. Currently, each university in Florida keeps a database of funded research for internal use, but these databases are disparate and dissimilar. The SAGE Expert Finder creates a single funded research data warehouse by incorporating a distributed database scheme, which can be searched by a variety of fields, including research topic, investigator name, funding agency, or university. Figure 15-2 represents the SAGE architecture. In this figure, the canisters in the Florida map represent each of disparate databases at each of the Florida universities.

The content of each database is pulled by a file transfer protocol (FTP) client application that automatically obtains and transfers the database contents of each participating university. The file transfer takes place according to a prescheduled transfer rule, to the SAGE database server represented by the canister DATABASE. The FTP client is customized to each university, and it is marked by the abbreviations that represent each university: University of West Florida (UWF), Florida Agricultural and Mechanical University (FAMU), University of North Florida (UNF), Florida State University (FSU), University of Florida (UF), University of Central Florida (UCF), Florida Atlantic University (FAU), Florida International University (FIU), and Florida Gulf Coast University (FGCU). After the information is in the SAGE server,

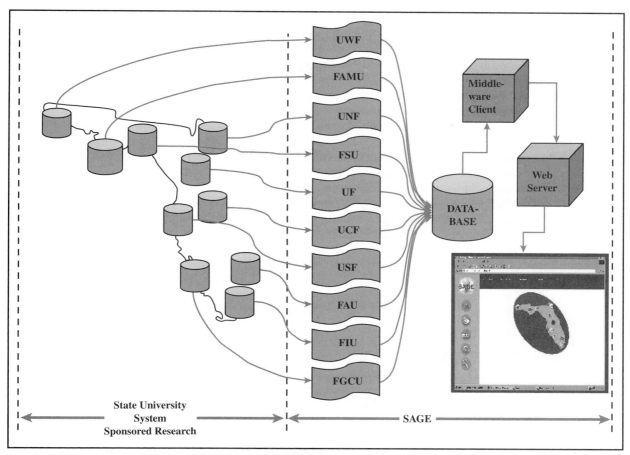

❬❭ ❬❭ ❬❭   FIGURE 15-2 SAGE Architecture

the next steps involve the migration of the data to the SQL server format, followed by cleansing and transforming the data to a relational format.

The SAGE system combines the unified database by masking multiple databases as if they were one. This methodology provides flexibility to users and the database administrator, regardless of the type of program used to collect the information at the source. One of the advantages of SAGE is that there is only one user point of entry at the Web-enabled interface. The main interfaces developed on the query engine use text fields to search the processed data for keywords, fields of expertise, names, or other applicable search fields. The application processes the end user's query and returns the pertinent information. The SAGE Expert Finder also includes an interactive data dictionary or thesaurus upon user request, and launches a query for similar words.

The development of SAGE was marked by two design requirements: minimize the impact on each of the universities' offices of sponsored research that collect most of the required data, and validate the data used to identify experts. For this reason, the system was designed to receive the content in its native form and to make necessary data cleansing at the SAGE server site. The strength of SAGE lies in the fact that it validates the data at the source, using the assumption that researchers who successfully obtain funded research grants are indeed experts in their fields. A number of database systems exist on the Web that claim to help them locate experts with a defined profile, such as Community of Science.[7] However, most of these tools rely on people assessing their own skills, against a predefined taxonomy, which is inherently unreliable and hard to maintain up to date. Figure 15-3 illustrates the technologies used to develop SAGE.

One of the technical challenges faced during the design and implementation of the SAGE project was that the source databases of funded research from the various universities were dissimilar in design and file format. The manipulation of the source data was one of the most important issues, because the credibility of the system would ultimately depend on the consistency and accuracy of the information. Manipulating the data included the process of cleansing the data, followed by the data transformation into the relational model, and ultimately the databases migration to a consistent format. One of the most important research contributions of SAGE is the merging of interorganizational database systems.

SAGE has been on-line since August 16, 1999 at www.sage.fiu.edu. SAGE's daily number of hits has increased since the day of its rollout to the current level of around 42 hits per day by February of 2003. Of these, about 64% originate from commercial domains (.com and .net), 13% from special organizations (.org), 6.5% from educational

❖ ❖ ❖ **FIGURE 15-3** Technologies to Implement SAGE

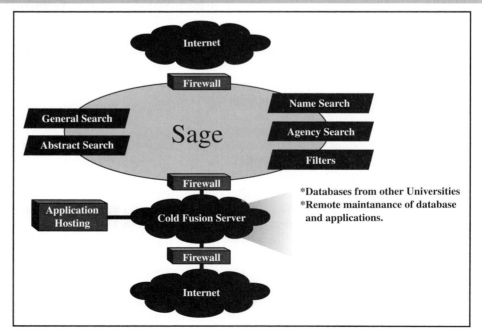

---

[7] www.communityofscience.com

domains (.edu), 5.5% from U.S. government domains (.gov and .mil), 7% from foreign domains, and 4% from other domains. SAGE visitors come from the United States and from around the world, including Japan, Canada, United Kingdom, Germany, France, Korea, Austria, Switzerland, Bahamas, and Mexico. SAGE is currently used by NASA to identify researchers to be invited to conferences and receive announcements, small businesses that need to identify research collaborators when pursuing SBIR and STTR grants, businesses that need to identify experts who could assist in solving technical problems, and researchers who need to identify potential collaborators.

## ◇◇ ◇◇ ◇◇ Case Study: Overview of Expert Seeker in Locating Experts at the National Aeronautics and Space Administration

This section presents insights and lessons learned from the development of Expert Seeker [Becerra-Fernandez, 2000b, 2001], an organizational EL KM system used to locate experts at NASA. To accompany the discussions presented in this section, please refer to the **Expert Seeker** demo found in the CD accompanying this book.

The main difference between Expert Seeker and SAGE is that the former searches for expertise at NASA (KSC and Goddard Space Flight Center [GSFC]), whereas the latter is on the Web and seeks expertise at various universities. Expert Seeker interfaces to SAGE, which allows for specifying a search scope that is not bound by the organization, but may include the base of researchers who work at different universities. Another important difference between SAGE and Expert Seeker is that the latter enables the user to search for much more detailed information concerning the experts' achievements, including information, skills and competencies, and proficiency level for each of the skills and competencies.

Previous KM studies at KSC affirmed the need for a center-wide repository that would provide KSC employees with Intranet-based access to experts with specific backgrounds [Becerra-Fernandez, 1998]. To further create synergies between the efforts to develop Expert Seeker at KSC, a similar effort was funded to prototype Expert Seeker at GSFC. It was expected that the knowledge taxonomy for GSFC would differ from the one for KSC. However, this requirement did not pose a concern, because Expert Seeker could be developed so the software can be "configured" with a customizable knowledge taxonomy. Expert Seeker offers NASA experts more visibility and at the same time allows interested parties to identify available expertise within NASA, and is especially useful when organizing cross-functional teams.

The Expert Seeker ELS is accessed via NASA's Intranet, and provides a Web-based unified interface to access experts with specific competencies within the organization. The main interfaces on the query engine in Expert Seeker uses text fields to search the repository by fields of expertise, names, or other applicable search fields. Expert Seeker unifies a myriad of structured, semistructured, and unstructured data collections to create an expert's profile repository that can easily be searched via a Web-based interface facilitating communication via a point of contact. The development of Expert Seeker required the utilization of existing structured data as well as semistructured and unstructured Web-based information as much as possible. It uses the data in existing human resources databases for information such as employee's formal educational background, the X.500 directory for point-of-contact information, a skills database that profiles each employee's competency areas, and the Goal Performance Evaluation System (GPES). Information concerning skills and competencies, as well as proficiency levels for the skills and competencies needs to be collected, to a large extent, through self-assessment. Figure 15-4 depicts the architecture of Expert Seeker, and Table 15-3 describes the data sources for Expert Seeker. Furthermore, other related information deemed important in the generation of an expert profile not currently stored in an in-house database system can be user-supplied, such as employee's picture, project participation data, hobbies, and volunteer or civic activities.

Recognizing that there are significant shortcomings to self-assessment, the system relies on technology to update employees' profiles, and thus is less dependent on self-assessed data. For example, Expert Seeker uses the Global Performance Evaluation System (GPES), an in-house performance evaluation tool, to mine employees'

◆◇ ◇◆ ◇◆ **FIGURE 15-4** Expert Seeker Architecture

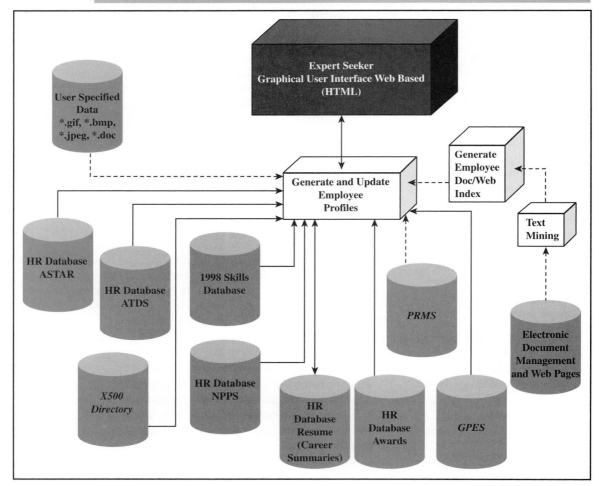

**TABLE 15-3   Description of the Data Sources for Expert Seeker**

| Source | Description |
|---|---|
| User-specified data | This information is optionally user-supplied; for example, experts can opt to provide career summaries that may be used by Expert Seeker to augment the expertise search; a database table to hold this information was created and linked to the system, initially populated from the NPPS human resources database; other user-supplied data could include pictures, publications, patents, hobbies, civic activities, etc. |
| ASTAR | This human resources database view provides the experts' in-house training courses |
| ATDS | This human resources database view provides the experts' workshops and academic classes employees are planning to take |
| X.500 | This database view provides the experts' general employee data such as first name, last name, work address, phone, organization, fax, and email; X.500's unique identifier is also used to cross-reference employees in different databases |
| Skills database | This database view provides a set of skills and subskills that are used by Expert Seeker to index the expertise search; the KSC Core Competency team defined this set of skills and subskills as a refinement to a previous center-wide skills assessment |
| NPPS database | This human resources database view provides the experts' formal education, including professional degrees and the corresponding academic institutions; NPPS is also the source the employees' department, used by the directorate search mode; the contents of this database were also used to initially populate the career summary section table |
| KPro | This database view is populated with project participation information through a new project management system under development at NASA/KSC |
| GPES | The Goal Performance Evaluation System (GPES) is a system developed at KSC; this database view serves as the data source for profile information such as employees' achievements; GPES replaces the Skills Database because GPES is also populated with KSC's strategic competencies and levels of expertise |
| Data mining | Expert Seeker expertise search is augmented through the use of data mining algorithms, which build an expert's profile based on information published by employees on their Web pages; similarly, a document repository could be mined for expertise using these algorithms |
| SAGE | The Searchable Answer Generating Environment (SAGE) is an expertise-locator system developed and hosted at the Florida International University Knowledge Management Laboratory to identify experts within Florida's universities; Expert Seeker users can define the search scope to be within KSC or to expand it to universities in Florida; the latter means that Expert Seeker would launch an expert search to SAGE, and the results of this search are integrated into one output at the Expert Seeker GUI |

accomplishments and automatically update their profiles. Typically, employees find it difficult to make time to keep their resumes updated. Performance evaluations, on the other hand, are without a doubt, part of everybody's job. Therefore, it makes perfect sense to use this tool to unobtrusively keep the employees profiles up to date. Future developments for EL systems may incorporate advanced technologies, such as DM and intelligent agent technologies, to automatically identify experts within as well as outside the organization.

## ◇ ◇ ◇ Knowledge Management Systems to Share Tacit Knowledge

The systems discussed so far assist organizations in sharing explicit knowledge. To create a cultural environment that encourages the sharing of knowledge, some organizations are creating knowledge communities [Dignum, 2002]. As we discussed in Chapter 3, a **CoP,** also known as a *knowledge network*, is an organic and self-organized group of individuals who are dispersed geographically or organizationally but communicate regularly to discuss issues of mutual interest. Two examples of CoPs mentioned in that chapter are a tech-club at DaimlerChrysler, which includes a group of engineers who don't work in the same unit but meet regularly to discuss problems related to their area of expertise; and a strategic community of IT professionals at Xerox, who frequently meet to promote knowledge sharing.

Many studies have demonstrated that any technological support for knowledge exchange requires users to believe they know and can trust one another. One company that is taking steps in this direction is Achmea,[8] one of the top insurance and financial services companies in the Netherlands. The company encourages direct contacts between participants in its knowledge community, through formalized workshops. Through these workshops the company ensures the creation, maintenance, and uniformity of domain knowledge; and at the same time enables members to appreciate other colleagues, thus contributing to develop a feeling of community.

Communities are groups of people who come together to share and learn from one another and who are held together by a common interest in a body of knowledge. Communities come together either face-to-face or virtually, and are driven by a desire and need to share problems, experiences, insights, templates, tools, and best practices [McDermott, 2000]. This section concentrates on systems used to share tacit knowledge, specifically to support CoPs. According to McDermott, people come together in CoPs because they are passionately interested in the topic and can receive direct value from participating in the community, because they are emotionally connected to the community, or because they want to learn new tools and techniques. Communities grow out of their members' natural networks; and follow five stages of development: planning, start-up, growth, sustenance, and closure. Although CoPs are not new phenomena, the Internet has enabled the proliferation of virtual communities, facilitated through the same collaborative technologies described in

---

[8]www.achmea.com/

an earlier section of this chapter. By 2000, at IBM the CoPs numbered around 60, and more than 20,000 employees had participated in a community [Gongla and Rizzuto, 2001].

Whereas knowledge repositories support primarily codified and explicitly captured knowledge, virtual CoPs are supported through technology that enables interaction and conversations among its members. Interaction technology can support structured (and perhaps more explicated) communication, such as in discussion groups and Web-based forums, to unstructured (and perhaps more tacit) communication, such as in videoconferencing.

For example, in Vignette 15-1 we mentioned the World Bank's initiative to establish CoPs as a powerful venue for sharing global experiences while at the same time adapting them to meet local challenges. For example, the *K4D Community* combines experts from across sectors, networks, and regions of the World Bank, to share knowledge related to capacity development in each of the different regions of the world. At the World Bank, technology is considered a critical building block for CoP, but only as support to the social aspects of sharing knowledge, which are building trust, personal communication, and face-to-face meetings. At the World Bank, technology is adapted to the needs of the community and the tools that support their CoP include document repositories, debriefings to identify lessons learned, an Internet-based broadcasting station, newsletters, printed publications, and Web sites. Specifically, the World Bank developed a Web site that supports virtual discussions called the *Development Forum*, an electronic venue for dialogue and knowledge sharing on issues of sustainable development. Participants of this forum must adhere to a set of rules,[9] namely:

1. *Personal identification.* Participants should include their name in all messages posted to the discussion, and never represent themselves as another person.
2. *Conduct.* Participants may not post libelous or defamatory messages or materials, or links to such materials. They may not post messages or materials that are obscene, violent, abusive, threatening, or designed to harass or intimidate another person.
3. *Liability and responsibility.* Participants are legally responsible, and solely responsible, for any content posted to a discussion. They may only post materials that they have the right or permission to distribute electronically. The sponsors of the Development Forum are not responsible from any liability arising from users' posting of any materials to the Forum Dialogues.
4. *Accuracy.* The World Bank, as sponsor of the Development Forum, cannot and does not guarantee the accuracy of any statements made in, or materials posted to, the Forum by participants.
5. *Attribution.* Participants in the Development Forum, including participants in the Development Dialogues and the authors of contributions to the Speakers' Corner, are assumed to be speaking in their personal capacity, unless they explicitly state that their contribution represents the views of their organization. For this reason, participants in the Forum should not quote the postings of other participants as representing the views of the organizations to which those other participants belong.

---

[9] www.worldbank.org/devforum/rules.html

6. ***Copyright and fair use.*** As a participant in the Development Forum, participants retain the copyright of any materials (of their own creation) posted to the Forum. However, users authorize other participants in the Forum to make personal and customary use of that work, including creating links to or reposting such materials to other Internet discussion sites, but not otherwise to reproduce or disseminate those materials unless you give permission. Participants must always identify the source and author of materials downloaded from the Forum if it is reposted elsewhere.

CoPs have been observed to impact organizational performance [Lesser and Storck, 2001] in four areas:

1. ***Decreasing new employee's learning curves.*** CoPs can help new employees identify subject matter experts in the organization who can guide them to the proper resources, and thus foster relationships with more senior employees. CoPs can help develop mentor–protégé relationships that can help employees to develop their careers and to understand the larger organizational context of their individual tasks.

2. ***Enabling the organization to respond faster to customer needs and inquiries.*** CoPs can help identify experts that can address customer issues. Furthermore, because many communities maintain electronic document repositories, relevant codified knowledge can often be reused.

3. ***Reducing rework and preventing to reinvent the wheel.*** CoPs are able to locate, access, and apply existing knowledge in new situations. Repositories serve as common virtual workspace to store, organize, and download presentations, tools, and other valuable materials. Metadata are used to identify authors and subject matter experts. Most repositories include human moderation. For example, the sponsors of World Bank's Development Forum retain the right to refuse to post any message that they consider to be in violation of the rules, and may opt to publish the messages posted to the Forum in whole or in part. CoPs help create trust within the organization, by helping individuals build reputations both as experts and for their willingness to help others.

4. ***Spawning new ideas for products and services.*** CoPs serve as a forum in which employees are able to share perspectives about a topic. Discussing diverse views within the community can often spark innovation. Furthermore, CoPs provide a safe environment where people feel comfortable about sharing their experiences.

In short, CoPs are effective mechanisms for tacit knowledge sharing that can provide significant value to organizations. The role of management is to carefully craft interventions that are likely to support the formation and development of CoPs.

## SUMMARY ◇ ◇ ◇

In this chapter, we discuss what knowledge sharing systems are, including design considerations and specific types of such systems. Specific attention was placed on the two systems most frequently discussed in the KM literature: lessons learned systems and expertise locator (EL) systems. The lessons learned process was discussed. Also we discussed in detail EL systems, including design considerations and two representative case studies. The experience gained from the development of two such systems is presented: SAGE Expert Finder, an EL system to locate experts in Florida; and Expert Seeker, an EL system used to identify experts at NASA. The chapter concludes with a discussion on systems to share tacit knowledge through communities of practice.

## Review Questions  ◇ ◇ ◇

1.  Describe the crucial requirements for the successful implementation of knowledge sharing systems.
2.  Discuss the different types of knowledge sharing systems.
3.  Explain the lessons-learned (LL) process.
4.  Explain the role that taxonomies play in knowledge sharing systems.
5.  Explain the differentiating characteristics of the EL system developed at Hewlett Packard, NSA, and Microsoft.
6.  Discuss the role that communities of practice (CoPs) play in sharing tacit knowledge.

## Application Exercises  ◇ ◇ ◇

1.  Identify examples of knowledge sharing systems in use in your organization. What are some of the intelligent technologies that enable those systems?
2.  Design a knowledge sharing system to support your business needs. Describe the type of system and the foundation technologies that you would use to develop such a system.
3.  Describe the non-technical issues that you may face during the implementation of the system designed in the previous question.
4.  Design the system architecture for the system described in Question 2 above.
5.  Identify three recent examples in the literature of knowledge sharing systems.

## Key Terms  ◇ ◇ ◇

- alert systems—p. 306
- authority files—p. 313
- communities of practice (CoPs)—p. 320
- corporate memory—p. 299
- expertise locator (EL) systems—p. 299
- Expert Seeker—p. 317
- knowledge sharing systems— p. 301
- knowledge taxonomies—p. 313
- lessons-learned (LL) systems— p. 306
- not-invented-here (NIH) syndrome—p. 305
- ontologies—p. 313
- organizational knowledge— p. 299
- Searchable Answer Generating Environment (SAGE)—p. 314
- semantic networks—p. 313

## References  ◇ ◇ ◇

Abecker, A., Bernardi, A., Hinkelmann, K., Kuhn, O., and Sintek, M. 1998. Towards a technology for organizational memories. *IEEE Intelligent Systems and Their Applications,* 13(3) May/June, pp. 30–34.

Becerra-Fernandez, I. 1998. Corporate Memory Project. Final Report, NASA grant No. NAG10-0232, pp. 12–25.

Becerra-Fernandez, I. 1999. Searchable Answer Generating Environment (SAGE): A Knowledge Management System for Searching for Experts in Florida. Proc. 12th Annual Int. Florida Artificial Intelligence Research Symp. — Knowledge Management Track, Orlando, FL, May.

Becerra-Fernandez, I. 2000a. The role of artificial intelligence technologies in the implementation of people-finder knowledge management systems. *Knowledge Based Systems*, special issue on Artificial Intelligence in Knowledge Management, 13(5), 315–320. October.

Becerra-Fernandez, I. 2000b. Facilitating the Online Search of Experts at NASA using Expert Seeker People-Finder. In Proc. 3rd Int. Conf. on Practical Aspects of Knowledge Management, Basel, Switzerland.

Becerra-Fernandez, I. 2001. Locating expertise at NASA—Developing a tool to leverage human capital. *Knowledge Management Review*, 4(4), 34–37.

Davenport, T. 1996. Knowledge Management at Hewlett Packard. Available on-line at www.bus.utexas.edu/kman/hpcase.htm.

Davenport, T. 1997. Knowledge Management Case Study: Knowledge Management at Microsoft. Available on-line at: http://kman.bus.utexas.edu/kman/microsoft.htm.

Dignum, V. 2002. A Knowledge Sharing Model for Peer Collaboration in the Non-Life Insurance Domain. In Proc. 1st German Workshop on Experience Management, Berlin, Germany.

Gongla, P., and Rizutto, C. 2001. Evolving communities of practice: IBM Global Services experience. *IBM Systems Journal,* 4(4), 842—862.

Khun, O., and Abecker, A. 1997. Corporate memories for knowledge management in industrial practice: Prospects and challenges. *Journal of Universal Computer Science*, 3(8), 929–954.

Lesser, E., and Storck, J. 2001. Communities of practice and organizational performance. *IBM Systems Journal,* 40(4), 831–841.

Mc Dermott, R. 2000. Community development as a natural step. *KM Review*, November/December.

Mitchell, M. 2001. Share and share alike. *Darwin Magazine,* February.

O'Leary, D.E. 1999. Knowledge Management for best practices. *Intelligence*, 4(10), 12–24.

Roberts-Witt, S. 2002. A "Eureka!" moment at Xerox. *PC Magazine, March.*

Secchi, P., Ciaschi, R., and Spence, D. 1999. A Concept for an ESA Lessons Learned System, In Secchi, P. (Ed.), *Proc. Alerts and LL: An Effective Way to Prevent Failures and Problems (Technical Report WPP-167).* ESTEC, Noordwijk, The Netherlands.

Weber, R., Aha, D.W., and Becerra-Fernandez, I. 2001. Intelligent Lessons Learned Systems. *International Journal of Expert Systems Research & Applications*, 20(1), 17–34.

Wiig, K. 1993. *Thinking About Thinking—How People and Organizations Create, Represent, and Use Knowledge.* Schema Press, Arlington, TX.

Wright, A., and Spencer, W. 1999. The National Security Agency (NSA) Networked Knowledge and Skills Management System. Presentation at Delphi's International Knowledge Management Summit (IKMS), San Diego, CA.

# CHAPTER 16

# Knowledge Application Systems

## *Systems That Utilize Knowledge*

### ◇◇◇ Introduction

In the last chapter we discussed knowledge sharing systems. In this chapter, we describe what **knowledge application systems** are and how they are developed, and relay experiences of how organizations have implemented such systems. As we discussed in Chapter 3, knowledge application systems support the process through which individuals utilize the knowledge possessed by other individuals without actually acquiring, or learning, that knowledge. Both mechanisms and technologies can support knowledge application systems by facilitating the knowledge management (KM) processes of **routines** and **direction.** Knowledge application systems are typically enabled by intelligent technologies for knowledge application, as we present earlier in Chapters 7 to 9.

You may recall that knowledge application *mechanisms* facilitate direction (e.g., hierarchical relationships, help desks, and support centers) and routines (e.g., organizational policies, work practices, and standards). On the other hand, technologies supporting direction and routines include expert systems, decision support, advisor systems, fault diagnosis (or troubleshooting) systems, and help desk systems. These systems may support direction, as in the case of a field service technician seeking to troubleshoot a particular product; or may support routines, as in the case of a customer service representative who may need to identify alternative product delivery mechanisms while preparing the shipment of an order. Many of these systems are enabled by the use of intelligent technologies, such as **case-based reasoning (CBR)** (see Chapter 9), rule-based systems (see Chapter 8), enterprise systems, and traditional management information systems. Both knowledge application mechanisms and technologies can facilitate direction and routines within or across organizations.

For a quick overview of what knowledge application systems are and how they are used, let us look at Vignette 16-1 for a brief case study of how NEC redefined the way

VIGNETTE 16-1

### Applying Organizational Experiences to Produce Quality Software

NEC[1] is a leading global company that manufactures cutting edge products for the broadband networking and mobile Internet market. In 1981, NEC recognized the need to extend its quality control (QC) activity to the domain of software development. To accomplish this goal, the company established a company-wide corporate structure to assist employees in applying the principles of software quality control. QC activities typically resulted in a case report that outlined the problem analysis, its possible root cause, the corrective actions taken, and the results of the corrective actions.

By 1991, the company had collected over 25,000 such cases in an effort to apply the productivity improvements across the organization. Initially the case reports were stored in a book, and later in a searchable database, but people found it difficult to search and apply the QC cases. NEC then decided to implement the software quality control advisor (SQUAD), based on CBR technology, to improve user access and application of the reported QC cases. The cases in SQUAD are nominated through a committee that reviews each case and selects the best cases. Cases are selected on the basis of the quality of the analysis, significance of the results, and how generalizable the problem is.

Adequate incentives were established to encourage employee participation. Initially about 3,000 cases were submitted each year and later new submissions decreased to about 1,000 cases a year. The significant drop in the rate of new case submissions came about because most typical cases were already reported in the system. By 1994, the system represented about 24,000 cases and served over 150,000 users.

Some of the success factors that marked the development of SQUAD included low-development cost, because its development only required 4 person-months. Furthermore, the development of SQUAD supported incremental modifications, because it allowed for cases to incrementally be included in the case database. By 1991, it was estimated that SQUAD had already paid off to the organization over $100 million per year. For further details about SQUAD, refer to Kitano and Shimazu [1996].

---

[1] www.nec.com

the organization is able to apply its collective experience to better produce high-quality software.

## ◆ ◆ ◆ Technologies for Knowledge Application Systems

Traditionally, the development of knowledge-based systems had been based on the use of rules or models to represent the **domain knowledge.** As we discussed in Chapters 7, 8, and 10, the development of such systems requires the collaboration of a subject matter expert with a knowledge engineer (KE), the latter responsible for the elicitation and representation of the expert's cognitive model. Although the rules approach to knowledge representation has produced many examples of successful expert systems, for example, the Web-based advisor system presented in a later section, many knowledge application systems are increasingly based on the implementation of CBR technology (see Chapter 9).

CBR, rules, and models are not the only type of intelligent technology underpinning the development of knowledge application systems. Other important technologies used to develop these systems are worth mentioning, namely, **constraint-based reasoning, model-based reasoning,** and **diagrammatic reasoning.** These technologies are described in Chapter 7. These technologies are radically different from rule-based or CBR systems and have very specific application areas.

As a point of interest to the reader, there are variants of CBR, such as **exemplar-based reasoning, instance-based reasoning,** and **analogy-based reasoning.** These different variations of CBR are also described below [Aamodt and Plaza, 1994; Leake, 1996]:

1. ***Exemplar-based reasoning.*** These systems seek to solve problems through classification, that is, finding the right class for the unclassified exemplar. Essentially the class of the most similar past case then becomes the solution to the classification problem, and the set of classes are the possible solutions to the problem [Kibler and Aha, 1987].
2. ***Instance-based reasoning.*** These systems require a large number of instances (or cases) that are typically simple; that is, they are defined by a small set of attribute vectors. The major focus of study of these systems is automated learning, requiring no user involvement [Aha et al., 1991].
3. ***Analogy-based reasoning.*** These systems are typically used to solve new problems based on past cases from a different domain [Aamodt and Plaza, 1994; Veloso and Carbonnell, 1993]. Analogy-based reasoning focuses on case reuse, also called the **mapping problem,** that is, finding a way to map the solution of the analogue case to the present problem.

In summary, rule-based systems and CBR, as well as constraint-based reasoning, model-based reasoning, and diagrammatic reasoning, are all technologies used to develop knowledge application systems. The applicability of each technology is dictated primarily by the characteristics of the domain as described above. Table 16-1 summarizes the technologies to develop knowledge application systems, and the characteristics of the domain that define their applicability. The next sections describe specific types of knowledge application systems, based on the aforementioned technologies.

As we mentioned above, it has become increasingly clear that the most popular technique for the implementation of knowledge application systems in businesses today is CBR. The reasons why CBR is more commonly used in the development of such systems include the fact that CBR implementations are, at least on the surface, more intuitive. In addition, CBR implementations take advantage of explicit knowledge that may already exist in the organization, for example, in problem reports (PRs). In the next section we describe how to implement knowledge applications systems. For

| TABLE 16-1 Technologies for Knowledge Application Systems | |
|---|---|
| *Technology* | *Domain Characteristics* |
| Rule-based systems | Applicable when the domain knowledge can be defined by a manageable set of rules or heuristics. |
| Case-based reasoning | Applicable in weak-theory domains, that is, where an expert either does not exist, or does not fully understand the domain. Also applicable if the experience base spans an entire organization, instead of a single individual. |
| Constraint-based reasoning | Applicable in domains that are defined by constraints, or what cannot be done. |
| Model-based reasoning (MBR) | Applicable when designing a system based on the description of the internal workings of an engineered system. This knowledge is typically available from design specifications, drawings, and books, and which can be used to recognize and diagnose its abnormal operation. |
| Diagrammatic reasoning | Applicable when the domain is best represented by diagrams and imagery, such as when solving geometric problems. |

◇ ◇ ◇ ◇

the reasons mentioned above, we will assume that the underpinning technology for the knowledge application system will be CBR, although the methodology applies to any of the technologies mentioned earlier.

## ◇ ◇ ◇ Developing Knowledge Application Systems

In this section we describe how to build a knowledge application system. We make extensive use of examples and vignettes to enhance the learning experience. The different types of knowledge application systems, and specific examples are presented in the next four sections.

Briefly reviewing Chapter 9, CBR is an artificial intelligence (AI) technique designed to mimic human problem solving. CBR is based on Schank's [1982] model of dynamic memory. Its goal is to mimic the way humans solve problems. When faced with a new problem, humans search their memories for past problems resembling the current problem, and adapt the prior solution to fit the current problem. CBR is a method of analogical reasoning that utilizes old cases or experiences in an effort to solve problems, critique solutions, explain anomalous situations, or interpret situations [Kolodner, 1991, 1993; Leake, 1996; Aamodt and Plaza, 1994; Watson, 2003]. Remembering our discussion in Chapter 9, a typical case-based knowledge application system consists of the following processes:

1. *Search the case library for similar cases.* This implies utilizing a search engine that examines only the appropriate cases, and not the entire case library, because it may be quite large.
2. *Select and retrieve the most similar cases.* New problems are solved by first retrieving previously experienced cases. This implies having a means to compare

each examined case to the current problem, quantify their similarity, and some-how rank them in decreasing order of similarity.

3. ***Adapt the solution for the most similar case.*** If the current problem and the most similar case are not similar enough, then the solution may have to be adapted to fit the needs of the current problem. The new problem can be solved with the aid of an old solution that has been adapted to the new problem.

4. ***Apply the generated solution and obtain feedback.*** Once a solution or classification is generated by the system, it must be applied to the problem. Its effect on the problem is fed back to the CBR system for classification of its solution (as success or failure).

5. ***Add the newly solved problem to the case library.*** The new experience is likely to be useful in future problem solving. This step requires identifying whether the new case is worth adding to the library, and placing it in the appropriate location in the case library.

Again reviewing our discussion from Chapter 9, there are several advantages to using CBR over rules or models for developing knowledge application systems. These advantages come to light when the relationship between the case attributes and the solution or outcome is not understood well enough to represent it in rules. Alternatively, CBR systems are advantageous when the ratio of cases that are exceptions to the rule is high, because rule-based systems become impractical in such applications. CBR is especially useful in such situations because it incorporates the solution of a newly entered case. In such situations methods for adaptation are used, providing the user with steps to combine and derive a solution from the collection of retrieved solutions.

The effective implementation of the knowledge application system requires a carefully thought-out methodology. The **Case Method cycle** [Kitano and Shimazu, 1996] is a methodology that describes an iterative approach to effectively develop CBR and knowledge application systems in general. The Case Method describes the following six processes:

1. ***System development process.*** This process is based on standard software engineering approaches, and its goal is to develop a knowledge application system that stores new cases and retrieves relevant cases.

2. ***Case library development process.*** The goal of this process is to develop and maintain a large-scale case library that adequately supports the domain in question.

3. ***System operation process.*** This process is based on standard software engineering and relational database management procedures. Its goal is to define the installation, deployment, and user support of the knowledge application system.

4. ***Database mining process.*** This process uses rule inferencing techniques and statistical analysis (as described in Chapters 12 and 13) to analyze the case library. This step could help infer new relationships between the data, which could be articulated to enhance the knowledge application system.

5. ***Management process.*** This process describes how the project task force will be formed and what organizational support will be provided to the project.

**6.** ***Knowledge transfer process.*** This process describes the incentive systems that will be implemented to encourage user acceptance and support of the knowledge application system. This step ensures that users feel compelled to augment the case library with new cases.

In terms of actually developing the case library (step 2 above), the process can also be described in terms of the following subprocesses [Kitano and Shimazu, 1996]:

**1.** ***Case collection.*** This process entails the collection of seed cases, which provide an initial view of the application. For example, for the SQUAD system we describe in Vignette 16-1, the developers started with 100 seed cases. These seed cases were used to define a format for the collection of future cases and for the design of the database structure. Seed cases typically do not follow a predefined structure, whereas the subsequent collection of cases follow the defined format. The number of seed cases may vary according to the application, as we see in this chapter, and may even be generated artificially by creating permutations of the cases available, as discussed in the case study in a later section.

**2.** ***Attribute-value extraction and hierarchy formation.*** This step (described in detail in Chapter 9) is essential for indexing and organizing the case library. The goal of this phase is to extract the attributes that define the case representation and indexing. This phase seeks to create a list of attributes that define each case, a list of values for each attribute, and a possible grouping of such attributes. In addition, the relationships among the attributes must also be defined. After the hierarchy is defined, the relative importance of each attribute is determined. This decision is typically reflective of the implementation domain. This phase results in a concept hierarchy created for each attribute, assigned with similarities between values. Also, this step requires mapping a hierarchy into a relational database or flat case library.

**3.** ***Feedback.*** This phase provides necessary feedback to those supplying the cases to the CBR system, so the quality of the cases can be improved.

The use of the Case Method in CBR development has been shown to result in significant reduction in system development workload and costs [Kitano and Shimazu, 1996]. For example, use of the Case Method during the development of SQUAD resulted in a savings of six person-months from the expected development time for the entire system. Furthermore, the workload required for the system maintenance was reduced to less than 10% of the initial workload.

Knowledge application systems not only apply a solution to a similar problem but also serve as a framework for **creative reasoning** [Leake, 1996]. For example, analogy-based reasoning could provide the initial ideas in solving new problems. Case memories can provide humans with the experience base they may lack. Faced with a problem, experts may recall experiences from the case library, and perform the adaptation and evaluation of the solutions that are sometimes relegated to the knowledge application systems. This is the emphasis of the SQUAD system presented in Vignette 16-1.

Knowledge application systems have enabled the implementation of decision support systems to support design tasks in diverse domains such as architecture, engineering, and lesson planning [Domeshek and Kolodner, 1991, 1992, 1993; Griffith and

Demeshek, 1996]. These decision support systems, also called **case-based design aids (CBDAs),** help human designers by making available a broad range of commentated designs. CBDAs can serve to illustrate critical design issues, explain design guidelines, and provide suggestions or warnings concerning specific design solutions. One of the critical components in the development of such systems is the supporting indexing system used to perform the relevant case search (refer to Chapter 9 for a brief discussion on case searching techniques).

Finally, case libraries can serve to accumulate organizational experiences, and can often be viewed as a corporate memory. For example, the case library for a help desk system could be considered a corporate memory of organizational experiences related to customer support. The same thing can be said of a rule-base supporting an expert system.

## ◇ ◇ ◇  Types of Knowledge Application Systems

Recall that knowledge application systems include advisor systems, fault diagnosis or troubleshooting systems, expert systems, help desk systems, and decision support systems in general.

One area where knowledge application systems are specifically important is in the implementation of help desk technologies. For example, Compaq[2] implemented a help desk support technology named SMART [Acorn and Walden, 1992], to assist help desk employees track calls and resolve customer service problems. Compaq's SMART system was developed to support its customer service department when handling user calls through its toll-free number. SMART is an integrated call tracking and problem-solving system, supported by hundreds of cases that help resolve diagnostic problems resulting from the use of Compaq products [Allen, 1994]. The system automatically retrieves from the case library historical cases similar to the one currently faced by the customer. The customer service representative then uses that solution to help customers solve the problem at hand. SMART developers reported an increase from 50% to 87% of the problems that could be resolved directly by the first level of customer support. The implementation of SMART at Compaq paid for itself in 1 year with the productivity improvements it brought to the company.

Fault diagnosis is increasingly becoming a major emphasis for the development of knowledge applications systems, as we discuss in a later section. Fault diagnosis has been one of the main focuses of intelligent system implementations. One of the earliest successful implementations of knowledge application systems for the diagnosis and recovery of faults in large multistation machine tools, was CABER at Lockheed Martin[3] [Mark et al., 1996]. Although these milling machines are equipped with self-diagnostic capabilities, typically they resolved only 20% to 40% of the systems faults. The expectation for the CABER system was that it must help identify how the equipment experienced the fault, and how the faulted state could be safely exited. Typically, an equipment fault results in a call to the field-service engineer. For the creation of the

---

[2]www.compaq.com
[3]www.lockheedmartin.com/

case library that supports this system, Lockheed counted over 10,000 records collected by the field-service engineers. CABER augmented the self-diagnostic capabilities of the milling machine, which provided junior field-service engineers with the necessary tools to resolve the fault and reduce machine downtime.

In addition, Compaq also developed a fault diagnosis system for its PageMarq printer line known as QuickSource [Nguyen et al., 1993]. A case base of over 500 diagnostic cases supported the QuickSource knowledge applications system. This system, designed to run in a Windows environment, was shipped with printers to enable customers to do their own diagnosis.

In the following three sections we discuss the development and implementation details for four knowledge application systems. The first system, SOS Advisor, is a Web-based expert system built using a set of rules. The reason heuristics are used for the implementation of this system is that a small number of rules can define the domain, that is, define the eligibility potential for companies interested in applying for a specific federal program. In later sections we describe the development of a knowledge application system based on CBR technology. The first knowledge application system to be discussed, Total Recall, was designed with the goal of reusing the solutions to software quality problems, because these problems recur throughout the organization. In a later section, another knowledge application system developed for NASA, is described which is somewhat different in the sense that it's designed to assist in the solution of new problems as they occur, by identifying similar problems that may have happened in the past and their corresponding solutions. Finally, we describe Generator Artificial Intelligence Diagnostics (GenAID), one of the earliest diagnostic knowledge application systems. GenAID is based on the use of rules and is still operational today.

We begin by describing the development of SOS Advisor.

## ◆>◆>◆> Case Study: SBIR/STTR Online System (SOS) Advisor A Web-Based Expert System to Profile Organizations

To accompany the discussions presented in this section, please refer to the SOS Advisor demo found in the CD accompanying this book.

The **SBIR/STTR Online System (SOS) Advisor** is a Web-based expert system used to identify potential applicants to the Small Business Innovation Research (SBIR) and Small Business Technology Transfer Research (STTR) programs. The purpose of the SOS Advisor is to optimize the time required to examine the potential eligibility of companies seeking SBIR/STTR funding. Established by Congress in 1982, the SBIR and STTR programs help NASA and other federal agencies develop innovative technologies by providing competitive research contracts to U.S.-owned small business companies with fewer than 500 employees. These programs also help by providing seed capital to increase private sector commercialization of innovations resulting from federal research and development.[4] The goal of the SOS Advisor is to optimize the time required to examine the potential eligibility

---

[4]http://technology.ksc.nasa.gov/WWWaccess/SBIR.html

for companies seeking SBIR/STTR funding. The SOS Advisor prompts users through an interactive questionnaire used to evaluate their potential eligibility to be an SBIR/STTR recipient. Users only need to click on *yes* or *no* to answer the 10 questions that frame the eligibility criteria.

On entering the Web site (www.sbir.fiu.edu), users are asked to register by providing their name, e-mail address, technology, and company uniform resource locator (URL). Once the user submits the registration form, the SOS Advisor questionnaire page is launched. The questionnaire consists of 10 questions used to determine the eligibility of the company. The profile questions are listed in Table 16-2, to which users can respond by selecting the radio button next to the *yes, no,* or *not sure.* Answering *not sure* prompts users for more information, necessary to define the potential candidate's eligibility for funding. To match the SBIR winners' profile, users are expected to answer according to the responses specified in Table 16-2. Question 6 is for information purposes only, because it does not constitute a necessary criterion for eligibility. Each question has a *Tip* icon that allows the user to obtain additional information related to the corresponding question, through the use of a pop-up window. In this manner users can learn about SBIR and STTR requirements, and the reasoning for each question. The one-page questionnaire format

### TABLE 16-2 SBIR/STTR Profile Framing Questions

| *Question* | *SBIR Winners' Profile* |
|---|---|
| 1. I would like to know if your company is independently owned and operated. | Yes |
| 2. Is this company located in the United States? | Yes |
| 3. Is this company owned by at least 51% U.S. citizens or permanent U.S. residents? | Yes |
| 4. Regarding your company size, does it have less than 500 employees? | Yes |
| 5. What about your proposed innovation? Has it been patented or does it have any patents pending? | No |
| 6. Could it be patented, copyrighted, or otherwise protected? | Don't Care |
| 7. Are you planning on using SBIR/STTR funding to conduct any of the following?<br>   a. Systems studies<br>   b. Market research<br>   c. Commercial development of existing products or proven concepts<br>   d. Studies<br>   e. Laboratory evaluations<br>   f. Modifications of existing products without innovative changes | No |
| 8. Does your technology area align with any of the following research areas of interest to NASA? | Yes |
| 9. Is there a likelihood of your proposed technology having a commercial application? | Yes |
| 10. Has your firm been paid or is currently being paid for equivalent commercial application? | No |

allows users to spend a minimum of time when answering the profile questions. Furthermore, the user has the opportunity to see at once all the questions and answers to review and modify the answers before submission. The *suggestions* field provides users with the option of providing feedback to the development team. Figure 16-1 describes the architecture of the SOS Advisor.

The user information provided and the corresponding answers to the questionnaire are stored in the SOS Advisor database and evaluated automatically by the SBIR/STTR Web advisor. Using a set of rules that evaluate the user responses, the advisor identifies whether the user profile matches the profile of an SBIR/STTR candidate. SOS Advisor then automatically sends an e-mail to the user, with the results of the evaluation. At the same time, if user profile match is positive, the system automatically notifies via e-mail the corresponding NASA personnel, with the user point of contact.

The rules that evaluate the user profiles were developed using a scripting code. The scripts evaluate the answers given and based on predefined rules to generate the user profiles. SOS Advisor has been on-line since March 1, 2000 and receives about 12 hits per day, and each user has visited the site approximately three times. The NASA Kennedy Space Center Commercialization Office refers most visitors of the SOS Advisor, because the SOS Advisor is linked to the Web page of that office.

❖❖ ❖❖ ❖❖ **FIGURE 16-1** SOS Advisor Architecture

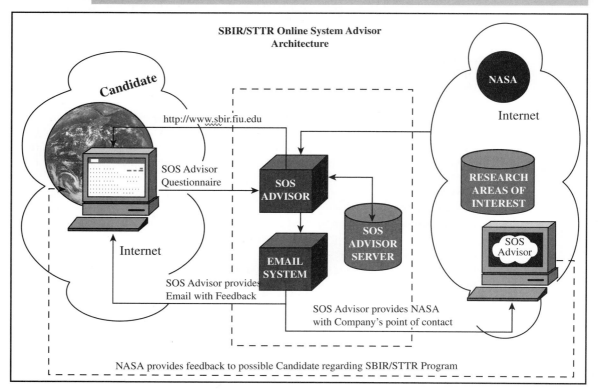

Based on the user's answers to the questionnaire, the SOS Advisor is able to determine whether the user profile indeed matches that of an SBIR/STTR recipient, and provides sufficient information to educate potential applicants about related funding opportunities. However, the SOS Advisor System endures certain limitations, namely, that many Web site visitors do not take the time to complete the questionnaire. Since its initial deployment of the Web, several modifications aimed at speeding up the application and increasing the user's trust on the application have been made to the tool, to increase the percentage of users completing the questionnaire. For example, the initial design of SOS Advisor presented the questionnaire over several screens, one per question. This original design was replaced with a one-screen questionnaire, speeding up the time required to complete it. To increase user's trust on the application, the graphical user interface (GUI) background was modified to follow an outer space theme, alluding to the NASA theme. Finally, a promise of confidentiality reading, "The information will be used to assess the organization's qualification criteria and to identify resources that could assist the organization in applying for the SBIR/STTR program. This information is considered private and will not be shared with any other organization," was included in the welcoming screen to assure users that their rights to privacy are to be respected. These considerations resulted in increased user acceptance of the application.

In summary, the SOS Advisor is a knowledge application system that helps to identify those companies whose profiles match that of an SBIR/STTR candidate, and to focus the resources of federally funded assistance programs. The system prompts users to answer a set of questions that describe whether the company meets the stipulated criteria defined for companies interested in the SBIR/STTR program. The system then uses a set of heuristics or rules to quickly examine each company's qualifications, instead of attempting to transfer the knowledge about the program requirements to each of the companies interested in applying for the program (although that option is available through launching the *Tip* section). For those companies with matching profiles, the SOS Advisor automatically sends the company's contact information to a NASA employee who identifies appropriate assistance resources available for the benefit of the inquiring company. In this way, the SOS Advisor helps minimize distractions to the NASA program representative caused by casual Cyber surfers, because it only forwards the information for the companies that match the qualification criteria. In addition, a by-product of this effort is the creation of a database with point-of-contact information for each company that completes the survey, which can be used to generate mailings and announcements of upcoming SBIR/STTR informative events.

The key importance of SOS Advisor is that it enables NASA to apply the knowledge about qualification requirements for the SBIR/STTTR program without tying up the time of NASA program representatives. Prior to the development of the SOS Advisor, NASA employees provided this information and performed the initial assessment of companies interested in the program. The NASA representatives repeatedly used their tacit knowledge base to perform the analysis. The SOS Advisor helps to apply this knowledge, freeing up the NASA employees to use their time so they can provide more personalized advice to those companies that meet the program's stipulated criteria.

In the next section, we discuss how knowledge technologies can be used to reuse organizational knowledge about software quality.

## ◆ ◆ ◆ Case Study: Product Quality Analysis for National Semiconductor

To accompany the discussions presented in this section, please refer to the National Semiconductor, Total Recall, demo found in the CD accompanying this book.[5]

National Semiconductor[6] was established in 1959 in Santa Clara, California. Since that time, with manufacturing sites around the world, the company has been a leader in the semiconductor industry. National Semiconductor had annual sales of $1.5 billion in fiscal 2002 and approximately 10,100 employees worldwide. National Semiconductor has set the pace for revolutionary electronics technologies, with 2,170 patents and over 10,000 products; this company's achievements range from the design and manufacture of early discrete transistors to the introduction of sophisticated integrated circuit product lines.

National Semiconductor's product quality record represents about a 22-ppm defect rate. Although this is an extraordinary quality record, today's environment requires semiconductor component deliveries with zero defects, enabling manufacturers to achieve lower costs and just-in-time (JIT) manufacturing schemes. Therefore, a rare failure is a cause of immediate concern for both National and the customer, because it's imperative to quickly determine and take corrective action; in particular, if the failure indicates that a manufacturing process is moving out of statistical control. National's customers demand rapid and complete failure analysis, as well as the adoption of corrective actions that ensure the accurate identification and solution for the root cause of the failure. The advanced technology and high degree of complexity in today's semiconductors make this analysis a major challenge. For this purpose, National depends on its Worldwide Quality Network, a centralized manufacturing quality assurance (QA) group. This group consists of engineers who use the **Product Quality Analysis (PQA)** process to focus on root cause determination and finding solutions to each of these failures.

To support the engineers involved in the PQA and other quality-related business processes, an in-house team at National developed the Advanced Quality and Reliability Information System (AQUARIS) in 1995, a tracking system that provided a searchable repository of PQAs. Some of the limitations of AQUARIS related to its inefficient ability to query similar past failures. The workflow associated with the PQA process is quite elaborate and can involve many analysis steps to determine the true causes of a device's failure or, in some cases, just a cursory analysis revealing that there is no problem with the part at all. In any event, these steps taken to analyze parts are carefully and methodically accomplished, and the interim and final results are captured and stored in the AQUARIS system. Many times, engineers engaged in the various stages of analysis make "hunch" decisions based on prior experiences or anecdotal information, which can significantly shorten the analysis cycle.

By 1999, it was recognized that AQUARIS did not provide an effective means of recalling information that could prevent unnecessary work from being performed, while at the same time promoting learning from prior failures. Engineers

---

[5]We acknowledge National Semiconductor, in particular, Art Hamilton, Mike Glynn, Mike Meltzer, and Amir Razavi, for the support in creating this section and the accompanying demo.
[6]www.national.com

would typically spend hours attempting to search on AQUARIS for similar past PQAs that they distantly remembered, based on some similarity to their current analysis. Typically because their search centered on retrieving recalled PQAs, it only focused on those with which they were previously involved and didn't include the work of others. Soon National recognized the need to better collect these experiences in a way that could be adequately applied by others, because written reports collected in AQUARIS did not provide an efficient means to extract and apply this knowledge when needed.

To respond to this challenge, National developed a knowledge application system based on the use of CBR technology. The development team adapted and expanded the back-end relational database that had driven AQUARIS to provide integration with the CBR system. The overall application, titled the **Total Recall** system, can be viewed as consisting of four components and the Web client.

Figure 16-2 illustrates the Total Recall system architecture. Users typically enter PQAs into the application server, and the users' workflow is illustrated with the dark arrows labeled as *User operation* in Figure 16-2. The Total Recall database is used to collect the results from the testing performed in the different PQA activities. Data from the Total Recall database are used to create the CBR case library. Note that not all PQAs produce new cases for the case library. A **nomination process** to the case library administrator is used to denote *potential* cases for the case library, illustrated by the hollow arrows labeled as *Admin Only* in Figure 16-2.

The case library stores the experience gained from the PQA process, as a collection of cases. During an active analysis, the Total Recall system relays queries to the CBR server by gathering information entered up to that point. The CBR server responds to the query with an ordered set of cases sorted by declining similarity. The

❖ ❖ ❖ **FIGURE 16-2** Total Recall System Architecture

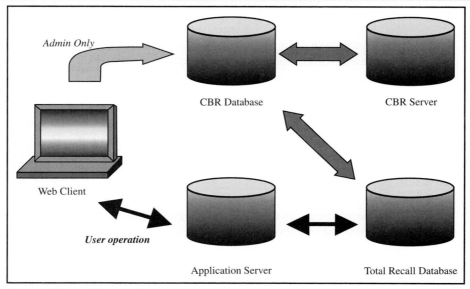

*Courtesy:* National Semiconductor.

**footprint number** identifies the cases in the CBR server, and the Total Recall application performs an additional search to translate these footprint numbers into the original PQA and device serial numbers that are more meaningful to the user. This information then allows the engineers to retrieve, on-line, the corresponding PQA reports. Engineers can then study the reports identified as similar to the case at hand, and decide whether the failure mechanism and corrective actions described for these earlier failures apply to their current situation. The engineer makes the final decision to adopt or adapt these findings.

Each basic component of Total Recall is described as follows:

1. ***Application server.*** The main server for the Total Recall application. This server performs data manipulation and user presentation. This component is the result of the system development process, described in an earlier section.
2. ***Total Recall database.*** Maintains all the information related to the testing results of the PQA process.
3. ***Case library.*** A separate database containing CBR representation of cases, including mapping information that relates the case footprint numbers to specific devices analyzed during PQA processing. This component is the result of the case library development process, described in an earlier section.
4. ***CBR server.*** The final case library and CBR engine.

When a CBR query is made, it is made from the Application server to the CBR engine. The CBR engine responds with a set of footprint numbers that represent the set of cases that are similar to the case in the query. Other devices on other PQAs may have failed in a similar way. Instead of treating these as separate cases, they are considered **reference cases.** The same footprint number is also used to identify these reference cases.

As mentioned before, when engineers complete a new PQA analysis, they decide whether they will nominate the PQA for possible inclusion in the case base. The Total Recall system at this point attempts to take advantage of the engineers' current knowledge of the failure, by allowing a thorough refinement of the case description. At this point the case base administrator performs the final evaluation of the nominated case, by searching the case library to identify whether similar cases already exist in the library. In general, it is preferred not to have numerous similar cases in the case library to provide users with manageable search results. If multiple cases reflecting the same type of failure and analysis are to be included in the case library, one is designated as the footprint case whereas the others are designated as reference cases. Figure 16-3 presents the details of how the CBR database is populated. The case library administrator can make the decision to treat newly nominated cases as a new footprint or as a reference case to an existing case. Also, this decision may be left to an engineering technical review board.

One of the most time-consuming tasks required for the implementation of Total Recall was the initial population of the case library. A subset of PQAs from AQUARIS was evaluated and the corresponding test data had to be cleansed and augmented prior to manually representing them as cases in the new system. This task also presented significant cultural challenges because it required the involvement of failure analysis engineers to review each potential case at a technical level. This task represented significant

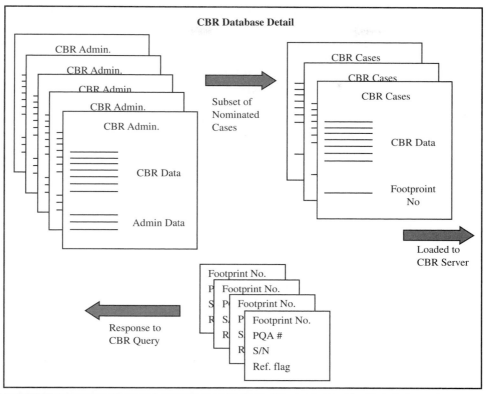

❖ ❖ ❖ **FIGURE 16-3 Details of the CBR Database**

*Courtesy:* National Semiconductor.

additional work requirement from this group, so only limited success could be claimed. In addition, lack of adequate CBR training and commitment from the users could also be attributed to the low level of support from this group. The initial case library represented approximately 200 cases, which were barely enough to perform the initial testing. The size of the case library was expected to grow substantially during the implementation of Total Recall. This was not expected to impact the application adversely, given the system's structured architecture.

In terms of its user interface, Total Recall mimics much of the AQUARIS workflow, with Web-based functionality and options required to capture new information, such as activities and explicit, related observations. Testing included the analysis of prior-solved cases through Total Recall. Engineers familiar with these cases then correlated these results with prior results. The testing process confirmed that the results of using Total Recall were consistent with the prior-case solutions.

Although the team at National is still faced with the evaluation of the usefulness of Total Recall, the benefits it offers are already prompting other developments at the company. For example, other organizational subunits are considering the use of CBR to support the company's external Web site in helping customers select devices that most closely meet their circuit needs. Systems like Total Recall are not intended to eliminate the analysis engineer. The Total Recall system acts as a cognitive prosthesis for the engineer, who is able to make a faster and perhaps more accurate prognosis of the failure case on hand.

The key importance of Total Recall is that it enables application of the knowledge gained from completed failure analyses performed throughout the worldwide quality organization. Prior to the development of Total Recall, only some of this information was kept in the AQUARIS database. The AQUARIS database was not a useful platform for knowledge application, because it was hard to identify and apply prior relevant knowledge. The Total Recall system helps to apply knowledge resulting from the software-enabled quality process. This knowledge can be applied to prevent unnecessary work from being performed, while promoting learning from prior failures. For more details on the Total Recall system, refer to Watson [2003].

In the next section, we see how knowledge application systems can assist the problem-solving process, even when these are new problems instead of recurring old problems as in Total Recall.

## <> <> <> Case Study: Out-of-Family Disposition System for Shuttle Processing

To accompany the discussions presented in this section, please refer to the NASA Shuttle demo found in the CD accompanying this book.

The Shuttle Processing Directorate of KSC provides preflight, launch, landing, and recovery services for KSC. Within the directorate, the Shuttle vehicle engineering department is responsible for the engineering management and technical direction of preflight, launch, landing, and recovery activities for all Space Shuttle vehicles and integration of payloads. An important function of this group is to perform the **out-of-family disposition (OFD) process,** which deals with any operation or performance outside the expected range that has not been previously experienced. These anomalies are described as out-of-family in the sense that they are new anomalies, and differentiated from in-family anomalies that have previously occurred. In the OFD process, new problems (which we reference as cases) are referenced, solved, and documented. Just like in problem solving, drawing analogies to similar prior cases helps to solve new problems. Therefore, this process lends itself to the adoption of knowledge application technologies, and documenting these anomalies in a way that makes the solutions to these problems available to the rest of the organization. As more unfamiliar cases get documented within the knowledge application system, the case database grows and becomes more comprehensive.

To build the OFD prototype, a sample set of 12 OFD **problem reports (PRs)** were collected, each describing an anomaly identified during the processing of the Space Shuttle, together with the anomaly resolution. The OFD PRs comprise a cover page with 36 entries that describe details for the OFD anomaly. Part of the report also details the description and requirement of the troubleshooting plan, damaged part specifications, and alternative replacement parts. PRs are typically from 10 to 70 pages in length, and do not follow a prescribed format. The final pages of the report included the most reasonable rationale, which details the most likely reason for the failure, as

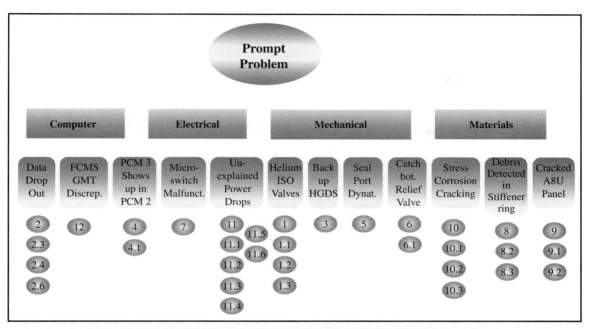

◈ ◈ ◈   FIGURE 16-4 4th Order Distribution Tree for the OFD Problem Reports

well as the most reasonable repair plan and justification. Also, the PR includes engineering orders for replacement parts, as well as related part specifications. Finally, the OFD PR includes a problem summary and conclusion. Each of the 12 OFD PRs were used to build a case in the case library.

The 12 OFD PRs were very different from one another. The steps in the creation of the case library were:

1. Identify and establish a set of categories or clusters to stratify them through analysis of their similarities and differences. In our example, we found the PRs grouped into four categories. This resulted in a fourth-order **distribution tree** (Figure 16-4). The most appropriate problem categories identified were computer, electrical, mechanical, and materials. Given that this was only a prototype based on a total of only 12 PRs, there was only an average of two to three cases corresponding to each problem category.

2. Analyze each PR to identify a case title, a description, a set of characterizing questions and answers, and a resulting action. Building the case library required combining information from the sections of the PR, because the reporting format of the PR is different from the way cases are stored in the case library. For example, for each case in the library, the description of the action taken was deduced from a combination of the PR sections describing the most reasonable rationale, summary, and conclusion.

3. Develop a set of descriptive questions for each case, which need to be in natural language format. Some CBR software packages require that the set of descriptive questions for each case must be normalized, to ensure that the similarity

function can work properly. The objective of the similarity function is to identify from the case database those cases that are similar to the case under analysis by the end user. Consider, for example, the Electrical category in Figure 16-4. Normalization means that cases 4, 7, and 11 should be described by a similar number of question–answer pairs. However, cases that are considerably different from other cases (like those catalogued in different clusters) can be defined with fewer questions because retrieval conflicts are less likely to occur.

4. Just as experts draw on their wide experiences to infer solutions to new problems, case-based systems work best when the case library is large enough to be representative of the total set of possible anomalies. As such, to develop a working prototype, the application developers were compelled to add permutations of the OFD problem reports to the case library, so that the additional cases improved the system's ability of finding a relevant solution. With a total of 12 cases, permutations of these original reports were developed to allow the library to represent a larger subset of possible anomalies. These permutations were created through the definition of variations for each question–answer pair that didn't correspond to the PR in question. Referring back to Figure 16-4, each PR corresponds to case numbers 1 through 12. In this example, the case corresponding to the **data-drop-out** PR appears as case 2, and the permutations corresponding to this case appear as 2.3, 2.4, and 2.6. The diagnosing solution for case 2 is found after answering *yes* or *no* to the set questions that accurately describe the data-drop-out problem. The permutations for case 2 correspond to a differing answer to the questions that essentially describe the case. This process of adding permuted cases resulted in a total set of 34 cases in the case library.

5. Following the development of the case library, the case library must be validated to ensure the proper execution of the application. The validation process requires that none of the following conditions exist in the case library, which essentially diminishes the accuracy of the application:

   a. *Disjunctions* (i.e., otherwise identical cases with separate solutions). Disjunctive cases must be combined into a single case.

   b. *Internal disjunctions.* These are characterized by situations in which a single case in a cluster contains multiple questions that are not answered in any other case in the same cluster. To resolve **internal disjunctions,** combine these questions into a single question with multiple answers, which allows the system to match a conversation's query containing either answer, and also reduces the number of questions in the cases.

   c. *Subsumed cases.* These **subsumed cases** are characterized by one case being a logical specialization of another and having the same solution. In these circumstances, eliminate the more specific case.

   d. *Automated testing functionality.* Finally, some case authoring tools provide the ability to validate the case library through an automated testing functionality. This functionality allows for verification if the retrieval precision for the case library is acceptable.

Figure 16-5 shows the information contained within each case in the case library. The background of the screen shows the list of cases within the library. When double-clicking on any case, a window containing all the reference information appears in the front. The

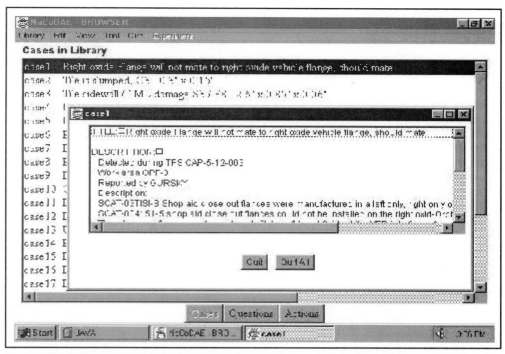

<> <> <> **FIGURE 16-5** OFD Case Database

small window shows data referencing for case 1. Figure 16-6 shows the application software in its search mode. The user inputs the topic of trouble in the description box. After this is done, the software will output all relevant cases in a ranked order inside the Ranked Cases box. Cases are given a rank score according to their relevance to the description topic. The application also outputs all relevant questions that are to be answered by the user to further constrain the search to the most relevant topic. These questions are also ranked according to their relevance to the topic. Once the user has answered the questions, a single most relevant case is identified. Figure 16-6 presents the screen with the Dialogue box, which shows output of the search, title, and description of the most relevant case (highest ranking case), and the steps and actions needed to solve the case. More information about this case study can be found in Becerra-Fernandez and Aha [1998].

The key importance of the OFD system is that it enables one to apply the knowledge gained through solving prior problems, when solving new anomalies experienced during the Space Shuttle processing process. The OFD system helps to apply knowledge to prevent unnecessary work from being performed, while promoting learning from prior failures. Prior to the development of the OFD system, this information remained in the tacit knowledge base of the engineer in charge of the process. Because NASA enjoys the advantage of having a relatively stable workforce, engineers use their own knowledge base to identify similar cases that they have solved in the past. However, as downsizing continues to be part of the federal landscape, systems like the OFD are essential as a platform for knowledge application to identify and apply prior relevant knowledge.

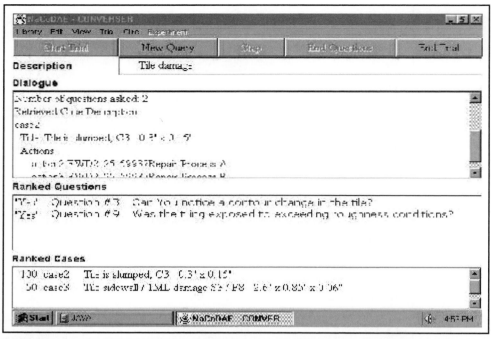

❮❯ ❮❯ ❮❯ **FIGURE 16-6** Search Results

In the next section, we discuss how rule-based systems can be instrumental for the design of troubleshooting systems that have stood the test of time.

## ❮❯ ❮❯ ❮❯ Case Study: GenAID a Knowledge Application System for Early Fault Detection at Westinghouse

Since the creation in the early 1970s of MYCIN, one of the earliest medical diagnosis systems designed to determine the infectious agent in a patient's blood and specify a treatment, a great number of knowledge application systems over diverse domains have been developed. Some of these were originally intended to be research prototypes, whose purpose was merely to show the applicability of the technology or to illustrate an alternative problem-solving strategy within the application domain. Other systems reached a certain stage in their development and, for a variety of reasons (e.g., cost or lack of management interest), did not progress into operational systems.

One of the earliest knowledge application systems developed as a commercial product for external users who paid for its use, was the Westinghouse GenAID system [Gonzalez, 1986]. Westinghouse Electric Corporation (now a part of Siemens Corporation), a manufacturer of large power generation equipment, developed this system in the early 1980s. Westinghouse decided that a market existed for a system to help its customers decrease the downtime of their turbine generators through the early detection of potentially serious abnormal operating conditions.

From a financial standpoint, this goal presented a potential for significant cost savings to the Westinghouse clients. A large, base-loaded (i.e., continuously operated) power plant during the peak load seasons (winter and summer) has a typical downtime cost ranging from $60,000 to $250,000 per day, depending on the size and the type of the plant. This daily cost reflects just the difference in cost for replacement power needed to supply the Westinghouse customer's load (because that power must come from less efficient plants in its own system or must be purchased from neighboring utilities, usually at a premium). This daily cost does not take into account the cost of repairing the broken unit. The magnitude of this problem becomes apparent when you realize that a major incident can cause downtimes ranging from 3 to 6 months!

The basis for GenAID was that many of these so-called major incidents actually started out as relatively minor faults that went undetected for a comparatively long time. This neglect caused the problem to become serious and, subsequently, led to a major incident. Had the problem been detected early, corrective action could have been taken to drastically reduce the outage from several months to 2 or 3 days (or even less).

Power generation equipment is typically well instrumented with sensors that are monitored continuously by a data acquisition system. If the data were to be inspected periodically by a knowledgeable individual (an expert), these incipient failures could be detected in time to take corrective action. The problem is that power plant personnel do not typically have the expertise to properly interpret these sets of readings. By providing this expertise to a typical power station, presumably, major destructive incidents could be avoided.

Westinghouse first attempted to solve this problem in the late 1970s with a microprocessor-based system using probabilistic analysis. The system worked well for up to 10 possible malfunctions, but had a number of serious limitations. Some of these include difficulty in representing the knowledge required by the statistical solution and the inability to handle more than one malfunction at a time. Additionally, computations became too complex for the system when more than 10 malfunctions were represented. For these reasons, the focus of the research turned to knowledge-based systems, which at the time (1979), were in their infancy.

In 1980, Westinghouse embarked on the development of a system that would accurately represent the knowledge concerning generators' malfunctions and their repair. Westinghouse R&D laboratories in Pittsburgh and the Robotics Institute at Carnegie-Mellon University jointly developed the resulting product, called *Process Diagnostic System (PDS)*. The first device chosen for commercial application of on-line diagnostics was the electric generator. GenAID represents the combination of PDS and the specific diagnostic knowledge used by experts to detect problems in these generators. GenAID originally resided at a central location in Orlando, Florida, where it accepted data directly from each of the plant sites across the United States on a semicontinuous basis, and diagnosed any developing malfunctions in real time. Because of limitations in the sensors monitoring the generators, the input data have some associated uncertainty that cause the results produced by GenAID to rarely be absolutely certain. As a result, all diagnoses produced are qualified by a numerical value representing the likelihood of the problem existing. This value is called the *confidence factor*, and each specific diagnosis has one. These results were then transmitted to the plant site over a data link, for use by the plant operators. GenAID now resides at each of the local power stations utilizing

Westinghouse generators, instead of being centrally located, with all diagnoses displayed internally to the plant operators.

Development on the GenAID knowledge base began in 1983 with limited deployment starting 1 year later. The development was completed in 1987. By 1990, there were 10 generators connected to the system with 4 others in the process of installation. GenAID currently serves 13 generator units across the United States. The PDS shell has been upgraded, and is now called PCPDS, because it was modified to run on general-purpose personal computers (PCs) Although PCPDS retains much of the PDS original operational characteristics, its user interface has been completely revamped to reflect the latest concepts in GUIs. The typical installation contains in the neighborhood of 2,500 rules.

Since its development, GenAID has been successful in diagnosing a number of problems that might have otherwise gone undetected and resulted in serious incidents. As a result, Siemens–Westinghouse has extended this concept to other equipment it manufactures, such as steam turbines and gas turbines. The most recent expert system developed and offered by Siemens–Westinghouse diagnoses gas turbine engines in power generating stations. Called GTAID, this knowledge-based system performs the same function as GenAID and is very similar in structure. It currently serves approximately 15 units throughout the United States and its use is growing rapidly in popularity.

In fact, GenAID is a prototypical knowledge application system. Its development required the elicitation of important knowledge possessed by human experts, capturing this knowledge electronically, and then the ability to apply it in a way that multiplied manifold the original utility of that knowledge by placing it in an automatic monitoring and diagnostic system.

## ◆ ◆ ◆ Limitations of Knowledge Application Systems

There are some practical limitations to the development of knowledge application systems. These relate to the fact that most of these systems are developed to serve a task-specific domain problem, and are typically not integrated with the organization's enterprise systems. Other limitations also exist, for example, for knowledge application systems based on CBR technologies; the following limitations apply [Kitano and Shimazu, 1996]:

1. *Security.* Cases may include sensitive information. Knowledge application systems must consider the incorporation of security measures, including access control according to the user's organizational role. If knowledge application systems do not incorporate security measures, systems may not realize their maximum value.
2. *Scalability.* Knowledge application systems must represent a large enough number of cases so that the majority of the new experiences are represented in the case-based system. This means the knowledge application system must reach saturation prior to its deployment. Reaching system saturation means that most typical cases would have already been reported in the system. The number of cases necessary to reach the saturation point changes according to the domain. For SQUAD, discussed in an earlier section, reaching this point required the inclusion of about 3,000 cases each year, a number that later reduced to 1,000 per year. The more complex the domain is, the higher the importance of keeping the growth of the case base viable. Clearly, the continual growth of the case library also requires the use of complex indexing schemes, which may result in decreased system stability.

**3. *Speed.*** As the size of the case library grows to a more comprehensive representation of real environments, computing and searching costs also increase. Therefore, developers of knowledge application systems must consider the use of complex indexing schemes that guarantee acceptable case retrieval times and performance levels.

In addition, knowledge application systems may not be able to solve all the problems that come across. In particular, diagnosing problems may be increasingly difficult in complex environments, as evidenced by the Space Shuttle Columbia tragedy. Diagnosing everything that went wrong or might go wrong in such environments may not be possible with systems like the ones described above. New technologies will need to be developed to prevent incidents in complex engineering environments.

Some rule-based systems could suffer from other limitations, namely, the lack of scalability. Other technologies offer a different set of limitations. In essence, the benefits that the implementation of knowledge application systems bring to the organization outweigh their limitations, and they will continue to provide competitive advantages to those organizations that continue to implement them.

## SUMMARY ◇ ◇ ◇

In this chapter, we discuss what knowledge application systems are, along with design considerations, and specific types of intelligent technologies that enable such systems. The Case Method cycle, a methodology to effectively develop knowledge application systems, is presented. Also, we discuss different types of knowledge application systems: expert systems, help desk systems, and fault diagnosis systems. Four case studies that describe the implementation of knowledge application systems are presented, each based on different intelligent technologies and designed to accomplish different goals: provide advice, fault detection, and creative reasoning. The first system is based on the use of rules, to advise potential applicants to the SBIR/STTR program whether they meet the program's criteria. The second system, based on CBR technology, helps engineers diagnose faulty chips. The third system helps NASA engineers find solutions to new problems faced while processing the Space Shuttle, assuming that new problems could be related to or be a combination of old problems. The fourth system uses rules to troubleshoot electrical generators in real time. Finally, limitations of knowledge application systems are discussed.

## KEY TERMS ◇ ◇ ◇

- analogy-based reasoning—p. 327
- attribute-value extraction—p. 330
- case-based design aids (CBDA)—p. 331
- case-based reasoning (CBR)—p. 325
- case library—p. 338
- Case Method cycle—p. 329

- constraint-based reasoning—p. 327
- creative reasoning—p. 330
- data drop out—p. 342
- diagrammatic reasoning—p. 327
- direction—p. 325
- distribution tree—p. 341
- domain knowledge—p. 326
- exemplar-based reasoning—p. 327

- footprint number—p. 338
- instance-based reasoning—p. 327
- internal disjunctions—p. 342
- knowledge application systems—p. 325
- mapping problem—p. 327
- model-based reasoning (MBR)—p. 327
- nomination process—p. 337

- out-of-family disposition (OFD) process — p. 340
- problem reports (PRs) — p. 340
- product quality analysis (PQA) — p. 336
- reference cases — p. 338
- routines — p. 325
- SBIR/STTR Online System (SOS) Advisor — p. 332
- subsumed cases — p. 342
- Total Recall system — p. 337

## REVIEW QUESTIONS ◆ ◇ ◆ ◇ ◆ ◇

1. What are some of the intelligent technologies that provide the foundation for the creation of knowledge application systems?
2. Describe the four steps in the CBR process.
3. Describe the steps and the importance of the Case Method cycle.
4. Explain the case library development process.
5. What are some of the limitations of knowledge application systems?

## APPLICATION EXERCISES ◆ ◇ ◆ ◇ ◆ ◇

1. Identify examples of knowledge application systems in use in your organization. What are some of the intelligent technologies that enable those systems?
2. Design a knowledge application system to support your business needs. Describe the type of system and the foundation technologies that you would use to develop such a system.
3. Design the system architecture for the system described in Question 2 above.
4. Identify three recent examples in the literature of knowledge application systems.

## REFERENCES ◆ ◇ ◆ ◇ ◆ ◇

Aamodt, A., and Plaza, E. 1994. Case-based reasoning: Foundational issues, methodological variations, and system approaches. *AI Communications,* 7(1), 39–52.

Acorn, T., and Walden, S. 1992. SMART: Support Management Automated Reasoning Technology for Compaq Customer Service. In Proceedings 4th Innovative Applications of Artificial Intelligence Conf., San Jose, CA.

Aha, D., Kibler, D., and Albert, M. 1991. Instance-based learning algorithms. *Machine Learning,* 6(1), 37–66.

Allen, B. 1994. Case-based reasoning: Business applications. *Communications of the ACM,* 37(3), 40–42.

Becerra-Fernandez, I., and Aha, D. 1998. Case-Based Problem Solving for Knowledge Management Systems. In Proc. 12th Annual Int. Florida Artificial Intelligence Research Symp. (FLAIRS): Knowledge Management Track, Orlando, FL, May.

Chandrasekaran, B., Narayanan, H., and Iwasaki, Y. 1993. Reasoning with diagrammatic representations. *AI Magazine,* 14(2), 49–56.

Davis, R. 1984. Diagnostic reasoning based on structure and behavior. *Artificial Intelligence,* 24(1–3), 347–410.

de Kleer, J. 1976. Local Methods for Localizing Faults in Electronic Circuits. Memo 394, MIT Artificial Intelligence Laboratory, Cambridge, MA.

Domeshek, E., and Kolodner, J. 1991. Toward a case-based aid for architecture. Toward a case-based aid for conceptual design. *International Journal of Expert Systems,* 4(2), 201–220.

Domeshek, E., and Kolodner, J. 1992. A case-based design aid for architecture. In Gero, J.S. (Ed.), *Artificial Inteligence in Design* 92. Kluwer, Norwell, MA, pp. 487–516.

Domeshek, E., and Kolodner, J. 1993. Using the points of large cases. *Artificial Intelligence for Engineering Design, Analysis, and Manufacturing,* 7(2), 87–96.

Genesereth, M. 1984. The use of design descriptions in automated diagnosis. *Artificial Intelligence,* 24(1), 411–436.

Gonzalez, A.J., Osborne, R.L., Kemper, C., and Lowenfeld, S. 1986. On-line diagnosis of turbine generators using artificial intelligence. *IEEE Transactions on Energy Conversion,* EC-1(2) June, 68–74.

Griffith, A., and Domeshek, E. 1996. Indexing evaluations of buildings to aid conceptual design. In

Leake, D. (Ed.), *Case-Based Reasoning Experiences, Lessons, and Future Directions.* AAAI/MIT Press, Menlo Park, CA, pp. 68–80.

Glasgow, J., Narayanan, H., and Chandrasekaran, B. (Eds.). 1995. *Diagrammatic Reasoning: Cognitive Computational Perspectives.* MIT Press, Cambridge, MA.

Kibler, D., and Aha, D. 1987. Learning representative exemplars of concepts: An initial study. Proc. 4th Int. Workshop on Machine Learning, UC-Irvine, CA, June, pp. 24–29.

Kitano, K. 1993. Challenges for Massive Parallelism. Proc. 13th Annual Conf. on Artificial Intelligence (IJCAI-93), Chabery, France, Morgan Kauffman, San Francisco, CA, pp. 813–834.

Kitano, H., and Shimazu, H. 1996. The experience-sharing architecture: A case study in corporate-wide case-based software quality control. In Leake, D. (Ed.), *Case-Based Reasoning Experiences, Lessons, and Future Directions.* AAAI/MIT Press, Menlo Park, CA, pp. 235–268.

Kolodner, J. 1991. Improving human decision making through case-based decision aiding. *AI Magazine,* 12(2), 52–68.

Kolodner, J. 1993. *Case-Based Reasoning.* Morgan Kaufmann, San Francisco, CA.

Leake, D. 1996. CBR in context: The present and future. In Leake, D. (Ed.), *Case-Based Reasoning: Experiences, Lesson, and Future Dire*ctions. AAAI/MIT Press, Menlo Park, CA, pp. 3–30.

Patton, R.J., Frank, P.M., and Clark, R.N. (Eds.). 2000. *Issues of Fault Diagnosis for Dynamic Systems.* Springer-Verlag, Berlin.

Magnani, L., Nersessian, N.J., and Thagard, P. (Eds.). 1999. *Model-Based Reasoning in Scientific Discovery.* Kluwer/Academic Press, New York.

Mark, W., Simoudis, E. and Hinkle, D. 1996. CBR: Expectations and results. In Leake, D. (Ed.), *Case-Based Reasoning Experiences, Lessons, and Future Directions.* AAAI/MIT Press, Menlo Park, CA, pp. 269–294.

Ngyen, T., Czerwishki, M., and Lee, D. 1993. COM-PAQ QuickSource: Providing the consumer with the power of artificial intelligence. In Proc. 5th Innovative Applications of Artificial Intelligence Conf., July 11–15, Washington, DC.

Schank, R. 1982. *Dynamic Memory: A Theory of Learning in Computers and People.* Cambridge University Press, New York.

Tsang, E. 1994. *Foundations of Constraint Satisfaction.* Academic Press, London.

Veloso, M., and Carbonnel, J. 1993. Derivational analogy in PRODIGY. *Machine Learning,* 10(3), 249–278.

Watson, I. 2003. *Applying Case-Based Reasoning Techniques for Enterprise Systems.* Morgan Kauffmann, San Francisco, CA.

# The Future of Knowledge Management

## ◇ ◇ ◇ Introduction

As we can see throughout this book, the knowledge management (KM) goals are for the members of an organization to discover, capture, share, and apply their knowledge. Ultimately, these KM goals translate into positive contributions to the organization's bottom line. Knowledge is first created in people's minds. First, KM practices identify ways to encourage and stimulate the ability of employees to develop new knowledge. Second, KM methodologies and technologies enable effective ways to elicit, represent, organize, reuse, and renew this knowledge. Third, KM is not distanced from the knowledge owners, but instead it celebrates and recognizes their position as experts in the organization. This, in effect, is the essence of KM. Thus, effective KM results in positive effects on the organization. However, knowledge sharing could also bring forth certain risks, namely, that the knowledge falls into the wrong hands, either maliciously or accidentally. Given the value of the knowledge, and the reliance that an organization places on this knowledge, losing this knowledge could have severe negative consequences for the organization. Therefore, knowledge must be protected. This epilogue discusses the importance of protecting intellectual capital.

This chapter also discusses the future of KM. In the future, KM systems are expected to help decision makers make more humane decisions and deal with **wicked problems.** We anticipate a future where people and advanced technology may continue to work together, enabling knowledge integration across diverse domains, and resulting in considerably higher payoffs.

As KM becomes widely accepted in corporate organizations, it may increasingly become critical for corporate managers to institute safeguards for ensuring the security and adequate use of this knowledge. In the next section, we discuss some of the issues involved with this topic.

## ◇ ◇ ◇ Protecting Intellectual Property

**Intellectual property (IP)** can be defined as any results of a human intellectual process that has inherent value to the individual or organization that sponsored the process. IP

### Dow Chemical's KM Initiative Captures Big Returns

On November 1994, Dow Chemical's KM initiative under the direction of then director of intellectual asset management Gordon Petrash, achieved worldwide notoriety on the cover of *Fortune Magazine* [Stewart, 1994]. Petrash recognized that the intellectual capital represented in the company's 29,000 unused patents represented an underutilized opportunity that could bring back huge returns to the organization.

Unused patents can represent a sizable investment to an organization, because the expense associated with keeping the patents current could be quite high. Petrash's group first decided to develop a concerted effort to evaluate these patents. Patents were assessed to determine whether they could be used, sold, or abandoned. During this process, Petrash was able to save the organization close to $1 million in licensing fees that were currently expended on patents that would return no value to the organization.

◆◇ ◆◇ ◆◇

includes inventions, designs, processes, organizational structures, strategic plans, marketing plans, computer programs, algorithms, literary works, music scores, and works of art, among many others. KM proposes the effective use of IP, which can represent significant value to an organization. Loss of such property can damage the organization just as much as losing real capital property. In fact, in many cases intellectual property is an organization's most valuable asset. Companies whose investments in intellectual capital are growing may report high returns on equity and assets, even while reporting low earnings-to-book-value [Lev and Sougiannis, 1989]. In fact, one of the KM initiatives actively pursued by Dow Chemical was harvesting little-used patents and intellectual assets [Davenport and Prusak, 1998]. Vignette E-1 describes Dow Chemical's approach to KM.

As we discuss in the prior chapters, during the knowledge sharing process organizations capture this knowledge through documents that are stored in Web-based knowledge repositories. The more codifiable this knowledge is, and the more it is documented and distributed, the greater is the risk of losing this knowledge. Intellectual property losses can happen in many ways, including the following:

1. Employee turnover. The employee may leave the organization to be hired by a competitor. The employee may deliberately or accidentally share their knowledge with their new employer.
2. Physical theft of sensitive proprietary documents, either by outsiders or by insiders may occur.
3. Inadvertent disclosure to third parties without a nondisclosure agreement may occur.
4. Reverse engineering or close examination of company's products may be done.
5. The Web repository security is breached and unauthorized access to the proprietary documents takes place.
6. Unauthorized parties intercept electronic mail (e-mail), fax, telephone conversation, or other communications for the purpose of illicitly acquiring knowledge.

**7.** Attempts may be made by insiders or outsiders to corrupt documents or databases with false data, information, or knowledge. This could be done directly via *hacking* into a database and effecting unauthorized modifications, or indirectly via a virus. This is a variation of the electronic breach of the data problem in item 5, but it is somewhat different in that the actions can destroy the system in question. There are significant criminal implications with this act.

Note that the first four types of IP loss are not related to technology, whereas the last three are. Also, some of the intellectual capital losses are related to legal practices used to acquire sensitive competitive intelligence (items 1, 3, and 4), whereas the law prosecutes others (items 2, 5, 6, and 7). Clearly, the losses related to technology are easier to prove, and therefore easier to prosecute. Companies can take a number of steps to protect their organizations against IP losses as follows:

1. *Nondisclosure agreements.* A **nondisclosure agreement** is a contract between an organization that owns the IP and outside individuals to whom the organization's sensitive and proprietary information is disclosed on the condition that they maintain it as confidential. Divulging this knowledge to a third party constitutes a breach of confidentiality, and the offending party can be sued for damages. Employees of the organization owning the IP are by definition expected to maintain confidentiality, not only while they are actively employed by that organization but also after they terminate their association, for whatever reason. Nondisclosure agreements can serve to protect against loss of knowledge via employee turnover as well as via covered disclosure to outsiders.

2. *Patents.* **Patents** are the oldest and most traditional means of protecting inventions. They grew out of the need to encourage exceptionally bright people to invent products and processes that benefit humankind. Patents do this by giving exclusive rights (a monopoly) to any product containing the patented works to the inventor, with all rights therewith. This means that an inventor, for a fixed period of either 16 or 20 years from patent issuance, can control the duplication of the patented works or process. Patent law can be quite complex in what can and cannot be patented, at what time, and for how long. However, as long as a patent is not overturned, it provides the most secure of protections. Unfortunately, this protection is only exercised through court action taken by the patent holder against the individual or organization allegedly infringing the patent. In some cases, small inventors holding valid patents cannot successfully sue large corporate entities with large legal staffs. Patents are excellent vehicles for protecting knowledge about technical innovations and products. They can protect against reverse engineering of a product as well as unauthorized acquisition of any design or other documents that detail the nature of the invention. In fact, loss of such documents is considered immaterial, because the design of the patented invention is already part of the public record by virtue of its patented nature.

3. *Copyrights.* Whereas patents protect the ideas behind the invention (the so-called *claims)* **copyrights** protect the expression of the work. They have been traditionally used to protect literary works, works of art, architecture, and music. However, they can also be used to protect computer programs, albeit weakly. The advantage is that while

patents require a rather rigorous process to be granted, a copyright can be done by merely stating on a copy of the body of the work that it is copyrighted. Registration of the copyrighted work with the government in the United States is not required, although it is highly advisable. Other countries require registration. This is done with the symbol ©. Copyrights typically last for the life of the creator plus up to 50 more years, depending on the country of filing. A copyright holder maintains the rights to publish, broadcast, reproduce, or copy the work. The holders also have the exclusive right to translate their work into another language, either wholly or in part. Copyrights can protect stolen or illicitly obtained IP only if it is valuable in its expression. For example, computer programs may fall into that category.

4.  ***Trade secrets.***  An organization may choose not to patent an invention, but instead keep it as a **trade secret**. This invention may not fulfill all the criteria for patent ability. Alternatively, the organization may want to avoid the legal process required to protect IP. Stealing trade secrets is illegal and punishable by law if the damaged organization takes legal action. However, the said organization must make a strong effort to maintain confidentiality to maintain its legal rights. Organizations may accomplish this by instituting reasonable safeguards of its IP. Lacking that, a court may decide that it was not a very important trade secret to begin with.

We have discussed legal avenues of IP protection. However, once the organization resorts to legal remedies, the damage has already been done and it most likely can only aspire to **damage recovery.** An effective KM initiative must include institutionalizing policies and safeguards that prevent the loss of IP in the first place. Installing firewalls in computer systems, access controls, and protecting all the sensitive information through encryption can go a long way toward this. Furthermore, organizations should clearly educate their employees of their responsibility for confidentiality, and the consequences they could suffer if they violate this confidentiality, whether accidentally or purposely.

## ◆ ◆ ◆ Knowledge Management: A New Paradigm for Decision Making

The development of management information systems, decision support systems, and KM systems has been influenced by the works of five prominent philosophers, namely, Leibniz, Locke, Kant, Hegel, and Singer [Churchman, 1971]. Based on Churchman's definition of *inquiring organizations,*[1] Courtney [2001] defines a new paradigm for decision making in today's complex and wicked organizational contexts. In the conventional decision-making process, the emphasis is first on recognizing the problem, and then on defining it in terms of a model. Alternative solutions are then analyzed, and the best solution is selected and implemented. Thus, KM systems have successfully supported solving semistructured problems, those characterized by a limited number of factors and a certain future.

Recent developments in KM systems also have extended the reach of those involved in the solution, through group support systems. However, the jury is still out on how well

---

[1]This also means learning organizations.

KM systems provide support to problems that are characterized as wicked [Rittel and Webber, 1973]. Wicked problems are unique and difficult to formulate. Their solutions are good or bad (instead of true or false), and generate waves of consequence over time. Solutions to wicked problems are "one-shot," and so there is no opportunity to learn from prior mistakes and solutions cannot be undone. Moreover, solutions to wicked problems are not a numerable set of solutions, and many may have no solutions.

For example, a project plan for an enterprise resource planning (ERP) system implementation is a wicked problem. ERP system implementations are one-shot, in the sense that organizations typically only implement them once. Therefore, there is no opportunity to learn over time how to successfully implement these systems. Usually organizations only find out whether their implementation was good or bad on the deployment or go-live date, and at this point bad implementations result in disastrous economic consequences for the organization.

The fact is that as globalization expands, the number of stakeholders affected by the organization increases; each one is affected by different customs, laws, behaviors, and environmental concerns. Globalization also leads to wicked planning problems for organizations, and methods to help make decisions in such situations are greatly needed. The new paradigm for KM support, suggested by Courtney [2001], defines the decision-making process as starting with the recognition that the problem exists, then instead of proceeding immediately into analysis, the process consists of developing multiple perspectives. These multiple perspectives consider the following:

1. *Technical perspective.* This consists of analyzing the alternatives and implementing the chosen alternative. This perspective is the only one relevant to existing decision support and KM systems.
2. *Personal and individual perspective.* Complex problems involve a multiplicity of actors. Each sees the problem differently and generates a different perspective, based on individual experiences, intuition, personality, and attitudes about risk.
3. *Organizational and social perspective.* Complex problems involve various organizations. Organizations also each view the problem in a different fashion, and thus generate a different perspective. Organizations may also consist of diverse members with different interests.
4. *Ethics and aesthetics perspective.* Complex problems involve business ethics and aesthetic issues that are so high they require the involvement of key stakeholders, because there are no simple solutions. Perhaps the utilitarian emphasis of the Industrial Age neglected the spirituality of the *rational man* and contributed to the demise of ethics and aesthetics in decision making today [Courtney, 2001].

This new paradigm bases decisions on the use of these multiple perspectives. The prior mechanical view of decision-making environments minimizes the importance of relationships, collaboration, and trust in the organization. Personal relationships define organizational boundaries to a large extent. The future calls for the development of KM systems that support the human aspects of decisions: the personal, organizational, ethical, and aesthetic perspectives.

Thus, KM systems should help decision makers initiate more humane decisions and enable them to deal with wicked problems.

# ◇ ◇ ◇ Looking at the Future

The future of KM will be highlighted by three continuing trends: (1) KM will benefit from progress in information technologies (ITs), (2) KM will continue the shift toward integrating knowledge from a variety of different perspectives, and (3) KM will continue to make trade-offs in numerous important areas.

First, in the future, KM will benefit from continual, and even more dynamic, progress in ITs. Improvements in cost to performance ratios of IT have caused the cost of digitizing information to approach zero, and the cost of coordinating across individuals, organizational subunits, or organizations to approach zero as well [Grover and Segars, 1996]. IT progress also includes developments in autonomous, software-based agents.

Considerable progress is expected in the way in which the agents will evolve (i.e., change, develop, and act). Such *evolutionary agents* may be dramatically different in their abilities to: (1) build theories and create a world of their own; (2) assume any virtual identity they wish; (3) possess free will; and (4) develop a moral code and a value system of their own. However, these future evolutionary agents will probably still be limited, for example, because emotion and love cannot be programmed [Kendall, 1996]. In addition, progress in mobile technologies and increasing miniaturization will enable all customers and durable products to be addressable, wherever they might be [Watson et al., 1996]. Thus, the future of KM will be dramatically different due to the inevitable, unpredictable over any long period of time, and quantum changes in IT.

Second, in the future, KM will continue the shift toward bringing together, and effectively integrating, knowledge from a variety of different perspectives. KM originated at the individual level, focusing on the training and learning of individuals. Over time, the emphasis of KM shifted to groups and entire organizations, and now examples of interorganizational impacts of KM are becoming increasingly common. This trend in the impact of KM is expected to continue with its use across networks of organizations and governments, enabling collaborations across historical adversaries and integrating knowledge across highly diverse perspectives and disciplines.

Finally, in the future, KM will continue to make trade-offs in numerous important areas. One such trade-off pertains to the use of ITs for sharing. The same communication technologies that support the sharing of knowledge within an organization also enable the knowledge to leak outside the organization to its competing firms. A related trade-off concerns technological and organizational barriers to such **knowledge leakage.** These barriers, while preventing knowledge leakage, may also inhibit the ability of the organization's own employees to seek knowledge from individuals outside the organization, who may be able to provide them with helpful advice. A third trade-off relates to storing employees' knowledge using ITs. Advanced ITs help capture and store employee's knowledge, thereby reducing knowledge loss when expert employees leave the organization. However, the same technologies may also reduce the ability, as well as the motivation, to share that knowledge with others in the organization. A fourth trade-off concerns the balance between technology and people. It is essential to maintain a balance between using technology as substitutes for people (e.g., software agents) and using technology to enable collaboration from a wider range of people within and across organizations.

In conclusion, the future of KM is one where people and advanced technology will continue to work together, enabling knowledge integration across diverse domains, and producing considerably higher payoffs. However, the new opportunities and greater benefits will require careful managing of people and technologies, synthesizing of multiple perspectives, and effectively dealing with a variety of trade-offs. The future of KM will clearly be exciting due to the new opportunities and options, but interesting challenges definitely lay ahead for knowledge managers.

## KEY TERMS ◆◇ ◆◇ ◆◇

- copyrights—p. 352
- damage recovery—p. 353
- intellectual property (IP)—p. 350
- knowledge leakage—p. 355
- nondisclosure agreement—p. 352
- patents—p. 352
- trade secret—p. 353
- wicked problems—p. 350

## REFERENCES ◆◇ ◆◇ ◆◇

Churchman, C. 1971. *The Design of Inquiring Systems: Basic Concepts of Systems and Organization,* Basic Books, New York.

Courtney, J. 2001. Decision making and knowledge management in inquiring organizations: Toward a new decision-making paradigm for DSS. *Decision Support Systems,* 31, 17–38.

Davenport, T., and Prusak, L. 1998. *Working Knowledge: How Organizations Manage What They Know.* Harvard Business School Press, Boston, MA.

Grover, V., and Segars, A.H. 1996. IT: The next 1100102 years. *Database,* 27(4) Fall, 45–57.

Kendall, K.E. 1996. Artificial intelligence and Götterdämerung: The evolutionary paradigm of the future. *Database,* 27(4) Fall, 99–115.

Lev, B., and Sougiannis, T. 1989. The capitalization, amortization, and value-relevance of R&D. *Journal of Accounting and Economics,* 21(1), February, 107–138.

Rittel, H., and Webber, M. 1973. Dilemmas in a general theory of planning. *Policy Sciences,* 4, 155–169.

Stewart, T. 1994. Intellectual capital: Your company's most valuable asset. *Fortune Magazine,* 10, 68–73.

Watson, R.T., Pitt, L.F., and Bethom, P.R. 1996. Service: The future of information technology. *Database,* 27(4) Fall, 58–67.

# Appendix A

## ◆ ◆ ◆ ◆ Basic Computer Networks ◆ ◆ ◆ ◆

### The Digital Computer

It is a well-accepted fact that the rapid development of the digital computer and accompanying software has propelled the booming interest in knowledge management (KM) by business organizations worldwide. Computers can serve to store information and knowledge, represent it, and reuse it. The techniques we see in the previous five chapters attest to this ability. However, KM was not one of the traditional uses of digital computers.

The digital computer, originally invented by and for scientists and engineers, was designed to quickly and accurately compute mathematical calculations that were at the time (and still are) very daunting if done by hand. Solving such mathematical equations through a computer has allowed scientists and engineers to simulate increasingly complex physical phenomena. This has facilitated the design and development of modern devices without the need to build expensive prototypes. Furthermore, their computational ability has helped us to understand previously unknown phenomena, from the German Enigma code during World War II to large weather systems such as hurricanes or nuclear reactions.

At some point, someone discovered that this new device could be used to acquire, store, and retrieve large quantities of data very effectively and efficiently. Hence, databases became another major traditional use of digital computers.

Finally, computers' ability to make (simple) decisions very quickly led to their use as control devices. This is the third traditional use for computers. It is difficult to find many modern devices without an embedded computer controlling some facet of the device's operation.

Nevertheless, as anyone who uses e-mail and the World Wide Web knows, the main contribution of computing technology nowadays could arguably be its ability to serve as a fast, powerful, reliable, and affordable medium for communication. The Internet is the most obvious contributor to this. In this appendix we introduce the reader to the technology that has been so successful in fostering faster and more effective communications among people through computers.

### Computer Communications: Networks

Communication between computers allows them to efficiently share data as well as programs without the need to resort to external tapes, physically porting it over to the other computer. This other computer might be a hundred feet or a hundred miles away.

It is no surprise that direct connection of large computers was the first mode of communication developed. It only made sense. If humans, being intelligent creatures, thrived by communicating with each other over a telephone line, why could computers not do the same? Connection via direct telephone lines preceded the advent of the Internet by several decades. However, problems arose with this approach as more and more computers wished to interconnect. The main problem was that, to connect all computers together, direct communications among all of them became impossible—a combinatorial explosion. This gave rise to computer networks in which several computers are connected together so that they are able to share data and programs with each other without having to directly connect each pair of computers.

Furthermore, it was determined that, even in a network, two computers actively connected while they interacted would eliminate the ability of the other computers in the network to communicate. The other computers would have to wait until the session between the two actively communicating computers was terminated before other communication could take place. This gave rise to a connectionless form of communication, where the two computers communicating would not need to be directly connected in order to communicate. This is called a *packetized* form of communication, where there is no direct connection between two computers monopolizing the medium. In such packet-switching networks, the sending computer creates a *packet* of information it wishes to send to another computer. It can be either a request for information or a response to a request. It can include data or a program to be executed by the requesting computer. A packet has a maximum size that is variable depending on the type of network. Therefore, if the message is larger than the maximum size, more than one packet may have to be created and sent independently. The ability to break up long messages into discrete packets permits smaller units of data to traverse the transmission medium. Each packet contains a *header* with the address of the computer or computers it wants to receive the message, and a *body*, which contains the message itself. How that packet is sent and received depends on the network scheme used.

Two general types of networks exist—local area networks (LANs) and wide area networks (WANs). The main difference between them is the area encompassed by the network, dictated by the distance between the computers in the network. However, the long distance introduces some difficulties as a result of the electrical attenuation suffered by the signal over long distances.

Several schemes exist to implement LANs. The most common is Ethernet, where a cable connects all computers to a bus medium (a cable) that carries the packets between the computers (Figure A-1). One computer (or rather, a process therein) composes packets and sends them to one or more computers in the network. Each computer in the network receives and copies the packet from the Ethernet medium, and looks at the address on the packet header. If the address agrees with its own address, it accepts and processes the message. Otherwise, it neglects it. Computers can only emit packets when there is no other traffic in the network. This avoids interference and crossing traffic. Because these messages are transmitted very rapidly, it does not take much of a lull in communications to allow a computer to emit a packet into the network.

One popular alternative to Ethernet is the Token Ring network. In this system, all computers are connected in a closed ring of cable medium. In comparison, the Ethernet network is open ended, bringing some undesirable effects with message reflection from the open end if not terminated properly. The packet of information in a token ring network can only be sent by the computer with permission to send. That is, the sending computer must have the *token*. Only one computer—the one with the token—has permission to send packets at any

◆◇ ◇◆ ◇◆ **FIGURE A-1**

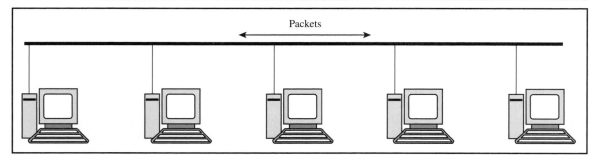

Packets

one time. The sending computer sends a packet out into the network medium; it is received by the next computer, which examines its address to determine destination. If it is indeed the destination, it copies the message and sends it on to the next computer in the ring. Otherwise, it merely sends it on without copying. Once the packet makes the complete round and returns to the computer that sent it (remember, it is a ring), the sending computer compares the packet received to the one sent. If not identical, an error has been detected and it sends the original packet again. If, on the other hand, the packet is received intact, the transmission process ends and the sending computer then passes the token to the next computer to allow it to send a message if it wants to. The token

makes its way around and around the ring providing each computer successively with the opportunity to send messages. Figure A-2 represents a token ring connection.

Communication can also be extended over a wide geographic area, to include branches of companies located in different buildings in a city, or in different cities in a country. This extends the concept of a LAN beyond the originally intended local areas such as an office. Such long-distance networking is done using modems and repeaters. This is the essence of WANs. Nevertheless, whether near or far, the network includes only computers purposely included in the network.

Networked computers can share files and programs without having to store copies in each

❖ ❖ ❖  **FIGURE A-2**

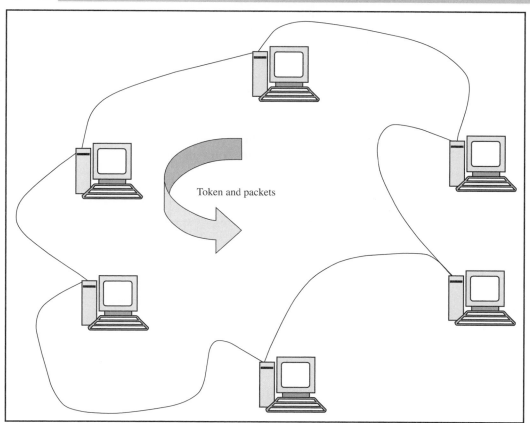

Token and packets

individual computer. This is important for large software systems to which several people contribute on an ongoing basis, such as databases. Networked computers can also exchange e-mail, allowing the users to communicate asynchronously. Nevertheless, such communication was limited only to computers in the network. Even for large networks, this limited the communication to several thousand people at most—quite acceptable for intercompany communications, but not for communicating with those in the world outside the network. Furthermore, as organizations began forming multiple networks (accounting, sales, finance networks), it became evident that there needed to be a communication link between computers (people) connected to the different networks. These networks could be composed of different computers and based on several different networking architectures and technologies. A universal communication service was required that enabled such communication in a fast and reliable manner—security came later. In this next section we discuss what is now called the Internet.

### The Internet

In the 1970s, the U.S. Defense Advanced Research Projects Agency (DARPA) developed a network of networks to address this issue. Initially called ARPA-net, this network of net-

works relies on routing messages from one network to the next. The basic idea behind the Internet is as follows: each network has a gateway that communicates with the outside world as well as with its internal network. A router located at this gateway receives messages (packets), interprets their final destination, and forwards them to another router that either is the final destination or is on the way to its own LAN or WAN for final delivery. If the packet is intended for a computer on the router's own network, then it sends it to its own internal network. Figure A-3 depicts an Internet as a network of networks.

The ground-breaking research sponsored by DARPA developed the Internet's architecture. This architecture—arguably the de facto standard for computer networks—follows a layered approach, where five layers are defined and specified. These are:

1. *Physical layer.* This layer includes the actual, physical hardware required to effect the transfer of packets in the network. This includes specification of the routers, switches, network interface cards, and hubs located throughout the Internet, and the interconnecting cables and connectors.

2. *Network interface layer.* This layer defines how to organize data into frames (packets) to prepare them for transmission.

◆▷ ◁▷ ◆▷ **FIGURE A-3**

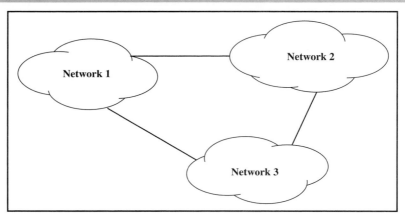

3. ***Internet layer.*** This layer specifies the format for the packets, the addresses, and how to route the packets through the multiple routers a packet typically sees on its way from the source computer to the destination computer. These protocols operate in the source and destination computers, as well as in the routers in between. This layer makes the decisions on how to route the packets arriving at a router. The path taken by such packets are a result of these decisions.

4. ***Transport layer.*** This layer concentrates on providing fast and reliable transfer of the packets from source to destination. The users of this protocol are the many application processes running on host computers connected to the Internet and independently wishing to send and receive messages via the Internet. The naïve version of the transport protocol is called the *user datagram protocol (UDP)*. It is a simple, best-effort, connectionless protocol that merely sends the packet into the network and hopes for the best. Alternatively, the transmission control protocol (TCP) works to ensure reliable, sequenced delivery of the packets.

5. ***Application layer.*** This last layer specifies how users' software should use the Internet.

The resulting networking technology is commonly called *transmission control protocol* and *Internet protocol (TCP/IP)*. These protocols represent the protocols of layers 3 and 4 of the list above. Many Internet-working schemes such as Novell NetWare, AppleTalk, NetBIOS, SNA, and others employ TCP/IP protocols.

TCP/IP, in reality, represents a suite of protocols required to connect to the Internet. Protocols in diplomatic circles are defined as the way to do things that both sides fully expect and understand. This standard set of common practices allows diplomats to communicate in an expected fashion, and thereby to avoid embarrassing and potentially dangerous misunderstandings. In the same way, the protocols found in TCP/IP define and specify the expectations for any computer or network that wishes to connect to the Internet. For the purposes of this book, the application layer is the most important of the five layers. We discuss it a bit further later in this appendix.

However, the Internet is more than merely sending and receiving packets of information. The modern Internet has several services it provides to users, such as e-mail and file transferring. Designing and operating an Internet that has no owner, just customers, is a difficult task. Although not without problems, the Internet stands as a monument to the success of what people can accomplish in unregulated, nongovernmental enterprises built and designed without a (direct) profit motive. Even more impressive is that its organizers have had to do this in the short span of 15 years, and while under the ever-present pressure of phenomenal growth.

One significant feature of the Internet is that all computers connected to it have unique addresses. These addresses are unique just like a house address is unambiguous in most parts of the world. More interestingly, it would be impossible to use the actual physical addresses of the interconnected computers to identify them, because individual manufacturers have their own way of identifying their products. Therefore, the addresses provided by the Internet are logical addresses—they are not related to their hardware addresses, but merely mapped to them by software. This means that we could replace the computer attached to a network interface card and have the same logical address for a different computer without disrupting the operation of the network.

These addresses are 32-bit words divided into two parts. The first part is the prefix, and it identifies the name of the network to which a computer is connected. The second part is the suffix, and it identifies the name of the specific computer inside that network. These addresses are known throughout the entire Internet. Every router needs to know the prefix to decide to which other router to forward a packet, or whether it is to be sent to a computer in its own network. The suffix only needs to be known by the gateway router for a particular network to know where to send a message with its network as the destination.

The addresses of all routers are kept in 13 *root servers*, as they are called, which contain all the addresses in the Internet. These 13 servers are located in various locations throughout the world, most of them in the continental United States. Internet addresses are composed of four fields separated by dots (appropriately called *dot notation*). These four fields have several options depending on the size of the network represented by the address. Discussion of this is beyond the scope of this chapter. Suffice it to say that it represents four 3-digit (max) integers separated by a dot. For example, an Internet address for a computer could be 132.14.128.2. The last field is called the high-level field, and it can only be one of a few values, depending on the type of organization to which the computer owner belongs. When an e-mail message is to be sent, the address of the recipient must be included in the header to allow the routing process to successfully forward it to its correct destination.

Fortunately, the Internet governing body permits these rather meaningless (to humans) addresses to be associated (mapped) to more meaningful ones that can be easily interpreted by humans, while still retaining the dot notation format. For example, an address similar to the one seen above can be mapped into isl.engr.ucf.edu. This address is the name of the mail server computer at the Intelligent Systems Laboratory at the University of Central Florida. Therefore, an electronic address to gonzalez at the UCF ISL can be gonzalez@isl.engr.ucf.edu. In this case, we are assuming that gonzalez is the account name for Avelino Gonzalez, who has this account at the ISL network at the University of Central Florida.

### Applications Layer

As mentioned previously, of the five layers making up the Internet architecture, the last layer, the applications layer, affects KM most. In this section, we discuss it in greater detail.

This layer is responsible for the most important services provided by the Internet — e-mail and file transfer. Although there are several other services, these are the most relevant to KM.

### Electronic Mail

Electronic mail (e-mail) has become the most popular way to communicate with other people around the world or around the corner. Given the increased dependency on computers, it is likely that the communicants will be "on" the computer at some time most days, therefore, having the ability to check for and respond to e-mail. E-mail is an asynchronous type of communication where significant information can be exchanged (unlike phone mail). Additionally, documents extraneous to the message itself can be easily attached, just like we would mail a book with a cover letter to someone via air mail.

The ability to communicate asynchronously with just about anyone in the world that has an electronic address has significantly encouraged knowledge exchange. People think nothing of dropping an e-mail to a stranger asking a question. Yet, they would never dream of calling this person on the phone (even if they have the person's phone number). The indirectness and relative impersonality of e-mail encourages exchange. Organizations interested in managing corporate knowledge have seized on this tendency to increase communication among its employees and distribute critical knowledge.

Sending e-mail consists of composing and sending a packet of information to the recipient's account name (gonzalez) at the computer where the recipient has this account (isl.engr.ucf.edu). The packet or packets contain the message as well as any attachments. Of course, long messages with large attachments may require several packets to communicate the entire body. The packet or packets make their way through the different routers until they reach the gateway router for the network where the target computer is located. Often, the different packets making up the same message arrive at their destination via different routes, depending on the network traffic at the time.

The Internet uses the simple mail transfer protocol (SMTP) to effect the transfer of packets containing e-mail. Although seemingly simple (its very name suggests it!), SMTP handles several detailed processes that make reliable e-mail a reality. This includes asking the destination mail server whether the destination mailbox exists. If it does not, it "bounces" the message to its sender, indicating that it never reached its destination, and that the sender must not assume receipt. Additionally, it saves a copy of the message until the recipient router has confirmed receipt. Otherwise, it will transmit it again to ensure receipt.

The incoming mail server in this network places this message in the recipient's mailbox for the recipient to open, read, and process. If the message is sent to a recipient in the same computer, only the person's account name is needed. If it is not, then the entire address of the mail server is required to permit the message to make its way from router to router in the Internet to its final destination. Mail-handling software, such as Microsoft's Outlook or Qualcomm's Eudora among many others, are used to manage the mail. They facilitate the opening and reading of incoming messages, replying to them, and composing new messages. They can be used to store and index old messages and can serve to download attachments.

### File Transfer

This is arguably the second most important service provided by the Internet. It is used to transfer copies of a file (document, picture, film, or program) to another computer via the Internet. Before the advent of computer communications, this transfer was restricted to downloading the files into magnetic media such as tapes or floppy disks, and then physically porting the medium to the other computer for another download to the destination computer's hard disk. With the availability and ease of connection of the Internet, this is no longer necessary, because large files can be quickly and easily downloaded via the Internet. But there are difficulties. The transfer system has to accommodate heterogeneous files as well as source and destination computers. Furthermore, a user on one computer may not have log in access in the other computer, compli-

cating the accessing of the file to be transferred. The file transfer protocol (FTP) ensures that this process is successful.

FTP running on one computer (the client) starts by establishing a connection to the computer with which it wants to transfer files (in either direction)—the server. FTP provides the client with several commands, most of which are not necessary for typical transfer operations. The protocol depends on opening a logical connection with the other computer. Of course, this connection is not like the direct connections discussed earlier. It still makes use of packets to transfer the file. FTP opens a logical connection by having the client computer log on the server computer. The client in the originating computer requests the transfer of a particular file and FTP supervises the transfer. The client computer does this by invoking the appropriate FTP commands to either retrieve (download) the desired documents, or place documents on the server (upload). The client may also wish to specify the format of the file to be transferred (binary, ASCII, etc.). When the transfer is complete, FTP so indicates to the client, who can now choose to close the connection or transfer another file. If the client chooses to close the connection, FTP causes it to log off the server, and closes the FTP window. FTP is a command line type of interface, much like DOS. It is also not highly informative about the causes of failure to transfer.

If the client does not have rights to log on the server computer, the owner of the documents to be transferred can permit them to be transferred by placing them on an anonymous FTP site. Clients can log on to the server as anonymous users, using a log in name and password that only permit them access to a particular subdirectory where the available files are located. The anonymous client has no privileges other than to download files found within, or sometimes to upload files to the same directory. Anonymous FTP must be specifically set up in the server for this to be an alternative. Typically, the login name will be "anonymous" and the password will be anything entered. The users are generally asked, as a courtesy, to enter their e-mail address as the password in order to keep track of the transfers.

A user of FTP does not have to be human. A process running in a connected computer can invoke FTP. FTP must then be able to interact with the connected computer during the file transfer process and to close the connection when the process is completed.

### Other Services Provided by the Applications Layer

There are other services provided by the applications layer protocols. Although less significant than e-mail and file transfer, these services are nevertheless important in their own right. We shall discuss these briefly.

The most important of these less important services is Telnet. Telnet allows someone in a remote computer to access (log in) other computers in the network or in other networks. The Telnet software establishes a client–server relationship between the Telnet software running on the local computer and that running on the remote computer. Telnet handles the data transfers involved in making the remote computer think that the data is being supplied by a local user.

Another simple but useful service is the Ping service. Ping allows a user in one computer to test for connectivity between the two computers. Ping sends a short message to the other computer requesting an echo. The receiving program immediately sends a response to the sending computer, which then records the receipt of the echoes. Ping then measures the time elapsed between transmission of echo request and receipt of echo. If the procedure takes too long, Ping assumes that it was not received and so indicates to the user.

# Glossary

**Access control** Mechanisms and policies that restrict access to computer resources.

**Active Web documents** Web documents received by a client from the World Wide Web (WWW) server, which contain programs that execute on the clients computer, continually changing the display.

**Adaptation** Process of modifying a historical solution to solve the current problem when the current problem is not identical to the historical problem associated with that solution.

**Aggregate sets** Sets whose components all work in synergism for the benefit of the set. For example, an automobile is an aggregate set of its parts.

**Algorithmic** Step-by-step problem-solving procedure for solving a problem in a finite number of steps.

**Application layer** Specifies how users' software should use the Internet.

**Application linking** When the enterprise shares business processes and data between two or more information technology (IT) applications.

**Artificial intelligence (AI)** AI refers to the science that provides computers with the ability to solve problems not easily solved through algorithmic models. John McCarthy coined the term in 1956.

**Artificial Neural Networks (ANNs)** Type of artificial intelligence mechanism that attempts to simulate human intelligence by recreating the connective physiology of the human brain. Neural nets can learn to map information between two vector spaces: *input* and *output*. Neural nets can be used to solve a large variety of problems, provided that it is possible to formulate the problem in terms of vector space mapping.

**Associational expertise** Knowledge or heuristic ability acquired mostly through human experience and elicited through the knowledge engineering process. Generally associates input patterns to certain outputs.

**Associational knowledge** *See* Associational expertise.

**Authorizer's assistant** A knowledge-based system that assists the credit authorization staff determine the credit level for credit card customers. The system takes information from a number of databases and approves or disapproves a telephone request from a merchant to authorize a large purchase from a cardholder.

**Auxiliary memory** Transfer of pages of data between a computer's main memory and a secondary medium of memory.

**Back propagation** Algorithm for efficiently calculating the error gradient of a neural network, which can then be used as the basis of learning.

**Backward reasoning** Reasoning from conclusions, or goals, to the inputs.

**Balanced Scorecard Method** Developed by Robert Kaplan and David Norton in 1992; an analysis technique designed to translate an organization's mission statement and overall business strategy into specific, quantifiable goals, and to monitor the organization's performance in terms of achieving these goals.

**Benchmarking** Designing a standard test for the purposes of fairly comparing the performance of different hardware and/or software systems.

**Best practices** Assessment recommending the most appropriate way of handing a certain type of task, based on an observation of the way that several organizations handle that task.

**Bidirectional reasoning** Uses forward reasoning to propagate belief from the inputs and generate

**365**

conclusions, and backward reasoning to confirm the conclusions generated dynamically.

**Blocks world** Early AI system. It simulated a robot arm to move blocks on a table, demonstrating the feasibility of automated task planning.

**Campaign management software** Software used to manage and monitor a company's communications with its customers.

**Case** Documented historical occurrence of a solution to a past problem used for comparison to current problems. This is the basis of case-based reasoning (CBR).

**Case library** Database of historical cases containing the universe of knowledge in a CBR system.

**Case-based reasoning (CBR)** An artificial intelligence technique that uses historical solutions to problems similar to the current one to design a solution for the current problem.

**Case-based substitution** The process of substituting a part of a historical solution deemed incompatible with the current problem with one that is compatible.

**Choosing parameters from a menu** Method in which the database system presents a list of parameters from which you can choose. This is perhaps the easiest way to pose a query because the menus guide you, but it is also the least flexible.

**Churn** Turnover of users, for example, on an on-line service, especially after the expiration of a free trial period.

**Classification** Grouping together of data sets according to some predefined similarity shared by all members of that set.

**Clickstream analysis** Virtual trail that a user leaves behind while surfing the Internet. A clickstream is a record of a user's activity on the Internet, including every Web site and every page of every Web site that the user visits, how long the user was on a page or site, in what order the pages were visited, any news groups that the user participates in, and even the e-mail addresses of mail that the user sends and receives. Both ISPs and individual Web sites are capable of tracking a user's clickstream.

**Client** Client part of the client–server architecture. Typically, a client is an application that runs on a personal computer or workstation and relies on a server to perform some operations. For example, an e-mail client is an application that enables you to send and receive e-mail.

**Close-ended questions** Questions asked of an expert that require a short answer or a number for answers. These are used for gathering specific problem-solving knowledge.

**Cluster analysis** Grouping together of data sets according to a natural but undefined parameter shared by all members of the set.

**Clustering techniques** The general definition for techniques that discover clusters in large data sets.

**Codifiability** Reflects the extent to which knowledge can be articulated or codified, even if the resulting codified knowledge might be difficult to impart to another individual.

**Collaborative-based filtering** Recommends items that similar people (to the one being studied) have liked in the past.

**Combination** Explicit to explicit knowledge conversion, involving the synthesis of multiple bodies of explicit knowledge (data or information) to create new, more complex sets of explicit knowledge. It is a process of systemizing concepts into a knowledge system. This may take place during activities such as sorting, adding, combining, and categorizing knowledge.

**Common knowledge** Organization's cumulative experiences in comprehending a category of knowledge and activities, and the organizing principles that support communication and coordination. It provides unity to the organization, and includes a common language and vocabulary, recognition of individual knowledge domains, common cognitive schema, shared norms, and elements of specialized knowledge common across individuals sharing knowledge.

**Common virtual system** Pinnacle of enterprise application integration (EAI); all aspects of enterprise computing are tied together so that they appear as a unified application.

**Community of practice** Organic and self-organized group of individuals who are dispersed geographically or organizationally but communicate regularly to discuss issues of mutual interest.

**Competitive intelligence** Term that indicates knowledge leading to competitive advantages for a business organization.

**Concept learning system** Algorithm that classifies a set of example data by building an inductive tree and distributing the examples throughout the tree.

**Constrained processing tasks** Artificial tasks given to experts for the purpose of observing them and learning from their performances. The expert is typically constrained in terms of time available for the solution.

**Constraint-based reasoning** An artificial intelligence technique that uses what cannot be done to guide the process of finding a solution. Useful in naturally constrained tasks such as planning and scheduling.

**Content-based filtering** Recommendations based on what a person has liked in the past.

**Context-Based Intelligent Tactical Knowledge Acquisition (CITKA)** An automated knowledge elicitation tool for acquiring tactical knowledge directly from experts. Based upon context-based reasoning.

**Context-based reasoning (CxBR)** An efficient human behavior representation technique that assumes that all tactical human activity can be decomposed into context-sensitive blocks of knowledge.

**Contextually specific knowledge** Knowledge of particular circumstances of time and place in which work is to be performed. It pertains to the organization and the organizational subunit within which tasks are performed.

**Contingency view of KM** Suggests that no one approach to managing knowledge is best under all circumstances.

**Cooker** Knowledge-based system that assists in the maintenance and diagnosis of soup-making equipment. It uses a personal computer as the delivery platform.

**Copyrights** The legal ability to protect the expression of an idea. Common in protecting artistic content such as art, music, and architecture. The creator retains the rights to the creation for his/her lifetime + 50 years in the United States.

**Critic** Rules used for adapting the solution of a similar historical case to the current problem in CBR.

**Cross-Industry Standard Process for Data Mining (CRISP-DM)** Industry-neutral and tool-neutral standard process for data mining. Starting from the knowledge discovery processes used in industry today and responding directly to user requirements, this standard defined and validated a DM process that is applicable in diverse industry sectors.

**Curve fitting** Derivation of a mathematical expression (a function) that closely describes a set of data.

**Customer relationship management (CRM)** Entails all aspects of interaction a company has with its customer, whether they are sales or services related. Computerization has changed the way companies are approaching their CRM strategies because it has also changed consumer-buying behavior. With each new advance in technology, especially the proliferation of self-service channels like the Web, more of the relationship is managed electronically. Organizations are therefore looking for ways to personalize on-line experiences (a process also referred to as mass customization) through tools such as help-desk software, e-mail organizers, and Web development applications.

**Daemons** Functions attached to a frame that assist in obtaining values for slots, or in maintaining consistency in the frame system.

**Damage recovery** A legal term that awards monetary compensation to an aggrieved party whose intellectual property was illegally stolen, corrupted, or taken away. The aggrieved party has to have incurred monetary damages from such a loss.

**Data** Comprise facts, observations, or perceptions (which may or may not be correct). Alone, data represent raw numbers or assertions, and may therefore be devoid of context, meaning, or intent.

**Data mining (DM)** Class of database applications that look for hidden patterns in a group of data. For example, DM software can help retail companies find customers with common interests. DM software does not just change the presentation, but actually discovers previously unknown relationships among the data.

**Data preparation** The process of preparing the data in a database for use in data mining. This includes placing it in an appropriate data structure as well as eliminating outlier points.

**Data quality (DQ)** IS research area that aims to ensure the quality of data in databases. DQ typically investigates database definitions, modeling, and control.

**Data tombs** Data stores that are effectively write-only; data is deposited to merely rest in peace, since in all likelihood it will never be accessed again.

**Data warehouse** Collection of data designed to support management decision making. Data warehouses contain a wide variety of data that present a coherent picture of business conditions at a single point in time. The development of a data warehouse includes development of systems to extract data from operating systems plus installation of a warehouse database system that provides managers flexible access to the data. The term *data warehousing* generally refers to combining many different databases across an entire enterprise. A data mart is defined as a database, or collection of databases, designed to help managers make strategic decisions about their business. Whereas a data warehouse combines databases across an entire enterprise, *data marts* are usually smaller and focus on a particular subject or department. Some data marts, called *dependent data marts,* are subsets of larger data warehouses.

**Database** Large collection of data organized for rapid search and retrieval or programs that manage data and can be used to store, retrieve, and sort information. You can think of a database as an electronic filing system. A relational database stores data in the form of related tables. Relational databases are powerful because they require few assumptions about how data is related or how it will be extracted from the database. As a result, the same database can be viewed in many different ways.

**Database linking** Databases that share information and duplicate information as needed.

**Declarative knowledge** Focuses on beliefs about relationships among variables. Characterized as "know what," it can be stated in the form of propositions, expected correlations, or formulas relating concepts represented as variables.

**Deep expertise** Highly theoretical knowledge, acquired through formal training and hands-on problem solving.

**Deployment** Implementing the live model within an organization to aid the decision-making process.

**Developer's interface** The suite of tools and displays that allow a knowledge engineer to view the internal components of a knowledge-based system for the purpose of developing or testing it.

**Development environment** Program used for developing the knowledge for the knowledge-based system, and providing the inference mechanism used to exercise the knowledge to solve a problem or answer a question posed by the end user.

**Diagrammatic reasoning** An artificial intelligence technique that reasons from the diagrams employed to represent knowledge.

**Direction** Process through which the individual possessing the knowledge directs the action of another individual without transferring to that person the knowledge underlying the direction.

**Discriminant analysis** Technique used primarily in market research and credit analysis to build a predictive model based on linear combinations of predictor variables that are either continuous or categorical.

**Document management systems** Computer systems that provide a Web-based repository accessible from multiple points. These systems also provide a collaborative environment for several clients to work on a document simultaneously.

**Domain expert** Individual who is both experienced and knowledgeable about a particular application domain.

**Domain knowledge** Relevant knowledge about a problem domain. Knowledge is embedded in the operators of the solution space.

**Downsizing** To reduce in number or size.

**Dynamic Web documents** Web pages created by the Web server in response to the specific request by the client.

**Dynamic** Actions that take place at the moment they are needed, not in advance.

**Economy of scale** Causes the amount of a firm's output to increase, while its average costs (i.e., total costs divided by the output) decline.

**Economy of scope** When the total cost of a firm that is producing two (or more) different products is less than sum of the costs that would be incurred if each product was produced separately by a different company.

**Effectiveness** Performing the most suitable processes and making the best possible decisions.

**Efficiency** Performing the processes quickly and in a low-cost fashion.

**Eliza** Early AI implementation. It used a natural language interface to act as an artificial psychoanalyst, carrying on a dialogue with a patient.

**EMYCIN** Knowledge-based system shell, developed by removing the domain specific knowledge from MYCIN.

**Encryption** Translation of data into a secret code. Encryption is the most effective way to achieve data security. To read an encrypted file, one must have access to a secret key or password that enables you to *decrypt* it. Unencrypted data is called *plain text*; encrypted data is referred to as *cipher text*.

**End–user** Person for whom the product was designed. Different from the person who programs, services, or installs the product.

**Enterprise application integration (EAI) technology** Unrestricted sharing of data and business processes throughout the networked applications or data sources in an organization. Early software programs in areas such as inventory control, human resources, sales automation and database management were designed to run independently, with no interaction between the systems. They were custom built in the technology of the day for a specific need, and were often proprietary systems. As enterprises grow and recognize the need for their information and applications to have the ability to be transferred across and shared between systems, companies are investing in EAI to streamline processes and keep all the elements of the enterprise interconnected.

**Enterprise resource planning (ERP) system** Business management system that integrates all facets of the business, including planning, manufacturing, sales, and marketing into a single integrated application that executes on a single database to support the entire enterprise. As the ERP methodology has become more popular, software applications have emerged to help business managers implement ERP in business activities such as inventory control, order tracking, customer service, finance, and human resources.

**Enterprise system** Literally, a business organization. In the computer industry, the term is often used to describe any large organization that utilizes computers. An intranet, for example, is a good example of an enterprise computing system.

**Ethernet** A type of network in which a cable connects all computers to a bus medium (a cable) that carries the packets between the computers. One computer (or rather, a process therein) composes packets and sends them to one or more computers in the network. Each computer in the network receives and copies the packet from the Ethernet medium, and examines at the address on the packet header. If the address agrees with its own address, it accepts and processes it. Otherwise, it neglects it.

**Evaluation** Evaluating a case in the case library for similarity with the current problem.

**Exchange** Used for communicating or transferring explicit knowledge between individuals, groups, and organizations.

**Experience management** A new IS special interest group that unites the case-base reasoning and knowledge management special interest groups.

**Expertise** Knowledge of higher quality (i.e., specific knowledge at its best). One who possesses expertise is able to perform a task much better than those who do not.

**Explicit knowledge** Knowledge that has been expressed into words and numbers. Such knowledge can be shared formally and systematically in the form of data, specifications, manuals, drawings, audio and video tapes, programs, patents, etc.

**Externalization** Converting tacit knowledge into explicit forms such as words, concepts, visuals, or figurative language (e.g., metaphors, analogies, and narratives).

**Facets** Subdivisions of a frame slot containing various types of information related to the slot.

**Facilitator** Leader or chairperson of a brainstorming session.

**Fact base** Data structure that holds all assertions made, either provided by the system or as inputs. These assertions serve as facts for matching premises in an inference chain.

**File Transfer Protocol (FTP)** Used to transfer copies of a file (document, picture, film, or program) to another computer via the Internet.

**Firewall** System designed to prevent unauthorized access to or from a private network. Firewalls can be implemented in both hardware and software, or a combination of both. Firewalls are frequently used to prevent unauthorized Internet users from accessing private networks connected to the Internet, especially *intranets*. All messages entering or leaving the intranet pass through the firewall, which examines each message and blocks those that do not meet the specified security criteria.

**Flat case libraries** Case library organization where all cases lie at the same single hierarchical level in the case library.

**Forward reasoning** Reasoning from inputs to conclusions.

**Frames** Structured framework for representing knowledge best organized as attribute value pairs. The framework is composed of slots.

**Fuzzy sets** Set theory that defines sets for which membership can be defined in degrees of membership. Used to represent imprecision and uncertainty in the world.

**GenAID** An expert system that remotely monitors and diagnoses the status of large electrical generators in real time. It issues a diagnosis with a confidence factor whenever the machine begins operating outside its normal operating conditions. It is presently in commercial operation at various sites throughout the United States.

**General knowledge** Possessed by a large number of individuals and can be transferred easily across individuals.

**General knowledge-gathering interview sessions** Interview sessions designed to elicit general domain knowledge from the expert.

**General problem solver (GPS)** Early AI system, which demonstrated ability to solve problems by searching for an answer in a solution space.

**Goal state** Final desired state of a problem in the solution space.

**Graphic user interface (GUI)** Program interface that takes advantage of the computer's graphics capabilities to make the program easier to use. Well-designed graphic user interfaces can free the user from learning complex command languages. On the other hand, many users find that they work more effectively with a command-driven interface, especially if they already know the command language.

**Groupware** Class of software that helps groups of colleagues (workgroups) attached to a local area network organize their activities.

**GUIDON** Instructional program teaching students therapy for patients with bacterial infections. GUIDON is a descendant of MYCIN and was developed as a research tool at Stanford University.

**Hacking** Pejorative sense of *hacker*, becoming more prominent largely because the popular press has co-opted the term to refer to individuals who gain unauthorized access to computer systems for the purpose of stealing and corrupting data.

**Header** The part of the packet that indicates the intended recipient of the packet and its encoded information.

**Heterogeneous networks** Networks consisting of computers with different processors and/or different operating systems.

**Heuristic functions** Used in solution space searches to compute the desirability of moving on to each of the possible next states based on some general knowledge. These states are ranked in order of decreasing desirability.

**Heuristic search** Search that uses heuristic functions as a guide to determine where in the problem space to search next.

**Heuristics** Commonsense knowledge drawn from experience to solve problems. They represent rules of thumb and other such shortcuts to the solution that are only learned through experience. This is in contrast to *algorithmic programming,* which is based on a deterministic sequence of steps procedures. Heuristic programs do not always reach the very best result but usually produce a good result.

**Hierarchical** Systems that are organized in the shape of a pyramid, with each row of objects linked to objects directly beneath it. Hierarchical systems pervade everyday life. The army, for example, which has generals at the top of the pyramid and privates at the bottom, is a hierarchical system. Similarly, the system for classifying plants and animals according to species, family, genus, and so on, is also hierarchical.

**Human computer interface (HCI)** Interface between a human and a computer; for example, a command line interface, a graphic user interface, and virtual reality interfaces.

**Hypertext Markup Language (HTML)** Standard representation for text and graphics that allows the browser to interpret the intentions of the Web page designer.

**Hypertext Transfer Protocol (HTTP)** Transfer protocol used for exchanging hypertext.

**Indexing** Act of classifying and providing an index to make items easier to retrieve in CBR.

**Induction tree** A data structure that represents the associations derived in inductive learning in a connected, acyclical manner.

**Inductive learning** The ability of a system to learn associations by examining examples supplied to it sequentially.

**Inference chain** Sequence of rules in a rule-based system where the assertions of an upstream rule serve as the facts to match the premises of downstream rules.

**Inference engine** An algorithm that controls the means through which knowledge is manipulated to derive new inferences.

**Inference mechanism** Another name for an inference engine.

**Inferential DM** Models that explain the relationships that exist in data. They may indicate the driving factors for stock market movements, or show failure factors in printed circuit board production.

**Information I** Includes data that possess context, relevance, and purpose. Information typically involves the manipulation of raw data to obtain a more meaningful indication of trends or patterns in the data.

**Information retrieval (IR)** The process of accessing information from either a database, a data acquisition system, or some other repository of knowledge, information, or data.

**Information technology (IT)** Broad subject concerned with all aspects of managing and processing information, especially within a large organization or company. Because computers are central to information management, computer departments within companies and universities are often called *IT departments*. Some companies refer to this department as information systems (IS) or Management information systems (MIS).

**Inheritance** Ability in frames and objects to conserve representational effort by having children frames contain all attributes and values possessed by the parent frame.

**Initial state** Starting problem definition in a problem space.

**Innovation** Performing a process in a creative and novel fashion that improves effectiveness and efficiency, or at least marketability.

**Innovators** Those who brainstorm the solutions to the customer's problem.

**Intangible assets** Refers to assets that are intangible but have value, such as knowledge about customers' preferences.

**Intellectual capital** Knowledge that can be exploited for some moneymaking or other useful purpose. The term combines the idea of the intellect or brainpower with the economic concept of capital, the saving of entitled benefits so that they can be invested in producing more goods and services.

**Intellectual property (IP)** Refers to right of ownership of ideas, designs, and other products of intellectual activity that have value in the marketplace.

**Intelligent program** Concept where the end user sees the knowledge-based system as a black box that provides intelligent problem-solving capability, without the ability to see its components. Composed of a knowledge base, an inference engine and a development environment.

**Internalization** Conversion of explicit knowledge into tacit knowledge. It represents the traditional notion of learning.

**Internet** A computer network protocol that permits the interconnection of many heterogeneous networks into one large network.

**Internet Layer** Makes the decisions on how to route the packets arriving at a router.

**Interpage structures** Evaluates the arrangement of the various HTML or XML tags that connect one page to another.

**Interviews** Time of interaction with experts for the purposes of eliciting their knowledge.

**Intrapage structures** Evaluates the arrangement of the various HTML or XML tags within a page.

**Inverse document frequency (IDF)** Highlights terms that are frequently used in one document, but infrequently used across the collection of documents.

**Iterative** Programming term that refers to a cyclic process that executes a block of instructions repeatedly until some criteria is satisfied by one or more variables within the loop.

**Java** Programming language specifically designed to allow it to execute in any type of computer. This makes programs written in Java easily exchanged through the Internet.

**Just-in-time (JIT) manufacturing** Ideal method of manufacturing with minimal waste, short cycle times, and fast communication that can respond rapidly to changing circumstances.

**Kick-off interview** First interview in the process of knowledge elicitation.

**K-means clustering** A statistical method used to define natural clusters of data.

**Knowledge** Knowledge in an area is defined as justified beliefs about relationships among concepts relevant to that particular area. Intrinsically different from information.

**Knowledge acquisition tool** A software system capable of eliciting knowledge from an expert through an intelligent and autonomous dialogue.

**Knowledge base** A body of knowledge codified in a way that can be manipulated by an inference engine for the purpose of deriving new inferences.

**Knowledge application** The process of using relevant knowledge that has been discovered, captured, or shared to make decisions and perform tasks.

**Knowledge capture** Process of eliciting knowledge (either explicit or tacit) that resides within people, artifacts, or organizational entities; and representing it in an electronic form such as a knowledge-based system, for later reuse or retrieval.

**Knowledge discovery** Development of new tacit or explicit knowledge from data and information or from synthesis of prior knowledge.

**Knowledge discovery in databases (KDD)** Process of data selecting, data cleansing, transferring to a data mining (DM) technique, applying the DM technique, validating the results of the DM technique, and finally interpreting them for the user.

**Knowledge elicitation** Process of obtaining tacit knowledge from an expert for the purposes of making that knowledge explicit.

**Knowledge engineering** Process of developing a knowledge-based system.

**Knowledge leakage** The loss of intellectual property by a careless or unfortunate organization.

**Knowledge management (KM)** Performing the activities involved in discovering, capturing, sharing, and applying knowledge in terms of resources, documents, and people skills, so as to enhance, in a cost-effective fashion, the impact of knowledge on the unit's goal achievement.

**Knowledge management infrastructure** Long-term foundation on which knowledge management resides. It includes five main components: organization culture, organization structure, communities of practice, information technology infrastructure, and common knowledge.

**Knowledge management mechanisms** Organizational or structural means used to promote knowledge management. These mechanisms may (or may not) utilize technology, but they do involve some kind of organizational arrangement or social or structural means of facilitating KM.

**Knowledge management processes** Broad processes that help in discovering, capturing, sharing, and applying knowledge.

**Knowledge management solutions** Variety of ways in which knowledge management can be facilitated. KM solutions may be divided into (1) KM processes; (2) KM systems; (3) KM mechanisms and technologies; and (4) KM infrastructure.

**Knowledge management systems** Integration of technologies and mechanisms to support KM processes.

**Knowledge sharing** Process through which explicit or tacit knowledge is communicated to other individuals.

**Knowledge-based systems** Computerized system that uses domain knowledge to arrive at a solution to a problem within that domain. This solution is essentially the same as one concluded by a person knowledgeable about the domain, when confronted with the same problem.

**Lateral thinking** Use of an entirely different approach to solve a problem. In any self-organizing system there is a need to escape from a local optimum to move toward a more global optimum. The techniques of lateral thinking, such as provocation, are designed to help that change.

**Learning** Process of improving one's performance by experiencing an activity or observing someone else experience that activity. Learning has been one goal of artificially intelligent systems.

**Limited information tasks** Artificial tasks given to an expert to perform with limited information. These tasks are used to place experts in situations where they are challenged. The tasks also serve to observe the expert in problem solving without danger of failure.

**Linear regression** Statistical procedure for predicting the value of a dependent variable from an independent variable when the relationship between the variables can be described with a linear model.

**Linguistic analysis** *See* Natural Language Processing (NLP).

**Local area networks (LANs)** A network encompassing a relatively small area, such as an office, or a co-located department.

**Logistic regression** Statistical procedure that uses a general linear model as its theoretical underpinning, calculates regression coefficients, and tries to fit cases to a line to predict a categorical variable, such as predicting whether people will renew a service.

**Machine learning** Ability of computers to automatically acquire new knowledge, for example, learning from past cases or experience, from the computer's own experiences, or from exploration.

**Many-on-many interviews** Interview sessions in which several knowledge engineers interact with several experts.

**Many-on-one interviews** Interview sessions in which several knowledge engineers interact with only one expert.

**Market basket analysis** Algorithm that examines a long list of transactions to determine which items are most frequently purchased together.

**Metadata** Data about data. Metadata describes how and when and by whom a particular set of data was collected, and how the data is formatted. Metadata is essential for understanding information stored in data warehouses.

**Metaphor** One thing perceived as representing another, a symbol.

**Method of least squares** Statistical method of finding the best fitting straight line or other theoretically derived curve for a group of experimental data points.

**Model-based reasoning (MBR)** Intelligent reasoning technique that uses a model of an engineered system to simulate its normal behavior. The simulated operation is compared with the behavior of a real system and noted discrepancies can lead to a diagnosis.

**Model-guided repair** Use of models to guide the adaptation of historical cases to current problems in case-based reasoning.

**Moore's law** A popular rule of thumb that states that the computational power of computers (specifically the number of transistors on CPUs) will double every 18 months.

**Motor skills expertise** Physical instead of cognitive knowledge. This type of knowledge is difficult for knowledge-based systems to emulate. Examples include riding a bicycle or hitting a baseball.

**Multivariate correlation** Correlation of data described by more than one variable.

**MYCIN** Early knowledge-based system developed in the early 1970s. The system was developed to diagnose and specify treatments for blood disorders through a Q&A session with a physician. The most significant and renowned research system, for it pioneered the separation of the knowledge from the way it is used.

**Narrative** Narrated account; a story.

**Narrowcast** Sending data to a specific list of recipients. Cable television is an example of narrowcasting because the cable TV signals are sent only to homes that have subscribed to the cable service. In contrast, traditional network TV uses a broadcast model in which the signals are transmitted everywhere, and anyone with an antenna can receive them.

**Natural language processing (NLP)** Branch of artificial intelligence that deals with analyzing, understanding, and generating the languages that humans use naturally to interface with computers in both written and spoken contexts.

**Network Interface Layer** Defines how to organize data into frames (packets) to prepare them for transmission.

**Nondisclosure agreement** Signed by the holder of intellectual property and another party to whom the secret property is to be disclosed. Places restrictions on the signers to maintain confidentiality with the secrets to be disclosed.

**Nonlinear correlation** Correlation between data sets that do not conform to a linear relation.

**Normalization** Data processing method applied to all data in a set that produces a specific statistical property. For example, monthly expenditures can be divided by total expenditures, to produce a normalized value that represents a percentage.

**Object-oriented programming (OOP)** Special type of programming that combines data structures with functions to create reusable objects.

**Observables** Physical property, such as weight or temperature, that can be observed or measured directly, as distinguished from a quantity, such as work or entropy, that must be derived from observed quantities.

**Observational elicitation** Process of observing an expert perform a task to learn that process for performing the task. This can be quiet observation, or interactive.

**One-line diagram** Drawing depicting the general connectivity of an engineered system.

**One-on-many interviews** Interview sessions in which one knowledge engineer interacts with several experts.

**One-on-one interview** Interview in which only one knowledge engineer and one expert participate.

**On-line analytical processing (OLAP)** Category of software tools that provides analysis of data stored in a database. OLAP tools enable users to analyze different dimensions of multidimensional data. For example, it provides time series and trend analysis views. The chief component of OLAP is the OLAP server, which is located between a client and a database management system (DBMS). The OLAP server understands how data is organized in the database and has special functions for analyzing the data. There are OLAP servers available for nearly all the major database systems. In essence, OLAP enables systems to summarize, aggregate, or selectively extract data from different points of view.

**Ontology** Description of the concepts and relationships that can exist for an agent or a community of agents.

**Open-ended questions** Questions asked of the expert that require a narrative or long explanation. These are used for gathering general domain knowledge.

**Output–input–middle method** Method used to organize knowledge elicited during expert interviews.

**Packet** A finite length string of bits sent across the communication medium. The bits encode the data to be transmitted as well as a header that indicates the addresses to be sent to.

**Paired-leaf analysis** A data mining technique in which minimally different data points are compared to determine this difference.

**Parameter adjustment** Adjusting the value of an attribute in order to adapt a historical solution to a current problem in case-based reasoning.

**Patents** The legal ability to protect inventions and novel designs for the purpose of encouraging innovation for the benefit of mankind. Typically valid for 16 to 20 years.

**Pattern matching** Comparing two patterns to determine whether they match according to some predefined criteria.

**Physical layer** Includes the actual, physical hardware required to effect the transfer of packets in the network. This includes specification of the routers, switches, network interface cards, and hubs located throughout the Internet, and the interconnecting cables and connectors.

**Ping** Allows a user in one computer to test for connectivity between the two computers.

**Predictive DM** Models that make predictions of output conditions given a set of input conditions.

**Problem space** The universe of possible states assumable by the problem. A set of operators defined for that problem space could be used to direct the state of the problem.

**Problem-specific database** Another name for the fact base in a knowledge-based system.

**Procedural knowledge** Focuses on beliefs relating sequences of steps or actions to desired (or undesired) outcomes. This knowledge may be viewed as "know how."

**Proposition** A statement of the expected presence or absence of relationship between two or more variables.

**Prospector** Knowledge-based system that assists geologists in identifying geologic formations that may contain mineral deposits. It elicited, preserved, and reused geologic formation knowledge to assist in mineral exploration.

**Prototype** Original type, form, or instance serving as a basis or standard for later stages.

**Proxy server** Server located between a client application, such as a Web browser, and a real server. It intercepts all requests to the real server to see whether it can fulfill the requests itself. If it cannot, it forwards the request to the real server.

**Qualitative KM assessments** Efforts aimed at developing a broad understanding of how well the KM efforts are working, without quantifying the level of the benefits and costs.

**Quantitative KM assessments** Producing specific numerical scores indicating how well an organization, an organizational subunit, or an individual is performing with respect to KM. These assessments may be based on a survey, in financial terms, such as the ROI or cost savings, or may include such ratios or percentages as employee retention rate.

**Query** Request for information from a database.

**Query by example (QBE)** Method in which the system presents a blank record and lets you specify the fields and values that define the query.

**Query language** Many database systems that require a user to make requests for information in the form of a stylized query that must be written in a special query language. This is the most complex method because it forces the user to learn a specialized language, but it is also the most powerful.

**Random search** Search having no specific pattern, purpose, or objective.

**Recontextualized knowledge** Existing knowledge recreated using alternative and innovative knowledge technologies and mechanisms.

**Remindings** The original basis for case-based reasoning. Represents patterns that bring back memories in a human about a similar problem solved in the past.

**Repertory grids** Table associating attributes of several subjects with respect to two diametrically opposed extremes. These grids are used to organize elicited knowledge and can be easily automated.

**Retrieval** Obtaining a case from the library that matches the description of the current problem.

**Reverse engineering** Process of recreating a design by analyzing a final product. Reverse engineering is common in both hardware and software.

**Role reversal** Elicitation technique where the expert and the knowledge engineer exchange roles and the expert interviews the knowledge engineer. This technique can serve to verify already elicited knowledge.

**Routines** Involve the utilization of knowledge embedded in procedures, rules, and norms that guide future behavior.

**Rule induction algorithms** Data mining techniques that generate rules from inspection of a sequence of examples. Typically associated with inductive learning techniques.

**Rule interpretation** The process of matching a rule's patterns with those found in the fact base. If a match is found to exist, the rule may be executed and its derivations asserted into the fact base.

**Search–retrieve—propose** Process on which CBR is founded. A case is sought, compared to the current problem, and retrieved if it is similar; and its solution is proposed as the solution to the current problem.

**Security** Techniques for ensuring that data stored in a computer cannot be read by unauthorized users or compromised. Most security measures involve data encryption and passwords. Data encryption is the translation of data into a form that is unintelligible without a deciphering mechanism. A password is a secret word or phrase that gives a user access to a particular program or system.

**Semantic analysis** Semantics means, in linguistic terms, the study of meanings. Semantic analysis is a computer-based technique to automatically extract meaning and annotate documents, Web pages, and even multimedia information.

**Server** Computer or device on a network that manages network resources. For example, a file server is a computer and storage device dedicated to storing files. Any user on the network can store files on the server. A print server is a computer that manages one or more printers, and a network server is a computer that manages network traffic. A database server that processes database queries.

**Set membership function** Functions that assign a potential member item a degree of membership in a fuzzy set.

**Shell** Development environment designed to exercise domain knowledge expressed as rules, and to arrive at solutions or answers to questions.

**Similarity functions** Functions that compare a sequence of historical cases with the current problem definition to determine the degree of similarity. This is the fundamental process in case-based reasoning.

**Simple Mail Transfer Protocol** SMTP handles several detailed processes that make reliable e-mail a reality.

**Slot** Attribute of a frame to which a value or set of values is assigned. A slot consists of facets.

**Socialization** Involves integration of multiple streams of tacit knowledge for the creation of new knowledge, and tacit to tacit knowledge conversion. Socialization is the process of sharing experiences and thereby creating tacit knowledge such as shared mental models and technical skills.

**Solution space** Contains the actions, states, or beliefs that represent the status of the problem. The solution is a sequence of steps through these actions, beliefs, or states starting from the initial state to the goal state.

**Specific knowledge** Knowledge that is possessed by a very limited number of individuals, and is expensive to transfer.

**Specific problem-solving, knowledge-gathering interview sessions** Interview sessions where the objective is to gather specific problem-solving knowledge.

**Stakeholder** One who has a share or an interest, as in an enterprise.

**Static Web documents** Web documents designed *a priori,* consisting of nonactive HTML.

**Stemming algorithm** Used to remove the suffix of a word.

**Stoplists** Used to eliminate words that are not good concept descriptions; group of words that are not considered to have any indexing value. These include common words such as "and," "the," and "there."

**Storage law** States that data storage capacity doubles every 9 months. This law has been in operation for over 10 years now.

**Storytelling** Act or practice of telling a story.

**Strategic knowledge** Pertains to the long-term positioning of the organization in terms of its corporate vision and strategies for achieving that vision.

**Structural capital** Everything that remains when the employees go home: databases, customer files, software, manuals, trademarks, and organizational structures.

**Structured knowledge** Knowledge best represented through attribute value pairs; knowledge not conditional in nature.

**Subject matter expert (SME)** Another name for a domain expert.

**Support knowledge** Relates to organizational infrastructure and facilitates day-to-day operations.

**Surrogates** Replacing someone else or used instead of something else.

**Sustainable competitive advantage** A firm's competitive advantage that is not temporary, but that can persist.

**Symbol manipulation** Using symbols for solving problems; basis of symbolic AI.

**Synergy** Interaction of two or more agents or forces so that their combined effect is greater than the sum of their individual effects.

**Systematic blind search** Follows a systematic, exhaustive method to find target; does not use any knowledge; can be very time consuming.

**Tacit knowledge** Includes insights, intuitions, and hunches. It is difficult to express and formalize, and therefore is difficult to share.

**Tactical knowledge** Knowledge used to determine a course of action to achieve a specific goal in a dynamically changing environment; pertains to the short-term positioning of the organization relative to its markets, competitors, and suppliers.

**Talking head (or avatar)** Image selected to represent oneself. Talking heads could be a photograph, a cartoon character, or an animated image driven by the user's voice including lip synchronization.

**Tangible measure** A metric that is concrete, as opposed to insubstantial.

**Target sell** Describes a firm's strategy to sell to a specific consumer market.

**Task interdependence** Indicates the extent to which the subunit's achievement of its goals depends on the efforts of other subunits.

**Task uncertainty** Represents the extent to which the organizational subunit encounters difficulty in predicting the nature of its tasks. High uncertainty implies changing problems and tasks, which reduces the unit's ability to develop routines.

**Teachability** Reflects the extent to which the knowledge can be taught to other individuals, through training, apprenticeship, and so on.

**Technically specific knowledge** Deep knowledge about a specific area. It includes knowledge about the tools and techniques that may be used to address problems in that area.

**Ten-fold (n-fold) cross-validation** Cross-validation and bootstrapping, both methods for estimating generalization error based on resampling. For 10 (n) fold cross-validation the database is divided, with random selection of examples, into 10 (n) partitions (folds) of equal sizes.

**Term frequency (TF)** How frequently a term occurs in the text.

**Term frequency inverse document frequency (TFIDF)** Information retrieval technique based on a vector space model where a vector is used to represent a document or query, and is used to calculate the importance of terms appearing in documents.

**Test case database** A set of inputs whose solution is known and well accepted. Used to test software to ensure it produces the correct results. Part of the software validation effort.

**Text mining** Automatically reading large documents of text, and deriving knowledge from the process.

**Token** A symbolic packet that permits the computer holding it to transmit. *See* Token ring networks.

**Token Ring network** A network type in which all computers are connected in a closed ring of cable medium. A token is passed sequentially from one computer to another. The computer holding the token is able to make one transmission before it passes the token to the next computer in the ring.

**Tracing a goal** The process of inspecting which rules are able to set the value of a goal, and

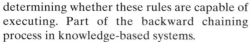

determining whether these rules are capable of executing. Part of the backward chaining process in knowledge-based systems.

**Trade secret** Intellectual property that an organization has chosen to not overtly protect through patents or copyrights. Protected by law from loss if appropriately protected.

**Transmission Control Protocol (TCP)** A more complex transmission protocol that works to ensure reliable, sequenced delivery of the packets.

**Uniform Resource Locator (URL)** Format for specifying Internet addresses; the global address of documents and other resources on the World Wide Web.

**Universalistic view of KM** Implies that there is a single best approach of managing knowledge, which should be adopted by all organizations in all circumstances.

**User Datagram Protocol (UDP)** A simple, best-effort, connectionless protocol that merely sends the packet into the network and hopes for the best.

**User interface** Screen and dialogue format seen by the user when working with a particular computer program.

**Value-added products** New or improved products that provide a significant additional value as compared with earlier products. Value-added products benefit from knowledge management due to increased knowledge or enhanced organizational process innovation.

**Virus** Program or piece of code that is loaded onto a computer without the owner's knowledge and which runs against the owner's wishes. Viruses can also replicate themselves. All computer viruses are man-made. A simple virus that can copy itself repeatedly is relatively easy to produce. Even such a simple virus is dangerous because it can quickly use all available memory and bring the system to a halt. An even more dangerous type of virus is one capable of transmitting itself across networks and bypassing security systems.

**Weak-theory domains** Domains where robust theoretical explanations do not exist, or if they exist, contain uncertainty.

**Web content mining** Discovers what a Web page is about and how to uncover new knowledge from it.

**Web crawlers** Computer programs that visit Web sites continuously and regularly, acquiring information for use in search engines.

**Web mining** Web crawling with on-line text mining.

**Web structure mining** Examines how Web documents are structured; attempts to discover the model underlying the link structures of the Web.

**Web usage mining** Identification of patterns in user navigation through Web surfing.

**wide area networks (WANs)** A network encompassing a larger geographic area, such as between two distant buildings in the same city or in different cities. Requires special devices to bridge the large area.

**Workflow management (WfM) system** System that provides procedural automation of a business process by managing the sequence of work activities and by managing the required resources (people, data, and applications) associated with the various activity steps. Computer programs that provide a method of capturing the steps, which lead to the completion of a project within a fixed time frame.

**World Wide Web (WWW)** Format that enables large-scale storage of documents to be easily accessed by a user via a browser.

**XCON** One of the earliest commercially successful knowledge-based systems. XCON assisted in the configuration of newly ordered VAX computer systems. The system was developed by Digital Equipment Corporation (DEC) in conjunction with Carnegie-Mellon University. XCON elicited, preserved, and reused the knowledge of human configurators of computer systems to automate and duplicate their functions.

## Sources

www.webopedia.com
www.onelook.com
www.knowledgepoint.com.au
www.whatis.com
www.vnulearning.com
www.geek.com
dictionary.cambridge.org
http://dictionary.reference.com/
http://www.crisp-dm.org/
www.dictionary.com
www.yourdictionary.com
Nonaka, I., and Takeuchi, H. 1995. *The Knowledge Creating Company: How Japanese Companies Create the Dynasties of Innovation.*
*American Heritage Dictionary of the English Language.* 4th ed., 2000.

*Oxford American Desk Dictionary,* 2nd ed., 2001.
Oxford University Press,
The Computational Beauty of Nature—
(http://mitpress.mit.edu/books/FLAOH/cbnhtml/
glossary.html)
http://aa.uncwil.edu/ward/chm25502/glossary.htm

http://www.shai.com/ai_general/glossary.htm
http://bioparadigma.narod.ru/hidden_history/
M.htm
www.edwdebono.com
www.cio.com
*Communications of the ACM*

# Index